THE RO
STOI
COMP
DISCOGRAPHY

THE ROLLING STONES COMPLETE DISCOGRAPHY

ALAN CLAYSON

UNIVERSE

First published in the United States of America in 2006 by
Universe Publishing
a division of Rizzoli International Publications, Inc.
300 Park Avenue South
New York, NY 10010
www.rizzoliusa.com

Originally published in Great Britain in 2006 as
The Rolling Stones Album File and Complete Discography by
Cassell Illustrated
a division of Octopus Publishing Group Limited
2-4 Heron Quays, London E14 4JP

ISBN-10: 0-7893-1499-1
ISBN-13: 978-0-7893-1499-4

Library of Congress Control Number: 2006903209

2006 2007 2008 2009 / 10 9 8 7 6 5 4 3 2 1

Design: Design 23

Printed in China

CONTENTS

The Rolling Stones on Record

After their first single touched its tantalising high of No. 21 in the British charts, who could have assumed that The Rolling Stones were anything other than a classic local group who'd caught the lightning once and would probably resume apprenticeships, college courses and 'proper' jobs within a year? They were, after all, just one of many peas from the same pod with sheepdog fringes who could crank out 'Money', 'Poison Ivy' and a good half of the Chuck Berry songbook. Indeed, it was a Berry number, 'Come On', that had been recorded as cheaply as possible and pushed out as that debut Stones 45.

No beat group was built to last, let alone to dominate concert platforms for the next half-century and to continue to release records, some of them hits, when most of its personnel was in their sixties? 'We're a terrible band really,' smiled drummer Charlie Watts, 'but we are the oldest. That's some sort of distinction, isn't it?'

Indeed it is, particularly as the original intention – to play rhythm and blues in home counties clubland – had been so humble. Yet soon after their formation in 1962, the Stones were having much the same effect on their audiences as The Beatles had had on theirs in Liverpool. With both R&B credibility, teen appeal and a clever co-manager in Andrew Loog Oldham, their cash flow was such that bass guitarist Bill Wyman, a married father, was able to think of packing in his day job as a storekeeper, and 19-year-old singer Mick Jagger of not finishing his degree at the London School of Economics.

A recommendation by George Harrison resulted in the Decca record company signing the Stones, whose long-haired, unkempt rebel image came to the attention of a shocked nation after a brief but necessary period of conformity in uniform stage costumes. Their motley dissimilarity to most other early 60s pop stars was most apparent in the cascading girlish tresses that flickered across surly, blemished complexions on *Top Of The Pops*. When these cartoon beatniks flashed into the nation's living rooms provincial teenagers were as nonplussed as their parents although worse was to come in the shape of The Pretty Things, the Stones' blood-brothers and, fleetingly, hit-parade rivals.

This was the other side of The Beatles coin. Unlike the lovable Moptopped Mersey Marvels, the Stones and The Pretty Things would *never* be invited to appear on any Royal Variety Show especially after a story filtered round that Jagger was to undergo a sex-change operation so that he could wed one of his colleagues. This tale was undercut by those about the group's tally of illegitimate children. More verifiable were reports that only fire hoses could quell the tumult at their recitals.

The trials of various personnel for insulting behaviour and drugs offences were yet to come, as was the feeling by some pundits that the Stones had swum out of their depth with 1967's psychedelic *Their Satanic Majesties Request*. More commensurate with their return to touring after a long lay-off were 'Jumping Jack Flash' and also in 1968, *Beggar's Banquet*, self-styled leader Brian Jones's last album before he was asked to leave by Jagger and guitarist Keith Richards – the Napoleon to Brian's Snowball – who, as the Stones' Lennon and McCartney, had snatched control of the group's destiny from him.

Like Elvis Presley, Bob Dylan and Frank Zappa, the Stones racked up far heftier sales in the decades after they'd made their most prominent mark. The repercussions of their records in the 60s resound still, having gouged so deep a wound in pop that whatever their makers got up to in the years left to them need be barely relevant. Yet the hits kept coming and, if augmented by horn sections *et al*, the group concentrated on the possible, drawing on the eternal verities of Jagger's half-caste singing, Richards' forceful rhythm, Wyman's stark throb and Watts' economic cohesion.

Their absence from the UK chart in 1977, however, was critical ammunition for certain quarters of the music press who, waxing sycophantically about the glories of punk, damned the Stones with faint praise without acknowledging their precedents of outrage. This storm was weathered as the group carried on with much the same sort of music they'd played since the early 70s. On the boards ambles down memory lane were spiced with more recent smashes; Jagger was as poutingly athletic as ever and the group still made a most glorious row.

Their stage performances will remain for all to see on video, DVD and whatever visual media are yet to come, but the Stones' principal legacy lies in the records they made together rather than the solo efforts by individual members made before and after a non-decisive sundering in the mid-80s. The parts never equalled the whole but the whole didn't always equal the whole either. Witness the sub-standard album tracks and singles that were foisted mostly on foreign consumers in the mid-60s.

The Stones' discography also proved to be chronologically messy at times, notably after they defected from Decca in 1970. Therefore, to facilitate both a run-on effect and the easier location of factual information, I have divided this work of reference into seven sections beginning with the British LPs up to 1967 when the difference in content between these and US releases bearing the same titles were minimal. There follows a lengthy listing of British and US albums from 1967 to the present with an overview of each and a track-by-track commentary that should serve as a biography in its account of the circumstances under which the music was made, the other people involved in making it, and the estimation of artistic motive. I have also attempted to clear up discrepancies such as the authorship of certain songs – and shatter some minor myths. Also, since there is so much material, I have tried to avoid re-telling a lot of the old stories.

The remaining segments round up the often cheapskate US-only output, the compilations and a miscellany of collectable oddities and solo offerings by the group's mainstays that should be of interest to both the Rolling Stones novice and to the fan who, like me, was there at the beginning, suffocating under bedclothes in the graveyard hours with a transistor radio to my ear in case Radio Luxembourg spun 'Come On' again.

Alan Clayson

THE BRITISH ALBUMS

mono LK 4605

THE ROLLING STONES

UK Release: 17 April 1964
Producer: Andrew Loog Oldham

Decca LK 4605
Running Time: 33:34

SIDE ONE: Route 66; I Just Wanna Make Love To You; Honest I Do; Mona; Now I've Got A Witness; Little By Little.

SIDE TWO: I'm A King Bee; Carol; Tell Me (You're Coming Back); Can I Get A Witness; You Can Make It If You Try; Walking The Dog.

By early 1963 the classic Rolling Stones line-up had found each other. Sharing small stages with Mick Jagger, Brian Jones, Keith Richards and pianist Ian Stewart, an amalgamation of members of two rehearsal groups, were Charlie Watts, once of Blues Incorporated, UK's first all-blues outfit, and Bill Wyman, who replaced Dick Taylor. With singer Phil May, Dick was to go on to form The Pretty Things. They were briefly on terms of fluctuating equality with the Stones as belligerently unkempt degenerates, detested by adults.

As such, the Stones cut appositely baleful figures on the front photograph of an eponymous debut LP. However, anyone awaiting seething musical outrage was disappointed. Its content was weighty with routine if exciting versions of rhythm and blues standards and equal to the maiden albums yet to come by The Animals, The Yardbirds, The Kinks, The Downliners Sect, Them, The Pretty Things, Dave Berry and The Spencer Davis Group, and the first two Beatles LPs put together.

However, unlike *Please Please Me*, if not *With The Beatles*, *The Rolling Stones* didn't include any of their three 45 rpm chart entries even though these had paved the way for the climb of the LP to No. 19 in the UK *singles* chart. This remarkable feat prompted the publication of a glossy monthly periodical devoted solely to the Stones. Only The Beatles and Gerry and the Pacemakers for four editions, had also been accorded that honour.

Like their singles, *The Rolling Stones* had been taped during a break in a remorseless schedule of driving to strange towns, strange venues and strange beds. Most of the sessions also transgressed Musicians Union stipulations by running over into open-ended graveyard hours during which there was room for such experiments as Watts swathing his drums with an overcoat.

Yet these were minor innovations in what was principally a culmination of everything that had gone before. Most pivotal to this had been a residency from January 1963 at the Crawdaddy, a club that convened in the functions room of a Richmond pub. 'It wasn't until much later that you realized you were involved in the start of such a vast thing that swept world-wide,' reminisced Jane Relf, a teenager who'd been among the multitudes that had grown weekly from the mere handful at the Stones' first Sunday night at the club. Ever-tighter clusters of girls in fishnet, suede and leather would block the view for the dismayed R&B enthusiast who recalled a dodgy support act at the Marquee, the National Jazz Federation's main London venue, only a few months earlier.

A kind of committed gaiety from an increasingly more uproarious crowd had lent an inspirational framework to performances that covered a waterfront from country blues to the latest from Chuck Berry, who was still a chart contender. In between lay works by Elmore James, Muddy Waters, Jimmy Reed, Rufus Thomas and Bo Diddley, and irresistible concessions to rock'n'roll and what was becoming known as soul.

Riding roughshod over tempo refinements, complicated dynamic shifts or, indeed, anything that needed too much thought, a few verse-chorus transitions were cluttered. Certain numbers were a fraction too bombastic but so what? The group's casually cataclysmic effect at the Crawdaddy was food for thought among the frayed jeans, CND badges and beatnik beards towards the back. Indeed, some of their wearers were to join the Stones in the Top 50 within a year.

Thus the Stones emerged as hot property now that the music industry's search for, if not *the* New Beatles, then *a* New Beatles, was shifting from the north back to the more convenient capital. For Georgio Gomelsky, the Crawdaddy's promoter, it was a foregone conclusion that he would become the Stones' manager. After all, it was he who had pulled strings so that IPC, a studio recommended by Ian Stewart, waived charging the group by the hour. Moreover, as a power on the National Jazz Federation, Gomelsky had cultivated a connection with Brian Epstein, The Beatles' man of affairs. This manifested itself most tangibly when Georgio engineered a trip to the Crawdaddy by the Fab Four.

As Georgio had foreseen, the Stones' more revered peers took a potentially useful shine to them. However, one of several pop journalists that Gomelsky had also invited to the club mentioned the Stones to Andrew Loog Oldham, soon to be one of about half-a-dozen pop svengalis in Britain who truly counted for anything. When briefly a cog in Brian Epstein's publicity machine, he had come to understand that Epstein's manipulation of The Beatles and his other chartbusting acts was the tip of an iceberg that would make more fortunes than had ever been known in the history of recorded sound.

Oldham felt ready, therefore, to go for the jugular as soon as he'd found a Beatles-sized vehicle with which to do so. He intended also to produce its records and be more than the usual *éminence grise* behind merchandising ballyhoo. He didn't know much about rhythm and blues, but he did know what he'd like to exploit and the Stones seemed as likely to be the next titans of teen as any other in this new breed of guitar groups.

On one Crawdaddy evening in April 1963, he rubbed his chin behind the massed females positioned stage-front to better gawk at Mick, Brian – 'an incredible blond, hulking hunk,' thought Oldham – and, in more qualified fashion, the other four. Next, as Andrew had neither the cash to launch the Stones nationally nor the clout to enchant record-company representatives to listen to the group, he brought someone with both these assets to another Crawdaddy sweatbath the following week.

Eric Easton wasn't an obvious person to supplicate as a possible co-manager. Nearing his forties, this former end-of-the-pier organist ran a cautious West End booking agency for entertainers that veered towards the middle-of-the-road. Yet he hadn't let personal dislike of transient pop stars and their teenage devotees prevent him from turning a hard-nosed penny when the opportunity knocked.

At the Crawdaddy Easton didn't behave as either an unsmiling pedant or as if visiting another planet. However, he wasn't sure what someone like Dick Rowe, head of A&R at Decca, one of the country's four main record companies, would feel about that grotesque-looking lead singer and his half-caste nasalings. Whatever doubts Eric had about Mick Jagger, his young sidekick was more uncertain about the Stones' keyboard player. To put it bluntly, Ian Stewart's face didn't fit. To drummer Jim McCarty, two months away from joining The Yardbirds, 'Ian always reminded me of Hoss Cartwright in *Bonanza*'. A comparison with the obese and dim-witted character in the 60s cowboy TV series is unkind, but Oldham had another worry: 'I didn't know a really successful group with six people in it. The public can't count up to six.'

It was thought prudent to thrust any misgivings aside when Oldham and Easton suggested a formal meeting. As self-appointed leader, Brian Jones did most of the talking on the group's behalf, hearing fine words when Andrew put them on an artistic par with The Beatles. It was Jones too who signed the official agreement, permitting Andrew and Eric to take official charge of his Rolling Stones' professional lives for the next three years.

Attending to a family bereavement overseas when Oldham and Easton pounced, Georgio Gomelsky was saddened by what he saw as the group reneging on 'a verbal understanding, I felt tremendously let down.' Neither could he be blamed for hurling a metaphorical stone at the departing back of the one he had thought had been the deception's central character: 'I never like to work with monsters, no matter how talented. Jones should have had treatment. His responses were never those of a normal person.'

Following any signpost that pointed in the direction of fame and wealth, Brian was quite prepared to sacrifice Mick and Ian if needs must. 'Easton said to Brian, "I don't think Jagger is any good",' snarled Ian Stewart, 'and so Brian said, "OK, we'll just get rid of him." I felt sure Brian would have done it.'

So would Dick Rowe when he summoned Easton and Oldham to Decca's riverside offices in May 1963. No one there knew what to make of young Andrew as he swept aside such obstacles as demo tapes and auditions. Decca could keep its West Hampstead studios, he told Rowe. The Stones would be making their first disc and those that came after elsewhere. Furthermore, they wouldn't need a Decca staff producer either. He'd take care of all that.

In a half nelson because the Stones' pressure-cooker reputation was filtering too fast from the Crawdaddy, Decca had no choice but to fix a ghastly corporate smile as this upstart called the shots. By the following weekend a three-year recording deal guaranteed the group and its handlers a royalty of six per cent between them, a lot more than EMI had granted their precious Beatles.

Ian Stewart's euphoria at this development was undercut by a management directive that under no circumstances was he to be seen either in photographs of the group or on the boards with them any more. It was a cruel necessity but he'd remain part of the team Brian Jones assured him – as if Brian were still in a position to decide such matters.

After he'd come to terms with this banishment, Stewart hovered unseen somewhere in the hierarchy between the humblest equipment-humper and the Jagger-Jones-Richards axis.

'He was the glue that held all the bits together,' was to be Keith's epitaph following Ian's death in 1985, 'Very few people realise how important he was to the Stones.'

Richards had been the subject of another adjustment when the Stones were on the point of take-off. His surname was to be 'Richard' now, giving him an implied affiliation with Cliff, Britain's most successful solo pop idol. With an irresolute nod, Keith, like the others, went along with both this and the sidelining of Ian. Later it transpired that Andrew Loog Oldham was not only younger than all his charges but, chuckled Richards, 'he had the same naïve experience – or lack of it – that we had. He didn't know what was going on nor did we. We just learned as we went along.'

Route 66 (Troup) 2.20
Mick Jagger: lead vocals
Brian Jones and Keith Richards: guitars
Bill Wyman: bass guitar
Charlie Watts: drums, tambourine
This is the most famous composition by US film actor and jazz pianist Bobby Troup. '(Get Your Kicks On) Route 66' that was penned by Troup in 1946 was to become a close second with 'Hoochie Coochie Man' to 'I Got My Mojo Working' as the British R&B movement's anthem. It was possible to ruin a school atlas by trying to figure out in Biro exactly how it 'winds from Chicago to LA'. The only version on which you could make out all the words was by Bing Crosby and the Andrews Sisters. This was not the prototype for the Stones' more frenetic and Chuck Berry-esque 'Route 66'.

I Just Wanna Make Love To You (Dixon) 2.17
Mick Jagger: lead vocals
Brian Jones: harmonica, tambourine
Charlie Watts: drums
Keith Richards: guitar
Bill Wyman: bass guitar
The words of this speeded-up blues by Willie Dixon, omnipresent double-bass player at Chicago's legendary Chess Records, were considered *risque* in 1964. Yet a fractional widening of vibrato during a sustained note on Jones's harmonica was as loaded as the lewdest of Jagger's vocal innuendos.

Honest I Do (Reed) 2.09
Mick Jagger: lead vocals, harmonica
Bill Wyman: bass guitar
Brian Jones and Keith Richards: guitars
Charlie Watts: drums
The antithesis of the hollered ferocity of Muddy Waters and Howlin' Wolf, Chicago contemporary Jimmy Reed's relaxed, slurred blues singing left its mark on the teenage Jagger, who would quote Jimmy Reed titles and lyrics as if they were proverbs. The Stones' commendable revival sticks closely to the arrangement on Mick's imported *I'm Jimmy Reed* LP.

Mona (McDaniel) 3.33

Mick Jagger: lead vocals, harmonica
Brian Jones and Keith Richards: guitars
Bill Wyman: bass guitar
Charlie Watts: drums, tambourine

Entitled 'I Need You Baby' on some pressings, this was drenched in reverberation and riven with the relentless shave-and-a-haircut-six-pence rhythm patented by Bo Diddley (Elias McDaniel) on whom the Stones leaned almost as heavily as they did on Chuck Berry. Diddley was among the all-American headliners on the group's first national tour, and was accompanied by Wyman and Watts on an edition of the BBC Light Programme's weekly pop magazine *Saturday Club* prior to his return to the USA.

Now I've Got A Witness (Nanker-Phelge) 2.29

Mick Jagger: tambourine
Brian Jones: harmonica
Keith Richards: guitar
Bill Wyman: bass guitar
Charlie Watts: drums
Ian Stewart: organ

The sub-title 'Like Uncle Phil And Uncle Gene' refers to two visitors to the sessions. The most self-important was a weedy New Yorker named Phil Spector, renowned for his spatial wall-of-sound production of hits by, among others, beehive-and-net-petticoat female vocal groups The Crystals and The Ronettes. The other was Gene Pitney, besuited and short-haired, one of the few North American singing stars to make the British charts during the beat boom. This salaam to him and Spector was a 12-bar instrumental with Jones extemporising on mouth-organ over a riff borrowed from Tommy Tucker's just-released 'Hi-Heel Sneakers'. This, and future output of this nature, was attributed to Nanker-Phelge, a corporate name for items to which all Stones personnel contributed. Phelge was after a former flatmate of Jones, Jagger and Richards, and Nanker was Brian's word for a particularly horrible face he liked to pull.

Little By Little (Nanker-Phelge-Spector) 2.39

Mick Jagger: lead vocals, harmonica
Bill Wyman: bass guitar
Ian Stewart and Gene Pitney: piano
Brian Jones and Keith Richards: guitars
Charlie Watts: drums
Allan Clarke and Graham Nash: percussion

This jammed rehash of Jimmy Reed's 'Shame Shame Shame' needed lyrics and these were collated in a studio alcove by Jagger and Phil Spector in the time it took the other Stones to record the backing. Clarke and Nash were mainstays of The Hollies, the biggest fish to be hooked in Manchester after Liverpool had been drained of its major talents by the London A&R invaders.

I'm A King Bee (Moore) 2.35

Mick Jagger: lead vocals
Keith Richards: guitar
Charlie Watts: drums
Brian Jones: slide guitar
Bill Wyman: bass guitar

While he wasn't trying consciously to copy Slim Harpo (James Moore), Jagger's emulation of the Louisiana blues giant's laconic style and his expressive harmonica blowing show Mick had absorbed too much of it by osmosis to escape being an imitator. Yet he copes well with the insidiously feverish lechery over an appropriate backing epitomised by a suggestive lowdown riff from Keith.

Carol (Berry) 2.33

Mick Jagger: lead vocals
Brian Jones and Keith Richards: guitars
Bill Wyman: bass guitar
Charlie Watts: drums

Of all the grand old men of classic rock, the first and foremost for the Stones, particularly Keith Richards was, and always would be, Chuck Berry. With melodies and R&B chord patterns powering often erudite verses celebrating the pleasures available to US adolescents, Chuck had become more than a cult celebrity in Britain by the time the Stones paid homage with this lively near-Xerox of a 1958 Berry A side.

Tell Me (You're Coming Back) (Jagger-Richards) 3.48

Mick Jagger: lead vocals
Brian Jones and Keith Richards: guitars
Ian Stewart: piano
Bill Wyman: bass guitar
Charlie Watts: drums, tambourine
Brian Jones and Bill Wyman: backing vocals

Response to the only true original, a slightly drippy teenage ballad, on the LP ranged from the *New Musical Express*'s 'a sad song which will compel people to listen to the words' to *Melody Maker*'s in-house grumpy old man Bob Dawburn cold-shouldering it as 'second-hand Liverpool'. Mick and Keith's breaking cover as a songwriting duo had been down to Andrew Loog Oldham's steady incitement. One immediate result of his nagging, 'That Girl Belongs To Yesterday' explored the same area as 'Tell Me' and was a British Top Ten hit for Gene Pitney, compounding the stereotyping of him as a merchant of melancholy. As the Stones' first US single, 'Tell Me' reached No. 24 on Pitney's side of the Atlantic.

Can I Get A Witness (Holland-Dozier-Holland) 2.55

Mick Jagger: lead vocals, tambourine
Keith Richards: guitar
Charlie Watts: drums
Brian Jones: harmonica
Bill Wyman: bass guitar
Ian Stewart: organ

Tamla Motown, a promising black soul label from Detroit, manoeuvred Marvin Gaye, its latest signing, into the US Hot 100 in 1963. 'Can I Get A Witness' was still hanging on in there but meant nothing in Britain when the Stones decided to cover it. Jagger's slightly strained vocal may have been the result of his dash to a high-street shop to purchase the sheet music.

You Can Make It If You Try (Jarrett) 2.01

Mick Jagger: lead vocals
Brian Jones and Keith Richards: guitars
Ian Stewart: organ
Bill Wyman: bass guitar
Charlie Watts: drums
Brian Jones and Keith Richards: backing vocals

Perhaps they'd be reluctant to acknowledge it, but all the Stones had fundamentally scholarly natures that dictated researching deep beneath the veneer of the music they enjoyed. Jones, for example, had bought Paul Oliver's *Blues Fell This Morning*, then a standard work, as soon as it was published in 1960 and had worked his way through as much of its bibliography as could be ordered from a public library. Meanwhile Jagger put himself on the mailing lists of untold US record labels like Excello, Aladdin, Atlantic and Imperial. Even when British firms began issuing R&B singles, letters arrived from Mick entreating them to release more. This item by Gene Allison leaked into Britain in 1958 and thence to obscurity although it crossed over from the US sepia chart to spend a solitary week in the mainstream Top 40.

Walking The Dog (Thomas) 3.10

Mick Jagger: lead vocals
Brian Jones and Keith Richards: guitars
Bill Wyman: bass guitar
Charlie Watts: drums

As an Australasia-only single, this try at a recent US smash by Rufus Thomas reached that continent's Top Ten. Back home it remained an album track, giving an intended Decca version on 45 by Liverpool's Kingsize Taylor and the Dominoes a clearer run. It also provided Brian Jones with artistic ammunition when the issue of who was and wasn't allowed to sing onstage came to a head in 1965. 'Brian could sing,' thundered a former girlfriend, Pat Andrews, 'but Mick, Keith and Andrew told him he was rubbish at it.' This may not have had much to do with the quality of Jones's light baritone that had been tuneful enough to harmonise and engage in call-and-response with Jagger, most conspicuously on 'Walking The Dog' that also embraced his aptly piercing whistles. 'Brian was meant to be doing that,' said Dave Berry who was on the bill of a Rolling Stones tour in 1965, 'but he kept shying away from the microphone which annoyed the others.'

THE ROLLING STONES NO. 2

UK Release: 30 January 1965
Producer: Andrew Loog Oldham

Decca LK 4661
Running Time: 36:58

SIDE ONE: Everybody Needs Somebody To Love; Down Home Girl; You Can't Catch Me; Time Is On My Side; What A Shame; Grown Up Wrong.

SIDE TWO: Down The Road Apiece; Under The Boardwalk; I Can't Be Satisfied; Pain In My Heart; Off The Hook; Susie Q.

The highlight of The Rolling Stones first US tour, that occupied them for most of June 1964, wasn't public as they seized the opportunity to record much of their second LP in Chicago, a metropolis that seemed to hirsute young Englishmen cartoon-like in its contradiction of familiar mystery. A Woolworth's reared up in North Clark Street – scene of the St. Valentine's Day Massacre – Coca-Cola tasted just the same, and pizza was the Windy City's answer to fish-and-chips. Yet the sights and sounds in the streets – the ones the Stones were able to walk – were so diverting they could be hours ambling just a mile from Chess Studios at 2120, South Michegan Avenue.

'I'd go back there tomorrow just to do some straight session work,' said Brian Jones of the building where Chicago blues lived as pungently and as pragmatically as it did when performed by a down-and-out busker on State Street. Inside Chess, the Stones were putty in the hands of the same house team that had forged the definitive works of Waters, Wolf, Diddley and Berry. Indeed, the venerated Muddy chanced to be present when the Stones were working on his downbeat 'I Can't Be Satisfied'.

The group returned for further work at Chess during a second trip to North America that autumn where wonderment at all things British had peaked in the 1964 week when The Beatles occupied *nine* positions in the Canadian Top Ten. This British Invasion was an eventuality predicted by Gene Pitney when he'd touched down in New York in late 1963. Audience screams during his slot on ITV's *Thank Your Lucky Stars* that had The Rolling Stones on the same programme, were still ringing in his ears. Yet, as a phenomenon, it had less to do with the musicians themselves than the behaviour of a public that, convinced of something incredible, exhibited a fanaticism for it that left the British themselves swallowing dust.

After Uncle Sam had capitulated, the rest of the world was a walkover. Once, a group had as much chance of getting a disc in the charts of even the local newspaper as the lead singer had of being knighted. But these days everything is different. There you were, miming your latest hit on *Brisbane Tonight* or, like Frank Allen of The Searchers, touring New Zealand with the Stones: 'I stood watching them, mesmerised by the energy if not overawed by the expertise. A fan by my side remarked that Keith Richards could make his guitar talk. I could see what he meant. I could almost hear the guitar saying, "Take your hands off me, you clumsy oaf" but it was impressive, of that there was no doubt. This was not so much a demonstration of music as a display of sex and power and, on that level, it worked to perfection.'

Keith's riposte to Frank might have been, 'I've always done things on a fairly instinctive basis. I think brains have got in the way of too many things, especially something as basic as what we're doing'.

Primitivism wasn't the way of The Searchers. They'd wished they were in hell rather than Hamburg at first. It had been punishing seasons in that city's red-light district clubland that had toughened them up in readiness for what lay ahead.

Similarly, their first month of hard graft in the States had been the Stones' Hamburg in that it was often arduous but contained hidden blessings. Hitless there, the group had been obliged to melt the *sang-froid* of non-screaming curiosity-seekers, and were indeed found wanting on a couple of poorly attended occasions. But other audiences, crucially those at two performances at New York's prestigious Carnegie Hall, felt a compulsion to dance only a few bars into the first number. They were eating from the palm of Jagger's hand by the finish on the evidence of the bedlam back in the dressing rooms.

Nevertheless, while the likes of The Searchers, The Dave Clark Five, The Kinks and The Animals had settled into the Top Ten, the Stones were still struggling as US chart propositions when they undertook their second jaunt. This time, however, it was more like a re-run of British beat hysteria what with a show at Loew's Theatre, Providence, being stopped after four numbers. This was not untypical. However, when the Stones ventured into the heart of the deep south bible belt, 'Doth not nature itself teach you that if a man have long hair, it is a shame unto him?' (I Corinthians xi.14) was quoted by redneck whites with a hatred of

DECCA

commies, blacks and gays like this new breed of musical Limey longhairs.

A few snatched hours of serenity round a Savannah swimming pool were interrupted when, recounted Keith Richards, 'we were arrested for topless bathing. Some people were driving by and swore that there was a load of chicks leaping in and out of the pool with just a pair of drawers on. So the cops came zooming in to bust these chicks – and, of course, the closer they got, the more stupid they must have felt especially when they heard these *sarf* London accents'.

Yet in back-street dance halls in Houston or Lexington, you'd come across many an outfit that so far as it dared, had grown out its crew-cuts and ditched stage costumes and big smiles for a motley taciturnity. Although the Stones had been relatively slow to gain ground in North America, during the interval between their first and second visits, they had amassed widespread grassroots support. In the north too, there were myriad Anglophile garage bands who, with dubious musical ability, had borrowed from the Stones' dialectic. This sometimes involved vocalists aping Mick Jagger's vocal style broken by handclaps above the head and kicking one leg backwards as if dancing a half-hearted Charleston.

Jagger added considerably to his arsenal of physical gyrations when the Stones were among many other weavers of the rich tapestry of mid-60s pop at Santa Monica Auditorium in late October 1964. They were there to participate in the huge Teen-Age Music International (TAMI) show entitled *Gather No Moss* when screened at a cinema near you. Mick is said to have smoked the entire contents of a packet of cigarettes as the group's allotted time approached. His nervousness wasn't just because it was being filmed for posterity. It was because he was consigned to be preceded by James Brown, who'd be totally justified in describing himself as 'the Godfather of Soul'. Watching Brown hurl a hand-mic into the air, swivel round, do the splits, jump upright and catch the mic in the space of two effortless seconds would have cowed any callow beat-group singer, chart-riding and frantic, waiting in the wings and pondering how long his entrance could be delayed to allow the Brown-inflamed crowd to cool down.

'You had to be the biggest dreamer in the world to think you could export our stuff to America,' agreed a pessimistic Keith Richards. Yet typifying the underlying affability of pop's most optimistic period, James deigned to join the assembled TAMI cast for a finale centred on the Stones. He was to be most courteous when Jagger and Richards were conducted into his backstage presence at the Harlem Apollo that was to Brown what the Crawdaddy had been to his callers. 'They were standing there like scared teenagers,' remembered Ronnie Spector of the Ronettes, 'They introduced themselves. He shook their hands and that's all there was to it. I don't think James even knew who these weird English guys were, but Mick and Keith were practically shaking.'

Later, Brown would protest that he brought Jagger onto the stage and introduced him to the Apollo's black audience; that the Stones 'got over real good' at the Santa Monica spectacular and that he thought of them as 'brothers'. Likewise, protest singer-in-transition Bob Dylan hung out with Brian Jones and was pleased to hear that Mick preferred the 'House Of The Rising Sun' on the first Dylan LP to The Animals' million-selling version, and would deride as phoney Barry McGuire's all-purpose 'Eve Of Destruction', the hit song of 1965 when protest was all the rage. It was a back-handed compliment of sorts that Dylan, believed Jagger was 'good but too fashionable to stay as popular as he is'.

All manner of US showbiz personalities would be paying artist-to-artist respects to incoming British pop celebrities, among them Frank Sinatra, shaking hands and chatting affably with Keith Richards and Andrew Loog Oldham when they looked in at a session at Hollywood's Western Recording Studio. They were scouting for a suitable West Coast location to tape further tracks for what would be one of Britain's biggest-selling LPs of 1965.

Everybody Needs Somebody To Love (Burke-Wexler-Russell) 5.03
Mick Jagger: all vocals
Brian Jones and Keith Richards: guitars
Ian Stewart: piano
Bill Wyman: bass guitar
Charlie Watts: drums
Mick Jagger and Jack Nitzsche: percussion

The Stones were fond enough of Philadelphia gospel singer-turned-soul-man Solomon Burke's output to record three of his songs. This one from 1964 wasn't a hit for him but, via the group's endorsement, it became to Burke what 'Rock Around The Clock' was to Bill Haley. Delivered by Jagger in the secular but testifying manner that was to connect stylistically with turn-of-the-millenium rap, it was a stage fixture for a long while, although performance quality depended much upon the mood of the hour. Its riff-and-chord sequence were to be grafted onto 1965's 'Whatcha Gonna Do About It' by The Small Faces.

Down Home Girl (Lieber-Butler) 4.11
Mick Jagger: lead vocals
Brian Jones and Keith Richards: guitars
Jack Nitzsche: piano
Bill Wyman: bass guitar
Charlie Watts: drums
Mick Jagger and Keith Richards: backing vocals

Co-written by Jerry Lieber who, with Mike Stoller, provisioned Elvis Presley, The Coasters and The Drifters with chart fodder, this is a citified perspective on country blues, made-to-measure for Alvin Robinson. His version flopped but was improved upon by the Stones with help from Jack Nitzsche, Phil Spector's arranger and maker of mostly instrumental discs under his own name. He was ominpresent at Hollywood's RCA Studios where this and other *Rolling Stones No. 2* items were completed.

You Can't Catch Me (Berry) 3.38
Mick Jagger: lead vocals
Brian Jones and Keith Richards: guitars
Ian Stewart: organ
Bill Wyman: bass guitar
Charlie Watts: drums

A straightforward revival of a 1957 A side by Chuck Berry, this blasted open memory banks for Bill Wyman who'd first experienced Berry when Chuck duck-walked through the number in 1957's *Rock Rock Rock*, a celluloid conveyor-belt of lip-synched pop diversity connected by a vacuous story-line.

Time Is On My Side (Meade) 2.52
Mick Jagger: lead vocals
Brian Jones and Keith Richards: guitars
Ian Stewart: organ
Brian Jones: backing vocals
Charlie Watts: drums
Bill Wyman: bass guitar, six-string bass
Meade was the pen-name of Jerry Ragovoy, another of the Philadelphia soul crowd who wrote and produced this uplifting ballad for Irma Thomas. The Stones copied the arrangement but still impregnated it with an individuality exemplified by Jagger's emotion-charged spoken passage. A simultaneous cover by The Moody Blues was issued as the B side of their 'I Don't Want To Go On Without You'.

What A Shame (Jagger-Richards) 3.03
Mick Jagger: lead vocals, harmonica
Keith Richards: guitar
Charlie Watts: drums
Brian Jones: slide guitar
Bill Wyman: bass guitar
Ian Stewart: piano
A muggy afternoon special from the Jagger-Richards songwriting factory, this is lifted slightly from the lacklustre by Wyman's lively bass line.

Grown Up Wrong (Jagger-Richards) 2.03
Mick Jagger: lead vocals, harmonica
Keith Richards: guitar
Charlie Watts: drums
Brian Jones: slide guitar
Bill Wyman: bass guitar
Mick Jagger and Keith Richards: backing vocals
An insubstantial but royalty-earning ditty for Mick and Keith, albeit one that Andrew Loog Oldham couldn't place with any other artist.

Down The Road Apiece (Raye) 2.55
Mick Jagger: lead vocals
Brian Jones and Keith Richards: guitars
Ian Stewart: piano
Bill Wyman: bass guitar
Charlie Watts: drums
This 1941 hit by Ray McKinley was revived by Chuck Berry, reason enough for the Stones to try it in similar rocked-up fashion.

Under The Boardwalk (Resnick-Young) 2.46
Mick Jagger: lead vocals
Keith Richards: guitar
Charlie Watts: drums
Brian Jones: percussion
Bill Wyman: bass guitar
Mick Jagger and Keith Richards: backing vocals

Contemporary reviews described this as a beat-ballad or rockaballad although it came from a soul source, namely a recent single by The Drifters, then in the throes of a run of mostly US chartbusters for Atlantic. This label was to loom large in the legend of the Stones whose 'Under The Boardwalk' was a hit 45 in Australia.

I Can't Be Satisfied (Morganfield) 3.26
Mick Jagger: lead vocals
Keith Richards: guitar
Charlie Watts: drums
Brian Jones: slide guitar
Bill Wyman: bass guitar

This English reproduction of a Muddy Waters number featured what Jones was to cite as 'one of the best guitar solos I've ever managed'. It confirmed Alexis Korner of Blues Incorporated's opinion that Brian was one of the finest British bottleneck players he'd ever heard. Although selected for *The Rolling Stones No. 2*, it didn't appear on its US counterpart, *The Rolling Stones Now!* This was because North American LPs tend to include fewer tracks, but why was 'I Can't Be Satisfied' one of the omissions? 'Grown Up Wrong' and 'What A Shame' could have gone without any hardship. Such an affront, however unintentional, fuelled Brian's growing paranoia about how dispensable a Stone he was becoming.

Pain In My Heart (Neville) 2.11
Mick Jagger: lead vocals
Brian Jones and Keith Richards: guitars
Jack Nitzsche: keyboards
Charlie Watts: drums
Bill Wyman: bass guitar, six-string bass

Taken at an attractively funereal pace, this was a reworking of the latest by Georgia soul shouter Otis Redding, another Atlantic signing. As well as 'Pain In My Heart', the Stones were to record three more items associated with Redding who, in reciprocation, had the gall to overhaul their 'Satisfaction' as a single within weeks of it being the first of many US No. 1's for the group.

Off The Hook (Jagger-Richards) 2.33
Mick Jagger: lead vocals
Brian Jones and Keith Richards: guitars
Bill Wyman: bass guitar
Charlie Watts: drums

A see-sawing *ostinato* is central to a lyrical nutshelling of a swain's failed attempt to ring his loved one, owing to her permanently engaged telephone line. Issued as an A side in some foreign territories, this was easily the most attractive Jagger-Richard opus on the LP although that's not saying very much. It opened the Stones' section of the TAMI extravaganza.

Susie Q (Broadwater-Hawkins-Lewis) 1.50
Mick Jagger: lead vocals
Brian Jones and Keith Richards: guitars
Bill Wyman: bass guitar
Charlie Watts: drums

This was left over from sessions for the first album. Though it added an awry lead guitar part by Richards it was, as was often the case, less robust than the original, a US Top 30 entry in 1957 by Dale Hawkins who recorded for Chess subsidiary Checker.

OUT OF OUR HEADS

UK Release: 24 September 1965
Intl CD No: ABKCO 94302
Running Time: 29:38

Decca LK/SKL 4733
Producer: Andrew Loog Oldham

SIDE ONE: She Said Yeah; Mercy Mercy; Hitch Hike; That's How Strong My Love Is; Good Times; Gotta Get Away; Talkin' 'Bout You.

SIDE TWO: Cry To Me; Oh Baby (We Got A Good Thing Goin'); Heart Of Stone; The Under Assistant West Coast Promotion Man; I'm Free.

A stop-gap measure, short on needle-time, *Out Of Our Heads* was created on the drip over several months in different studios in Britain and the USA. As well as being the last Rolling Stones LP to embrace a Nanker-Phelge composing credit, it was also the last to contain a preponderance of non-originals, most of them reflecting the US soul music that was to be heard in the West End clubs that Mick Jagger, Brian Jones and Keith Richards were frequenting outside working hours.

Their increasingly more splendid domestic record-players would also pulsate to the Betty Everetts, Don Covays and Chuck Jacksons as well as the more illustrious Marvin Gayes, Wilson Picketts and (Little) Stevie Wonders. Before saturation plugging on Britain's new pirate radio stations eased them into the lower rungs of the charts, Mick, Brian, Keith and the others had long been *au fait* with eruditions like 'Harlem Shuffle' by Bob And Earl, Chuck Jackson's 'Any Day Now' and the originals of such UK covers as The Hollies' 'Just One Look' (Doris Troy) and The Fourmost's 'Baby I Need Your Loving' (The Four Tops).

The Stones tried a few themselves to mainly tepid critical reaction after copies of *Out Of Our Heads* washed up round reviewers' typewriters. The most vitriolic assessment was 'samey and boring' by *Disc & Music Echo*. Signs of danger were perceptible too in its failure to top the LP chart, spending less than half the time in the Top 20 as 1964's eponymous debut.

A change of basic tactics was in order. A more prolific and higher standard of self-penned songs to match growing technological confidence was needed. Andrew Loog Oldham's

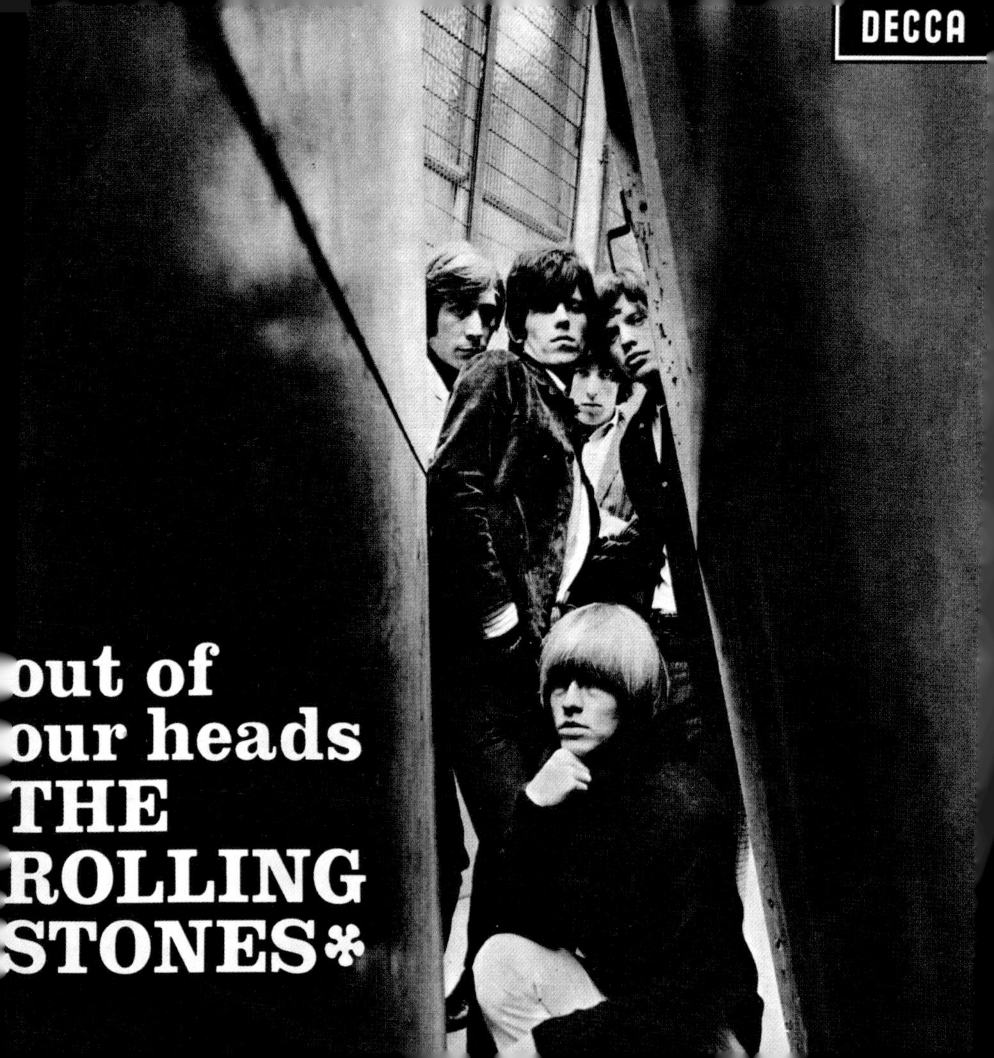
DECCA
out of
our heads
THE
ROLLING
STONES*

questionable skills as a record producer had been untried when first he and the group had gathered together in a studio. Now his directives at the mixing panel were dotted with erudite jargon as he decreed theoretical apportionment of trackage, shortlisting of devices and effects and general operational definition, while getting down to specifics like learned procrastinations over, perhaps, the level of acoustic overspill allowable on Charlie's floor-tom.

Meanwhile William Hickey, the *Daily Express* tittle-tattler, noted 'there's no harm these days in knowing a Rolling Stone. Some of their best friends are in fact fledglings from the upper classes'. Chauffeur-driven vehicles disgorged A-list celebrities of the calibre of Lionel Bart, Diana Dors and Judy Garland outside the Belgravia apartment block where Brian Jones dwelt with The Pretty Things ('sleeping with the enemy', to use Phil May's playful expression).

Across the Atlantic, the Stones were also clasped to the metaphorical bosom of Andy Warhol, ruler of New York's Factory, an arts laboratory hinged on his mannered revelling in consumerism, mass production and the emptiness of glamour. Warhol brought humour and topicality back into art via the earnest superficiality of soup-cans, Brillo pads, comic-strip philosophy interesting-but-boring films like *Chelsea Girls*. His mixed-media events spawned The Velvet Underground whose emotional vocabulary rippled across decades of pop through an unprecedented coverage of drug addiction, sexual taboos and mental instability.

In the Big Apple too, a hundred-foot illuminated portrait of the Stones in Times Square ensured a good turn-out at a press conference to kick off their fourth North American tour in the autumn of 1965. It was alleged by local guitarist Lee Underwood that a freelance photographer named Linda Eastman spent the subsequent night with Jagger 'and wrote about it in an American teen magazine'. If it ever existed, the article in question has not come to light, nor has any proof that a liaison between Mick and the soon-to-be Mrs. Paul McCartney went further than a wistful embrace beneath the stars at the conclusion of an evening out.

More importantly, the Stones had also hooked up with Ahmet and Nesuhi Ertegun, supremos of Atlantic Records that vied with Tamla Motown as the USA's foremost soul label, and a yapping disc-jockey with the *nom de turntable* Murray The K. The brashest and possibly the most powerful of them all, he'd had the unmitigated audacity to style himself 'the sixth Rolling Stone' and before that 'the fifth Beatle'. Nevertheless, he had his uses. It was Murray, for instance, who turned the Stones onto many of the soul tracks they covered.

That was jolly decent of Murray The K, but others of his countrymen expected more than a thank you for their kindnesses. With a mouth that spewed forth estimates at a moment's notice, Allen Klein, an accountant-manager from New Jersey, reminded The Kinks' Ray Davies of 'an archetypal villain in a film'. The fawning reverence of Klein's employees was tempered by innumerable derogatory *bon mots* from former clients. Yet, in his capacity as Loog Oldham's newly hired administrative trouble-shooter, Allen's wheedling of a jaw-droppingly high advance for the Stones from Decca was to impress Paul McCartney. And to Ringo Starr he'd come across as 'a powerful man and also, no matter what anyone says, he's fair.' A prophecy that Klein would represent The Beatles before the swinging sixties were out came almost as true as another that he would shake the Stones from the grasp of Oldham and Eric Easton.

She Said Yeah (Christy-Jackson) 1.34
Mick Jagger: lead vocals
Brian Jones and Keith Richards: guitars
Keith Richards: backing vocals
Bill Wyman: bass guitar
Charlie Watts: drums
The Beatles rated Larry Williams, a singing pianist from New Orleans of Little Richard persuasion, and it was on Paul McCartney's recommendation that the Stones delivered an astounding fast-tempo overhaul of a 1959 Williams A side. McCartney was to try it himself in 1999, and The Animals had already included a rather thuggish arrangement on their 1964 debut LP, but the Stones treatment was the ultimate one.

Mercy Mercy (Covay-Miller) 2.45
Mick Jagger: lead vocals
Brian Jones and Keith Richards: guitars
Keith Richards: backing vocals
Bill Wyman: bass guitar
Charlie Watts: drums
This Chess piece had been a US hit for Atlantic in 1964 by Don Covay, one of Jagger's favourite soul artists who, with Larry Williams, had owed much to Little Richard at the beginning of his career. He had also been in a 50s black vocal group, The Rainbows, with Marvin Gaye. On 'Mercy Mercy', Jagger's talent for vacuuming the characteristics of a given vocalist without descending to caricature was tested thoroughly and not found wanting.

Hitch Hike (Gaye-Stevenson-Paul) 2.25
Mick Jagger: lead vocals
Brian Jones and Keith Richards: guitars
Ian Stewart: piano
Bill Wyman: bass guitar
Charlie Watts: drums
Keith Richards: backing vocals
In 1963, Marvin Gaye's debut 45 was proferred as an alternative to the Twist, along with the Fly, the Locomotion, the ungainly Turkey Trot, the Madison, the back-breaking Limbo, the Mickey's Monkey *ad nauseum*. The Hitch Hike was still in vogue when the Stones decided to consume *Out Of Our Heads* grooves with it at RCA studios – with a guitar solo that lived a separate life from the rest of the number.

That's How Strong My Love Is (Jamison) 2.25

Mick Jagger: lead vocals
Keith Richards: guitar
Charlie Watts: drums
Brian Jones: organ
Bill Wyman: bass guitar
Jack Nitzsche: keyboards

This Otis Redding B side had been in the shops mere weeks when the Stones covered it, utilising the same slow build-up, but minus Redding's accompanying horns. To the average British dolly-bird shuffling about in the gloom beyond the footlights in a provincial palais, Otis Redding was little more than just a name in mid-1965. So far as she was concerned, the Stones' 'That's How Strong My Love Is' was the *only* version.

Good Times (Cooke) 1.58

Mick Jagger: lead vocals
Brian Jones and Keith Richards: guitars
Brian Jones: marimba
Bill Wyman: bass guitar
Charlie Watts: drums, percussion
Jack Nitzsche: organ
Mick Jagger, Keith Richards and Bill Wyman: backing vocals

Alhough his tambourine bashing was a trace element on other *Out Of Our Heads* items, Woody Alexander wasn't needed on a rendition of ear-grabbing 'Good Times', a 1964 single by his business partner, the late Sam Cooke who, like Don Covay, emerged from a gospel choir as a protege of Little Richard. In the Stones' hands, Cooke's US smash was more than just album filler but not potent enough for the group to work it into the stage act.

Gotta Get Away (Jagger-Richards) 2.06

Mick Jagger: lead vocals
Brian Jones and Keith Richards: guitars
Woody Alexander: tambourine
Bill Wyman: bass guitar
Charlie Watts: drums
Mick Jagger and Keith Richards: backing vocals

This was an improvement on the previous LP's 'What A Shame', that was also positioned surreptitiously as the penultimate track on Side One. However, it is both musically and lyrically a paler shoot from the same stem as 'So Much In Love', a sardonic Jagger-Richards opus for Scotland's Mighty Avengers who had snatched slight UK chart honours with it in 1964.

Talkin' 'Bout You (Berry) 2.31
Mick Jagger: lead vocals
Brian Jones and Keith Richards: guitars
Ian Stewart: piano
Bill Wyman: bass guitar
Charlie Watts: drums
Keith Richards: backing vocals
A proficient Chuck Berry cover had reared up on each Stones studio album thus far, but this near-impromptu selection from one of his albums was to be the last Berry number they'd issue on vinyl until 1970.

Cry To Me (Russell) 3.09
Mick Jagger: lead vocals
Brian Jones and Keith Richards: guitars
Ian Stewart: piano
Jack Nitzsche: organ
Bill Wyman: bass guitar
Charlie Watts: drums
Brian Jones and Keith Richards: backing vocals
Popularised by Solomon Burke, this placatory ballad from 1962 was the antithesis of 'Everybody Needs Somebody To Love'. A stronger version was to be The Pretty Things' final Top 20 strike. While the Stones suffered global acclaim and supertax the Things began decades of struggle that would have destroyed a lesser outfit. But there had been an uproarious *esprit de corps* moment on 7 March 1965 when, following a stopped show at the Palace Theatre in Manchester, Keith and Mick taxied across the city to leap onstage with the Things, who chanced to be playing the Manchester Cavern that evening. Among numbers on which Jagger duetted with Phil May was 'Cry To Me'.

Oh Baby (We Got A Good Thing Goin') (Ozen) 2.08
Mick Jagger: lead vocals
Brian Jones and Keith Richards: guitars
Ian Stewart: piano
Bill Wyman: bass guitar
Charlie Watts: drums
A slow blues by Barbara Lynn Ozen – no, I'd never heard of her either – was transformed into something more danceable with guitars holding their own behind a slightly embittered lead vocal.

Heart Of Stone (Jagger-Richards) 2.50

Mick Jagger: lead vocals
Brian Jones and Keith Richards: guitars
Mick Jagger and Keith Richards: backing vocals
Bill Wyman: bass guitar
Charlie Watts: drums
Jack Nitzsche: piano, tambourine

Nine months earlier, this had been the second Stones 45 to penetrate the US Top 20, but was not made available to a chagrined home following until it appeared on *Out Of Our Heads* much later in the year. A blues adjusted to the beat boom, it was a jaded warning to a nice girl by the very lout her parents wouldn't have in the house.

The Under Assistant West Coast Promotion Man (Nanker-Phelge) 3.07

Mick Jagger: lead vocals, harmonica
Bill Wyman: bass guitar
Ian Stewart: piano
Brian Jones and Keith Richards: guitars
Charlie Watts: drums
Woody Alexander: tambourine

Via means peculiar to himself, Jagger was becoming as fluent and as individual a lyricist as Berry or Dylan – as demonstrated on a dig at a finger-clicking, hep-to-the-jive Californian publicist that he'd met on a recent US expedition.

I'm Free (Jagger-Richards) 2.24

Mick Jagger: lead vocals
Brian Jones and Keith Richards: guitars
Ian Stewart: piano
Jack Nitzsche: organ
Bill Wyman: bass guitar
Charlie Watts: drums
Mick Jagger and Keith Richards: backing vocals
Woody Alexander: tambourine

This encapsulation of the free-spirited mood of swinging London belonged only to speculation over a communal cigarette behind school bike sheds in the provinces where the fog of repression that had followed the Second World War was still clearing. Nevertheless, if not as resonant a rallying cry as 'Satisfaction' or 'Get Of Off My Cloud' – that it B-sided in the USA – 'I'm Free' was a more directly articulate speech of the heart. The Stones were still performing it on stage in the early 70s.

AFTERMATH

UK Release: 15 April 1966
Intl CD No: ABKCO 94772
Running Time: 53:22

Decca LK/SKL 4786
Producer: Andrew Loog Oldham

SIDE ONE: Mother's Little Helper; Stupid Girl; Lady Jane; Under My Thumb; Dontcha Bother Me; Goin' Home.

SIDE TWO: Flight 505; High And Dry; Out Of Time; It's Not Easy; I Am Waiting; Take It Or Leave It; Think; What To Do.

Brian Jones was as multi-faceted a musician as Steve Winwood, Manfred Mann's Mike Vickers, Alan Blakely of The Tremeloes and when playing sax and keyboards simultaneously, Graham Bond. By mid-1966, Jones was playing up to six different instruments during the course of any given Rolling Stones concert or on any single album.

'All he wanted to do was dabble at other instruments,' Ian Stewart muttered darkly, 'he hardly touched the guitar'. This was far from strictly true, although Keith Richards was to insist too that 'it was down to me to lay down all the guitar tracks while Brian would be leaping about on the the marimba or the dulcimer'. Over the next three years Jones was to knit these and all manner of quaint instrumentation into the fabric of Rolling Stones discs. And never more so than for *Aftermath*, reckoned by many to be the group's most inventive and original collection. Certainly Jones would never again work so fully according to his considerable capacities.

Brian Jones should have been in his element, but often he added his musical icing just as the cake was baked. He spoke of *Aftermath* and its follow-up, *Between The Buttons*, without pride as he weighed up the easy money against being in what was as much of a hard-sell pop act as The Dave Clark Five or Herman's Hermits.

Another bone of contention was that a little over two years after their little 'Tell Me' for the first album, Richards and Jagger – never that receptive to the compositions of colleagues – had been sufficiently self-assured to write all 14 tracks on *Aftermath*. They arrived at the studio with detailed demo tapes or, like painters dabbing at a hanging canvas

AFTER
-MATH
UK

minutes before the gallery opens, nothing more than half-finished music with odds and ends of lyrics. It seemed to Brian that he, Bill, Charlie and Ian were there solely to lend power to their patterns and chords and rhymes. 'I try to help them get what they want,' averred Watts, who would extend his percussive skills beyond the limitations of the drum kit and tambourine at selected points on *Aftermath* that was a conscious musical progression from the previous patchworks of R&B-soul stand-bys and uneasy originals.

When the daring new LP restored the group to No. 1 in Britain and reached No. 2 in the States, it became clear that both the Stones and their self-contained songwriting team were as sound an investment for Decca as The Beatles and Lennon-McCartney were for EMI. However, artistically and as an aural abstraction of the times, *Aftermath* ranked not with John, Paul, George and Ringo's recent *Rubber Soul* album so much as The Kinks' contemporaneous *Face To Face*.

Like both The Kinks, The Beatles and every other group that counted, the Stones had noted Bob Dylan singing through his nostrils about myriad less wistful topics than protest and boy meets girl. When the underground monthly *Oz* was launched in Britain, one edition contained a mind-boggling word-for-word analysis of his 12-minute 'Desolation Row' by an obsessive who, in order to prove a pet theory, had placed an ad in an *Oz*-like New York journal for a Dylan urine sample.

You'd have had some search to find a corresponding Jagger-ologist. But as the principal wordsmith in his and Keith's creative liaison, he was at one with Phil May's comment 'we couldn't sing about chain-gangs because we'd never been on one. We were trying to get our language onto record using R&B as a framework and later finding a new direction.'

Jagger claimed 'to write about 12 songs in two weeks on tour. It gives you lots of ideas. You're just totally into it. You get back from a show, have something to eat, a few beers and just go to your room and write. At home, you don't want to do anything but read and things like that'.

He extended himself further as producer of Chris Farlowe, hitherto a blues and soul singer from north London, who'd done next to nothing in the charts but was appreciated by other artists for a curdled baritone enhanced with strangled gasps and anguished roars that enabled him to take on items like 'In The Midnight Hour' and sound as thrilled as Wilson Pickett, its black originator, about the prospect of a tryst beneath the stars.

1966 began for Chris with his 'Think' from the yet unreleased *Aftermath*, creating a stir.

Next, another Jagger-Richards number, 'Out Of Time', dragged Georgie Fame from No. 1 that summer. A guitar-shaped swimming pool each could have been ordered by Mick and Keith on the strength of Farlowe's aided triumph, and at least a diving board apiece for David Garrick's 'Lady Jane' and The Searchers' improvement on 'Take It Or Leave It', two other chart-penetrating covers from *Aftermath*.

Jagger praised Garrick to his face but wasn't especially complimentary in an interview about a 'Lady Jane' that was as lushly orchestrated as the *Aftermath* one wasn't. In doing so, Mick hurt himself financially as well as David. Consequently he kept quiet about other syndications such as 'I Am Waiting' by The Quiet Five, Wayne Gibson's 'Under My Thumb' and 'Mother's Little Helper' from a Gene Latter, who was accorded a modicom of press exposure by alleging that Jagger had stolen his stage act.

Mother's Little Helper (Jagger-Richards) 2.45
Mick Jagger: lead vocals
Keith Richards: guitar
Brian Jones: mandolin, slide guitar
Bill Wyman: bass guitar
Charlie Watts: drums
Jack Nitzsche: 12-string guitar
Dulcimer, bottleneck guitar and a 12-string tuned to a lower octave are played in unison to create a wiry, sitar-like effect on an enduring scrutiny of the prescribed habit-forming tablets that hasten a frantic housewife's 'busy dying day'. As a US-only 45, 'Mother's Little Helper' reached No. 8.

Stupid Girl (Jagger-Richards) 2.55
Mick Jagger: lead vocals
Bill Wyman: bass guitar
Brian Jones and Keith Richards: guitars
Charlie Watts: drums
Ian Stewart: organ
Mick Jagger and Keith Richards: backing vocals
The lyrics were supposedly symptomatic of Jagger's fading love for his girlfriend, Chrissie Shrimpton, younger sister of the fashion model Jean Shrimpton. Musically this has a touch of Manfred Mann about it.

Lady Jane (Jagger-Richards) 3.08
Mick Jagger: lead vocals
Brian Jones: dulcimer, harpsichord
Keith Richards: guitar
Bill Wyman: bass guitar
Charlie Watts: drums, marimba
This was as far removed from Waters, Berry and Diddley as any Stones fan from the Crawdaddy era could have imagined. Sounding like Elizabethan jongleurs and presented as such when plugging the *ballade* on *Thank Your Lucky Stars,* the group backed Jagger's fine enunciation of his devotion to his betrothed, another of the same social standing, plus one who might be a servant girl. This was the first *Aftermath* item to feature the vintage dulcimer, a mediaeval stringed instrument struck with hand-held hammers that was presented to Brian Jones by Irish-American protest singer Richard Farina. Jones also played harpsichord here and on other *Aftermath* tracks. This instrument's impact on pop has been blunted by the fine line between ear-catching extraneousness and its association with renaissance music. However, it had been heard on The Yardbirds' million-selling 'For Your Love' in 1965, and an

electric model had been employed throughout The Kinks' *Face To Face*. Alhough it was the B side of 'Mother's Little Helper', 'Lady Jane' slipped into the US Top 30 in her own right.

Under My Thumb (Jagger-Richards) 3.41
Mick Jagger: lead vocals
Keith Richards: guitar
Charlie Watts: drums
Brian Jones: marimba
Bill Wyman: bass guitar
Ian Stewart: piano
In the face of mitherings about its domineering sexual arrogance, one of the album's high points was still in the concert set 15 years later although the curiously circular effect of the constant marimba riff was emulated on guitar. In 1969, a subdued arrangement was included in the fabled open-air show in London's Hyde Park by the Blind Faith supergroup.

Dontcha Bother Me (Jagger-Richards) 2.41
Mick Jagger: lead vocals, harmonica
Keith Richards: guitar
Ian Stewart: piano
Brian Jones: slide guitar
Bill Wyman: bass guitar
Charlie Watts: drums, tambourine
If not a stand-out track, a sour blues shuffle suits further ill-tempered verses about an unsatisfactory girlfriend.

Goin' Home (Jagger-Richards) 11.13
Mick Jagger: lead vocals
Keith Richards: guitar
Charlie Watts: drums, tambourine
Brian Jones: harmonica
Bill Wyman: bass guitar
Ian Stewart: piano
Part of the second section of the longest Stones track ever recorded succeeded The Who's 'Anyway Anyhow Anywhere' as the opening theme to ITV's *Ready Steady Go*, the most atmospheric pop series of the 60s. In the control booth at the RCA studio, Andrew Oldham felt that it was, as he put it '*the* take', and chose to let the tape roll on for minutes past where a fade-out might have been expected, indicating through the glass that the group should play on to catch 'a musical moment of the forever'. Only Dylan's 'Desolation Row', the finale of 1965's *Highway 61 Revisited*, had approached the quarter-hour mark. Keith Richards said it 'released everyone from that whole three-minute thing.'

Flight 505 (Jagger-Richards) 3.27

Mick Jagger: lead vocals
Brian Jones and Keith Richards: guitars
Ian Stewart: piano
Brian Jones and Bill Wyman: keyboards
Bill Wyman: bass guitar
Charlie Watts: drums
Mick Jagger and Keith Richards: backing vocals

The 'Satisfaction' riff is quoted during Stewart's solo piano intro to a piece inspired by some of the paint-peeling antiquities that lifted the group from A to B and fuelled misgivings about air transport – especially in the light of the crashes that had already killed Buddy Holly, Patsy Cline and Jim Reeves.

High And Dry (Jagger-Richards) 3.08

Mick Jagger: lead vocals
Keith Richards: guitar
Charlie Watts: percussion
Brian Jones: harmonica
Bill Wyman: double-bass

The Stones take on skiffle in a track that tended to grow on the listener after about the 20th spin. Of the different stylistic shades of skiffle, 'High And Dry' leans heaviest on the hillbilly sounds of the Appalachian highlands where early English settlers had stabilized a conservative repertoire that, with minimal melodic variation, was the opposite of jazz.

Out Of Time (Jagger-Richards) 5.37

Mick Jagger: lead vocals
Brian Jones: marimba, saxophone
Charlie Watts: drums, percussion
Keith Richards: guitar
Bill Wyman: bass guitar, xylophone
Ian Stewart: organ
Mick Jagger and Keith Richards: backing vocals

With the same infallible exactitude as he had on 'Under My Thumb', Jones hits a tricky ostinato that follows a descending chord sequence on the marimba, a wooden xylophone he'd brought back from a recent holiday in Morocco. This was carried by lush strings on the Chris Farlowe interpretation of a lyric deriding an old lover whose affection the vocalist can't be bothered to rekindle.

It's Not Easy (Jagger-Richards) 2.56

Mick Jagger: lead vocals
Brian Jones and Keith Richards: guitars
Ian Stewart: organ
Bill Wyman: bass guitar
Charlie Watts: drums
Mick Jagger, Keith Richards and Brian Jones: backing vocals

As both a song and a performance, this is OK but nothing brilliant. Its principal attributes are skittish backing vocals and the trump of Bill Wyman's fuzz-toned bass.

I Am Waiting (Jagger-Richards) 3.11

Mick Jagger: lead vocals
Brian Jones: hand bells, dulcimer
Charlie Watts: drums, percussion
Keith Richards: guitar
Bill Wyman: bass guitar
Mick Jagger and Keith Richards: backing vocals

If not an outstanding track in itself, this leapt into sharper focus than it may have warranted when mimed on television more than once during the extensive publicity blitz. Quiet, measured and perplexing verses snap into two fast bridge sections. 'If you have a question about the lyric, ask Mick,' shrugged Keith, 'That's his department.' While Richards appeared to suggest that he attended to the music and Jagger the words, their concordat was less cut-and-dried Rodgers and Hammerstein with defined demarcation lines than Lennon-McCartney where creative functions dissolved and merged, often under immense market pressures.

Take It Or Leave It (Jagger-Richards) 2.47

Mick Jagger: lead vocals
Brian Jones: harpsichord, hand bells
Charlie Watts: drums
Keith Richards: guitar
Bill Wyman: bass guitar
Jack Nitzsche: organ

Partly because it lent itself so readily to The Searchers' fusion of Merseybeat and contemporary folk and melodic three-part harmonies, this throwback to the genesis of the beat boom has a charm that the sense that the Stones couldn't wait for the end of that particular session, has never dispelled.

Think (Jagger-Richards) 3.09

Mick Jagger: lead vocals
Brian Jones and Keith Richards: guitars
Ian Stewart: piano
Bill Wyman: bass guitar
Charlie Watts: drums
Keith Richards: backing vocals

Recorded in Hollywood in early December 1965, this served as a useful demo for Chris Farlowe's chart debut. His punchy horn section was indicated by Richards' guitar lines that were fed through a device called a fuzz box, reputedly the first in Britain, that he had brought back from the Stones' first US trip. When designed by Gibson in 1962, the Maestro Fuzztone had been intended to make a guitar sound like a saxophone but through Keith its blackboard-scratching hoarseness was assuming a personality of its own.

What To Do (Jagger-Richards) 2.32

Mick Jagger: lead vocals
Brian Jones and Keith Richards: guitars
Ian Stewart: piano
Bill Wyman: bass guitar
Charlie Watts: drums
Keith Richards and Brian Jones: backing vocals

Brian and Keith's Beach Boys-esque *baw-baw-baw*s support Jagger on a number that, whatever its merits in isolation, seems dull when set against many of those that went before. As *Aftermath* was almost twice the length of each of the albums that preceded it, 'What To Do' rather over-painted the musical canvas.

BETWEEN THE BUTTONS

UK Release: 20 January 1967
Intl CD No: ABKCO 95002
Running Time: 38:44

Decca LK/SKL 4852
Producer: Andrew Loog Oldham

SIDE ONE: Yesterday's Papers; My Obsession; Back Street Girl; Connection; She Smiled Sweetly; Cool Calm And Collected.

SIDE TWO: All Sold Out; Please Go Home; Who's Been Sleeping Here; Complicated; Miss Amanda Jones; Something Happened To Me Yesterday.

Charlie Watts' most visible contribution to *Between The Buttons* was adorning the back cover with a six-frame cartoon loaded with pokes at the posturing hypocrisy of the record industry: the fake sincerity, the mental sluggishness, the backstabbing, the cloth-eared ignorance. Meanwhile, at the centre of the group photograph on the front, Brian Jones's provocatively creepy face was asking to be punched.

With some justification Jones thought that the LP marked time artistically after the quantum jump that was *Aftermath*, even though the discerning Frank Zappa thought that *Between The Buttons* was an important piece of social comment at the time.

Partly self-inflicted, Jones was now less integrated into the creative process. This aggravated a sense of isolation particularly as it was beyond him to come up with a composition of his own that the Stones might consider recording, let alone one or two per album, as John Entwistle did with The Who, or George Harrison did with The Beatles.

Marianne Faithfull, 1964's recipient of Richards and Jagger's Gene Pitney-sized hit 'As Tears Go By', was amused by 'Brian's phantom songs', the consequence of his 'manic scribbing in notebooks, followed by pages being ripped out. Recording, erasing, recording, erasing, reels unspooling all over the floor, the offending tapes being hurled across the room.'

Frustrated and resentful, Brian's confidence eroded daily and he began absenting himself from recording dates – in Los Angeles during August 1966 and back in London that

THE ROLLING STONES
BETWE
TH
BUTTO

autumn – and yet there appeared to be no end to his talents as a multi-instrumentalist.

There'd be much to praise too on *Between The Buttons* about Jagger's libretto, that drew from him a range of vocal expression from bitter-sweetly sinister on 'Back Street Girl' to his jocular valediction in 'Something Happened To Me Yesterday'. He was devoid of vowel purity and plummy eloquence. Instead, you got sometimes slurred diction and battered nuances dredged from a throat with vocal cords and muscles beyond remedy. After four years of straining a disjointed range past its limits through public-address systems of variable quality, the voice that resulted was not unattractive, even grimly charming. Who cared if he weren't much of a warbler? At the very least Mick Jagger always sounded like Mick Jagger.

A couple of tracks amounted to Jagger-Richards duets. Soon, Keith alone, rather than with Bill, Mick and Brian, would be evident on harmonies that were integrations into the lead vocal rather than accompanying responses, indicating perhaps lessons learnt from the small chorales of The Beatles, The Hollies, The Searchers and The Byrds. In the first instance, Keith had steered clear of the microphone both in the studio and on the boards. Partly this was because the choirboy he once was had been dejected by having to gulp when straining to hear himself in the days before on-stage monitors. He'd been finicky about pitch from his earliest youth during musical evenings at his grandfather's. 'If I didn't sing a grace note,' remembered his mother, 'Keith would tell me to do it properly. He'd know it was wrong. It's something that's just built into him'.

Yesterday's Papers (Jagger-Richards) 2.04

Mick Jagger: lead vocals
Keith Richards: guitar
Charlie Watts: drums
Brian Jones: mellotron
Bill Wyman: bass guitar
Mick Jagger and Keith Richards: backing vocals

Smothered in reverberation, an effective rhythm guitar interlude separates verses that apparently were to do with Jagger's faded love for Chrissie Shrimpton who was seeking comfort in the arms of Steve Marriott, singing guitarist in The Small Faces. Marianne Faithfull was now sharing the bed of 'the most fashionably modish young man in London,' according to a condescending *Evening Standard*. 'We are told Mick Jagger is the voice of today, a today person, symptomatic of our society. Cecil Beaton paints him, says he is reminded of Nijinsky, of renaissance angels; magazines report that he is a friend of Princess Margaret; gossip columns tell us what parties he failed to turn up at'.

My Obsession (Jagger-Richards) 3.17

Mick Jagger: lead vocals
Keith Richards: guitar, bass guitar
Ian Stewart: piano
Charlie Watts: drums
Bill Wyman: bass guitar, organ
Mick Jagger and Keith Richards: backing vocals

Watts' stylistic frugality was entirely appropriate for this forceful if advisedly veiled outlining of erotic fixations. Brian Wilson, The Beach Boys' presiding genius, was present at the session in Hollywood and was nonplussed by 'a hell of a party in progress. Tables overflowed with booze, drugs and food. Girls were everywhere'.

Back Street Girl (Jagger-Richards) 3.27

Mick Jagger: lead vocals
Brian Jones: piano-accordion, dulcimer
Charlie Watts: drums
Keith Richards: guitar
Bill Wyman: bass guitar
Nicky Hopkins: keyboards

Brian's piano-accordion brought a mordant Jacques Brel-esque *belgitude* to an address by a respectable family man to his rather common and coarse mistress. If not quite a chanson in the grandest tradition, it ranks with 'Lady Jane' as a thoughtful venture into unprecedented territory.

Connection (Jagger-Richards) 2.08

Keith Richards and Mick Jagger: lead vocals
Keith Richards: guitar
Ian Stewart: piano
Bill Wyman: bass guitar, organ
Charlie Watts: drums
Charlie Watts and Mick Jagger: percussion

Keith's nicotine-tortured baritone is louder than Mick's on a number that seems to contain references to the non-prescription drugs that helped time pass quicker in this bandroom or on that long-haul flight. If all too aware of Purple Hearts, Black Bombers and like pep pills, marijuana (pot) had been a bit too cloak and dagger for most 60s pop stars until no less than The Beatles had giggled through the shooting of *Help!* in the haze of its short-lived magic. Pot came to be used increasingly as a herbal handmaiden to creativity. Richards resurrected 'Connection' in the late 1980s when on the road to promote his first solo album.

She Smiled Sweetly (Jagger-Richards) 2.44

Mick Jagger: lead vocals
Bill Wyman: bass guitar
Jack Nitzsche: keyboards
Keith Richards: organ
Charlie Watts: drums

Without a solitary guitar within earshot, this marked Richards' first vinyl offering on another instrument, namely the plain church organ that pounds away beneath probably the soppiest love lyric Jagger ever sang on a Stones disc. When signed to Decca for a one-off maiden 45, Love Affair that was soon to be one of the biggest groups on Britain's 'scream circuit', chose 'She Smiled Sweetly' as its A side. It may have been because the group adhered too closely to the arrangement on an already successful LP that their version sold poorly.

Cool Calm And Collected (Jagger-Richards) 4.17

Mick Jagger: lead vocals, harmonica
Keith Richards: guitar
Charlie Watts: drums
Brian Jones: kazoo, sitar
Bill Wyman: bass guitar
Nicky Hopkins: piano

An intrinsically English rave-up, broken only by the breath of the orient on its hook-line, this is a warped construction of a song that 30 years earlier might have wowed 'em in Britain's now-outmoded music halls. Honky-tonk pub piano dominates an accelerated coda.

All Sold Out (Jagger-Richards) 2.17
Mick Jagger: lead vocals
Keith Richards: guitar
Charlie Watts: drums, congas, percussion
Brian Jones: flute
Bill Wyman: bass guitar
Bill Wyman and Brian Jones: keyboards
Mick Jagger and Keith Richards: backing vocals
Weighty percussion manages to maintain a precise backbeat and permit a swipe at some unhappy girl gliding on a seething musical wind and a fade-out that intimates that the group may have been swept into a blow of 'Goin' Home' length. Some researchers maintain that the flute was actually a sound generated on a Mellotron, a newish synthesiser-like keyboard instrument.

Please Go Home (Jagger-Richards) 3.17
Mick Jagger: lead vocals, maraccas
Bill Wyman: bass guitar
Charlie Watts: drums
Brian Jones: theramin
Keith Richards: guitar, backing vocals
Over a Bo Diddley beat, the vocal fades in and out of echo and the psychedelic age is further telegraphed by a weird and wonderful implement that Brian had stumbled upon at RCA Studios. The theramin was invented around 1920 by Leon Theramin, a Russian physics professor. With tone and single-note pitch adjustable by the movement of one hand back and forth around a hypersensitive antenna and the twiddling of a volume control with the other, the oscillating and unearthly wails that came from this device were to come into their own when used in horror movies and, most famously, on 'Good Vibrations' by The Beach Boys in 1966.

Who's Been Sleeping Here (Jagger-Richards) 3.55
Mick Jagger: lead vocals, maraccas
Keith Richards: guitar
Charlie Watts: drums
Brian Jones: guitar, harmonium
Bill Wyman: bass guitar
Jack Nitzsche: keyboards, tambourine
The *New Musical Express* noted shades of Dylan pervading imagery infused with literariness, incongruous connections and streams of consciousness gleaned through constant replay of *Bringing It All Back Home, Highway 61 Revisited* and that year's *Blonde On Blonde*.

Furthermore, just as the Stones had hardened Dylan's resolve to go electric in 1964, so his organic instrumental criteria affected 'Who's Been Sleeping Here'.

Complicated (Jagger-Richards) 3.15

Mick Jagger: lead vocals
Keith Richards: guitar
Charlie Watts: drums
Mick Jagger and Keith Richards: backing vocals
Brian Jones: keyboards
Bill Wyman: bass guitar
Charlie Watts, Bill Wyman and Mick Jagger: percussion

Musically, this is a sibling of 'All Sold Out', especially in the drum balance. Organ too is prominent in a number in which Jagger, for once, appears to display a rueful awe for an object of desire, perhaps because she's more lady-like and self-possessed than others he could mention.

Miss Amanda Jones (Jagger-Richards) 2.47

Mick Jagger: lead vocals
Keith Richards: guitar
Charlie Watts: drums
Brian Jones: harpsichord
Bill Wyman: bass guitar, organ
Ian Stewart: piano

Just as 'Please Go Home' was rooted in Diddley, this one connects to Chuck Berry in its essential instrumental feel. Ostensibly, the words are concerned with a girl for whom life begins at the discotheque. Myth has it, however, that Miss Amanda Jones was actually Amanda Lear, a tall, blonde jet-setter known to the Stones, who was to be launched as a 70s disco diva amid publicity that cast unfounded doubts about her gender.

Something Happened To Me Yesterday (Jagger-Richards) 4.55

Mick Jagger and Keith Richards: all vocals and whistling
Keith Richards: guitar
Brian Jones: guitar, keyboards, brass, woodwinds
Bill Wyman: bass guitar
Charlie Watts: drums

The result of multiple overdubs by Jones rather than a phallanx of session shellbacks playing at the same time. It sounds like a colliery silver band tootling beneath a comedy turn by Jagger and Richards thanking everyone who'd taken part and dispensing advice for pedestrians on the evening streets.

BRITISH AND US ALBUMS

THEIR SATANIC MAJESTIES REQUEST

UK Release: 8 December 1967
US Release: 9 December 1967
Intl CD No.: ABKCO 90022
Running Time: 44:08

Decca TXL/TXS 103
London NP/NPS 2
Producer: The Rolling Stones

SIDE ONE: Sing This All Together; Citadel; In Another Land; 2000 Man; Sing This All Together (See What Happens).

SIDE TWO: She's A Rainbow; The Lantern; Gomper; 2000 Light Years From Home; On With The Show.

The Rolling Stones were as culpable as anyone else of bandwagon-jumping: witness the basic *Sgt. Pepper's Lonely Hearts Club Band* formula for *Their Satanic Majesties Request*. This, the Stones' most nakedly psychedelic LP, quivered into reluctant life during the best-known drugs trial in pop, the aftermath of police invading Keith Richards' country house and uncovering enough substances to secure jail sentences for its owner and a visiting Mick Jagger, followed by dismissal on appeal within a week. Brian Jones would be awaiting trial for similar offences when studio sessions got underway in June 1967. 'It gave the Stones this image of being like a real bunch of dope fiends,' sniggered Jagger 20 years later.

A more profound upset of the Stones' equilibrium, however, was rooted in Richards stealing Jones's girlfriend, German actor Anita Pallenberg. Near-unbearable tension, onstage and off, was exacerbated by the first stirrings of a real-life enactment of that soap-opera cliche where the greater the antagonism between two characters, the greater the likelihood that they will become lovers. 'Mick really tried to put me down,' grimaced Anita, 'but there was no way that this crude guy was going to do a number on me. I found out that if you stand up to Mick, he crumbles'.

Carnal self-interest and other complications of personal affiliations informed the recording of the first Stones album without Andrew Oldham in charge. Tiring of ideas that were more intriguing intellectually than in ill-conceived practice, he was to ring Jagger from a telephone booth to wish him a happy rest-of-his-life.

'The reason he left,' proferred Mick, 'was because he thought we weren't concentrating and that we were being childish.' Now that Sir had left the classroom, the children started doing what they liked. 'It was a really fun moment,' agreed Mick, 'and there were some good songs on it. There's a lot of rubbish too – just too much time on our hands, too many drugs, no producer to tell us "Enough". Anyone let loose in the studio will produce stuff like that. It's like believing everything you do is great and not having any editing.'

But thanks in part to the likes of *Satanic Majesties*, pop was upgraded from ephemera to holy writ, the Word made vinyl in the comfort of your own home.

It has become an artefact that remains linked forever to psychedelic times past and maybe that's its lasting message. Listening to it decades later, a middle-aged hippy would almost smell the joss-sticks and see the *Satanic Majesties* sleeve being used as a working surface for rolling a spliff. Artistically too, it belongs very much to pop's fleeting classical period straddling genres as otherwise irreconcilable as music hall and John Cage electronic collages, just like The Beatles' less syncretic *Sgt. Pepper's Lonely Hearts Club Band*, replete with similarly elaborate and expensive packaging awash with real and imagined symbolism.

The Stones' absorption of psychedelia didn't smother entirely the blueswailing aggression of old as it had when, for instance, Steve Winwood from The Spencer Davis Group pixified 'Hole In My Shoe' with his new outfit Traffic. However, the Stones were to prove just as capable of nursery-rhyme tweeness, especially Jagger.

As well as being the central figure on the montage on the front of the sleeve, he was chief advocate of the musical content of what was supposed to be a continuous work with little or no spaces between tracks. Segues, cross-fades, *leitmotifs*, interlocking themes and the sustaining of a specific and recurring mood were much more far-reaching than simply stringing together a bunch of songs about, say, hot-rod cars as The Beach Boys had in 1963.

That was the original concept, anyway, but, with retrospective honesty, Keith Richards thought that 'basically, *Satanic Majesties* was a load of crap. It was really almost done semi-comatose, sort of "Do we really have to make an album?"' Yet one million Stones fans couldn't be wrong. How could anyone criticise an item of merchandise that was assured a gold disc before a note of it was recorded.

Sing This All Together (Jagger-Richards) 3.47

Mick Jagger: lead vocals
Keith Richards: guitar
Bill Wyman: bass guitar
Charlie Watts: drums
Brian Jones: brass and woodwinds
Nicky Hopkins: piano
Mick Jagger, Keith Richards, John Lennon and Paul McCartney: backing vocals
Charlie Watts and others: percussion

It could be argued that briefly The Stones were ahead of The Beatles in North America. Casting nervous backwards glances, the Merseysiders would snipe at the Stones in the press while sending an underling out mid-session to purchase their chief competitors' latest release. Nevertheless, both groups socialised outside working hours. Richards and Jagger, for example, were among party guests after The Beatles' concert before a record-breaking 56,000 at Shea Stadium in 1965, and were often sighted holding court with Lennon and McCartney in one of about ten fashionable London watering holes for which Top 20 *conquistadores* could select a night out.

It wasn't surprising, therefore, that Lennon and McCartney were delighted to add their voices to this desperate attempt at a ditty as catchy as The Beatles' flower-power singalong 'All You Need Is Love' on which Jagger and Richards were present, while Jones was to honk alto saxophone on two Beatles B sides, 'Baby You're A Rich Man' and knockabout 'You Know My Name'. Of Brian's hand in the latter, McCartney commented, 'He was a really ropey sax player. It happened to be exactly what we wanted. Brian was very good like that.'

Citadel (Jagger-Richards) 2.51
Mick Jagger: all vocals
Keith Richards: guitar
Bill Wyman: bass guitar
Charlie Watts: drums
Brian Jones: keyboards
Nicky Hopkins: piano
Mick Jagger and Rocky Dijon: percussion
Not for the first time, the Stones employ a rhythm guitar off-beat to propel a song, although tonally it becomes fractionally more dissonant with each verse. Based upon one of the writers' fascination with the 1926 silent movie *Metropolis*, this contradiction of a nostalgic look at an unnerving inner-city future also began the commercial discography of Rocky Dijon (Dzidzorna), whose conga-pattering was to enliven many other Stones tracks.

In Another Land (Wyman) 3.14
Bill Wyman: lead vocal, bass guitar, keyboards
Charlie Watts: drums
Steve Marriott: guitar
Nicky Hopkins: piano
Mick Jagger, Keith Richards and Steve Marriott: backing vocals
Studio assistants were growing accustomed to two or even three Stones either missing or very late arriving at any given session. Watts and Wyman were the only two there for this track's principal date during which Wyman decided to sing lead. They called on Steve Marriott, who was recording in an adjacent studio with his Small Faces, now the flagship act of Andrew Loog Oldham's record label, Immediate. Thus Wyman broke the songwriting monopoly that the Jagger-Richards team had established with *Aftermath*. Nevertheless, though 'In Another Land' was issued as a US single, only one more item penned solely by Bill would ever appear on a Stones disc. Speculating in artist management and record production he had, however, been able to off-load some of his works onto The End, Bobbie Miller and other unprofitable clients.

2000 Man (Jagger-Richards) 3.08
Mick Jagger: lead vocals
Keith Richards: guitar
Bill Wyman: bass guitar
Charlie Watts: drums
Brian Jones and Nicky Hopkins: keyboards
Mick Jagger and Keith Richards: backing vocals
Thanks to technical wizardry, a gentle vocal floats effortlessly over trenchant accompaniment. A catalyst here and throughout the rest of the LP is Nicky Hopkins, one of Screaming Lord Sutch's backing Savages prior to choosing the more comfortable and lucrative sphere of session work. The Kinks had immortalized Hopkins in the 1966 LP track, 'Session Man'. He'd also played on two *Between The Buttons* tracks.

Sing This All Together (See What Happens) (Jagger-Richards) 8.34
Mick Jagger: lead vocals
Keith Richards: guitar
Bill Wyman: bass guitar
Charlie Watts: drums
Brian Jones: keyboards, brass and woodwinds
Nicky Hopkins: piano
Charlie Watts, Mick Jagger, Brian Jones, and Keith Richards: percussion
On the chatty introit to a reprise of 'Sing This Song Altogether', it's possible to pick up on trifles such as a muffled 'Where's that joint?' but it might be 'Where's that johnny?'. The piece escapes song structure to continue in a vein akin to what an ordinary bloke in Aldershot, Alice Springs or Abilene might imagine the world sounds like on this LSD stuff that he'd been reading about in the papers. The end bit, apparently, is discernable as 'We Wish You A Merry Christmas' if you play it at 78 rpm.

She's A Rainbow (Jagger-Richards) 4.35

Mick Jagger: lead vocals
Keith Richards: guitar
Bill Wyman: bass guitar
Charlie Watts: drums
Brian Jones: keyboards
Nicky Hopkins: piano
Mick Jagger, Keith Richards, John Lennon and Paul McCartney: backing vocals
Mick Jagger and Brian Jones: percussion
Various: strings arranged by John Paul Jones

'You would do The Rolling Stones, The Everly Brothers, French rock'n'roll sessions, German ones, Engelbert, Tom Jones – and all in the same day quite often,' enumerated John Paul Jones, a session musician who was to join Led Zeppelin in 1968. Among his more absorbing commissions was scoring orchestral strings for 'She's A Rainbow'. This, however, was marred by him 'waiting for them forever. I just thought they were unprofessional and boring'. The result typified pop's gingerbread-castle hour as much as Traffic's 'Hole In My Shoe', 'Gnome' by The Pink Floyd and, particularly, Love's 'She Comes In Colours'.

The Lantern (Jagger-Richards) 4.23

Mick Jagger: all vocals
Keith Richards: guitar
Bill Wyman: bass guitar
Charlie Watts: drums
Brian Jones and Nicky Hopkins: keyboards
Charlie Watts and Mick Jagger: percussion

Church organ and a funereal bell – dunggggggg – begin some tired business that seems to be about karma, the transmutation of souls and the world of illusion. Though it could be nothing more than a negative metaphor to carry the melody in a year when even the bucolic Troggs were singing about 'the bamboo butterflies of yer mind'.

Gomper (Jagger-Richards) 5.09
Mick Jagger: lead vocals
Keith Richards: guitar
Bill Wyman: bass guitar
Charlie Watts: tabla
Brian Jones: mandolin, sitar
Brian Jones and Nicky Hopkins: keyboards
Mick Jagger and Keith Richards: backing vocals
The lyrics reveal more than cursory poring over hardbacks of a mystical, religious and aerie-faerie nature, purchased via the account that Jagger had at the arty Indica bookshop off London's Piccadilly. The instrumental second section of 'Gomper' sparkles with the oscillations of a newly acquired monophonic Moog synthesizer that previously could be hired only from US dealers.

2000 Light Years From Home (Jagger-Richards) 4.45
Mick Jagger: lead vocals, percussion
Keith Richards: guitar
Bill Wyman: bass guitar
Brian Jones and Bill Wyman: keyboards
Charlie Watts: drums
Nicky Hopkins: piano
Mick Jagger and Keith Richards: backing vocals
On the album's piece de resistance Brian Jones created a spooky counterpoint on 'a big old Mellotron' recalled engineer George Chkiantz, 'with a delay between the moment you pressed a note and achieving a sound'. A precursor of the space rock propagated by brand-leaders Hawkwind in the 70s, it was, supposedly, drafted by Jagger during his fleeting spell as a convict.

On With The Show (Jagger-Richards) 3.39
Mick Jagger: lead vocals
Keith Richards: guitar
Bill Wyman: bass guitar
Charlie Watts: drums
Brian Jones and Nicky Hopkins: keyboards
Mick Jagger, Keith Richards and others: backing vocals
Charlie Watts and Mick Jagger: percussion
With Mick on the pavement outside a night club, barking the show within to passers-by, this is the hippie cousin of gleeful 'Little Egypt' originally by The Coasters, but revived to top the Swedish charts by the Stones' London R&B contemporaries, The Downliners Sect in 1964.

BEGGARS BANQUET

UK Release: 6 December 1968
US Release: 7 December 1968
Intl CD No: ABKCO 95392
Running Time: 39:49

Decca LK/SKL 4955
London LL 3539/PS 539
Producer: Jimmy Miller

SIDE ONE: Sympathy For The Devil; No Expectations; Dear Doctor; Parachute Woman; Jigsaw Puzzle.

SIDE TWO: Street Fighting Man; Prodigal Son; Stray Cat Blues; Factory Girl; Salt Of The Earth.

Like Bob Dylan's *John Wesley Harding*, the unvarnished directness of *Beggars Banquet* especially in comparison to *Satanic Majesties*, helped steer pop away from backwards-running tapes, funny noises and self-conscious clutter that disguised many essentially inane artistic perceptions. Nonetheless, much of its rough edge was contrived via refinements in recorded sound since the first Rolling Stones album back in 1964.

One technique developed by Keith Richards was taping an acoustic guitar with attached magnetic pick-up through an amplifier onto his cassette recorder – one of the first privately purchased such machines in Britain – with so much overdrive that it sounded electric. On transference to the eight-track mixing desk in Olympic Sound, the studio now favoured whenever the Stones recorded in London, it also lent a gritty quality to finished products such as 'Street Fighting Man' on which the only solid-body instrument heard was the bass, also thrummed by Richards.

He found it necessary on other tracks to tune his six-string to an open chord. Most often it was G major, requiring the removal of the lowest string so that the dominant wouldn't, well, dominate. The conducting of such experiments at home had, he said, 'rejuvenated my enthusiasm for playing guitar because you'd put your fingers where you thought they'd go and you'd get accidents happening.'

During the transition between *Satanic Majesties* and *Beggars' Banquet* too, the group instigated a studio alliance with Jimmy Miller who'd been headhunted in 1966 to work with The Spencer Davis Group and then Traffic. Other British acts were keen to use him too. As a

Rolling Stones

Beggars Banquet

R.S.V.P.

would-be pop singer, the New Yorker's early ambition had been thwarted by a saddening fistful of flop singles for CBS. Accepting that he wasn't going to be the east coast's answer to Elvis Presley, 'I soon realised that the aspect of the business that I liked was being in the studio.' During the so-called British Invasion of his native soil Miller, with other entrepreneurial north Americans such as Allen Klein, songwriter Jackie de Shannon and producer Shel Talmy, anticipated correctly unprecedented demand for further Limey talent and flew the Atlantic in 1964 to stake his claim in the musical diggings.

When he first loosened his tie in the producer's chair for *Beggars Banquet* early in 1968, Jimmy Miller accepted that the group also should have a say in proceedings behind the glass-fronted booth of tape spools and switches. After all, they'd finished *Satanic Majesties* on their own. Richards in particular was sufficiently au fait with the workings of the console and secure enough in his prime position in the Stones hierarchy to make insightful recommendations, turn knobs, push faders and even to plan to take a lead vocal on the next album.

He also played both bass and lead guitar on *Beggar's Banquet's* most memorable selection, 'Sympathy For The Devil'. Every unforgiving minute of its completion over 'two very good nights' estimated Mick Jagger, was documented by Jean-Luc Godard. Although approaching his forties, Godard was still regarded as an enfant terrible of European cinema. 'Godard understands music better than any director, alive or dead', reckoned Mike Figgis, an acquaintance of Charlie Watts and an aspiring film-maker.

Jean-Luc was so captivated by the new Jagger-Richards song that he had abandoned the flick's working title, *One Plus One*, for *Sympathy For The Devil* by the time the picture was shown at the London Film Festival in November 1968. A slow-moving 99 minutes, it had been intended to contrast construction (the Stones creating 'Sympathy For The Devil') and destruction (a girl's suicide when deserted by her lover). But now it was remodelled with no linking narrative between footage from the recording sessions, Black Power militants in a Battersea car dump, a television interview with some woman (Eve Democracy) in a forest, her spraying graffiti all over London and a bloke reading excerpts from *Mein Kampf* in a pornographic bookshop.

It was an art statement, and very much of its era. 'Revolution is this year's flower power' was how Frank Zappa summed it up 1968. There was so much to spark off the general uprising, so many common denominators: the Soviet rape of Czechoslovakia; the assassinations of Martin Luther King and Robert Kennedy; a compounding of feminism; the continued slaughter and starvation of Mao Tse Tung's cultural purge; Ireland, bloody Ireland, and, of course, Vietnam. Thus kaftans were mothballed as their former wearers followed the crowd to violent demonstrations, riots, student sit-ins and disruptions of beauty pageants. Girls lost their marbles over Daniel Cohn-Bendit (Danny The Red), organiser of the situationist New Left political demonstrations in France, but not as much as they did over the late Cuban guerrillero Che Guevara.

Interviewed by Richard Branson, then editor of the leftish *Student* magazine, Jagger seemed to be all for pacifism and dissident popular opinion but made no doctrinal statement. However, he was to volunteer financial aid when the saga of the notorious Schoolkids edition of *Oz* climaxed at the Old Bailey. He also sunk cash into the British operation of San Francisco's groovily subversive *Rolling Stone* periodical, until then not readily available outside the States. Indeed, he settled down eagerly to his duties as newspaper proprietor, hoping that the UK publication was to be developed separately from its Californian template.

Jagger also seemed to be supportive of spiritual changes afoot circa 1968. For instance, he appeared on the cover of *The Process*, mouthpiece of the Church Of The Final Judgement, a magazine that, like *Oz*, was going the rounds of sixth-form common rooms. However, Marianne Faithfull who had articulated her perspective in an issue dedicated to Death regarded Mick as 'far too sensible and normal ever to have become seriously involved in black magic. "Sympathy For The Devil" was pure papier-mâché satanism'.

The craze for theatrical diabolism was traceable in Britain to Screaming Lord Sutch who began his act by being carried onto the boards in a coffin. It picked up speed when The Crazy World Of Arthur Brown, the toast of London's psychedelic dungeons, went public with 1967's 'Devil's Grip' before going for the jugular with chart-topping 'Fire!' in the summer of '68.

Perusing *Melody Maker* as a stockbroker would the *Financial Times*, Mick would remark, 'There's a big following for these hocus-pocus bands, so obviously the subject has a vast commercial potential'. So did *Beggars Banquet*, though, statistically, not as much as *Satanic Majesties* because while it also peaked at No. 3 in Britain, it spent less weeks in the charts. In the States *Satanic Majesties* had come within an ace of the top, but *Beggars Banquet* stalled at No. 5.

Sympathy For The Devil (Jagger-Richards) 6.18

Mick Jagger: lead vocals
Keith Richards and Brian Jones: guitars
Keith Richards: bass guitar
Mick Jagger, Keith Richards, Brian Jones, Bill Wyman, Marianne Faithfull, Anita Pallenberg, Nicky Hopkins and Jimmy Miller: backing vocals
Charlie Watts: drums
Bill Wyman and Rocky Dijon: percussion
Nicky Hopkins: piano

Jagger portrays himself as a fiendish figure on the fringe of the events detailed in 'Sympathy For The Devil' but sufficiently well-placed to stir kettles of fish for private amusement, whether a face in the crowd at Golgotha for the Crucifixion; in conference with Adolf Hitler 'when the blitzkrieg raged and the bodies stank', or behind the steering-wheel of JFK's Lincoln Limousine in Dallas. When the President's younger brother died at the trigger-jerk of another maniac in June 1968, the infallably pragmatic Jagger had made the line 'I shouted out, "Who killed John Kennedy!"' plural ('the Kennedys').

While he joined in the oo-oooo background chant and was allowed to hack negligible chords on an acoustic guitar, Brian Jones was reduced to just shaking maraccas when, on 12 December 1968, 'Sympathy For The Devil' was the penultimate number in The Rolling Stones' Rock'n'Roll Circus, a cancelled television spectacular that would gather dust for decades until it acquired historical interest. Furthermore, during long weeks of daily inspection of the accumulated celluloid miles, Jean-Luc Godard noticed Jones asking Jagger, 'What can I play?' 'Good question,' was the cutting riposte, 'What *can* you play, Brian?' The title of Little Richard's 1966 single, 'Get Down With It', provided a catch-phrase of a kind on *Beggars Banquet*. It was heard on this track and, truncated, on 'Street Fighting Man'. Finally, if deploring the overall quality of Jagger's lyrics, Bryan Ferry was to exhume 'Sympathy For The Devil' in quasi-'Monster Mash' fashion on a 1973 solo LP.

No Expectations (Jagger-Richards) 3.56

Mick Jagger: lead vocals
Keith Richards: guitar
Bill Wyman: bass guitar
Charlie Watts: drums
Brian Jones: slide guitar
Nicky Hopkins: piano

A Dickensian-sounding title is married to a rural blues in which some of the deliberation of a dream's slow motion owes much to Brian's contribution. Deputising for the otherwise unreliable Jones on an earlier take, Dave Mason was to assist on other tracks. He was at something of a loose end, having left Traffic from December 1967 to the following April to strike out on his own as both a freelance record producer and maker of a solo 45, 'Little Woman'.

Dear Doctor (Jagger-Richards) 3.21

Mick Jagger: lead vocals
Brian Jones: harmonica
Keith Richards and Dave Mason: guitars
Bill Wyman: bass guitar
Charlie Watts: drums
Nicky Hopkins: piano
Mick Jagger and Keith Richards: backing vocals

With a lyric that veers between the despair and gladness of an unwilling groom jilted by his bride, this is a comedy number that owes as much to C&W as blues. It sounds as if the Stones had fun recording it, conjuring up visions as it does of ale-choked mouths and flushed, happy faces in Olympic Sound as well as the one-shot novelty of such as 'The Runaway Train', The Singing Dogs, 'Yellow Submarine' or 'Something Happened To Me Yesterday'.

Parachute Woman (Jagger-Richards) 2.20

Mick Jagger: lead vocals, harmonica
Keith Richards: slide guitar
Brian Jones: guitar
Bill Wyman: bass guitar
Charlie Watts: drums
Nicky Hopkins: piano

Jimmy Miller was to praise Jones's slide playing on *Beggar's Banquet*, but on this track and elsewhere, Richards crossed what outsiders had understood to be a demarcation line by occupying the slide (or bottleneck) area, once Brian's exclusive preserve. There are echoes of both 'Goin' Home' from *Aftermath* and traditional 'Special Rider Blues' aka 'Hurry Sundown', a late 60s blues boom standard revived by New York's Insect Trust in 1968 and, two years later, by Hawkwind.

Jigsaw Puzzle (Jagger-Richards) 6.05

Mick Jagger: lead vocals
Keith Richards and Brian Jones: slide guitars
Charlie Watts: drums
Keith Richards: bass guitar
Bill Wyman and Brian Jones: keyboards
Nicky Hopkins: piano

This was mostly the work of Jagger, triggered maybe by him peering glumly from a window of his elegant Chelsea mews house at a rain-sodden early evening street where a vagrant, his mind rotted by meths, was trudging off to sleep on the Embankment in cardboard-boxed squalor. A gangster who in private life is a devoted husband and father, and a pop group with no choice but to go right on performing, also rear up as an overlong and lyrically fragmented piece progresses.

Street Fighting Man (Jagger-Richards) 3.15

Mick Jagger: lead vocals
Keith Richards: guitar, bass guitar
Nicky Hopkins: piano
Charlie Watts: drums
Brian Jones: sitar, tamboura
Dave Mason: percussion

A spin-off US single, this had been born of the general mood that summer. Jagger qualified its sentiments with 'It's stupid to think you can start a revolution with a record. I wish you could'. Nevertheless, while not as pointed a rallying cry as, say, The Kinks' 'Every Mother's Son' that peaceniks sang outside the White House during the Vietnam moratorium, 'Street Fighting Man' acquired million-selling outsider chic when banned by the BBC. Later, in the light of alarmist talk about the forthcoming 1968 National Democratic Convention various radio stations in Chicago where Mayor Daley had ordered police to 'shoot to kill' marching trouble-makers, it suffered the same fate. Towards the fade-out, we hear a plink-plonk emulation of Big Ben's chimes on a piano beneath the fingers of Nicky Hopkins who contributed more to the album than did Brian Jones.

Prodigal Son (Jagger-Richards) 2.51

Mick Jagger: lead vocals
Bill Wyman: bass guitar
Brian Jones: harmonica
Keith Richards: guitar
Charlie Watts: drums
Nicky Hopkins: piano

This holy blues, a straightforward account of the New Testament parable, was penned by a Rev. Robert Wilkins, a medicine show entertainer who yapped his spiel about snake-bite tonics and cure-all elixirs throughout the deep south between the wars. In 1952, 'Prodigal Son' was revived in hard country style by Hank Williams and his Drifting Cowboys, much admired by an adolescent Keith Richards.

Stray Cat Blues (Jagger-Richards) 4.37

Mick Jagger: lead vocals
Bill Wyman: bass guitar
Brian Jones: mellotron
Rocky Dijon: percussion
Keith Richards: guitar
Charlie Watts: drums
Nicky Hopkins: piano

The Stones had long been able to pick and choose from the perpetually loitering backstage Jezebels. Eventually, those members of the group who took such advantages gave up trying to guess if a given girl was under-age. A rhythm-guitar drive underlines lyrics that were the only barrier to making 'Stray Cat Blues' a most marketable single.

Factory Girl (Jagger-Richards) 2.08

Mick Jagger: lead vocals
Bill Wyman: bass guitar
Nicky Hopkins: piano
Rick Grech: violin
Keith Richards: guitar
Charlie Watts: tabla
Dave Mason: mandolin

While its music recreates that of a dust bowl string band of the depression, the words are very much Love On The Dole in industrial Lancashire at any time during the previous half-century. Rick Grech was a member of Family whose maiden LP, *Music From a Doll's House* happened to have been produced by Jimmy Miller and Dave Mason.

Salt Of The Earth (Jagger-Richards) 4.47

Mick Jagger and Keith Richards: lead vocals **Keith Richards:** guitar, slide guitar
Bill Wyman: bass guitar **Charlie Watts:** drums
Nicky Hopkins: piano **The Watts Street Gospel Choir:** backing vocals

Richards takes the first verse, Jagger the others on this anthem to the working classes by rich, sophisticated men long and perhaps guiltily detached from the everyday. Yet, because the Stones didn't pretend to be anything else, it didn't inflame raw nerves in the queue at the labour exchange. The female choir were from the depressed Watts suburb of Los Angeles where racial tension had smouldered into open riot during 1965's humid August. This was the subject of 'Trouble Comin' Every Day' by Frank Zappa who was to compose a burlesque of 'Salt Of The Earth' for 1971's *200 Motels* movie. Six weeks after 9/11 Richards and Jagger gave 'em 'Salt Of The Earth' when among Billy Idol, Destiny's Child, The Who, Bon Jovi, David Bowie and the rest of the artistes at Madison Square Garden, shaking fund-raising buckets against the terrorists.

LET IT BLEED

US Release: 28 November 1969
UK Release: 5 December 1969
Intl CD No: ABKCO 90042
Running Time: 42:26

London NP/NPS 4
Decca LK/SKL 5025
Producer: Jimmy Miller

SIDE ONE: Gimme Shelter; Love In Vain; Country Honk; Live With Me; Let It Bleed.

SIDE TWO: Midnight Rambler; You Got The Silver; Monkey Man; You Can't Always Get What You Want.

As well as the Jones-Anita Pallenberg-Richards business annihilating any cosy pretentions about The Rolling Stones as a five-man brotherhood, Brian Jones's related and apparently, near-perpetual drug-clouded state was mirrored in an increasing morosity as he was pushed further into the background by Mick Jagger and Keith Richards. Keith was 'in charge of recording sessions, more or less, in an oblique way,' according to Ian Stewart. 'He doesn't march into the studio and say, "Right! It's going to be this, that and the other". He just kicks off into something and most people follow him. He usually decides how each song is going to shape up.'

All the other Stones were becoming accustomed by now to life without Brian who was present at sessions only if his rising from a bed of dreams induced by prescribed tranquillizers coincided with a remembered recording date for *Let It Bleed*, an album that resulted from hundreds of hours (mostly in London's Olympic Sound) staggered over a year.

'He would turn up when he felt like it,' concurred Jimmy Miller. 'One night he showed up after he hadn't bothered to come to the previous four. He had a sitar and we were doing a blues song. There was no way a sitar was going to fit but I was happy that he was there. Mick and Keith, however, would come up to me and say, "Just tell him to clear off. He hasn't been here for days". I said 'Yeah, but the guy's got problems. Don't you think we have some responsibility to encourage him to show up and not tell him to go away when he does get here?' Their reply was, "You're new on the scene. We've been putting up with Brian's nonsense for the past two years.'

ROLLING STONES LET IT BLEED
DECCA
STONES - LET IT BLEED
THE Rolling Stones

Even Bill Wyman, the steady older man, was tiring of Brian Jones: 'I never disliked him as a person, although he was a bastard sometimes, but I found it impossible to get on with him musically. You couldn't rely on him, but he wasn't unique in that he was messed up. A lot of people in groups were messed up then.' Wyman gave an example: 'Brian's contribution to 'You Can't Always Get What You Want' was to lie on his stomach most of the night, reading an article on botany.'

As rain and dull weather span out 1968's harvest into November, a hastening conspiracy involved Allen Klein who was now both the Stones manager and one of the fiercest lions in the US showbiz jungle. Though all the cards weren't quite on the table yet, it was obvious that the group couldn't carry its self-styled founder any more and Brian, now referring to 'they' rather than 'we', couldn't envisage being a Stone for the rest of his life. He was bracing himself for a leap into the unknown.

Whether Brian Jones fell before he was pushed is academic. At his Sussex home early in the evening on the first Sunday in June 1969, it was one of a deputation consisting of Jagger, Richards and Charlie Watts who marshalled his words and dared make the speech everyone knew had to be made. The air was cleared at last, and the prevalent feeling was of release. An unsettled chapter in the respective careers of Brian and the group he'd helped form had just ended. Charlie, Keith and Mick drove off into the dusk, not forgetting to pull over at a telephone kiosk to ring Bill Wyman. The possibility of Jones rejoining one day had been mentioned, even if no one present regarded it as likely. But how could anyone have imagined that Brian had less than six months left?

For the Stones, vague contingency plans concerning a replacement had been in force for many months. As early as the previous summer they'd rehearsed with Los Angeles-born bottleneck guitar exponent and music archivist Ry Cooder, who'd been in London to assist with incidental music to the film *Performance* that starred Jagger and Anita Pallenberg.

Invited to Richards' house near Chichester, Cooder was initially flattered but not quite comfortable with the close attention his host paid to his playing. With some bitterness at the time, Cooder claimed co-authorship of Richards' and Jagger's 'Honky Tonk Women', a hit 45 in the summer of 1969 and its 'Country Honk' derivative, both recorded in the same period. Later, he said: 'It's of zero importance. There's nothing I can say about that without looking like a chump. If you want to know, ask Keith. The experience with the Stones showed me one thing, if you don't advance yourself, you'll find yourself left in the dust.'

This grievance had put the tin-lid on any possibility of home-loving Cooder remaining on a short-list of possible successors to Brian Jones. Nevertheless, his contributions to million-selling *Let It Bleed* were lauded by most reviewers. The cover illustrations were centred on a cake baked by the little-known Delia Smith, whose aptitude in the kitchen would manifest itself on television and in cookery books.

Gimme Shelter (Jagger-Richards) 4.31

Mick Jagger: lead vocals, harmonica
Keith Richards: guitar
Bill Wyman: bass guitar
Charlie Watts: drums
Nicky Hopkins: piano
Percussion: Jimmy Miller
Keith Richards and Merry Clayton: backing vocals

Clayton, who'd once traded strident 'heys' and 'yeahs' with Ray Charles in his backing group the Raelets, is more prominent than Jagger in places. However, this blood-and-thunder opus is more interesting for subtleties like Miller's scraping guiro and the wraith-like flutters of harmonica beneath a guitar solo that sounds like Chuck Berry tormented by monsters. 'Gimmie Shelter' – spelt 'Gimme Shelter' on most subsequent compilation albums – was to lend its title to the film of the Stones' US tour in 1969 and, a year later, to an album by Merry Clayton. Much later, the Stones' instrumental introit resurfaced in an ITV commercial for an automobile breakdown and relay service.

Love In Vain (Payne) 4.19

Mick Jagger: lead vocals
Keith Richards: guitar
Bill Wyman: bass guitar
Charlie Watts: drums
Ry Cooder: mandolin

As well as 'taking Ry Cooder for all I could get', Keith escorted him into Olympic Sound one spring evening in 1969 to shimmer mandolin on a C&W-tinged arrangement of Robert Johnson's 'Love In Vain', erroneously credited to 'Payne' alias Doris Troy, another *Let It Bleed* backing vocalist. The original rural blues was taped in 1937, a few months before Johnson's slow death by poison in his 20s. For all his youth, there are those who reckon he was the greatest musician ever to have walked the planet. Richards wouldn't go that far, but he was to avow that 'if Robert Johnson had lived into the era of electric guitar, he'd have killed us all. When you listen to him, the cat's got Bach going on down low and Mozart going on up high.'

Country Honk (Jagger-Richards) 3.07
Mick Jagger: lead vocals
Keith Richards: guitar
Bill Wyman: bass guitar
Charlie Watts: drums
Mick Taylor: slide guitar
Byron Berline: violin
Keith Richards and Nanette Newman: backing vocals
This silly C&W version of 1969's chart-topping 'Honky Tonk Women' is replete with parping car-horns, yee-hah exuberance and a bluegrass fiddler recommended by Gram Parsons with whom Keith Richards was keeping company. As a member of The Byrds, Parsons had been the main advocate of the group's stylistic transition from jingle-jangling acid folk to country-rock via 1968's *Sweetheart Of The Rodeo* LP.

Live With Me (Jagger-Richards) 3.33
Mick Jagger: lead vocals, guitar
Keith Richards: guitar, bass guitar
Charlie Watts: drums
Mick Taylor: guitar
Nicky Hopkins and Leon Russell: keyboards
Various: brass and woodwinds
At this stage Mick Taylor, once one of Hatfield's boss group The Gods, played as though he was a session hireling rather than an auditionee. This bland song was also the first but by no means the last time the Stones employed personnel from the ranks of Delaney and Bonnie and Friends. This was an amalgam mostly of Los Angeles session musicians whom Eric Clapton had endorsed with finance for a European tour and whose ranks he had joined as lead guitarist. For 'Live With Me', Leon Russell arranged a horn section of friends who, crowed the saxophonist, 'went on to back all the players who really do have a lot of influence.' Wyman and Watts were to back Russell on his eponymous debut album.

Let It Bleed (Jagger-Richards) 5.28
Mick Jagger: lead vocals
Keith Richards: guitar
Bill Wyman: bass guitar, autoharp
Charlie Watts: drums
Ian Stewart: piano
Perhaps it was to imprint the superficial worth of another of the album's weaker moments that this honky-tonkin', restricted-code ditty became the title track.

Midnight Rambler (Jagger-Richards) 6.53
Mick Jagger: lead vocals
Keith Richards: guitar
Brian Jones: percussion
Bill Wyman: bass guitar
Charlie Watts: drums

During this final fling by the old line-up, Jones is inaudible on an episodic musical melodrama. In this decelerated stop-start middle section is incorporated quoted dialogue from the police-station confessions of Albert de Salvo, the knife-wielding Boston Strangler.

You Got The Silver (Jagger-Richards) 2.50
Keith Richards: guitar, lead vocals
Brian Jones: autoharp
Bill Wyman: bass guitar
Charlie Watts: drums
Nicky Hopkins: keyboards

Zabriskie Point was one of the big rock movies of the turning decade. A slow-moving fantasy of wonderful young people running away from over-civilised old squares, its soundtrack included Keith Richards' first true lead vocal on disc. This musical ode to Anita Pallenberg apparently was penned during the shooting of *Performance* when she was preparing herself for bedroom scenes with Jagger.

Monkey Man (Jagger-Richards) 4.11
Mick Jagger: lead vocals
Keith Richards: guitar
Bill Wyman: bass guitar, vibraphone
Charlie Watts: drums
Nicky Hopkins: piano
Jimmy Miller: tambourine
Mick Jagger and Keith Richards: backing vocals

Impish and self-referential lyrics touch on the diabolism that the general public may have insisted it could sense emanating from the Stones who project themselves here as nice lads when you get to know them who only 'love to play the blues'. The song is divided by ensemble playing rather than an instrumental solo.

You Can't Always Get What You Want (Jagger-Richards) 7.29

Mick Jagger: lead vocals
Keith Richards: guitar
Bill Wyman: bass guitar
Jimmy Miller: drums
Al Kooper: keyboards, French horn
Percussion: Rocky Dijon
Doris Troy, Nanette Newman, Madeleine Bell and The London Bach Choir: backing vocals

During this outrageously grandloquent production – the first *Let It Bleed* opus to be completed – the choir, under the baton of Jack Nitzsche, carries the entire first verse on its own before acoustic guitar strumming and French horn herald Jagger's lyrical wanderings. The lyrics flit fitfully from some posh do to a conversation with a junkie at a local chemist, to the militant protest outside the US Embassy in London where Mick had been sighted on the periphery. An intriguing clotting of auxiliary personnel on the session in November 1968 included Al Kooper, Bob Dylan's organist after he went electric in 1964, and producer Miller, a drummer of such proficiency that he took over at Charlie Watts's kit. Then resident in London, Doris Troy's forthcoming 45, 'Ain't That Cute' produced by George Harrison, was to be *Melody Maker*'s Single Of The Year. The *Let It Bleed* studio date had come as a result of her teaming up for session work with Canadian expatriate Nanette Newman (alias Nanette Workman) and Madeleine Bell, a star of *Black Nativity* in London's West End and a solo recording artist since 1963. A severely edited cut of 'You Can't Always Get What You Want' formed the B side of 'Honky Tonk Women'.

GET YER YA-YAS OUT

UK Release: 4 September 1970
US Release: 4 September 1970
Intl CD No: ABKCO 90052
Running Time: 47:38

Decca SKL 5065
London NPS 5
Producers: The Rolling Stones and Glyn Johns

SIDE ONE: Jumpin' Jack Flash; Carol; Stray Cat Blues; Love In Vain; Midnight Rambler.

SIDE TWO: Sympathy For The Devil; Live With Me; Little Queenie; Honky Tonk Women; Street Fighting Man.

Elevated from engineer to co-producer for the only time on a Rolling Stones LP, 27-year-old Glyn Johns' console prowess was first applied to the group's sound at IPC in 1963 before Andrew Loog Oldham had even secured the Decca contract. Johns was then vocalist with The Presidents who enjoyed parochial renown in Sutton, the south London suburb where they'd once supported the Stones in a local pub.

Continuing to work with the outfit throughout the 60s and beyond, he was a friend as well as a professional colleague. The musicians attended his wedding reception three years after *Get Yer Ya-Yas Out* – the first Stones album with Brian Jones's replacement firmly in harness.

When Jones was in danger of going to jail again for drugs offences late in 1968, Allen Klein had calmed an alarmist media with 'There is absolutely no question of bringing in someone else'. Fortunately for Klein, it wasn't public knowledge that Dave Mason helped out on *Beggars Banquet*, and that other guitarists had been cropping up in discussions about a Stones tour pencilled in for 1969. Among these were 21-year-old ex-God Mick Taylor and latest wunderkind in John Mayall's Bluesbreakers and a former guitarist in the same outfit, Eric Clapton now that the last note of his Cream trio was about to resound at a farewell concert at London's Royal Albert Hall in November 1968.

During the previous June it had been announced that Mick Taylor was the chosen one and also that the Stones would play a show in London that would be free of charge! This was scheduled for Saturday 5 July in the natural amphitheatre beside the Serpentine, the artificial lake in Hyde Park.

Depending on what Sunday newspaper landed on your doormat, audience estimates for this would range from two hundred thousand to three-quarters of a million. However exaggerated, it was certainly the largest assembly for any cultural event ever accommodated by the capital. Nevertheless, only a day before there'd been talk of cancellation out of respect for Brian, who'd drowned in his swimming pool on the Thursday. The Stones' feelings about him ran too deep for simple analysis, but it was decided to turn the event into a send-off for Brian with an oration from Mick Jagger immediately before a dispelling of collective grief as the Stones launched into a set that appalled listeners with its careless tonality. Keith Richards was to admit, 'I was a bit shaky at first, but then I started enjoying myself.'

He also stole nervous glances at the increasing depth into which the Stones would plunge if they failed to live up to expectations when, after a three-year lay-off, the group resumed touring with a major coast-to-coast assault on North America starting in Colorado on 1 November 1969, that had sold out within hours.

The comeback was to finish on an ugly note when an attempt to recapture that Serpentine magic with a buckshee bash on 6 December 1969 at Altamont, a speedway race track an hour's drive from San Francisco. A 20-mile traffic jam and shortage of portable toilets were the least of it. With the benefit of hindsight, the first time in England should have been the only time because, while the Stones delivered more routinely solid goods than at Hyde Park, Altamont would be remembered by Keith Richards as 'chaos. I wouldn't say frightening, but definitely high in adrenaline. I was wondering who the hell was running the joint. 500, 000 people; guys are getting stabbed; the Hell's Angels are out of it on acid and Thunderbird wine. The only way you could cool it was by facing them down. The one thing you can't do is give way to fear or intimidation.' The event left four dead, one by murder with members of a chapter of the Hell's Angels the chief suspects.

Before the month was out, artificial snow cascaded onto ticket-holders at the Lyceum in the Strand when the Stones played their first home games since Hyde Park. However demonstrative their altruism on that summer's day, the purpose of these sold-out concerts was the same as that of any other rock group – to make a monetary killing.

'GET YER YA-YA'S OUT!'
The Rolling Stones in concert

There was also a tinge of a prodigals' return. Alhough the corrupted endeavour that was Altamont had been represented as an overall success in most of Britain's national newspapers, a harsher truth had resonated from an edition of *Rolling Stone* magazine that was devoted almost entirely to the event. Not a page went by without some vestige of blame sticking to the Stones.

This report had only just leaked into London and the full bitterness of what had occurred hadn't been understood by the majority of the crowds. Therefore, if there were any rancorous puzzlement, the Stones were still able to exact their customary submission from among the post-Woodstock flurry of long print dresses, pre-faded Levis embroidered with butterfly or toadstool motifs, clogs, bell-bottomed loon pants, cloche hats, grandad vests, air-force greatcoats and, even in the winter chill, stars-and-stripes singlets revealing underarm hair.

Here was consolation for the terrible end of the journey across North America: the acclamation of the great British public. That made up for the fall-out from Altamont and, in the New Year, the first Stones bootleg, *Live R Than You'll Ever Be*, taped at Oakland Coliseum, the third stop on the US trek. It defied every known copyright law but sold in sufficient quantities to qualify for a Billboard gold disc.

Live R Than You'll Ever Be compared so favourably with the official *Get Yer Ya-Yas Out* that it fuelled a rumour that the Stones had been responsible for their own bootleg. Yet *Ya-Yas* had been subject to much ironing out of faults back in London to the degree that Keith calculated that as much time was spent on this in-concert effort as on some of the studio albums.

Much of the fine-tuning concerned lead vocals because of Jagger's episodes of near-breathlessness during what amounted to a nightly equivalent of the London marathon. 'I certainly don't want to go on stage and just stand there' he laughed, 'I can hardly sing. I'm no Tom Jones, and I couldn't give a damn'.

As to the selected excerpts, the vinyl needle-time of *Get Yer Ya-Yas Out* had been pruned down from the nights of the 27 and 28 of November 1969 at New York's Madison Square Garden; whereas 'Jumping Jack Flash' and 'Love In Vain' came from a previous evening at Baltimore Civic Centre when the Stones also spent almost three hours on the boards.

A lot of attention was paid to the packaging too. Charlie Watts was photographed for the front cover prancing gleefully before a backdrop of a flat countryside landscape, top-hatted and with an electric guitar in either hand. Bearing Bill Wyman's four-string, a bass drum and a floor tom-tom, a donkey peers indifferently at him. While only the most hooked Stones devotee might have bothered to decipher this symbolism if that's what it was, *Get Yer Ya-Yas Out* topped the domestic chart and lingered for weeks in the US Top Ten that autumn.

Jagger's 'Charlie's good tonight, isn't he?' comment survived the editing but the drummer was still becoming accustomed to the lengthy and uproarious post-psychedelic rock extravaganzas. As Watts had noticed already, 'rock bands' no longer thought that a ten-minute slot on a scream-circuit package was sufficient.

Charlie had developed a swift acceptance of both this and of toiling behind his kit in North America's baseball parks and concrete coliseums. 'When they miked drums up,' he observed, 'it became a whole other world but they can't take away the character you develop in your relationship between the cymbal and the snare drum. Great players have that, but you get somebody else's version when you get a guy mixing you. It's very loud but flat.'

This attendant increase in onstage volume and the advent of monitor speakers also brought to the forefront the idiosyncracies of the Stones' approach to corporate rhythm. With Brian out of the way, and Mick Taylor seemingly as meek as a lamb, Keith Richards was becoming more than one of the four human walls of the cavorting Mick-as-Jumpin'-Jack-Flash's padded cell. Previously, many onlookers hadn't given him much notice, but it wasn't long before Jagger waved him in to hog the central microphone for at least one number.

During more typical Stones fare, the interaction between Richards and Taylor had already revealed a stronger differentiation between lead and rhythm than there'd been under the old regime of Brian and Keith, so much so that critics were lauding Keith's chord flaying as much as they were his and Taylor's dazzling solos. Suddenly, a rhythm guitarist no longer skulked in grey mediocrity beyond the main spotlight while the other fellow stupified listeners with his note-bending dexterity. 'Without Keith's rhythm guitar, there'd be no Rolling Stones,' declared Jack Nitzsche, 'What Keith does is play guitar without trying to be flash. It's all taste. Keith doesn't make a lot of faces.'

Unheeded was the lad's cry, 'I didn't say I was a rhythm guitarist. Other people made my reputation for me.' Nonetheless, the concept of the guitarists and singer being controlled *en bloc* by tempos defined strictly by bass and drums had always been a misnomer.

In the Stones' case, it boiled down to an onstage interaction hinged on the good-bad rawness of Richards's chord-slashing that was compulsively exquisite even to more proficient guitarists who could hear what was technically askew. As Bill Wyman put it: 'Our band does not follow the drummer. Our drummer follows the rhythm guitarist. Immediately, you've got something like a one-hundredth of a second delay between the guitar and Charlie's lovely drumming. Onstage, you have to follow Keith. You have no way of not following him. With Charlie following Keith, you have that very minute delay. The net result is that loose type of pulse that goes between Keith, Charlie and me.

'Keith knows in general that we're following him, so he doesn't care if he changes the beat around or isn't really aware of it. He'll drop a half or quarter bar somewhere and suddenly Charlie's playing on the beat instead of the backbeat. He'll be so surprised and be very uptight to get back in because it's very hard for a drummer to swap the beat, especially on the intros. He's got monitors but if you're not hearing too well with the screaming crowds, its very difficult to hear the accents, the difference between the soft and hard strokes. The problem is that he's often totally unaware that he's on the wrong beat, and he shuts his eyes and he's gone. Someone has to go up and kick the cymbal but I think that's a little of the charm of the Stones.'

Except where otherwise stated, the line up throughout is as follows:-
Mick Jagger: lead vocals, harmonica
Keith Richards: guitar, backing vocals
Bill Wyman: bass guitar
Charlie Watts: drums

As on all Rolling Stones in-concert albums, timing includes continuity and audience response.

Jumping Jack Flash (Jagger-Richards) 4.02
A cacophony of very London-sounding dialogue by Jagger and the Stones' own master-of-ceremonies, Sam Cutler, is the frontispiece to an opener that would be a hard yardstick for any group to follow.

Carol (Berry) 3.47
An affectionate trawl through the Chuck Berry item that was a fixture in the stage repertoire from the beginning until circa 1965. An unseen Ian Stewart is vamping the piano.

Stray Cat Blues (Jagger-Richards) 3.41
Jagger subtracts two years from the groupie's age in this brisk rendition of the *Beggars Banquet* track.

Love In Vain (Trad. arr Jagger-Richards) 4.57
Featuring a heart-swelling bottleneck solo by Mick Taylor, this was the only slow number. Inverting the principle that a drop of black makes white paint whiter, the Stones make a run of in-yer-face uptempo items all the more poignant by thus hanging fire a third of the way in. An alternative to 'Love In Vain' might have been 'Prodigal Son', in which Keith switched to acoustic and seated himself on one of two stools brought on to enable him and Mick to duet folk-club style while the other three took five. It was edited out of the album because on-stage pianissimos tended to be undercut by a ceaseless barrage of stamping, whistling and, worst of all, bawled request for the good old ones like '19th Nervous Breakdown', 'Paint It Black', anything loud.

Midnight Rambler (Jagger-Richards) 9.05
One of Jagger's eternal on-stage preferences, it let him take it down easy, build the tension to raving panic and finally, sweep into the wings leaving 'em wanting more. Road-drilled with all manner of tempo, dynamic and rhythmic refinements, this was stretched out closer to the quarter-hour mark at other stops on the tour as heard on a bootleg entitled 'We Didn't Really Get In On Until Detroit'.

Sympathy For The Devil (Jagger-Richards) 6.52
This begins with some female cawing for 'Paint It Black, Paint It Black!' and showcases a Richards solo that, if lacking the needle-sharpness of the studio version, is commensurate with the emergency of the live situation, almost as if he were playing it while parachuting from a high altitude.

Live With Me (Jagger-Richards) 3.03
Surely there were more interesting pickings from the miles of accumulated tape than this run-through of one of the most ordinary post-*Satanic Majesties* numbers the group ever recorded.

Little Queenie (Berry) 4.33
Two attempts at this Chuck Berry rocker were included on a tape sent to an unimpressed Alexis Korner in spring 1962 by Little Boy Blue and the Blue Boys, i.e. Jagger, Richards, Dick Taylor and student friends. This is the second number in the set to feature Ian Stewart on keyboards. 'Little Queenie' was still in the air 18 months later when a line was quoted on the fade-out of T Rex's UK chart-topper, 'Get It On'.

Honky Tonk Women (Jagger-Richards) 3.45
Like 'Jumping Jack Flash' also from the first Madison Square Gardens performance, this was a vast improvement on the way it was played at Hyde Park, though the audience went as ape over that as they did here.

Street Fighting Man (Jagger-Richards) 4.03
The amplifiers were flat-out on what managed to stay a few degrees short of a sound-picture of Genghis Khan carnage.

STICKY FINGERS

UK Release: 23 April 1971
US Release: 23 April 1971
Intl CD No: CBS CDCBS 450195 2
Running Time: 46:26

Rolling Stones Records COC 59100
Rolling Stones Records COC 59100
Producer: Jimmy Miller

SIDE ONE: Brown Sugar; Sway; Wild Horses; Can't You Hear Me Knocking; You Gotta Move.

SIDE TWO: Bitch; I Got The Blues; Sister Morphine; Dead Flowers; Moonlight Mile.

Among auxiliary players employed by The Rolling Stones on their first album of the new decade was Tennessee pianist Jim Dickinson who could improvise the orthodox 'Nashville sound' from a notation peculiar to studios in the USA's country music capital. However, before the translation of C&W into a late-20th-century commentary on the aspirations of middle America, today's Dolly Parton fan might have once proffered the excuse, 'I just had the radio on. I wasn't actually listening to it'.

But by the early 70s, the music previously associated with uneducated, bigoted rednecks and considered the most uncool and right-wing genre in pop, was being reassessed and recognised for its many virtues. As well as Gram Parsons' Byrds, Bob Dylan, Neil Young, Ringo Starr and ex-Monkee Mike Nesmith had all gone country. Furthermore, Jerry Lee Lewis had risen anew as a C&W star following a hit with 1968's 'Another Time Another Place'. And that same year, Johnny Cash, described as 'the Keith Richards of country music' after he'd assumed Hank Williams' crown as a drug-dizzied booker's risk, had earned the approbation of the hippie sub-culture for a professional liaison with Dylan and a televised concert before inmates of San Quentin. The discerning Frank Zappa declared himself a Cash fan too.

While respective audiences were becoming less biased against one or the other, Keith Richards had discussed possible fusions of country and classic rock with Gram Parsons while the latter was still a Byrd, initially during a lengthy debate one spring evening in a

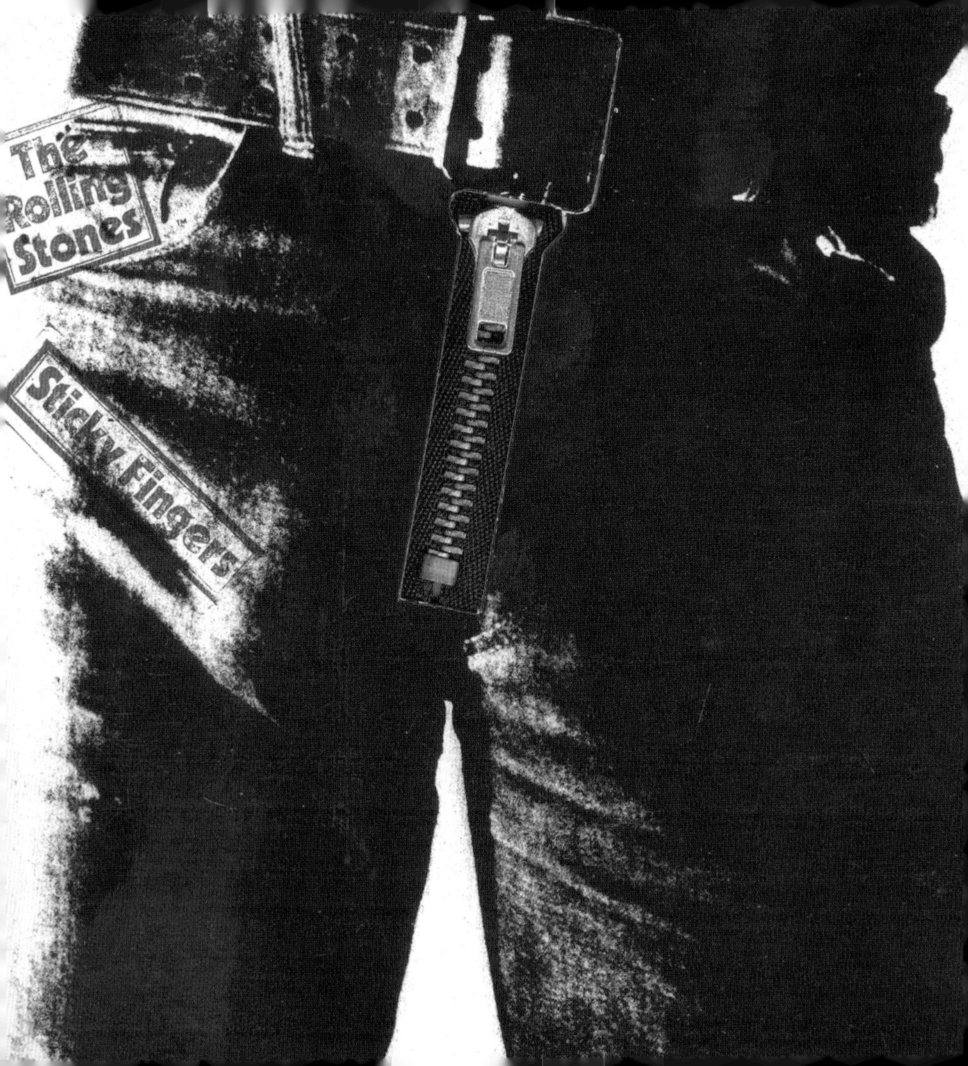
The Rolling Stones
Sticky Fingers

London night club in 1969. During the same boozy conversation, it transpired that Parsons was unhappy about The Byrds' forthcoming dates in aparthied-riven South Africa. 'On the spur of the moment, he decided to leave the band,' recalled Keith, 'so I had to put him up. We would get stoned, sit around with two guitars or a piano and be the happiest kids in the sandbox.' Coming with the territory was Gram's friend, Phil Kaufman who ran the Executive Nanny Service, a security firm who were to be employed by The Rolling Stones.

Kaufman had also served as road manager for The Flying Burrito Brothers, formed by Parsons and other ex-Byrds, who had been among the support acts at Altamont. He and Gram were present when three tracks that would find their way onto *Sticky Fingers* were taped mid-tour at rural Alabama's trendy eight-track Muscle Shoals complex – 'very laid-back and relaxed', said Leon Russell. The previous autumn, Russell had introduced saxophonist Bobby Keyes, who shared the same birthday to the year with Keith Richards, to the Stones.

As well as the ambles down Memory Lane and excerpts from *Let It Bleed*, the Stones were giving 'em no less than three Chuck Berry numbers and unfamiliar items from the album yet to come including 'Bitch', earmarked as the single on a motley album and 'Sister Morphine' which was an antiquity from mid-1968.

Although Richards found the emotional detachment to allow its selection for *Sticky Fingers*, 'Sister Morphine' was closer to the bone than it had once been. For some time he had been escaping into reveries induced by cocktails of cocaine and its more sinister sister narcotic, heroin. He imagined that he could give it up any time he liked. However, though not yet breakneck, his slide into heroin dependency had become unstoppable.

Keith's interest in business affairs was by now far less intense although his years in the music industry had fostered in him a grasp of financial technicalities that was less hesitant than most. 'Rock'n'roll is big business, you know,' he pontificated, 'Musicians who find themselves suddenly the focal point of millions and millions of dollars neither have the time nor inclination to be able to look after it properly'.

As the expiry date of the Decca contract – 31 July 1970 – crept closer, rumour darkened to a certainty that the Stones were not going to re-sign, partly because of what they saw as avaricious vacillation over perceived royalty discrepancies. Needless to say, Decca refuted this sullying of its good name but swallowing its ire, sent representatives to other major labels that were submitting their bids to one of the hottest properties in showbusiness.

That the metaphorical weather-vane was turning in the direction of Atlantic Records had been indicated in April when Mick and Keith tagged along with the company's boss Ahmet Ertegun to hear Screaming Lord Sutch at the Speakeasy. Sutch was the latest acquisition by a company that had been a bystander during the British Invasion, buoyed as it was by a bevy of hitmaking black soul singers before seizing The Spencer Davis Group in 1966.

More recently, Led Zeppelin, Yes and other British outfits concentrating principally on the US market, had melted into Atlantic's caress too. In a stronger position to dictate terms, the Stones were granted their own subsidiary label, Rolling Stones Records, complete with a logo that caricatured Mick Jagger's lips and tongue. If there were the slightest deviation from the ascribed riders and fringe benefits, wild horses wouldn't drag the Stones out to utter one solitary syllable or play a single note on a given album's behalf.

It was a tall order, but Atlantic was the label most prepared to obey. There was also the enticement of its historic stable of black R&B artists from The Coasters and The Drifters back in the 50s to a roster of hit-making soul singers. Among them were Wilson Pickett, Carla Thomas, Otis Redding and Don Covay, on both Atlantic and its subsidiary outlet, Stax. When the Stones had reached an agreeable compromise between monetary gain and an affiliation to music that had captured the imagination of their younger selves, the Erteguns recognised a sound investment as an in-person slot on Top Of The Pops oiled the wheels of a domestic chart climb for 'Brown Sugar', the debut Atlantic 45. On the same show, the group also plugged its 'Bitch' coupling, and 'Wild Horses' a ballad that was to be the second US Top 30 single from *Sticky Fingers*, that had absorbed just enough of prevailing fads to keep older fans turned on.

It sold millions, despite or because of perceived references to the hard drugs that had caught on within the Stones' inner circle. These surfaced in the lyrics as frequently as swear-words would later. 'Sister Morphine' was considered sufficiently venal for it to be expunged from the album's Spanish pressing. There was also concern about the packaging in a sleeve designed by Andy Warhol. Like a protruding square of plastic on the cover of *Satanic Majesties*, a real zip on the fly of the denim-clad male loins that graced the front obstructed the snug insertion into a wire record rack of what many fans still feel was the last truly great Stones LP.

Brown Sugar (Jagger-Richards) 3.50

Mick Jagger: lead vocals
Keith Richards and Mick Taylor: guitars
Ian Stewart: piano
Bill Wyman: bass guitar
Charlie Watts: drums
Bobby Keyes: saxophone

A rough draft of horn-laden 'Brown Sugar' had been penned by Jagger during the filming of *Ned Kelly* in which he played the title role. Its verses effused images of slave ships bound from West Africa to US clearing houses where cotton planters bought and branded the manacled cargo. Both below decks and in the stockades, the females were coaxed with whips into manifold rude activities with their white captors. Black US politician Reverend Jesse Jackson urged the instant removal of 'Brown Sugar' from radio playlists as it sliced as a wire through cheese to No.1, repeating the process in Britain. Drummers may be intrigued to know of Charlie's calculated deviation from the orthodox eight quavers in a bar on the hi-hat on 'Brown Sugar'. He omits the second beat of each measure.

Sway (Jagger-Richards) 3.51

Mick Jagger: lead vocals
Keith Richards, Mick Taylor and Mick Jagger: guitars
Bill Wyman: bass guitar
Nicky Hopkins: piano
Mick Jagger and Keith Richards: backing vocals
Paul Buckmaster: string arrangement

Nothing to do with the 1954 hit of the same title by crooner Dean Martin, an audible count-in pitches the Stones into a stirring, if self-loathing ballad, somewhere between slow and moderato. 'Sway' was the first item to be recorded in the Mobile, the Stones' own portable studio, set up on this occasion at Stargroves, Jagger's grand rural property in west Berkshire. Among others who were to use the Mobile during this period were The Who, Led Zeppelin and The Faces.

Wild Horses (Jagger-Richards) 5.42

Mick Jagger: lead vocals
Keith Richards and Mick Taylor: guitars
Jim Dickinson: piano
Bill Wyman: bass guitar
Charlie Watts: drums

Occasionally Richards and Gram Parsons spent nights in southern California's High Desert watching out for extra-terrestrials. Many hours passed with no signs from outer space, unless hallucinogenically induced, amid the surreal landscapes of this arcadia of desert bloom and sun-dappled woodland that was becoming lost in an encroaching urban sprawl spreading from Los Angeles. The area was on a par with Gauguin's South Sea island or Byron's Italy in its potential to inspire greatness or at least accommodate it. It's feasible that 'Wild Horses', a highlight of both *Sticky Fingers* and 1970's *Deluxe*, the second Flying Burrito Brothers' album, began there.

Jagger tidied up and added considerably to the lyrics and sang this countrified melancholia about Keith's reluctance to abandon relatively sedate domesticity to go on tour without affectation. The opening bars of the guitar solo places Chuck Berry in as strange a context as he was in 'Gimmie Shelter', and capture the essence of the Stones in downbeat mood.

Can't You Hear Me Knocking (Jagger-Richards) 7.15

Mick Jagger: lead vocals
Keith Richards and Mick Taylor: guitars
Billy Preston: organ
Jimmy Miller and Rocky Dijon: percussion
Bill Wyman: bass guitar
Charlie Watts: drums
Mick Jagger and Keith Richards: backing vocals

More than a touch of Santana prevailed on the wholly instrumental second section of a song that would have stood tall enough without it. This also marked the first appearance on a Stones disc of Billy Preston, a black Texan whose musical pedigree stretched back to stints as Little Richard's organist and the house band of Shindig, an American TV pop series of the mid-60s. After a stint with Ray Charles, he enjoyed a UK chart debut produced by George Harrison and, famously, played on The Beatles' 'Get Back' in 1969. A subsequent solo career as a singer would spawn two US No. 1s. Hired later as the Stones' musical director, Preston was to be permitted a lead vocal spot replete with fancy footwork and soulman exhibitionism while Jagger took a breather.

You Gotta Move (McDowell-Davis) 2.32
Mick Jagger: lead vocals
Bill Wyman: bass guitar, piano
Mick Taylor: slide guitar
Charlie Watts: drums
Keith Richards: guitar

With just a bass drum as the rhythmic pulse, the Stones revived a primitive and roots-affirming rural blues, a collaboration between street evangelist the Rev. Blind Gary Davis and the younger Mississippi Fred McDowell, a frequent visitor to Europe from the late 60s.

Bitch (Jagger-Richards) 3.36
Mick Jagger: lead vocals
Keith Richards and Mick Taylor: guitars
Jimmy Miller: percussion
Bobby Keyes and Jim Price: brass and woodwinds
Bill Wyman: piano
Charlie Watts: drums
Mick Jagger and Keith Richards: backing vocals

The horns punch out Keith's four-bar riff, both in ragged unison with his fretting and to underpin his solo between the final verse and the coda of a number that was relegated to a B-side in the States. Like bad would be, bitch was meant as a compliment and was the latest smart slang word to be imported from the streets of urban North America.

I Got The Blues (Jagger-Richards) 3.53
Mick Jagger: lead vocals
Keith Richards and Mick Taylor: guitars
Billy Preston: organ
Bobby Keyes and Jim Price: brass and woodwinds
Bill Wyman: bass guitar
Charlie Watts: drums

Although bearing a standardised title from another genre, this was nearer to Atlantic soul, notably via a horn section that could be mistaken for that of the lately reconstituted Bar-Kays, one of Stax's two all-purpose backing combos.

Sister Morphine (Jagger-Richards-Faithfull) 5.31
Mick Jagger: lead vocals
Keith Richards: guitars
Bill Wyman: bass guitar
Ry Cooder: slide guitar

Charlie Watts: drums

Jack Nitszche: piano

Just as Ry Cooder felt he deserved a writing credit for 'Honky Tonk Women' and Mick Taylor for 'Moonlight Mile', so Marianne Faithfull claimed authorship of lyrics proffered when Richards and Jagger were tinkering with the slow but captivating melody of 'Sister Morphine'. With Mick on acoustic guitar, she recorded 'Sister Morphine' as the B side of her final 60s single. Smelling of hospitals, the song pictures a fragile junkie on a ward mattress to the agitated clang of an ambulance bell. While the surroundngs fill him/her with nightmare reflections – 'why does the doctor have no face?' 'tomorrow I'll be dead', 'clean, white sheets stained red' – a sense of longing as much as wretchedness also permeates the atmosphere. On the orders of a fretting Decca executive who'd bothered listening to both sides, the Faithfull 45 was withdrawn from circulation.

Dead Flowers (Jagger-Richards) 4.03

Mick Jagger: lead vocals

Bill Wyman: bass guitar

Keith Richards and Mick Taylor: guitars

Charlie Watts: drums

Ian Stewart: piano

Mick Jagger and Keith Richards: backing vocals

A mickey-taking Jagger sounded as if he had inhaled the air round Nashville for months on end. C&W wasn't Ian Stewart's bag but because of the jokey nature of 'Dead Flowers' he didn't mind stepping in on piano. For a while, it was the opening number of the Stones' stage shows.

Moonlight Mile (Jagger-Richards) 5.56

Mick Jagger: lead vocals

Bill Wyman: bass guitar

Charlie Watts: drums

Mick Taylor: guitar

Jim Price: piano

Paul Buckmaster: string arrangment

Buckmaster of The Third Ear Band whose oboe, viola, bongo and 'cello undulations opened the Hyde Park show, scored the orchestral strings for 'Sway'. The incandescent encapsulation of a van's headlights signalled one more wearied deliverance from the treadmill of the road for someone who preferred to develop some flash of inspiration rather than fall asleep upright with the motorway roaring in his ears.

EXILE ON MAIN STREET

UK Release: 12 May 1972
US Release: 12 May 1972
Intl CD No: CBS CDCBS 450196 2
Running Time: 66:34

Rolling Stones Records COC 69100
Rolling Stones Records COC 2-2900
Producer: Jimmy Miller

SIDE ONE: Rocks Off; Rip This Joint; Hip Shake; Casino Boogie; Tumbling Dice.
SIDE THREE: Happy; Turd On The Run; Ventilator Blues; Just Wanna See His Face; Let It Loose.

SIDE TWO: Sweet Virginia; Torn And Frayed; Black Angel; Loving Cup.
SIDE FOUR: All Down The Line; Stop Breaking Down; Shine A Light; Soul Survivor.

Atlantic's huge advance, combined with the release of million-selling *Sticky Fingers*, had come not a moment too soon. The Inland Revenue had been challenging the Stones with a tax bill that had snowballed over seven years of international stardom. A sky-high bill demanded the group migrate overseas until the dust settled.

Through a combination of Mick Jagger's persistence and the weariness they all felt about the nasty situation, the Stones uprooted to the Cote D'Azur after what was publicised as a farewell tour of Britain in spring 1971.

When each individual member had found somewhere to live out there, life returned not to normal but to a relocated domestic routine broken by sessions at Nellcote, Keith Richards' coastal abode where basic tracks were laid down for what would turn out to be the Stones' only non-compilation double-album, *Exile On Main Street*.

Shuttered underground in the newly installed drum isolation booth, Charlie Watts thumped out take after rejected take, emerging occasionally to listen hard to a playback amid the spools and blinking dials. An ennui manifested itself in Charlie getting to know by sight individual sweet wrappers, and note their day-to-day journeyings up and down a ledge, where an empty bottle of Keith's whisky might also remain for weeks next to a discarded swap-stick made grubby from cleaning tape-heads.

Rolling
EXILE ON MAIN ST
"THE HUMAN CORKSCREW"
Joe Allen

Watts had stumbled on ever-more fathomless reserves of patience as the years passed: 'When we're recording, it's not a question of getting it over quickly. It's getting a take that the majority likes. This tends to take longer than it did when we first started. The consolation is that these days our records sound so much better. So far as I'm concerned, once I've done my bit, there's nothing else for me to do except hang about in the studio. It's okay if the boys have brought some people in to do overdubs or the girls are doing a back-up vocal track. Otherwise, it's just boring.'

Although more at the centre of affairs as an associate co-producer, Jagger seemed to be unenthusiastic about buckling down to *Exile On Main Street*. This had much to do with the pregnancy of his new wife Bianca; their zest for the social whirl in Paris; his newly discovered sensitivities about the shallow rituals of pop and the initial conjugal bliss. Indeed, there was much concern about Mick's increasingly compartmentalised life causing him to vanish from the sessions for days, often on what appeared to some to be the slightest excuse, to be with Bianca.

While others in the group's coterie said nothing about a woman they thought rather intimidating, Keith Richards could not contain his resentment. All the same, he had to admit that, whether Mick had pulled his weight during the recording or had found more interesting things to do, he went beyond the call of duty when *Exile On Main Street* was on the point of release by composing and singing verses with piano accompaniment entitled *'Exile On Main Street Blues'* that linked excerpts from the album on a flexi-disc given away with the *New Musical Express* on 29 April 1972.

This and British anti-pornography campaigner Mary Whitehouse's complaints to the BBC about the words to some of the tracks on the collection, assisted a passage into the charts, even though Jagger felt that '*Beggars Banquet* and *Let It Bleed* were better records. They're more compressed. When you put a double-album out, there's always going to be something that could have been left off. I'm being super critical, but the record lacks a little focus.' These remarks were made during another period when it wasn't all smiles between Mick and Keith and it's not difficult to imagine the latter's knuckles whitening as he read them.

After all, Richards had been responsible for the lion's share of the songs on *Exile On Main Street.* Not only that, but he had allowed the installation of recording equipment in the basement of what had been nicknamed 'Keith's Coffee House'. If there were a storm centre of the Stones' operation in exile, it was surely Nellcote where musicians and payroll courtiers conferred; journalists were turned away; freeloaders sponged and telephones rang from Los Angeles, London and New York.

Among the compensations for constraints on Keith's private life was that, free from the financial overheads of a hired studio, the electronic den below stairs enabled him to potter about with sound, tape the wackiest demos and to begin a day's recording with nothing prepared. While mixing and mastering was to take place in more sophisticated locations in the USA, every note of *Exile On Main Street*, was hand-tooled at Nellcote over 1971's blazing Cote D'Azur summer into its autumn when heavy air flopped over the place like a wet raincoat.

'Keith works on his own emotional rhythm pattern,' grinned Glyn Johns, summoned from Surrey, 'If he thinks it's necessary to spend three hours working on a riff, he'll do it while everyone else picks their noses. I've never seen him stop and explain something.'

Grasping the reins of what he called 'Stones Mach II', Richards had never been out on a longer limb, particularly as Jagger was absenting himself so much. This was regrettable but far from disasterous as Keith took more or less sole charge with not so much bossy hauteur as a known taciturn obstinancy. 'If things don't suit Keith, he won't go along with it,' sighed Bill Wyman, 'and that's the end of the subject. When asked why not, Keith would reply, "Because I don't want to".'

Debated precision thus deferred to the spirit of the moment and a home-made passion enhanced by Keith's increasingly more eccentric rhythmic shifts and the very surroundings in which, as more and more musical trimmings were discarded, direction and outcome shone through with the same sepia-tinged clarity as the discs' packaging. In this respect, Keith's hard listening to the incantations of pre-war bluesmen hadn't been wasted – particularly those of Robert Johnson: 'He was playing with rooms,' concluded Keith, 'I think that he was very, very aware of sound and a room, and where the sound of his guitar would bounce off the corner. He was into ambience.'

Exile On Main Street, Keith's baby, became the yardstick by which future Rolling Stones output would be measured. Alongside *Sgt. Pepper* and The Beach Boys' *Pet Sounds*, it was to be near the top of those 'Hundred Greatest Albums' polls that rear up periodically in the media. Yet *Exile On Main Street* wasn't greatly appreciated at the time of its release. It certainly wasn't regarded as the classic that today's pop journalists think it is.

While it made No.1 in the USA, it had been disparaged by *Rolling Stone* with 'too much of *Exile* is simply forgettable'. Adding injury to insult, it finished just outside the Top 30 in Billboard's best-selling LPs of 1972 list. Among higher placings was *Hot Rocks 1964-1971*, a greatest hits collection of pre-Atlantic Stones material that had spread itself thinly enough to sell more copies without rising above No. 4.

As a decent interval had passed since Altamont, no time was better for another US tour with some European dates, even if none of these could accommodate the same tens of thousands in one go. With appetites whetted by 'Tumbling Dice', the first of two *Exile On Main Street* singles in Billboard's springtime Top Ten, Uncle Sam's pop-pickers were awaiting a carnival of even greater magnitude than when The Rolling Stones last visited in 1969.

Rocks Off (Jagger-Richards) 4.32
Mick Jagger: lead vocals
Keith Richards and Mick Taylor: guitars
Nicky Hopkins: keyboards
Bobby Keyes and Jim Price: brass and woodwinds
Bill Wyman: bass guitar
Charlie Watts: drums

The chaps get off to a flying start with the up tempo, if not completely satisfying, antics of a pleasure-seeker with a dancing girl, as blasting horns and Richards, 'the Human Riff', interweave behind a vocal that exudes the breathy sentience of a man who has been sprinting.

Rip This Joint (Jagger-Richards) 2.23
Mick Jagger: lead vocals
Bill Wyman: bass guitar
Keith Richards and Mick Taylor: guitars
Charlie Watts: drums
Bill Plummer: double bass
Nicky Hopkins: keyboards
Bobby Keyes and Jim Price: brass and woodwinds

Though there are allusions to recent newsworthy events in the verses, this is much in the tradition of 'Shake Rattle And Roll', 'Flip Flop And Fly' and similar rock-a-boogie from the 50s as epitomised by the very employment of Bill Plummer, a Los Angeles session man, to slap that dissolute bull fiddle.

Hip Shake (Harpo) 2.59
Mick Jagger: lead vocals, harmonica
Keith Richards and Mick Taylor: guitars
Bill Wyman: bass guitar
Charlie Watts: drums
Nicky Hopkins: keyboards
Bobby Keyes: saxophone

Jagger's deep absorption of Slim Harpo is perceptible in this blues from the mid-50s. A contagious rockabilly backbeat gives credence to one pundit's summary of the form as 'the blues with acne'.

Casino Boogie (Jagger-Richards) 3.33

Mick Jagger: lead vocals
Keith Richards and Mick Taylor: guitars
Keith Richards: bass guitar
Charlie Watts: drums

Paving the way for 'Tumbling Dice' and encompassing a lengthy instrumental coda, this is a barrelhouse blues sidetracked to Monte Carlo, with certain words that the more upright of the form's more elderly practitioners and British expatriate gentlefolk wouldn't use. Incidentally, Joseph Hobson Jagger, one of Mick's immediate ancestors, allegedly inspired the music-hall favourite, 'The Man Who Broke The Bank At Monte Carlo' by figuring out the secret of a casino's roulette wheel.

Tumbling Dice (Jagger-Richards) 3.45

Mick Jagger: lead vocals
Keith Richards, Mick Taylor and Mick Jagger: guitars
Nicky Hopkins: keyboards
Clydie King, Vanetta Field and others: backing vocals
Charlie Watts: drums
Mick Taylor: bass guitar
Bobby Keyes and Jim Price: brass and woodwinds

Jagger commented 'those cymbals sound like dustbin lids' at the start of the mixing session. The problem was resolved and, if not a Stones classic, the resulting 45 was a palpable hit in most charts. Decades later it was still in a stage show that sometimes embraced passages as pre-ordained as a Broadway musical such as Mick's head turning abruptly in Keith's direction for the partner-in-crime phrase in one of the verses.

Sweet Virginia (Jagger-Richards) 4.25

Mick Jagger: lead vocals, harmonica
Bill Wyman: bass guitar
Ian Stewart: piano
Jimmy Miller: percussion
Mick Jagger, Keith Richards and Gram Parsons: backing vocals
Keith Richards and Mick Taylor: guitars
Charlie Watts: drums
Bill Plummer: double bass
Bobby Keyes and Jim Price: brass and woodwinds

At this beginning of *Exile On Main Street's* slow side, the vocal presence of Parsons is indicative of his continuing advice to the Stones about adding an ever more piquant boots-and-saddles ingredient to their stylistic cauldron. After all, what else is C&W but white man's blues? 'It was a logical step for The Rolling Stones to get into country music,' acknowledged Gram, 'because they've always been well into the old blues since they first began.'

Torn And Frayed (Jagger-Richards) 4.17

Mick Jagger: lead vocals
Keith Richards and Mick Taylor: guitars
Mick Taylor: bass guitar
Jim Price: organ
Charlie Watts: drums
Bill Wyman: synthesiser
Nicky Hopkins: piano
Al Perkins: pedal steel guitar

The swirl of pedal steel appeared to plague every other album heard in university campuses in the early 70s as did plodding laid-back tempo. Nevertheless, while catching this overall drift, the Stones still manage to apply a unique touch to a song about the ballrooms and smelly bordellos that were the frequent lot of a working band.

Black Angel (Jagger-Richards) 2.54

Mick Jagger: lead vocals, harmonica
Keith Richards and Mick Taylor: guitars
Bill Wyman: bass guitar
Charlie Watts: drums
Jimmy Miller: percussion
Richard Washington: steel drums

An element of socio-political journalism fired this non-doctrinal statement about the outcome of an appeal against the imprisonment for murder of the titular Black Panther, Angela Davis. The neo-acoustic backing was tough enough to direct attention away from the main difficulty with such a topical ditty: what becomes of it when the subject is no longer topical or the topic becomes tedious? The answer was to impose it on the concert set for as long as the general public was still interested in Angela Davis and her cause, and then never perform it again.

Loving Cup (Jagger-Richards) 4.23

Mick Jagger: lead vocals
Charlie Watts: drums
Bill Wyman: bass guitar, synthesiser
Keith Richards and Mick Taylor: guitars
Jimmy Miller: percussion
Nicky Hopkins: piano
Mick Jagger and Keith Richards: backing vocals
Bobby Keyes and Jim Price: brass and woodwinds

Composed too late for *Beggars Banquet*, this was premiered at Hyde Park and there had been no room for it on either of the two albums that followed. Lyrically, it may have stemmed from 'Just A Little Bit' by Memphis R&B entertainer Rosco Gordon that was a minor hit for Liverpool's Undertakers in 1964.

Happy (Jagger-Richards) 3.04
Keith Richards: lead vocals, bass guitar
Jimmy Miller: drums
Mick Jagger and Keith Richards: backing vocals
Keith Richards and Mick Taylor: guitars
Bobby Keyes: percussion

The first Stones 45 with someone other than Jagger as lead singer since 'In Another Land', this lived up to its name, musically and lyrically, in spite of all the husky vehemence born of Keith tearing the cellophane off up to five packets of cigarettes daily since adolescence. 'Happy' also confirmed commercial expectations, soaring high in the US Hot 100.

Turd On The Run (Jagger-Richards) 2.37
Mick Jagger: lead vocals, harmonica
Bill Wyman: bass guitar
Nicky Hopkins: keyboards
Keith Richards and Mick Taylor: guitars
Charlie Watts: drums
Bill Plummer: double bass

An off-putting title aside, this is a pleasant-enough ditty from the C&W end of the rock'n'roll spectrum – with the 'I gave you diamonds, you gave me disease' line encapsulating the thrust of the narrative. 'Turd On The Run' was one of two *Exile On Main Street* tracks acquired illicitly by a Los Angeles radio station that played both for the best part of a day.

Ventilator Blues (Jagger-Richards-Taylor) 3.24
Mick Jagger: lead vocals
Keith Richards and Mick Taylor: guitars
Keith Richards: dobro
Bobby Keyes and Jim Price: brass and woodwinds
Bill Wyman: bass guitar
Charlie Watts: drums
Nicky Hopkins: piano

A blues with standard chord changes, its composition may have been motivated by air-conditioning that barely coped with a stifling summer's prickly heat, growing by the minute in the studio.

Just Wanna See His Face (Jagger-Richards) 2.52

Mick Jagger: lead vocals
Keith Richards and Mick Taylor: guitars
Mick Taylor: bass guitar
Jimmy Miller: percussion
Clydie King, Vanetta Field and others: backing vocals
Keith Richards: piano
Charlie Watts: drums
Bill Plummer: double bass

While claiming to be an atheist in at least one interview, Jagger appreciated gospel music. On instant replay for several weeks in summer 1969 was 'Oh Happy Day', an 18th-century hymn arranged to chart-climbing effect by black US choir The Edwin Hawkins Singers. Next, he acquired the associated LP. His liking for the Singers came home to roost on this track in which the face mentioned is that of Jesus although the exhorter-congregation interplay is closer to that of a Missa Luba mass from deep in the Congo.

Let It Loose (Jagger-Richards) 5.17

Mick Jagger: lead vocals
Keith Richards and Mick Taylor: guitars
Nicky Hopkins: keyboards
Bobby Keyes and Jim Price: brass and woodwinds
Bill Wyman: bass guitar
Charlie Watts: drums
Clydie King, Shirley Goodman, Dr. John and others: backing vocals

'Let It Loose', 'the single most soulful thing the Stones ever recorded', was to earn Jagger place in *Mojo*'s '100 Great Voices And The Records That Prove It', but with the qualification that he 'was never a Van Morrison (or even a Stevie Winwood), but he could pull out the stops when the song warranted it, pushing himself beyond his usual posturings.' The most illustrious members of the accompanying chorale were Dr. John and Shirley Goodman, once half of Shirley and Lee, whose 'Let The Good Times Roll', became a much-revived rock'n'roll set-work. Later, she became a feathered, beaded chanteuse in a troupe led by Dr. John, who brought voodoo from the Louisiana everglades to late 60s pop. Known off-stage as Mac Rebennack, sometime Los Angeles session player, he was returning a favour as Jagger had sung on the Dr. John LP *The Sun, The Moon And The Herbs* a few months earlier.

All Down The Line (Jagger-Richards) 3.49
Mick Jagger: lead vocals
Keith Richards and Mick Taylor: guitars
Nicky Hopkins: piano
Bill Plummer: double bass
Bobby Keyes and Jim Price: brass and woodwinds
Bill Wyman: bass guitar
Charlie Watts: drums
Jimmy Miller: percussion
Kathi McDonald: backing vocals

This was completed in Sunset Sound Studios, Los Angeles with session singer McDonald, formerly one of Ike and Tina Turner's Ikettes, a vital layer of the onion. An ear-grabbing rock'n'soul opus, 'All Down The Line' satisfied every qualification of a 'Brown Sugar'-sized smash. If 'Happy', with which it was coupled, had flopped, perhaps it would have been re-promoted as the A side.

Stop Breaking Down (Johnson) 4.34
Mick Jagger: lead vocals, harmonica
Bill Wyman: bass guitar
Ian Stewart: piano
Keith Richards and Mick Taylor: guitars
Charlie Watts: drums

The second Robert Johnson item in the Stones' discography, this was not to become a blues-rock standard as 'Crossroads' and, to a lesser extent, 'Love In Vain' had done since their respective revivals by two world-famous groups. As well as expedient album reissues, Johnson had since precipitated frequently empty revaluation by music press hacks. Nevertheless, after he set up his own production company, Jagged Films, in 1996, Mick Jagger acquired the rights to a bio-pic treatment of Johnson's brief but eventful life.

Shine A Light (Jagger-Richards) 4.14
Mick Jagger: lead vocals
Keith Richards and Mick Taylor: guitars
Billy Preston: keyboards
Clydie King, Vanetta Field and others: backing vocals
Mick Taylor: bass guitar
Jimmy Miller: drums

This was recorded in nascent form during the *Let It Bleed* sessions. Here, it is given a gospel flavour thanks in no small part to the quality of the backing singers. Field was another ex-Ikette. In the 70s, she and King constituted two-thirds of The Blackberries, a female vocal group that, while recording artists in their own right, were hired to back all manner of other acts. To mainstream pop consumers they were synonymous with the British supergroup, Humble Pie.

Soul Survivor (Jagger-Richards) 3.49
Mick Jagger: lead vocals
Keith Richards and Mick Taylor: guitars
Mick Taylor: slide guitar
Keith Richards: bass guitar
Charlie Watts: drums
Nicky Hopkins: piano

A number about romance on the ocean wave, the initial seeds for its composition may have been sewn when viewing the blue curvature of the Mediterranean from Nellcote. The new resident spent many an afternoon on the rolling waves in his yacht, Mandrax, with only the phut of engine and groan of cordage to remind him of modern times on the mainland.

GOAT'S HEAD SOUP

UK Release: 31 August 1973 **Rolling Stones Records COC 59101**
US Release: 31 August 1973 **Rolling Stones Records COC 59101**
Intl CD No: CBS CDCBS 450207 2
Producer: Jimmy Miller
Running Time: 46:58

SIDE ONE: Dancing With Mr. D; 100 Years Ago; Coming Down Again; Doo Doo Doo Doo (Heartbreaker); Angie.

SIDE TWO: Silver Train; Hide Your Love; Winter; Can You Hear The Music; Star Star.

In 1973's summer term, California State University inaugurated a degree course in rock studies with The Rolling Stones the subject of at least one thesis. So began a long journey to some sort of officially recognised respectability for the group, who were then fresh from sessions for *Goat's Head Soup* at Dynamic Sound Studios in Kingston, Jamaica. It was to be mixed at Island Studios in London, owned by Chris Blackwell who was Kingston-born and bred. The golden goose of his record label, that was also called Island, was Traffic who were recording in Jamaica at the same time as the Stones. As well as being a pleasant escape from that wet British winter, the Commonwealth republic was favoured by Steve Winwood because 'Jamaican music is itself particularly English and African for obvious historical reasons, and that's what attracted me to it'.

Ska, bluebeat, calypso and further shades of West Indian sounds amalgamated into the primaeval atom of reggae that had become a turntable fixture at Mick Jagger's London home by the early 70s. To Gary Glitter, Jagger came across as 'an expert, and started explaining what was going on inside the rhythms and commenting on little subtleties of the mix.'

Keith Richards was even more passionate about reggae than Jagger, and so the Stones repaired to Jamaica to record their next album. Between hotel and studio they may have gazed from car windows at the city's poor quarters with often undernourished children descended from the black slaves at the lyrical core of 'Brown Sugar'. Mixing business with pleasure, they may have been shown a good time in local clubs, but the stay in Kingston wouldn't leave a pronounced mark on *Goat's Head Soup* as it would on later albums.

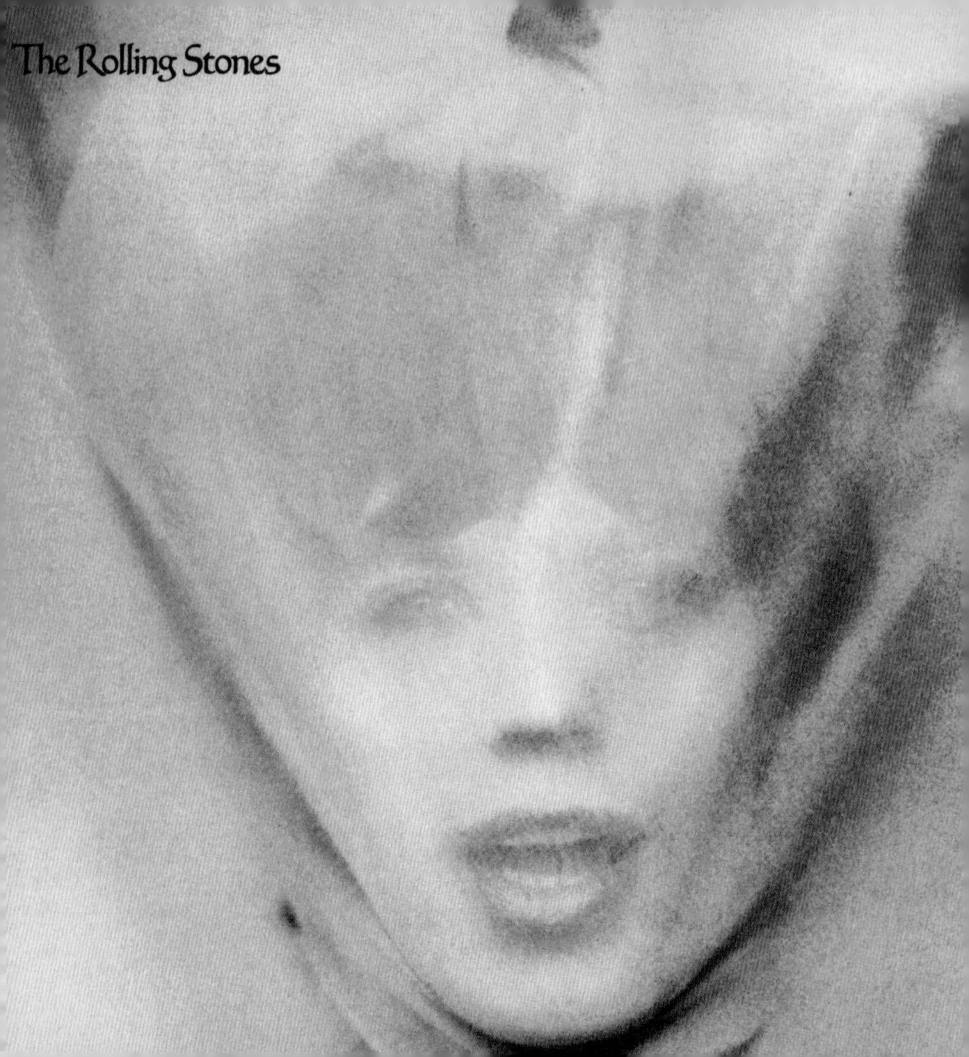
The Rolling Stones

Nonetheless, hands-on endorsement of Jamaica as a place to work by the Stones and Traffic, fully-integrated mainstays of rock's ruling class, also indicated correctly that West Indian sounds need be no longer an alien commodity to the general pop market. Keith Richards had been integrated easily into the society of the islands' most shunned sub-culture when he started hanging around with dread-locked Rastafarians in the sound-system dives of downtown Kingston, where massive sounds poured from huge speakers. When removed from unintelligible platitudes shouted over the racket, Keith spoke of producing Rastafarian acts for Rolling Stones Records in between drawing on spliffs laced with ganja provided by his new pals.

Ganja may have helped sustain the spiritual resolve of Rasta entertainers but by the mid-70s there was a strong hostility to certain illicit drugs expressed by many musicians, both in interview and record grooves. Frank Zappa, James Brown and even The Grateful Dead were warning of the dangers of hard drugs, but 'maybe I'll get a song out of it,' would be Keith Richards' reaction to one of the drugs charges that were punctuating his journey through the decade.

It was becoming a vicious circle for Keith. During intervals between this arrest and that court hearing, the substance at the heart of the matter, heroin, would work its questionable magic, staying the phantoms of distress and nudging away from the forefront of his thoughts an obsessive build up of a damning case against himself. By his own graphic admission, Richards had metamorphosed into 'a human chemical laboratory, almost like trying to commit suicide without any intention to do it – that stupid, stupid kind of suicide.'

He looked the part, especially after his teeth began to rot, and he took to wearing make-up to keep pace with the glam-rock boom in Britain. Hollow eyes were framed by purple-black blotches that remained even after he had cold-creamed away mascara that had trickled and dried. His emaciation and the corpse-grey colour that he radiated were exacerbated by an accumulation of fatigue caused by staying awake for hyperactive days on end, once allegedly managing a giddying nine without so much as a cat-nap. Gazing in a mirror, he saw ill health but his mind wandered to other subjects the moment he turned away.

An abiding image of the group on the road, post-*Exile On Main Street*, is a photograph taken in a customs area of Keith beneath a notice pleading for patience because 'A Drug-Free America Comes First!' The Stones had become sure enough of their standing in the continent to let *Goat's Head Soup* fend for itself without any accompanying tour. The only appearance there that year was January's hastily organised fund-raiser at the Los Angeles Forum. This was for the refugees of a Yuletide earthquake in Nicaragua's capital, Managua, where many of Bianca Jagger's relations lived. Tremors could be felt all along the spine of Central America.

Gathering together a mere fraction of the medicines and further foreign aid needed to cope with the disaster, Bianca and her man's shocked inspection of the aftermath of homelessness and spreading infection prompted the Stones to take a giant leap for Managua. From the Jaggers' personal resources poured more than the Forum show netted, that in turn generated a greater amount than George Harrison's more renowned Concerts For Bangla Desh. However, delivery of the cash was hindered by turgid US bureaucracy and interference from the affected country's corrupt government.

While Bianca appealed directly to the US Senate, Mick arranged a charity auction of Stones memorabilia days before the group's trek round Australasia and the Far East that was troubled by every fibre of red tape that could be used to prevent these decadent *ketos* from defiling Japan. Recently, Jagger had replied 'No, never' when asked by a US rock scribe if the Stones ever used drugs but, since 1969, he'd resumed a habit, noted by one fellow traveller, of having a supply of cocaine to hand, on-stage perspiration diminishing its effect, 'but I never saw him doing heroin'.

Such allegations, however mitigated, did not assist an easy passage round the globe. Neither was Jagger's proposal as the next single of a *Goat's Head Soup* ditty with a title derived from its delightful hook-line, 'Starfucker, starfucker, starfucker, starfucker, sta-ar!'. It was vetoed by Atlantic. A Radio One producer was reprimanded when, renamed 'Star Star', it was aired on the evening before the domestic release of the LP was heralded by a knees-up in the cafeteria of Blenheim Palace.

Even without the attendant fuss, *Goat's Head Soup* was a more commercially attractive proposition than *Exile On Main Street*. It also encompassed a miscellany of recycled ideas. For example, 'Hide Your Love', with Jagger singing to his own piano-pounding, wasn't unlike Boogie Bill Webb's 1952 country blues, 'I Ain't For It' in both content and delivery. From the Stones' own portfolio 'Dancing With Mr. D' was a sequel to 'Sympathy For The Devil'.

Dancing With Mr. D (Jagger-Richards) 4.53

Mick Jagger: lead vocals
Keith Richards and Mick Taylor: guitars
Nicky Hopkins: piano
Jimmy Miller, Rebop Kwaku Baah and others: percussion
Bill Wyman: bass guitar
Charlie Watts: drums
Billy Preston: clavinet
Mick Jagger, Keith Richards and Mick Taylor: backing vocals

I'm not saying there's anything sinister in this, but one of the engineers at the main session for this track became ill with a digestive complaint. Jimmy Miller was also poleaxed with the same affliction, but managed to finish the album. He never worked with the Stones again.

100 Years Ago (Jagger-Richards) 3.59

Mick Jagger: all vocals
Charlie Watts: drums
Nicky Hopkins: piano
Jimmy Miller: percussion
Bill Wyman: bass guitar
Mick Taylor: guitars
Billy Preston: clavinet

When captured for a hallucinatory moment in times past during a rural ramble, Jagger resisted being too prettily poetic over a charming reminiscence that builds to a slow-down before the next and final soft explosion.

Coming Down Again (Jagger-Richards) 5.54

Mick Jagger: lead vocals
Keith Richards and Mick Taylor: guitars
Nicky Hopkins: piano
Mick Jagger, Keith Richards and Mick Taylor: backing vocals
Bill Wyman: bass guitar
Charlie Watts: drums
Various: brass and woodwinds

This is conducive to the blissed-out afterglow of some pleasurable activity, so long as you don't listen too hard to lyrics that touch on faithlessness and related topics that could worry you into a state of mild paranoia.

Doo Doo Doo Doo (Heartbreaker) (Jagger-Richards) 3.27

Mick Jagger: lead vocals
Keith Richards and Mick Taylor: guitars
Billy Preston: keyboards
Mick Jagger, Keith Richards and Mick Taylor: backing vocals
Bill Wyman: bass guitar
Charlie Watts: drums
Various: brass and woodwinds

As a US single, this spent six weeks in the Top 20. Taylor's wah-wah six-string waxes almost vocal during musical snapshots of two avoidable urban tragedies: cops shooting a boy in a case of mistaken identity, and an ankle-socked girl found in a gutter, killed by a needle in a vein during what ought to have been her richest and most rewarding years.

Angie (Jagger-Richards) 4.33

Mick Jagger: lead vocals
Keith Richards and Mick Taylor: guitars
Nicky Hopkins: piano
Bill Wyman: bass guitar
Charlie Watts: drums
Nicky Harrison: string arrangement

A time-honoured strategy of using a girl's forename as a title as exemplified by 'Ramona', 'Charmaine', 'Peggy Sue', 'Claudette', 'Diane', 'Juliet', 'Michelle', 'Clair' and so on, was employed for 'Angie', the album's first single and a US chart-topper. It also stirred up an immediate and ill-founded rumour that it was a love song for Angela, David Bowie's wife. In London the couple had lived just round the corner from the Jaggers and the four of them had often been sighted on companionable outings together. Was Jagger up to no good with Mrs. Bowie? She insisted that he wasn't. In any case, 'Angie' was, reputedly, composed chiefly by Keith Richards. It would be to the pipe-organ strains of this rather than the traditional Wedding March that he walked his eldest daughter Dandelion, who'd renamed herself Angela, down the aisle when she wed in 2003.

Silver Train (Jagger-Richards) 4.27

Mick Jagger: all vocals and harmonica
Keith Richards, Mick Taylor and Mick Jagger: guitars
Bill Wyman: bass guitar
Charlie Watts: drums
Ian Stewart: piano
Jimmy Miller and Rebop Kwaku Baah: percussion

The Stones' performance in Hyde Park in 1969 began with 'I'm Yours And I'm Hers' by Johnny Winter who'd become a luminary of the 'blues boom'. Among enthusiast listeners to this boss-eyed, albino Texan's music were John Lennon and Keith Richards. Each was to pen a song in that style for Winter, respectively, 'Rock'n'Roll People' and 'Silver Train' which the Stones attempted in 1970 and, more successfully, when brewing up *Goat's Head Soup*. Winter's version was issued as a single shortly before the group's 'Silver Train' B sided 'Angie' in August 1973.

Hide Your Love (Jagger-Richards) 4.12

Mick Jagger: all vocals, piano
Bill Wyman: bass guitar
Bobby Keyes: saxophone
Keith Richards and Mick Taylor: guitars
Charlie Watts: drums
Jimmy Miller and Rebop Kwaku Baah: percussion

Seated at the piano, Jagger was the pivot of a jammed extemporisation, or that's the spirit that was immortalised on tape with Watts seeming to react instinctively, picking up the beat with his sticks, and Taylor tossing in a solo. Of the percussion ensemble, Baah had been a hand-drummer in Ginger Baker's Airforce and was then one of a 12-lane Traffic.

Winter (Jagger-Richards) 5.31

Mick Jagger: lead vocals
Mick Taylor and Mick Jagger: guitars
Nicky Hopkins: piano
Bill Wyman: bass guitar
Charlie Watts: drums
Nicky Harrison: string arrangement

Tinged with the antique symbolism of 'Who's Been Sleeping Here' (from *Between The Buttons*), this nothingness-to-eternity ballad was pronounced potentially brilliant by those who heard it in a comparatively raw state.

Can You Hear The Music (Jagger-Richards) 5.31

Mick Jagger: lead vocals
Keith Richards and Mick Taylor: guitars
Nicky Hopkins: piano
Mick Jagger, Keith Richards and Mick Taylor: backing vocals
Bill Wyman: bass guitar
Charlie Watts: drums
Jim Horn: flute
Jimmy Miller, Rebop Kwaku Baah and others: percussion

Quirky and psychedelic, this might have been lifted by time machine from *Satanic Majesties*. Alternatively, it may have been how the Stones would have sounded had Brian Jones managed to impose upon the modus operandi some of the more exotic visions he conjured up on creating the soundtrack to the German movie *Mort Und Totschlag* in 1966.

Star Star (Jagger-Richards) 4.25

Mick Jagger: lead vocals
Keith Richards and Mick Taylor: guitars
Ian Stewart: piano
Bill Wyman: bass guitar
Charlie Watts: drums
Bobby Keyes: saxophone

A galvanising squiggle of Chuck Berry persuasion by Richards plunged the Stones into the song that was the source of a media furore for lines that included a chorus riddled with the f-word. The verses also contained a bit about someone having oral sex with Hollywood actor Steve McQueen who, when told of the album's imminent release, said that it was OK by him. However, it's unlikely that John Wayne, an irregular Rolling Stones consumer, was able to comprehend a disobliging reference to himself in the same verse.

IT'S ONLY ROCK 'N ROLL

UK Release: 18 October 1974
US Release: 18 October 1974
Intl CD No: CBS CDCBS 450202 2
Producers: Mick Jagger and Keith Richards (The Glimmer Twins)

Rolling Stones Records COC 59103
Rolling Stones Records COC 79101
Running Time: 48:06

SIDE ONE: If You Can't Rock Me; Ain't Too Proud To Beg; It's Only Rock 'N' Roll; Till The Next Goodbye; Time Waits For No-One.

SIDE TWO: Luxury; Dance Little Sister; If You Really Want To Be My Friend; Short And Curlies; Fingerprint File.

Mick and Bianca Jagger spent the summer 1974 on Andy Warhol's Long Island estate where the late pop artist screenprinted an image of Mick in the same recurring style as his more widely exhibited portraits of Jacqueline Kennedy, Marilyn Monroe and Elizabeth Taylor. Warhol and Jagger were to autograph 250 portfolios of ten each for sale. They weren't cheap and neither was the rent on the house in the same vicinity where Mick and Bianca stayed initially from September to October.

As leaves turned brown, marital bonds, already loosened, continued to unbind, but the pair still tended to keep pace with each other's caprices, being photographed at the same premieres and covering the same exhibitions although Bianca was becoming increasingly disdainful about what she regarded as the shallowness of her spouses's cultural tastes. This provoked an indirect riposte in his composition of a song entitled 'It's Only Rock 'N Roll (But I Like It)'.

As he and Bianca grew further apart, Mick articulated some of his often bitter feelings when preparing material for the first self-produced Rolling Stones album since *Satanic Majesties*. Most listeners agreed that It's Only Rock 'n Roll was a holding operation. Tellingly, it was the first Stones LP not to reach the top in Britain since 1969 but it went to No.1 in the States as usual. There was an amusing video in which the group, dressed as sailors, mimed the title track in a confined space as soap-suds rose from floor to ceiling.

As musicians, they were men of respect – especially Mick Taylor. Joe Cocker finished below Mick Jagger in the World's Greatest Vocalist musicians' poll in the *New Musical Express*. If Mick hadn't also beaten John Lennon, Paul Rodgers of Free and Bob Dylan, he had, nevertheless, tied at fourth with Maggie Bell, an up-and-coming Glaswegian contralto of gutbucket persuasion.

The Rolling Stones could still take Top 30 strikes, if not No. 1s, for granted too. As a 1974 A side, 'It's Only Rock 'n Roll (But I Like It) hadn't sold millions, but had crept to No. 18 in the States and, in the wake of an orchestrated graffiti campaign across London, reached the Top Ten at home, becoming briefly something of a national catch-phrase. It also triggered an affectionate parody in 'It's Only Knock And Know-All' at the climax of *The Lamb Lies Down On Broadway*, a 1974 album by Genesis, whose chief show-off Peter Gabriel asked rhetorically, 'Is there a man alive who hasn't performed his Jaggerisms in front of the mirror? I know I have'. And so had other vocalists in the stadium rock hierarchy including Alice Cooper, Roger Daltrey, Ozzy Osbourne and Led Zeppelin's Robert Plant

There had been no chance to witness an in-person masterclass for more than a year from the final date of a European tour in October 1973. The *It's Only Rock 'N Roll* album wasn't taken on the road, and there was a distinct possibility that the follow-up, if it were ever completed, wouldn't be either, owing to an unexpected vacancy.

If You Can't Rock Me (Jagger-Richards) 3.37
Mick Jagger: lead vocals
Keith Richards and Mick Taylor: guitars
Ray Cooper: percussion
Keith Richards: bass guitar
Charlie Watts: drums
Billy Preston: piano, clavinet
Mick Jagger and Keith Richards: backing vocals
Apart from the insertion of a bass guitar solo, this makes for an unastonishing, if strident, start although Jagger's words might be read as a requiem for his marriage.

Ain't Too Proud To Beg (Whitfield-Holland) 3.31
Mick Jagger: lead vocals
Keith Richards and Mick Taylor: guitars
Billy Preston: piano
Mick Jagger and Keith Richards: backing vocals
Bill Wyman: bass guitar
Charlie Watts: drums
Ray Cooper and Ed Leach: percussion
Neither the first nor last Temptations hit to be processed by the Stones, this was issued as a US-only 45, reaching No. 17, four places beneath that of the original in 1966.

It's Only Rock 'n Roll (Jagger-Richards) 5.07
Mick Jagger: lead vocals
Keith Richards and Ronnie Wood: guitars
Kenny Jones: drums
Mick Jagger, Keith Richards, Mick Taylor and Ronnie Wood: backing vocals
Willie Weeks: bass guitar
Ian Stewart: piano
Like it was when Jimmy Miller took over on 'You Can't Always Get What You Want' and two *Exile On Main Street* tracks, Charlie Watts had long been sure enough of his position within the Stones to be quite amenable to similar corner-cutting, such as Kenny Jones of The Faces beating the skins on the album's spin-off 45 that resulted from a jolly musical evening in London attended by personnel from both groups. Neither did Bill Wyman mind the bass guitar being played by another invitee, Willie Weeks, a Californian session musician of nonchalant proficiency.

Till The Next Goodbye (Jagger-Richards) 4.37

Mick Jagger: lead vocals
Keith Richards and Mick Taylor: guitars
Mick Taylor: slide guitar
Mick Jagger, Keith Richards and Mick Taylor: backing vocals
Bill Wyman: bass guitar
Charlie Watts: drums
Nicky Hopkins: piano

Though set lyrically in New York, its prevailing mood was akin to the more generalized pop that Nashville, the Hollywood of Country Music, was cradling in the 70s.

Time Waits For No-One (Jagger-Richards) 6.38

Mick Jagger: lead vocals
Keith Richards and Mick Taylor: guitars
Mick Taylor: bass guitar
Ray Cooper: percussion
Bill Wyman: synthesiser
Charlie Watts: drums
Nicky Hopkins: piano
Mick Jagger and Keith Richards: backing vocals

In his stentorian vocal attack, Jagger could be mistaken for Van Morrison in the only item on the LP that would be selected and edited for 1981's *Sucking In The Seventies*, a Stones' album retropective. The track belonged as much to Mick Taylor as to Jagger for a lead guitar obligato that would be among his crowning achievements as a Stone.

Luxury (Jagger-Richards) 5.01

Mick Jagger: lead vocals
Keith Richards and Mick Taylor: guitars
Nicky Hopkins: piano
Mick Jagger and Keith Richards: backing vocals
Bill Wyman: bass guitar
Charlie Watts: drums
Ray Cooper: percussion

A wage slave's lament with more than a flavouring of the Caribbean, this was the closest the album came to showcasing a new face at Stones studio sessions, classically trained Ray Cooper. An in-demand session musician, he'd become a crony of the ex-Beatles and was to accompany Elton John as one of British pop's first ambassadors to Soviet Russia.

Dance Little Sister (Jagger-Richards) 4.11

Mick Jagger: lead vocals
Keith Richards and Mick Taylor: guitars
Ian Stewart: piano
Bill Wyman: bass guitar
Charlie Watts: drums

The younger sibling of animated 'Miss Amanda Jones' on *Between The Buttons*, this was almost too strong a B side to 'Ain't Too Proud To Beg', and was spun more times than its makers might have anticipated on North American FM radio, a medium that would remain amenable to the Stones even after the punk thunderclap resounded.

If You Really Want To Be My Friend (Jagger-Richards) 6.17

Mick Jagger: lead vocals
Keith Richards and Mick Taylor: guitars
Nicky Hopkins: piano
Charlie Watts: drums
Mick Taylor: bass guitar
Keith Richards and Blue Magic: backing vocals

The negro spiritual overtones of this paeon to a new love were stressed via the employment of Philadephia's Blue Magic who were signed to Atlantic in 1972 as accompanists to soul chanteuse Margie Joseph.

Short And Curlies (Jagger-Richards) 2.44

Mick Jagger: lead vocals
Keith Richards and Mick Taylor: guitars
Ian Stewart: piano
Mick Jagger, Keith Richards and Mick Taylor: backing vocals
Bill Wyman: bass guitar
Charlie Watts: drums

This was started and then abandoned in 1972. Two years later, the group added some overdubs and erased the old lead vocal to accommodate coarser lyrics.

Fingerprint File (Jagger-Richards) 6.33

Mick Jagger: lead vocals
Keith Richards, Mick Taylor and Mick Jagger: guitars
Billy Preston: synthesiser
Charlie Watts: drums
Bill Wyman: bass guitar and synthesiser
Nicky Hopkins: piano
Jolly Kunjappu: tablas

Jagger was responsible for the riff as well as the words that dwell on ceaseless shadowing by the FBI of a subject whose increasing alarm is expressed during a spoken passage from a telephone booth. Unlike that in 'Chantilly Lace' by The Big Bopper in 1957, this monologue contains little conscious humour. Indian percussionist Jolly Kunjappu was to rear up in a pop context again when ministering to the final track of Ringo Starr's *I Wanna Be Santa Claus* album in 1999.

METAMORPHOSIS

UK Release: 6 June 1975
US Release: 6 June 1975
Intl CD No: ABKCO 90062
Running Time: 48:05

Decca SKL 5212
ABKCO ANA 1
Producers: Andrew Loog Oldham, Jimmy Miller

SIDE ONE: Out Of Time; Don't Lie To Me; Some Things Just Stick In Your Mind; Each And Every Day Of The Year; Heart Of Stone; I'd Much Rather Be With The Boys; (Walkin' Thru') The Sleepy City; We're Wastin' Time; Try A Little Harder.

SIDE TWO: I Don't Know Why; If You Let Me; Jiving Sister Fanny; Downtown Suzie; Family; Memo From Turner; I'm Going Down.

A pressing matter for The Rolling Stones in the mid-70s was the difficult task of establishing an agreement with Allen Klein, now that the days of any open-handed conviviality around his desk were long gone. Once a hero who, on the group's behalf, had bullied Decca into parting with an eye-stretching advance royalty cheque back in 1965, he was now a villain of the darkest hue. Auditors appointed by the Stones had apparently uncovered enough proof of mismanagement of funds from his mazy balance sheets to justify a multi-million dollar law suit. Counter-suits and further mud-slinging were to ensure that it would take years for the writs to subside before the incoming monies could be divided among the disgruntled parties, a process summarised by Keith Richards as 'the price of an education'.

'Klein would probably sue if I told you my opinion of him,' snarled Mick Jagger, 'He's a person to be avoided as far as I'm concerned.' Jagger was long-faced too about a general reek of corruption that was pervading the entire industry. An American TV news channel commissioned *The Trouble With Rock*, a one-hour special that placed dirty dealings in the music business on a par with the scandal that had just led to US President Nixon's resignation. Mick was a talking head on the programme and was 'sure there's other industries in America that are far dirtier than the record industry', but associated allegations, however unfounded,

METAMORPHOSIS

by other of Allen Klein's charges had renewed the Stones' protracted determination to curtail his handling of their affairs both during and after his official tenure as manager. He remained, for instance, controller of all recordings from the Decca era. Some had been prised from the firm's vaults for issue in various formats since 1971, the most recent being *Metamorphosis* and its first spin-off single, the 'Out Of Time' that combined Jagger's lead vocal and the backing track of Chris Farlowe's UK No. 1 single.

By one of those odd coincidences that impinge periodically on pop, this 'Out Of Time' fought two simultaneously released revivals by Dan McCafferty of Nazareth and Arthur Brown as well as a repromotion of Chris Farlowe's version. None of them did especially well, although his fleeting re-entry into the UK Top 50 after eight years outside it, gave Farlowe's bank account a welcome shot in the arm. Nevertheless, all signposts pointed towards the snowballing swinging sixties nostalgia circuit for Chris. As his distant friend Mick could have advised him, a mere great voice wasn't enough to sustain contemporary interest.

To many, the Stones had never been or would never be as great as they'd been in the 60s. Yet there were fiscal advantages in this. As commodity began to assume more absolute sway over creativity, the history of pop was seized upon more tightly than ever as an avenue for shifting records. This was demonstrated by the chart performances of *Metamorphosis*, that while fizzling out at a lowly No. 45 at home, reached No. 8 in the States.

Moreover, most of the out-takes and alternative versions that filled the album were as entertaining as they were documentary because this haphazardly programmed motley array of tracks was a corruption of an original intention for Bill Wyman, the group's most meticulous archivist, to prepare an authorized audio anthology. It had even been given *The Black Box* as a working title. Instead, pragmatism ruled and Allen Klein rode roughshod over the idea, preferring a rushed compilation with a preponderance of royalty-earning group originals.

Most of side one consisted of demos of Mick and Keith's first attempts at composition. These had been produced principally at Decca's West Hampstead studios by Andrew Loog Oldham who wrote the Metamorphosis sleeve notes. Next, they'd been submitted to would-be pop stars grubbing round London's music publishing offices. Bobby Jameson, a fair-headed Paul McCartney lookalike tried, for instance, 'Each And Every Day Of The Year' with Keith credited as 'musical director'. Then there'd be '(Walkin' Thru' The) Sleepy City', an

A side by Rugby's Mighty Avengers, and 'I'd Much Rather Be With The Boys' attributed to Richards and Oldham by The Toggery Five, runners-up to The Bo Street Runners in a national talent contest organised by the producers of *Ready Steady Go* .

Financial rewards for Keith and Mick were meagre until 'My Only Girl' was revamped as 'That Girl Belongs To Yesterday' by Gene Pitney. This was a money-spinner, but Vashti's 'Some Things Just Stick In Your Mind' and 'We're Wastin' Time' by Liverpool comedian Jimmy Tarbuck either made deflated journeys into bargain bins or were hidden away on B sides.

The templates of these syndications were knocked together, assembly-line style, by whatever Stones were available plus session musicians with as close a knowledge of each other's work via countless daily record dates, punctuated by Musicians Union-regulated tea-breaks. It didn't matter who played what on what were essentially recordings that were never designed for public consumption.

Out Of Time (Jagger-Richards) 3.22
Mick Jagger: lead vocals, **Arthur Greenslade:** directed sessions musicians

After Andrew Loog Oldham co-founded Immediate, his own record label, in 1965, he was not able to sign the Stones, but there was nothing to stop the group's members functioning in a behind-the-scenes capacity as Jagger did as producer of Chris Farlowe. Mick was to graft his own lead vocal over keyboard-player Greenslade's orchestral scoring of his client's 'Out Of Time' just in case it could be put to monetary use in the future. If neither a skinflint nor over-extravagant by nature, Mick deplored waste.

Don't Lie To Me (Jagger-Richards) 2.00
Mick Jagger: lead vocals
Keith Richards and Brian Jones: guitars
Ian Stewart: piano
Bill Wyman: bass guitar
Charlie Watts: drums

Belying what was printed in brackets under the title on the album's label, this fusion of urban blues and nascent rock'n'roll was composed by the celebrated singing pianist Antoine 'Fats' Domino who recorded it as a single in New Orleans in 1951. The Stones 'Xerox' was taped at Chess studios during their US tour in 1964.

Some Things Just Stick In Your Mind (Jagger-Richards) 2.25 February 1964
Mick Jagger: lead vocals
Other Rolling Stones plus session musicians

Among reputed helpers on this July 1964 demo were guitarists John McLaughlin and Big Jim Sullivan. A jazz-rock colossus of the 70s, the former was then a 20-year-old Yorkshireman who had been in an outfit formed by chartbusting ex-Shadows Jet Harris and Tony Meehan. And the sometime leader of The Big Jim Sullivan Combo had first refusal of nearly all metropolitan record dates in the early 60s.

Each And Every Day Of The Year (Jagger-Richards) 2.48

Mick Jagger: lead vocals

Other Rolling Stones plus session musicians

This midsummer session in 1964 was engineered by future Led Zeppelin bass guitarist, John Paul Jones, who'd played alongside John McLaughlin with Jet Harris and Tony Meehan. When time permitted, Jones and McLaughlin were also seen on stage with Herbie Goins and the Night-Timers, fronted by a black ex-US serviceman. Led Zeppelin's guitarist-in-waiting Jimmy Page was also present on 'Each And Every Day Of The Year', fretting subordinate rhythm chords to the lead picking of Big Jim Sullivan. As a fish beneath the waves of the burgeoning beat boom, Page was soon to be on a par with Sullivan as one of the brightest stars in the London studio firmament.

Heart Of Stone (Jagger-Richards) 3.47

Mick Jagger: lead vocals

Keith Richards, Brian Jones, Mick Jagger and session musicians: backing vocals

Bill Wyman: bass guitar

Charlie Watts: drums

Jimmy Page: guitars

This was taped in London in August 1964. Richards was to parrot Page's solo to the quaver on the official Hollywood version three months later.

I'd Much Rather Be With The Boys (Oldham-Richards) 2.11

Mick Jagger: lead vocals

Other Rolling Stones plus session musicians

Penned during the Stones visit to Australasia at the beginning of 1965, this was recorded in haste soon after they'd readjusted to Greenwich Mean Time. Oldham's production assistants were Gus Dudgeon, whose skills were to help facilitate David Bowie's chart breakthrough, and Mike Leander, who produced Marianne Faithfull's 'As Tears Go By', and would be behind Paul Gadd's success in the 70s as glam-rock overlord Gary Glitter.

(Walkin' Thru') The Sleepy City (Jagger-Richards) 2.51

Mick Jagger: lead vocals

Other Rolling Stones plus session musicians

The drumming here was most likely Andy White, who had also been heard on 'Love Me Do' The Beatles' first 45, in 1962.

We're Wastin' Time (Jagger-Richards) 2.42
Mick Jagger: lead vocals
Other Rolling Stones plus session musicians

Instrumentally, this vague waltz-time fusion of Merseybeat and C&W was notable for someone – probably Big Jim Sullivan – finger-picking a 12-string acoustic guitar, still regarded as something of a novelty in the mid-60s.

Try A Little Harder (Jagger-Richards) 2.17
Mick Jagger: lead vocals
Other Rolling Stones plus session musicians

With an abundance of tambourine-and-snare drum and the female backing chorale, this attempt at ersatz soul might be Jagger with personnel from The Andrew Oldham Orchestra, assembled from London session shellbacks for easy-listening album melanges of mostly current hits and acclamatory originals such as 'There Are But Five Rolling Stones' and '365 Rolling Stones (One For Every Day Of The Year)'.

I Don't Know Why (Wonder-Riser-Hunter-Hardaway) 3.01
Mick Jagger: lead vocals
Keith Richards: guitar
Ian Stewart: piano
Bill Wyman: bass guitar
Charlie Watts: drums
Various: brass and woodwinds

Less than six weeks after he left the group, Brian Jones was found face-down at the bottom of his swimming pool in the small hours of 3 July 1969. While the rest of Britain slumbered, the Stones – minus Bill, who'd gone home – were told about Brian at Olympic Studios where they were mixing this apparently irresistible cover of a very recent Stevie Wonder Top 40 entry. As a single, the Stones' 'I Don't Know Why' won but the slightest chart honours.

If You Let Me (Jagger-Richards) 3.17
Mick Jagger: lead vocals
Keith Richards and Brian Jones: guitars
Ian Stewart: piano
Bill Wyman: bass guitar
Charlie Watts: drums

This acoustic ramble from the *Aftermath* period centres on a staccato hook-line and seems to be missing an instrumental solo in a non-vocal third verse. The bass line is strengthened by one-finger piano in a low octave.

Jiving Sister Fanny (Jagger-Richards) 3.24

Mick Jagger: lead vocals
Keith Richards and Mick Taylor: guitars
Nicky Hopkins: piano
Bill Wyman: bass guitar
Charlie Watts: drums
Various: brass and woodwinds

With echoes in the lyrics of 'Flea Brain', a Gene Vincent LP track from 1958, this attractive 12-bar trundle – left off *Let It Bleed* – may have proved more negotiable a spin-off single than either 'Out Of Time' or 'I Don't Know Why'.

Downtown Suzie (Wyman) 3.52 April 1968

Mick Jagger: lead vocals
Keith Richards: guitar and slide guitar
Jimmy Miller: percussion
Bill Wyman: bass guitar
Charlie Watts: drums
Mick Jagger and Keith Richards: backing vocals

Perhaps the funniest song in the Stones' catalogue, this appears to be a call-and-response account of the morning after a bender in some peculiar house of ill-repute. Radically re-arranged, this might have been suitable for Frank Sinatra, jackpot of all songwriters. Certainly, Wyman's oft-thwarted ambition as a composer provokes sympathy.

Family (Jagger-Richards) 4.05

Mick Jagger: lead vocals
Keith Richards: guitar
Jimmy Miller: percussion
Bill Wyman: bass guitar
Charlie Watts: drums

From June 1968, a narrative within two tempo variations of off-colour doings within a domestic circle could be interpreted by the man in the pub as an unfunny serenade about incest or as darkly humorous by a rock scribe trying to be cool.

Memo From Turner (Jagger-Richards) 2.45

Mick Jagger: lead vocals
Bill Wyman: bass guitar
Keith Richards and Al Kooper: guitars
Charlie Watts: drums

During the filming of *Performance*, Mick Jagger's first film acting role, it was necessary for him to cavort between bedsheets with co-star Anita Pallenberg. Riven with jealous imaginings, Keith Richards, then in the first flush of his romance with her, expressed his anguish by making this soundtrack opus sound amateurish when he deigned to turn up at the long-delayed session with the Stones. Session players including Ry Cooder had to be hired for the difficult task of layering a more acceptable backing onto a busy Jagger's vocal now isolated from the original effort. It was this version that was issued as a Decca 45 – Jagger's first solo release – in November 1970, to teeter on the edge of the British Top 30. The only non-Stone on the *Metamorphosis* rendition was Al Kooper who, as well as backing Bob Dylan, was also a mainstay of Blood, Sweat And Tears. With Chicago, they were the most famous rock equivalent of a 'brass band' – Kooper's own description in the sleeve notes of *Child Is Father To The Man,* the combo's first LP in 1968.

I'm Going Down (Jagger-Richards-Taylor) 2.52

Mick Jagger: lead vocals
Keith Richards and Mick Taylor: guitars
Charlie Watts: drums
Bill Plummer: upright bass
Rocky Dijon: congas
Bobby Keyes: saxophones

Of similar moderato pace to 'Tumbling Dice', this seems incomplete, chiefly because of what is probably only a guide vocal. It dates from the early months of Mick Taylor's period as a Stone.

BLACK AND BLUE

UK Release: 20 April 1976
US Release: 20 April 1976
Intl CD No: CBS CDCBS 450203 2
Running Time: 41:21

Rolling Stones Records COC 59106
Rolling Stones Records COC 79104
Producers: The Glimmer Twins

SIDE ONE: Hot Stuff; Hand Of Fate; Cherry Oh Baby; Memory Motel.

SIDE TWO: Hey Negrita; Melody; Fool To Cry; Crazy Mama.

After much heart-searching, Bob Marley and the Wailers – led by one described as the Mick Jagger of reggae – had spurned an offer with Keith Richards their principal champion, to open the show nightly for The Rolling Stones. They preferred to headline a US tour in their own right in 1975. Both acts chanced to be performing in Los Angeles on the same July night but an enthralled Stones deputation found the time to attend a Marley matinee at the city's Roxy Theatre.

The most practical recent evidence of the British group's capitivation with contemporary reggae, however, had been the imposition of moderato rhythms straight from a Kingston sound-system dance hall onto 'Luxury' from *It's Only Rock 'N Roll* and 'Cherry Oh Baby' on *Black And Blue*, the album that Richards would dismiss with 'rehearsing guitar players, that's what that one was about.'

Black And Blue had taken the Stones to a Munich studio as 1974 drew to its close, and to Rotterdam in the New Year for recording dates that served as auditions for a guitarist to supersede Mick Taylor who had never felt as if he quite belonged. Out of the blue, he had written a formal letter of resignation that was about his person when he and Jagger and Ronnie Wood of The Faces watched Eric Clapton play at the Hammersmith Odeon before drinks at Clapton's manager's home. Thus Taylor earned the distinction of being the second ex-member of the Stones with the same surname.

It would have been uncool for Jagger to have shown any kind of consternation either at the soiree or, after the news broke, when goaded about it by the media. However, it was to

THE ROLLING STONES
BLACK AND BLUE

be a long and sometimes mind-stultifying chore to whittle down a formidable list of possible replacements. Alexis Korner was present at the studio dates that served as try-outs, where among those under serious consideration for invitation were Robben Ford whose squittering wah-wah had enlivened George Harrison's only solo tour; Leslie West, another rated North American on whose latest album, *The Great Fatsby*, Jagger had strummed rhythm guitar; Mick Ronson, David Bowie's Yorkshire-born guitarist; sometime mainstay of Colosseum, Dave Clempson, and a detectably balding Steve Marriott, esteemed by Keith Richards as a stronger singer than Jagger.

Marriott was weary of a shallow megastardom accrued over 22 US tours with Humble Pie, the supergroup he'd formed after the demise of The Small Faces. Just before Christmas, he and Keith had been thrown together as guitarists on the slowed-down revival of 'Get Off Of My Cloud' that was the title song of a new Alexis Korner album. While Steve confided to a journalist that he valued artistic freedom to superstardom anyway, Damian Korner, Alexis's son, maintained that this assertion was contrary to a fervent desire to be a Stone.

Present on other *Get Off Of My Cloud* tracks, Marriott's Humble Pie cohort Peter Frampton was another possibility. Oiling the wheels would be his intended inclusion of an overhaul of 'Jumping Jack Flash' on the album that was the small beginning of solo success in North America later in the decade. The composing royalties from this were to provide the exact amount required for the purchase of a desired house in upstate New York.

Debating the Stones' future, the press put forward Eric Clapton, then at a vocational loose end, for the job as well as Rory Gallagher, former leader of the highly rated power trio Taste; Chris Spedding, respected studio shellback and soon-to-be one-hit-wonder with autumn 1975's 'Motorbikin' and Wilko Johnson, as renowned for his spasmodic movements onstage as his picking with Dr. Feelgood, a busy R&B outfit from Essex. What was Dick Taylor doing these days?

The search returned to the USA, boiling down to Harvey Mandel from Canned Heat and Wayne Perkins, a Texan who'd given a Bob Marley album, *Catch A Fire*, a hard-rock touch-up. He'd also just been playing on *Monkey Grip*, Bill Wyman's first solo L in 1974.

There was substance to some of these speculations. For a while, Perkins was in great favour with Richards, 'but he was American, and we had to own up we were an English band'. As English as Perkins wasn't, Jeff Beck, who pitched in at Rotterdam on a remaindered instrumental arrangement of Martha and the Vandellas' 'Heatwave', was Jagger's prime choice until the former Yardbird 'couldn't handle it because my mind wasn't into that way of doing things. I was working a million miles an hour compared to the way they were'.

Besides, when understanding more precisely what he'd be taking on, 'the sudden realisation that I might be a Rolling Stone frightened the hell out of me.' Rather than informing them face to face, Beck pushed a note reading 'Sorry lads, I got to go home' under the door of Jagger's hotel room. 'I hated to do it because Mick's such a lovely guy, but I was used to conceiving a notion, putting it on tape and having it finished by the evening. They had trouble turning up at the same time.' Beck also had a tendency not to get Stones humour, storming out of a session for a later Jagger solo LP when a roguish Mick pretended to instruct an engineer to erase a particularly startling guitar solo.

You could understand Jeff's disenchantment with the *Black And Blue* dates. Away from the privacy of the studio some Rolling Stones performances were starting up to five hours late nowadays. At the heart of the matter was Keith Richards keeping both musicians and audience waiting, a laid-back habit that Watts and Jagger in particular found annoying. Conducting himself as if a participant in a heavily subsidised travelling debauch, Richards was frequently missing minutes before the scheduled showtime. Flanked by retainers, he'd then retreat into a dressing room where he might become semi-comatose with further pills, powders, fluids and resins.

He always made it onto the boards eventually and, like chronic alcoholic Dylan Thomas pulling himself together for the duration of a poetry reading, Keith's mixture of stimulant intake and work walked a tightrope between straggling indiscipline and near-magical inspiration. Once, his eyelids dropped, his chin sagged onto his chest and he drifted into a gentle snore during a slow ballad, his fingers on automatic. Conversely, he'd recollect with quiet pride that 'I played on stage in Australia on acid in '72 or '73. It was one of the best shows I ever played.'

Stray paragraphs in tabloid newspapers hinted that Richards was taking occasional steps to shake off his increasingly graver heroin addiction under supervision but in denial, he had 'never considered I was actually pushing it anywhere near the danger limit, although later on, I realised that I was probably a lot closer than I ever admitted but it kept my feet on the ground, nearly underground, in fact.'

As such, he had become by the mid-70s the Stones' biggest asset and biggest liability. Whereas a 1973 bootleg bearing the title Keith Richard And His Rolling Stones emphasized an artistic pre-eminence, he was still holding up proceedings in both auditorium and studio with his muzzy and unconcerned attitude towards time-keeping. More specifically, a fire in his hotel suite maybe caused by smoking half-asleep in bed or a table lamp falling over, had tarred the other Stones with the same brush. The group had been unable to play in France until after Keith's suspended sentence late in 1973 put a full-stop to the repercussions of a drug-squad raid on Nellcote.

He was incorrigible, they muttered with annoyance rather than amusement now. A more recent bust on 26 June 1973 had uncovered cannabis, Chinese heroin and Mandrax plus a revolver, a shotgun and ammunition. A plea that these had been left there by others when he was overseas was not accepted at Marlborough Street Magistrates Court four months later, resulting in a fine for Richards and a conditional discharge for co-defendant Anita Pallenberg.

That same summer, a rumour had gone the rounds that Keith's condition and correlated reliability had deteriorated so much that he was either intending to leave the Stones or that there'd been an ultimatum disguised as friendly advice that he ought to take a sabbatical to sweat out his problem.

While Keith was yet to admit his drug dependency was serious, the decision about a new guitarist was held at arm's length by borrowing Ronnie Wood for the duration of the 1975 US tour that paralleled one by market competitors Led Zeppelin. North America was the only territory where either group could slip easily into a profit position far beyond the break-even point that was the norm in Europe.

From the full-page advertisement in *Rolling Stone* to the chartered flights, the glossy full-colour programme and the wages of the lowliest equipment humper, the dollar outlay was in millions, but you also made millions, especially if you were on the road in the wake of a chart strike like *Black And Blue,* which spent a month at the top in the States and at No. 2 in Britain. It had been helped on its way by the fuss about a Hollywood billboard of a bruised and bound half-naked lady to publicise it. This built up into an international media storm when an organisation called Women Against Violence Against Women spearheaded a mass protest.

Hot Stuff (Jagger-Richards) 5.20
Mick Jagger: lead vocals
Keith Richards and Harvey Mandel: guitars
Billy Preston: piano
Mick Jagger, Keith Richards, Ronnie Wood and Billy Preston: backing vocals
Bill Wyman: bass guitar
Charlie Watts: drums
Mick Jagger, Bill Wyman, Ian Stewart and Ollie Brown: percussion
Wyman plucked an almost defiantly simple bass line and Richards pedalled some wah-wah on this platter of foot-food that, as the US flip-side of 'Fool To Cry', was heard in every hip discotheque from New York to Chicago.

Hand Of Fate (Jagger-Richards) 4.28
Mick Jagger: lead vocals
Keith Richards and Wayne Perkins: guitars
Billy Preston: piano
Bill Wyman: bass guitar
Charlie Watts: drums
Ollie Brown: percussion
Its backing track recorded in Munich on 25 March 1975, this was the first Stones item to include Brown, Stevie Wonder's drummer, whose enlistment had been at Watts's instigation. However, the difference he made to this deceptively fast tale of a doomed murderer on the run is only faintly discernible.

Cherry Oh Baby (Donaldson) 3.53

Mick Jagger: lead vocals
Keith Richards and Ronnie Wood: guitars
Nicky Hopkins: keyboards
Bill Wyman: bass guitar
Charlie Watts: drums
Mick Jagger and Keith Richards: backing vocals

A hit in Jamaica for Eric Donaldson, this was a stab at reggae, once despised by Britain's so-called intelligentsia as skinhead music but now outflanking even blues as the new twisted voice of the underdog and students union disco accessory, thanks to mainstream acceptance of Bob Marley and, to a lesser degree, the likes of Ijahman, Toots and the Maytals and Burning Spear. Earlier white British attempts included 'Ob-la-di Ob-la-da' by both The Beatles and Marmalade, 'To Ransaan' by Blodwyn Pig, Cat Stevens' 'Can't Keep It In' and, in the US Top 20 in 1973, 'D'Yer Mak'er' by Led Zeppelin. One of Eric Clapton's best-selling singles would be a respectful version of Marley's 'I Shot The Sheriff', but in comparison to any of these examples, the Stones were the most authentic.

Memory Motel (Jagger-Richards) 7.07

Mick Jagger and Keith Richards: lead vocals
Keith Richards, Harvey Mandel and Wayne Perkins: guitars
Mick Jagger, Keith Richards and Billy Preston: keyboards
Bill Wyman: bass guitar
Charlie Watts: drums
Mick Jagger, Keith Richards, Ronnie Wood and Billy Preston: backing vocals

Marred, as other *Black And Blue* tracks were, by instrumental meandering, this drank from the same lyrical pool as Gene Pitney's 'Twenty-Four Hours From Tulsa', Frank Zappa's 'Road Ladies' and similar songs of travel laced with affairs of the heart. On what was the first true Jagger-Richards duet since 1968's 'Salt Of The Earth', Keith took the middle eight alone, but reverted to supporting harmonies on the verses.

Hey Negrita (Jagger-Richards) 4.58

Mick Jagger: lead vocals
Keith Richards and Ronnie Wood: guitars
Billy Preston: piano, organ
Ollie Brown: percussion
Bill Wyman: bass guitar
Charlie Watts: drums
Keith Richards, Ronnie Wood and Billy Preston: backing vocals

'Negrita' was Jagger's pet-name for his now estranged wife, who had suggested it as an appealing title of a song yet to be written. When it was – as a mid-tempo rocker – it served as a vehicle for Ronnie Wood's recording test.

Melody (Jagger-Richards) 5.47

Mick Jagger: lead vocals
Keith Richards and Ronnie Wood: guitars
Billy Preston: piano, organ
Ollie Brown: percussion
Various: brass and woodwinds, arranged by Arif Mardin
Bill Wyman: bass guitar
Charlie Watts: drums
Keith Richards, Ronnie Wood and Billy Preston: backing vocals

For this instance of the Stones at their most jazzy – with Watts scuffing his snare with brushes – it was felt by Wyman that Preston deserved a composing credit. The number also owed much to the scoring for horns by Mardin, whose elevation to Atlantic's vice-presidency gave practical recognition of the combined musical and supervisory skills that he had perfected through his studies at the respective Schools of Economics and Music in London and New York as well as his dexterity as a bebop pianist. Later in 1975, he'd be awarded a Grammy for guiding the talents of The Average White Band and for the transition from 60s teen idols to disco paladins of The Bee Gees.

Fool To Cry (Jagger-Richards) 5.04

Mick Jagger: lead vocals, piano
Charlie Watts: drums
Keith Richards and Wayne Perkins: guitars
Nicky Hopkins: piano and synthesiser

Evidence that Jagger's first marriage had floated into a choppy sea was tangible by 1976 and there was his daughter Jade to consider. Perhaps she was the muse – a child comforting a lonely parent – for this opus, a kind of Stones 'You've Lost That Lovin' Feeling'. Featuring Mick emoting to his own electric keyboard accompaniment and a melody not dissimilar to '100 Years Ago' from *Goat's Head Soup*, it was chosen to be the album's sole single, and was soon ensconced in Top 10 listings across the globe.

Crazy Mama (Jagger-Richards) 4.34

Mick Jagger: lead vocals
Keith Richards and Mick Jagger: guitars
Ollie Brown: percussion
Keith Richards, Ronnie Wood and Billy Preston: keyboards
Keith Richards: bass guitar
Charlie Watts: drums
Mick Jagger, Keith Richards and Billy Preston: backing vocals

Brown's contribution includes the cow-bell that makes the most rhythmic noise on this contrastingly up-tempo UK B side to 'Fool To Cry'.

LOVE YOU LIVE

UK Release: 23 September 1977
US Release: 23 September 1977
Intl CD No: CBS CDCBS 450208 2
Running Time: 42:49 40:32

Rolling Stones Records COC 89101
Rolling Stones Records COC 79104
Producers: The Glimmer Twins

SIDE ONE: Honky Tonk Women; If You Can't Rock Me/Get Off Of My Cloud; Happy.

SIDE TWO: Hot Stuff; Star Star; Tumbling Dice; Fingerprint File; You Gotta Move.

SIDE THREE: You Can't Always Get What You Want; Mannish Boy; Crackin' Up; Little Red Rooster; Around And Around.

SIDE FOUR: It's Only Rock 'n' Roll; Brown Sugar; Jumping Jack Flash; Sympathy For The Devil.

Taken from shows taped between 1975 and 1977, *Love You Live* was The Rolling Stones' third in-concert album. A double, it rose to No. 5 in the US list and No. 3 in Britain.

It was also the maiden release under a new distribution deal with EMI from February 1977 for six albums and publishing rights for everywhere except North America. Jagger commented, 'In this Jubilee Year, I think it is only fitting that we sign with a British company.'

As well as marking the 25th anniversary of Elizabeth II's accession, 1977 was as much of a pop watershed year as 1963 had been. The punk thunderclap had resounded and the Stones were being denounced by a fairweather music press as monied megastars forever in America, throwing a wobbler in the green room at the Los Angeles Forum because of a misunderstanding about dressing room amenities.

Musically too, they and their kind were out of sync with the inspired amateurism of rising acts as diverse as Television, The Ramones, The Sex Pistols, The Stranglers, Patti Smith, Wreckless Eric, The UK Subs, Squeeze, Cock Sparrer, The Police, The Clash, Adam and the Ants, France's Les Thugs and, from Wales, Y Trwynau Coch. 'We're another generation,' scowled Joey of the Ramones, 'They're rich and living in another world altogether'.

The Rolling Stones

LOVE YOU LIVE

On the West Indian island of Mustique, a hidden-away colony for British millionaires and blue-bloods, Jagger was a near-neighbour of Princess Margaret. Moreover, the Queen's younger sister had been more than just an acquaintance since the swinging sixties. In 1976, she had been in the VIP enclosure at a Stones concert at Earl's Court, and was photographed afterwards congratulating Mick on his performance. On Mustique, he was a periodic guest at what were composites of candle-lit regimental dinner and Polynesian *tamara* with other invitees from all walks of successful lives.

Small talk with Princess Margaret over dessert in a Caribbean twilight was a world away from punk-rock Britain where The Sex Pistols' second single, 'God Save The Queen', was not reflective of monarchist fervour. Nonetheless, when in London, Mick had taken the trouble to experience this street level sub-culture that everyone was talking about. Down in Oxford Street's 100 Club, Mick witnessed the Pistols' two-minute bursts of aural debris to appreciative Niagaras of spittle. At least it wasn't weak, this raw display of loathing, madness and retaliation, the very opposite of poker-faced professional cool. He eyed Johnny Rotten and his cronies with a hint of apprehension, even admiration, then left without looking back.

There was a certain déjà vu about aspects of the trend-setting Sex Pistols' career path. As many degrees beyond the Stones in outrageousness as the Stones had been beyond Presley, the Pistols became notorious for performances accompanied by violence. Like Andrew Loog Oldham had, Malcolm McLaren welcomed headline-hogging boorishness from his charges. Following a small Top 30 beginning with a maiden single, 'God Save The Queen' almost topped the UK charts, Yet, after two more hits in 1977, the public seemed to have got over the initial shock of The Sex Pistols, even accepting them as a tolerable part of the national furniture, even when Sid Vicious was arrested in New York for the murder of his girlfriend. A morning-after comment from ex-New York Doll Johnny Thunders surfaced in *Rolling Stone*: 'Well, he beat Keith Richards for the story of the year'.

Keith still made the front page in February 1977, not long after an idea of taping a Stones performance before a small audience went past discussion. The four-hundred capacity El Mocambo club in Toronto was the chosen venue. Keith was expected to drag himself from his moated farmhouse in Sussex to cross the Atlantic for rehearsals. He found this no easy task as he passed lethargic hours between heroin fixes. Hours and then days passed at Toronto International Airport for those appointed to ensure his undistracted passage to the Harbour Castle Hotel and on to a downtown warehouse with mains leads fanning out in all directions from an encampment of guitar cases, speaker cabinets and Charlie's drum kit assembled beneath dusty strip lights.

Plane after British plane landed and Richards was still shuttered away in Sussex. Then, on 24 February, just over a week before the reckoning, he shuffled through customs. Desperately weary, he dumped his luggage in the Harbour Castle suite and trudged straight into the bedroom for some shut-eye. The next day, a squeak of feedback from Keith's amplifier launched an unproblematic run-through of a mooted selection that delved as far back as their earliest Crawdaddy stumblings. Conducted by Richards' tempo announcements, nods and eye-contact, The Stones started to relax.

An overall mood of quiet confidence was, however, to be disrupted when, armed with a search warrant, a squad of Royal Canadian Mounted Police invaded Keith's hotel rooms as he lay in bed. It was so heart-sinkingly familiar to someone harassed over and over again in like fashion since the famous bust in 1967: the voices at the door, the uniforms, the execution of duty, the ransacking, the emptying of ashtrays into polyethylene bags, the uncovering of the dope (mostly heroin), the monotonal caution. This time, Keith dozed through most of it before, with a pincer-like squeeze on both arms, he was hastened outside.

Then there was the back-seat ride to the station; sitting sullen and white-faced on a wall bench; the mounting anxiety, and the illuminated desk on a raised platform where the sergeant filled in the booking slip. Under 'Charge', he wrote 'Possession of controlled drugs with intent to re-sell'. Canadian drug laws were stringent, harsh and effective. Richards could be facing decades in jail, reckoned the duty solicitor.

Just the ticket for the accused, therefore, was the endless scrutiny of tapes of the two El Mocambo concerts undertaken during the 1977 week of the latest trouble as well as ones in the States, Europe and elsewhere in Canada. These revealed to Keith and especially to Mick that there were only so many fantastic mixes of 'Around And Around' or 'Little Red Rooster' that could be endured in one evening. When the resulting album, *Love You Live* – a title at odds with punk – was mastered, Jagger sighed that 'nine months of listening to The Rolling Stones isn't my idea of heaven'.

A play-back of concerts on 5 and 6 June 1976 at Les Abattoirs in Paris, the source of most of *Love You Live,* was especially trying for Richards, a trouper of 'the show must go on' stamp, who insisted that the first of two hours or so of songs about hot stuff, only rock'n'roll and Jumpin' Jack Flash, went ahead despite the telephoned bombshell that very afternoon that his son Tara, who was less than three months old, was dying of influenza.

Understandably, he left the exploitation of *Love You Live* to Mick, who gave his blessing to a press kit containing a pair of rubber lips, visualising perhaps office jokers putting them on and doing a Jagger impression. Condoning such mockery of yourself was a cheap shot, but necessary.

Pop music was becoming like a dull but remunerative job that if he had completed his degree course at the London School of Economics in 1963, Jagger might have ended up doing until he retired. For every creative act, there was an infinity of tedious mechanical processes. Sometimes he couldn't wait for knocking-off time. 'My whole life isn't rock'n'roll,' he shrugged while weathering the punk storm, 'It's an absurd idea that it should be. It's no more than anybody's whole life should revolve around working in Woolworth's'.

Except where otherwise stated, the line up throughout is as follows:-

Mick Jagger: lead vocals, harmonica

Keith Richards: guitar, vocals

Bill Wyman: bass guitar

Charlie Watts: drums

Ronnie Wood: guitar

Ollie Brown: percussion

Ian Stewart and Billy Preston: keyboards

As on all Rolling Stones in-concert albums, timing includes continuity and audience response.

The Rolling Stones' performance on Side One is preceded by a taped one minute and 24 seconds of 'Fanfare For The Common Man' by the late Aaron Copeland.

Honky Tonk Women (Jagger-Richards) 3.19
Before the Stones set off on a summer tour of the Americas in 1975, Watts and Jagger collaborated on a stage design that was supposed to emulate the pageant of sunrise via the unfolding of a huge metal lotus flower containing the five principals plus conga-pounding Brown sharing Charlie's podium after they pitched into the opening 'Honky Tonk Women'. This device did not travel to Europe but the song did, as demonstrated by this version from Paris on 5 June 1976.

If You Can't Rock Me/Get Off Of My Cloud (Jagger-Richards) 5.00
A track from It's *Only Rock 'N Roll* mingles with a disco-ed good-old-good one as a vocal duet with Preston at the last of six shows at London's cavernous Earl's Court on 27 May 1976.

Happy (Jagger-Richards) 2.55
Keith pours out his US hit at Les Abattoirs on 5 June 1976. Those with a glimmer of his personal history might imagine that the bad tidings before the concert honed his singing to razor-sharp piquancy. By most accounts, he had been flitting fitfully off-stage from withdrawn moodiness to trying to conduct himself as if free from all care and responsibility.

Hot Stuff (Jagger-Richards) 4.35
Richards also found the emotional detachment to join in the Abattoirs fun during this dash through a track from the last studio album.

Star Star (Jagger-Richards) 4.10
The customers' direct participation at Les Abattoirs centred on a chorus in which they stressed the f-word with the same authority-baiting exultancy as their younger siblings would that of a certain syllable of The Sex Pistols' 'Pretty Vacant' when it impinged on international consciousness just over a year later. A 'Star Star' visual aid was the centre-stage inflation of a 20-foot long white phallus, wavering like a caber about to be tossed. It didn't always achieve a full erection, but this was laughed off by Mick who pretended to coax it from flaccidity as an occupational hazard of 'mass funny entertainment. It's like an un-art event.'

Tumbling Dice (Jagger-Richards) 4.00
Generally rougher than the hit single version, this begins with the lurch of Wood's bottleneck guitar.

Fingerprint File (Jagger-Richards) 5.17
Recorded at Toronto's Maple Leaf Gardens, this is over a minute shorter than the *It's Only Rock 'N Roll* arrangement.

You Gotta Move (McDowell-Davis) 4.19
A rapt crowd at Les Abattoirs overlooked any shortcomings in the strains of Jagger, Richards, Wood and Preston's near *a capella* transformation of this old blues from *Sticky Fingers*.

You Can't Always Get What You Want (Jagger-Richards) 7.42
To bring on a choir for the introduction of this stage fixture may have been like feeding a pig strawberries. Also, the sound of Al Kooper's French horn was synthesised by Preston during what was now a immovable fixture in the stage repertoire although 'Satisfaction' had been conspicuous by its absence throughout the entire jaunt.

Mannish Boy (McDaniel-Morganfield-London) 6.28
Back to the roots at the El Mocambo on 4 March 1977, ramshackle lucidity shines through as Richards, Wyman, Watts and Wood advance with the grace of fencing masters on a Muddy Waters number the Stones used to do at the Crawdaddy. A hi-hat beneath the riff stokes up the heat to a simmer for Jagger's vocal entry.

Crackin' Up (McDaniel) 5.40
Riding roughshod over tempo refinements, complicated dynamic shifts or indeed anything that needed too much thought, this Bo Diddley B side from 1959 had been performed by the Stones on the BBC Light Programme's *Saturday Club* on 17 July 1964 before its 12-year suspended animation.

Little Red Rooster (Dixon) 4.39
A repertory choice that had scarcely seen the light of day since the mid-60s, it slew the 300 souls that had won a radio contest to be at the El Mocambo for one of these 'Greatest Nights Anyone Could Ever Remember', as well as the special guests squeezed in, among them Margaret Trudeau, the Canadian Prime Minister's wayward wife.

Around And Around (Berry) 4.09
This final selection from the Canadian club sounds fine in a dated sort of way to a dated sort of person, though it leaves a peculiar afterglow of 1964's dusty old *Five By Five* British EP on which the Stones' version of the song was first committed to vinyl.

It's Only Rock 'N Roll (Jagger-Richards) 4.31
At the Maple Leaf Gardens, Jagger takes it down easy, indulges in a little rabble-rousing, builds up the tension to raving panic and leaves 'em wanting more.

Brown Sugar (Jagger-Richards) 3.11
Watts can take credit for the launching the 1975-1976 expedition from a flat-bed lorry that was driven slowly down New York's busiest thoroughfares. On the back, the Stones smashed out 'Brown Sugar' for a swelling trail of starstruck pedestrians. 'The old jazz bands used to do it,' elucidated Charlie, 'to publicise their gigs' and there was certainly a full turn-out for the second night in Paris where this rendition was recorded.

Jumping Jack Flash (Jagger-Richards) 4.03
If the first or second number in from Hyde Park to *Get Yer Ya-Yas Out*, this had become the traditional finale by the mid-70s. Later, it would be stretched out like toffee to last at least twice the length of the version presented here.

Sympathy For The Devil (Jagger-Richards) 7.51
From a recital at the LA Forum on 9 July 1975, this encore was an example of Jagger's attitude to his vocal limitations: 'The important thing about singing is to get the personality across. Forget the notes.'

SOME GIRLS

UK Release: 19 May 1978
US Release: 19 May 1978
Intl CD No: CBS CDCBS450197 2
Running Time: 40:47

Rolling Stones Records CUN 39108
Rolling Stones Records TP 39108
Producers: The Glimmer Twins

SIDE ONE: Miss You; When The Whip Comes Down; Just My Imagination (Running Away With Me); Some Girls; Lies.

SIDE TWO: Far Away Eyes; Respectable; Before They Make Me Run; Beast Of Burden; Shattered.

Trivia freaks will need to know that, via an EMI memo in spring 1978, Keith Richards ratified the restoration of the 's' at the end of his surname although it had long been printed on composing credits and elsewhere on record packaging. Of more import to a wider cultural world is the information that *Some Girls* was the first Rolling Stones studio LP with Ronnie Wood as an official member

Not so worried about the Stones' inconsistent and lackadaisical working methods as Jeff Beck, Wood (once Beck's bass player) had, with singer Rod Stewart, joined forces with what remained of The Small Faces after Steve Marriott's departure in 1969. With no attributive adjective now, The Faces had, after a sluggish start, emerged as one of the most popular concert attractions of the early 70s, but were going off the boil as a chart act, owing in part to the greater success of Stewart's parallel solo career. Another crack appeared when Wood was in the process of recording 1974's *I've Got My Own Album To Do*, a venture that was noteworthy for its big-name sleeve credits, with Keith Richards conspicuous on guitar, keyboards and backing vocals and as co-writer of three tracks.

Almost as a matter of course, Richards pitched in when, on 14 June 1974, Wood promoted his new LP with an all-star line-up accompanying him at Kilburn's Gaumont State Theatre, a further indication that the end was nigh for The Faces. However, the final hurdle to Ron becoming a temporary and then full-time Rolling Stone was that most of their 'It's Only Rock 'N Roll (But I Like It)' single had been realised in a party atmosphere at Wood's home studio in Richmond although its production was attributed to The Glimmer Twins (ie. Richards and Jagger).

Ronnie could never hope to penetrate Keith and Mick's caste-within-a-caste, but he was sufficiently well placed to recommend Ian MacLagan, another ex-Face now a highly waged jobbing keyboard player, as an auxiliary Stone. More to the point, during the making of *I've Got My Own Album To Do*, a restricted code had evolved quickly between Richards and Wood to the extent that utterances unamusing to anyone else would have them howling with laughter. In the way that close friends revile each other affectionately, Ronnie would describe Keith as 'a filthy swine. We're like naughty schoolboys. You'll never take that away from us'.

Richards' and Wood's liaison was closer to the former's fretboard concord with Brian Jones than the more pronounced lead-rhythm division with Mick Taylor. 'Both Ron and Keith are brilliant rhythm guitarists,' exclaimed Mick Jagger, 'It allows a certain cross-trading of riffs not previously possible.' It was there for all to hear in a stage act that was, beamed Keith 'less slick and sophisticated sounding than the other one at its best when everyone was in tune and could hear each other. This is a lot dirtier and rougher, and a lot more exciting'.

A certain extra-tonal piquancy emanated from Keith's guitar, customised to possess just five machine-heads. The new instrument also contained one of the properties of banjos and sitars, a vibrating sympathetic string that Keith observed 'got some kind of drone going. Ordinarily, when you change chords, the previous chord is completely dead.'

In the music media, the smart money was on Keith in a morbid sweepstake about the next live-fast-die-young pop idol to follow Brian Jones, Jimi Hendrix, Janis Joplin, Jim Morrison and similar unfortunates to the grave. However, since the Toronto bust, he seemed to have braked his excesses if you were to believe press statements that contained quotable gravities like, 'I have grimly determined to change my life and abstain from drug use'; promises made about million-dollar endowments to drug rehabilitation charities, and a photographer hired to take nice, smiling pictures of Keith that tempered a pasty complexion indicative of the Dracula hours he kept.

The campaign had followed the granting of bail chiefly on the grounds that Richards was either undergoing or about to undergo detoxification in a psychiatric clinic in New York. He'd

THE ROLLING STONES
Some Girls
PERMA-STYLED WASH -N- WEAR
READY FOR INSTANT WEAR
STYLE TST-79
Lies - lies you dirty Jezebel
Why, why, why why don't you go to Hell?
MISS YOU $6.99
STYLE No PBF 79
Pretty Baby
FREEDOM $6.99
100% CAREFREE WASH & WEAR
Some girls give me jewelry
STYLE No CT-79
Some GIRLS $6.99
RELAXED CURL
STYLE TS-79
GEORGIE Girl $6.99
TAPERED BACK
AFRO $6.99
100% CAREFREE WASH & WEAR
INSTANT BEAUTY
PERMA-STYLED
100% WASH & WEAR
6 in 1
KOOL -N- LIGHT
Beast of Burden $7.99
Wash and Wear
French girls they want Cartier
Heavenly BEAUTY $7.99
LIGHT COOL AIRY—
STYLE No. NC-89
IMAGINATION $7.99
FarAwayEyes
Laughter, joy, and loneliness and sex and sex and sex and sex
FREEDOM WIG
SOFT RELAXED CURLS
Some girls give me children
COOL-CAPLESS Comfortable
PERMA-STYLED
Miracle Fibre
NEVER NEED SETTING
New Lovely You
CAPLESS SKIN-TOP
BEAU CATCHER $8.99
KOOL -N- LIGHT
STYLE No. LIC-99
SHATTERED $8.99
Synthetic Japanese MODACRYLIC
STYLE No. LBC-99
BOY-CUT Shorty $8.99
Black girls just wanta get ...
'When the Whip Comes Down' $8.99
WIZ-WIG
SUPER FREEDOM
Italian girls want cars
100% MIRACLE FIBRE
BEAUTIFUL YOU in a few seconds
NEVER NEED SETTING
PERMA-STYLED
100% WASH & WEAR
Some Girls
6 WIGS in ONE $9.99
'Before They Make Me Run'
Gypsy $9.99
DR. CORTIZONES' APPROVED
LIES Gypsy $9.99
Skin-Crown $9.99
PERMANENT BUILT in HEIGHT
6 in 1
SOME GIRLS
RESPECTABLE $9.99

be seen smiling as he went in and out of counselling sessions where the treatment hinged principally on the electro-acupuncture that had proved successful for the similarly afflicted Pete Townshend and Eric Clapton.

Between appointments, he convalesced in South Salem, an estate in Westchester, not quite an hour's drive outside the city limits and within close proximity to open countryside. There, he'd look back at the events between arrest and bail as like a vague parody of *Midnight Express*. A drama of a US student sentenced to open-ended years in a squalid Turkish prison for a narcotics offence, it would be the hit movie of 1978 when, after two nail-biting postponements, Keith was scheduled to enter the dock at last on 23 October 1978.

History seemed to be repeating itself. That the trial was hanging over him like a sword of Damocles impeded his full executive involvement in *Some Girls* as the 1967 bust had in *Satanic Majesties*. A topical single concerning Keith's self-aggravated plight, 'Keith Don't Go' by Nils Lofgren, was released and a faction within the Stones' German fan base marched on the Canadian Embassy in Frankfurt to present a petition asking for clemency.

This was ineffectual and contingency plans for life without Richards remained in force with Jimmy Page a prime candidate to understudy him, according to media hearsay. 'We all know Keith could get nothing or life imprisonment,' philosophised Mick Jagger. 'If he got life, I would carry on with the band, but I'd be very upset. I'm sure Keith could write in prison. He'd have nothing else to do.'

Playing a lot of rhythm guitar on disc these days, Jagger had emerged as *Some Girls*' prime mover. Nevertheless, both he and Keith were on hand to waver and spring between too many completed tracks at a console in New York, where they also applied finishing touches to the ten final selections. Jagger felt that the Big Apple's open-all-night atmosphere 'gave the album an extra spur and hardness'. He was not alone in his praise. In 1974, George Harrison had observed, 'Some of my best songs were written there. It's great, in that it gives you 360-degree vision.' Steve Winwood was to find New York 'a fantastic place to work. There's a lot of energy. a lot of music there. There's a lot of drive to get things done, which I find very attractive. Maybe attractive isn't the right word.'

Miss You (Jagger-Richards) 4.48

Mick Jagger: lead vocals
Keith Richards, Ronnie Wood and Mick Jagger: guitars
Keith Richards and Ronnie Wood: backing vocals
Bill Wyman: bass guitar
Charlie Watts: drums
Ian MacLagan: piano
Mel Collins: saxophone
Sugar Blue: harmonica

This disco-smitten single was, in hard financial terms, bigger world-wide than anything else the Stones had ever released. Its catchy harmonica riff was whistled by the milkman and, when it blasted from John Lennon's car radio, he upped the volume further, remarking that Mick had got a great song from recent marital upheavals. Bianca may have agreed, but although he was reluctant to discuss its lyrical motive, Jagger explained that 'it's not really about a girl. To me, the feeling of longing is what the song is about.' In passing, Collins was once a member of King Crimson, while myth has it that Sugar Blue (James Whiting), a New Yorker, was discovered busking in a Parisian subway. Finally, Keith Richards played on a 1981 revival of 'Miss You' by venerable US soul singer Etta James.

When The Whip Comes Down (Jagger-Richards) 4.20

Mick Jagger: lead vocals
Keith Richards, Ronnie Wood and Mick Jagger: guitars
Mick Jagger, Keith Richards and Ronnie Wood: backing vocals
Bill Wyman: bass guitar
Charlie Watts: drums
Ronnie Wood: pedal steel guitar

Striding several steps further than, say, The Kinks' 'See My Friend' in 1965 with its bold intimation of bisexuality, this over-vigorous and relentless backing spells out a newcomer to New York's homosexual community's baptism of sado-masochistic fire. Even when a pupil at Dartford Grammar School, there had been spurious murmurings of lyricist Jagger's leanings in this direction but his main targets then and now were females more dauntingly free-spirited than the usual nice girl of the mid-50s saving herself for the wedding night.

Just My Imagination (Running Away With Me) (Whitfield-Strong) 4.38
Mick Jagger: lead vocals
Keith Richards, Ronnie Wood and Mick Jagger: guitars
Mick Jagger, Keith Richards and Ronnie Wood: backing vocals
Bill Wyman: bass guitar
Charlie Watts: drums
Ian MacLagan: organ

Despite its commercial potential, the Stones were reluctant to issue on 45 what was not, in any case, one of their own compositions. Besides, however convincing the *Some Girls* refashioning, the original by The Temptations had topped the US charts in 1971.

Some Girls (Jagger-Richards) 4.37
Mick Jagger: all vocals
Keith Richards, Ronnie Wood and Mick Jagger: guitars
Sugar Blue: harmonica
Keith Richards: bass guitar
Bill Wyman: synthesiser
Charlie Watts: drums

This raised feminist hackles for lyrical generalisations based on the singer's apparent knowledge of the carnal predelictions of particular racial types of female. He also in-joked about Bob Dylan's recent divorce for which the US songwriter was attempting to soften the blow of the resulting alimony with a lucrative and extensive world tour.

Lies (Jagger-Richards) 3.12
Mick Jagger: all vocals
Keith Richards, Ronnie Wood and Mick Jagger: guitars
Bill Wyman: bass guitar
Charlie Watts: drums

By 1978, punk was but a memory for the man in the street, although this opus, thrashed at speed, was very much infused by it as much as the Stones' 'She Said Yeah' and The Pretty Things' 'Honey I Need', also from 1965, had anticipated it.

Far Away Eyes (Jagger-Richards) 4.24

Mick Jagger: lead vocals
Keith Richards and Ronnie Wood: guitars
Ronnie Wood: pedal steel guitar
Mick Jagger, Keith Richards and Ronnie Wood: backing vocals
Bill Wyman: bass guitar
Charlie Watts: drums
Mick Jagger and Keith Richards: keyboards

The B side of 'Miss You' this was a C&W take-off, laced with pious fear and matey cameraderie with the Lord, rendered with humourous exuberance and in an apposite mid-Californian accent by Jagger.

Respectable (Jagger-Richards) 3.07

Mick Jagger: all vocals
Keith Richards and Ronnie Wood: guitars
Ronnie Wood: pedal steel guitar
Bill Wyman: bass guitar
Charlie Watts: drums

When this burst from a wayside cafe's juke-box, a casual listener's reaction was usually 'That's The Rolling Stones,' rather than 'That's "Respectable"'. Paying stricter attention, they might have noted a tuneful bass guitar section and verses about the high society circles in which the Stones were now orbiting. Jack Ford, with-it son of the US president, had attended the Washington DC stop on the group's last tour in the company of Andy Warhol and Bianca Jagger. Elsewhere, Raquel Welch, Charles Bronson and Liza Minelli had received ovations as they were shepherded to their reserved seats. As a UK single, 'Respectable' reached No. 23.

Before They Make Me Run (Jagger-Richards) 3.25

Keith Richards: lead vocals
Keith Richards and Ronnie Wood: guitars
Mick Jagger, Keith Richards and Ronnie Wood; slide guitar and backing vocals
Bill Wyman: bass guitar
Charlie Watts: drums

Keith's *Some Girls* party-piece, this was his first lead vocal excursion since 'Happy' from *Exile On Main Street*. Its verses were very much based on the events of the previous year or so as well as possibly the sudden demise of Gram Parsons in 1973, when he washed down morphine tablets with a quantity of tequila. Heroin and cocaine already in Parsons' bloodstream also assisted the promotion of a blackout of such depth that he never came round.

Beast Of Burden (Jagger-Richards) 4.25

Mick Jagger: lead vocals
Keith Richards and Ronnie Wood: guitars
Mick Jagger and Keith Richards: backing vocals
Bill Wyman: bass guitar
Charlie Watts: drums

To the most poignant melody on the album, this account of some poor but not uncomplaining fool coming back for more abuse may be regarded as almost the inverse of put-downs like 'Under My Thumb' and 'Out Of Time'. It also has overtones of Buddy Holly's 'pretty-pretty-pretty-pretty Peggy Sue' of 1957. As a single, an edit entered the US Top Ten. Six years later, a revival by Bette Midler, a US vocalist who injected archly kitsch cabaret into pop, slinked into the Hot 100 after Jagger appeared in the attendant video. During a Stones concert at Madison Square Garden in 1973, she'd been beside herself with ecstasy when 'I just saw what Mick was doing. Oh, the nerve! I stood there and shouted, "Please, oh please!" Oh, how I wanted him!'

Shattered (Jagger-Richards) 3.47

Mick Jagger: lead vocals
Keith Richards and Ronnie Wood: guitars
Mick Jagger, Keith Richards and Ronnie Wood: backing vocals
Ronnie Wood, Jimmy Miller, Rebop Kwaku Baah, Simon Kirke and others: percussion
Bill Wyman: bass guitar and synthesiser
Charlie Watts: drums
Ronnie Wood: pedal steel guitar

A rather too frenzied closer, it was technically impressive for its neatly dovetailed backing, but this was not a recipe for more than superfluous excitement. Simon Kirke was drummer with Free and its Bad Company derivation.

EMOTIONAL RESCUE

UK Release: 22 June 1980
US Release: 22 June 1980
Intl CD No: CBS CDCBS206 2
Running Time: 45:19

Rolling Stones Records CUN 39111
Rolling Stones Records CUN 16015
Producer: The Glimmer Twins

SIDE ONE: Dance; Summer Romance; Send It To Me; Let Me Go; Indian Girl.

SIDE TWO: Where The Boys Go; Down In The Hole; Emotional Rescue; She's So Cold; All About You.

Though Jagger could count royalty among his chums, he and three ex-Beatles had doled out impromptu and ragged cabaret on a makeshift stage, deep in the Surrey countryside, at Eric Clapton's star-studded wedding reception in 1979. He was also very receptive to jamming with Muddy Waters in a Chicago club on two occasions at the turn of the decade, the last one filmed and stored in the Stones' data base.

A clip would be incorporated into 1989's *25 X 5*, a self-made documentary sub-titled 'The Continuing Adventures Of The Rolling Stones'. Contradicting his punk-era ennui and a later statement to a tabloid journalist 'The band has done what it set out to do. It will disintegrate very slowly', The Rolling Stones remained belligerently alive.

In 1980, Jagger had been weighing up the cash benefits of pop against his self-picture as a musician. 'How long do you want to be in rock'n'roll?' a *Melody Maker* newshound had enquired. Mick's face – temporarily bearded to the cheek-bones – pinched in thought before a deliberated 'I dunno. Maybe forever.' Yet, later that same month, he'd reckon that 'rock'n'roll had no future. It's only recycled past.'

Is that what he thought of *Emotional Rescue*, the first Stones studio album to appear after the final act of Keith Richards' Canadian drug bust drama? This had unfolded in a Toronto courtroom on 23 October 1978 when plea bargaining had resulted in a decision that he was to admit to possession on the understanding that the more heinous accusation of trafficking with a narcotic wasn't to be pursued. Keith's defence also maintained this

THE ROLLING STONES EMOTIONAL RESCU

4 2 - △ + 2

'creative, tortured person, a major contributor to an art form' was a reformed character whose attempt to 'rid himself of this terrible problem' seemed to be working. As the Stones' principal lyricist, Jagger was blamed for the perceived drug references in songs such as 'Moonlight Mile', 'Can't You Hear Me Knocking', 'Torn And Frayed' and, still in the British Top 30, 'Respectable', with its line about 'taking heroin with the Duke of Kent'.

These and further arguments had a bearing on the judge's ruling that, as well as probation, a one-year suspended sentence and the continuation of his addiction cure, Keith was to undertake a form of community service by playing two free fund-raising concerts for the Canadian Institute for the Blind.

Richards fulfilled this most unusual legal obligation on 21 April 1979 when The Rolling Stones gave their only performances that year. They were supported by the newly formed New Barbarians, the brainchild of Ronnie Wood and Keith. One of its purposes, perhaps, was to provide the latter guitarist with occupational therapy by banishing convalescent sloth, and catapulting him back onto the concert bulletin while the Stones were off the road.

After a US tour by the New Barbarians had wound down, a footloose period of excursions back and forth across the Atlantic found Richards assisting on albums by such respected names as Booker T's guitarist Steve Cropper and reggae icon Peter Tosh. Tosh was present, but not actively participating when a ten-minute reggae-flavoured Jagger-Richards item, the hitherto-unissued 'Jah Is Not Dead', was finished at the lavish new Compass Point Studios in the Bahamas where the Stones had started work on *Emotional Rescue.*

Emotional Rescue swept with neo-mathematical precision to the top in Britain and the US, conveying even more of a sense of marking time than the superior *Between The Buttons*. 'There's hardly a melody here you haven't heard from the Stones before,' affirmed *Rolling Stone* of the album. 'This word-perfect, classic sounding, spiritless record is a message from the grave. I'm afraid that people won't be calling them survivors much longer'. Adoration, nevertheless, would be for life for the faithful, but after *Emotional Rescue*, many ceased buying Stones albums just to complete the set like Buffalo Bill annuals.

Dance (Jagger-Richards-Wood) 4.23

Mick Jagger: lead vocals
Keith Richards, Ronnie Wood and Mick Jagger: guitars
Bobby Keyes: saxophones
Bill Wyman: bass guitar
Charlie Watts: drums
Michael Shrieve: percussion

Richards visualised this as an instrumental with maybe perfunctory lyrics at most but the notion was capsized by Jagger's verbosity over a disco-esque backing fattened by Keyes's multi-tracked woodwinds and a rhythmic undercurrent by Shrieve, drummer with tijuana-rock exponents, Santana, then at a low ebb.

Summer Romance (Jagger-Richards) 3.16

Mick Jagger: lead vocals
Keith Richards and Ronnie Wood: guitars
Mick Jagger, Keith Richards, Ronnie Wood and Max Romeo: backing vocals
Bill Wyman: bass guitar
Charlie Watts: drums
Various: brass and woodwinds

Held over from *Some Girls* sessions in Paris, this re-mix makes the lead guitar more of a feature though not enough to obscure verses that evoke vague memories of post-war holiday camps that were hunting grounds for souls aching for romance.

Send It To Me (Jagger-Richards) 3.43

Mick Jagger: lead vocals
Keith Richards and Ronnie Wood: guitars
Sugar Blue: harmonica
Charlie Watts: drums
Ronnie Wood: bass guitar
Max Romeo: percussion

Third track, side one, might not have been the wisest positioning choice for a tepid opus of reggae persuasion. In parenthesis, Max Romeo was responsible for the BBC-banned 'Wet Dream' that reached the British Top Ten in summer 1969.

Let Me Go (Jagger-Richards) 3.50

Mick Jagger: lead vocals
Keith Richards and Ronnie Wood: guitars
Ronnie Wood: pedal steel guitar
Bill Wyman: bass guitar
Charlie Watts: drums
Bobby Keyes: saxophone

If not uninfluenced by the lyrical pre-occupations and melodic appeal of country-rock, there is also a perverse element of dub reggae in the way this item was processed at the console.

Indian Girl (Jagger-Richards) 4.23

Mick Jagger: lead vocals
Keith Richards and Ronnie Wood: guitars
Ronnie Wood: pedal steel guitar
Various: brass and woodwinds arranged by Jack Nitzsche
Bill Wyman: bass guitar
Charlie Watts: drums
Nicky Hopkins: piano
Max Romeo: xylophone

Though countrified almost to the point of sweetcorn, the lyrical scenarios are a west-African theatre of guerilla war.

Where The Boys Go (Jagger-Richards) 3.29

Mick Jagger: lead vocals
Keith Richards, Ronnie Wood and Mick Jagger: guitars
Mick Jagger, Keith Richards, Ronnie Wood and others: backing vocals
Bill Wyman: bass guitar
Charlie Watts: drums
Ian Stewart: piano

To fast accompaniment that embraces an apt tinge of 1977 disco movie *Saturday Night Fever*, in female voices among the backing singers, Jagger spits out in 'Oi! Oi!' cockney his perspective about a night on the beer that promises to climax with a knee-trembler in a pub's back alley.

Down In The Hole (Jagger-Richards) 3.58
Mick Jagger: lead vocals
Keith Richards and Ronnie Wood: guitars
Sugar Blue: harmonica
Bill Wyman: bass guitar
Charlie Watts: drums
It was back to stylised blues musically although the lyrics conjure up images of bartering in sex with occupation GIs after the fall of Germany in 1945.

Emotional Rescue (Jagger-Richards) 5.39
Mick Jagger: piano and lead vocals
Ronnie Wood: bass guitar
Charlie Watts: drums
Max Romeo: percussion
Keith Richards and Ronnie Wood: guitars
Bill Wyman: synthesiser
Ian Stewart: piano
Bobby Keyes: saxophone
The title track was released as a single the same month as the album, to penetrate Top Tens across the globe and actually got to No.1 in the Philippines. A hybrid of disco and ersatz reggae frames what seem like improvised lyrics by Jagger in a variety of different vocal ranges and intonations.

She's So Cold (Jagger-Richards) 4.14
Mick Jagger: lead vocals
Keith Richards and Ronnie Wood: guitars
Ronnie Wood: pedal steel guitar
Bobby Keyes: saxophone
Bill Wyman: bass guitar
Charlie Watts: drums
Michael Strieve: percussion
This was cast adrift on the vinyl oceans on 45 to hover for a few weeks around the wrong end of the Top 30s in Britain and the States. Richards and Wood barre over-familiar chord changes behind Jagger's frustrated eroticism.

All About You (Jagger-Richards) 4.18
Keith Richards: piano, lead vocals and bass guitar
Keith Richards and Ronnie Wood: backing vocals
Keith Richards and Ronnie Wood: guitars
Charlie Watts: drums

Possibly Richards' smoothest vocal performance on disc, this slow narrative concerns inexplicable love for a woman that logic says is no good for him. In the aftershock of the Toronto bother, he and Anita Pallenberg's lawyer 'lectured us that we were a bad influence on each other, and that if we were ever going to kick heroin, we would have to separate. That really ended it for us, although we occasionally saw each other for the sake of the children.'

TATTOO YOU

UK Release: 24 August 1981
US Release: 24 August 1981
Intl CD No: CBS CDCBS450198 2
Running Time: 43:00

Rolling Stones Records CUNS 39114
Rolling Stones Records COC 16052
Producers: The Glimmer Twins

SIDE ONE: Start Me Up; Hang Fire; Slave; Little T & A; Black Limousine; Neighbours.

SIDE TWO: Worried About You; Tops; Heaven; No Use In Crying; Waiting On A Friend.

As the 70s drew to a close, Mick Jagger spoke about downing tools as a Rolling Stone to intimates like David Bowie. An eavesdropper spread the tale that he was intending to devote himself solely to films, starting with a re-make of the 1959 farce, *Some Like It Hot*, with himself assuming the Jack Lemmon part and Bowie that of Tony Curtis. Another dismissed proposal was producing and acting in a celluloid adaptation of *Kalki*, a Gore Vidal play.

His procrastination appeared to be over when he agreed to the title role in *Fitzcarraldo* for German director Werner Herzog. In general circulation by 1983, the movie was praised by critics but Jagger's connection with it had dissipated within weeks of him arriving on location in Iquitos, three thousand miles from the Amazon delta. So remote was it that tropical disease was a way of life – and death. The cast were billeted in mosquito-ridden mud huts and loincloth-clad natives, descendants of headhunters, glowered, belaboured and stopped just short of open assault on the foreign intruders.

Initially, Mick mucked in, helping the crew lug and set up equipment while muttering his lines over and over again. One February day, however, he felt so sick and miserable that he dragged himself to the nearest airport and slipped smoothly into the skies and out of an intolerable situation.

Herzog chose to try again in May but by then his errant star was in the throes of readying himself for another album-tour-album sandwich. Come September, and the LP entitled *Tattoo You* plus its 'Start Me Up' 45 that was destined to be *Rolling Stones'* magazine's Single Of The Year, had been placed in their respective charts.

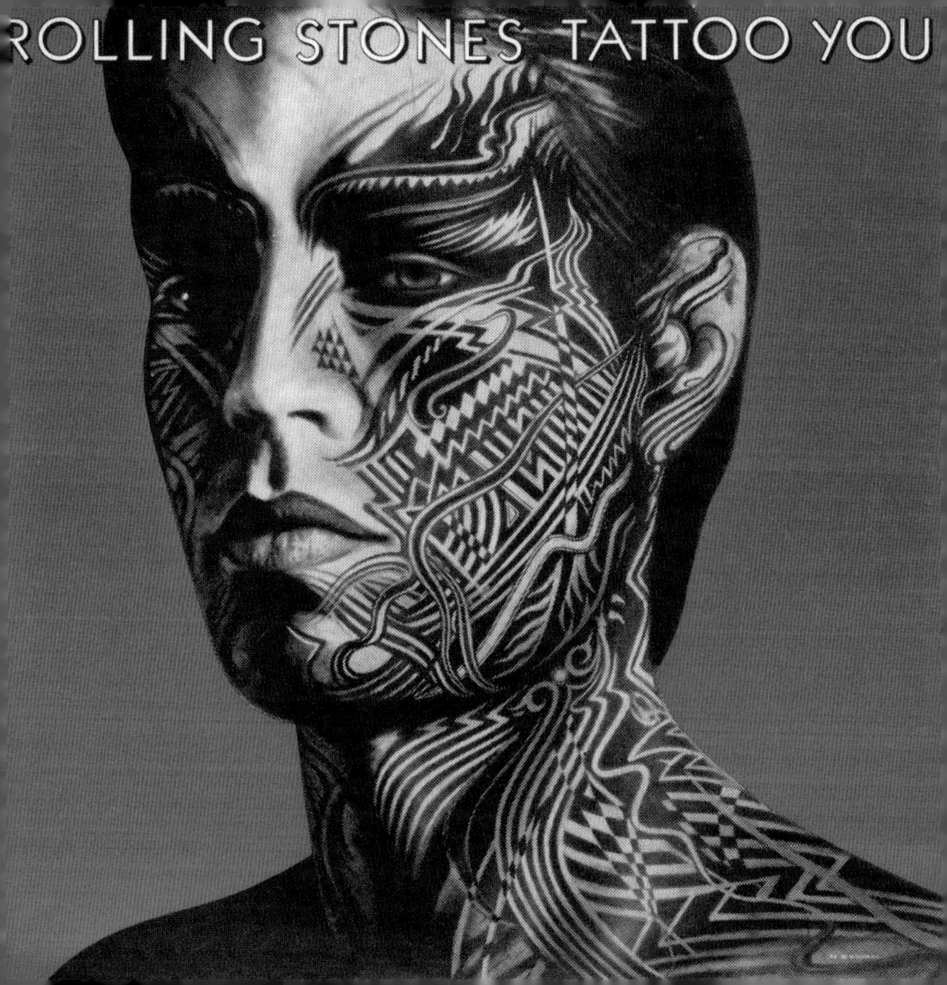
ROLLING STONES TATTOO YOU

Both discs had been rush-released in time for an imminent multi-national barnstormer, with every date of the US leg sold out. The album was culled from numerous hitherto unissued numbers from archives datable from the Mick Taylor years to Jagger-Richards compositions completed weeks before the tour got under way. It was then decided to divide *Tattoo You* into two distinct vinyl sides: rockers and ballads.

Not as barrel-scraping as it seemed on paper, the album was the last US No. 1 thus far and stopped one short of pole position in Britain.

Start Me Up (Jagger-Richards) 3.32
Mick Jagger: lead vocals
Keith Richards and Ronnie Wood: guitars
Mick Jagger, Keith Richards and Ronnie Wood: backing vocals
Bill Wyman: bass guitar
Charlie Watts: drums

It began life in April 1975 as 'Never Stop', a reggae outing with only reference vocals. This second attempt in 1978 explored more familiar Stones territory, and was blessed with instant familiarity. As a single issued the week before *Tattoo You* reached the shops, could anyone not have empathised with the fellows' mortification when only 'Endless Love' by Diana Ross and Lionel Richie prevented 'Start Me Up' from topping the US Hot 100 after three weeks at No. 2. It wasn't as big a hit in Britain, but it was a big hit all the same.

Hang Fire (Jagger-Richards) 2.21
Mick Jagger: lead vocals
Keith Richards and Ronnie Wood: guitars
Ian Stewart: piano
Bill Wyman: bass guitar
Charlie Watts: drums
Mick Jagger and Keith Richards: backing vocals

Of the same vintage as 'Start Me Up', this is one of those searing indictments of society. It was considered for inclusion on *Some Girls*, but its time came in April 1982 when, as a single, it irritated the US Top 20 in the early summer of 1982.

Slave (Jagger-Richards) 6.33

Mick Jagger: lead vocals
Keith Richards and Ronnie Wood: guitars
Billy Preston: organ
Sonny Rollins: saxophone
Bill Wyman: bass guitar
Charlie Watts: drums
Ollie Brown: percussion

This is two lost minutes from the *Black And Blue* period, although a longer version was to surface on the CD release. An early take featured Jeff Beck when he was one of the few rock guitarists capable of playing jazz fusion convincingly. He was impressed that the Stones had cajoled eminent hard-bop saxophonist Rollins to sit in with them.

Little T & A (Jagger-Richards) 3.23

Keith Richards: lead vocals and bass guitar
Charlie Watts: drums
Mick Jagger, Keith Richards and Ronnie Wood: backing vocals
Keith Richards and Ronnie Wood: guitars
Ian Stewart: piano

Taped in the Bahamas in 1979, this has an element of quasi-autobiography as exemplified by its observation that drug pushers were disgruntled because Keith was no longer interested in hard drugs. T & A, incidentally, stood for tits and arse.

Black Limousine (Jagger-Richards-Wood) 3.31

Mick Jagger: lead vocals, harmonica
Charlie Watts: drums
Ian Stewart: piano
Keith Richards and Ronnie Wood: guitars
Bill Wyman: bass guitar

Lead vocals were added in 1978 and a solo by Wood in 1981, although the backing track of this blues-boogie item had been 'in the can' for eight years before its emergence on *Tattoo You.*

Neighbours (Jagger-Richards) 3.31

Mick Jagger: lead vocals
Keith Richards and Ronnie Wood: guitars
Bobby Keyes: saxophone
Bill Wyman: bass guitar
Charlie Watts: drums
Sonny Rollins: saxophone

On one side of the vocalist's dwelling is a brothel while on the other a homicidal husband dismembers his wife's corpse. These observations were sung to an arrangement in hard-rock style with prominent snare drum. The repeated 'is it any wonder?' phrase may have been a nod towards 'Fame', a US chart-topper in 1975 for David Bowie that was co-written by John Lennon who was shot dead in New York on 8 December 1980. Accosted for a comment outside the Paris studio where the Stones were putting the finishing touches to *Tattoo You*, Jagger was not ready, he said, 'to make a casual remark right now at such an awful moment for his family', Lennon's slaying also summoned fears of a copycat killing, perhaps during the forthcoming Stones tour.

Worried About You (Jagger-Richards) 5.17

Mick Jagger: lead vocals
Keith Richards and Wayne Perkins: guitars
Billy Preston: piano
Mick Jagger, Keith Richards and Ronnie Wood: backing vocals
Bill Wyman: bass guitar
Charlie Watts: drums
Ollie Brown: percussion

Jagger vacillates between falsetto and low growl on this tuneful and slowish item from the Mick Taylor-Ronnie Wood interregnum. The guitar solo is by Perkins when he was the clear favourite to succeed Taylor.

Tops (Jagger-Richards) 3.45

Mick Jagger: lead vocals
Keith Richards and Mick Taylor: guitars
Nicky Hopkins: piano
Bill Wyman: bass guitar
Charlie Watts: drums

Uncredited on the *Tattoo You* package, Taylor, through his solicitor, demanded and received royalties for this 1972 opus with lyrical allusions to the casting couch as a means to 'take you to the top'.

Heaven (Jagger-Richards) 4.22

Mick Jagger: guitar, lead vocals
Charlie Watts: drums
Bill Wyman: guitar, bass guitar and synthesiser
Chris Kimsey: piano

Richards and Wood arrived too late to participate in this track from the Pathe-Marconi studio in Paris that works sensually more than intellectually. It had me groping for adjectives like serene, caressing and atmospheric. Assisting Jagger in the compilation of *Tattoo You*, Kimsey was roped in to tinkle the ivories here.

No Use In Crying (Jagger-Richards) 3.25

Mick Jagger: guitar, lead vocals
Bill Wyman: bass guitar
Mick Jagger, Keith Richards and Ronnie Wood: backing vocals
Keith Richards and Ronnie Wood: guitars
Charlie Watts: drums
Nicky Hopkins: piano, organ

Slightly eccentric stereo placement is one of the more notable aspects of an echo-laden track from 1979 that the Stones could have recorded in their sleep.

Waiting On A Friend (Jagger-Richards) 4.34

Mick Jagger: lead vocals
Keith Richards and Mick Taylor: guitars
Jimmy Miller: percussion
Mick Jagger, Keith Richards and Ronnie Wood: backing vocals
Bill Wyman: bass guitar
Charlie Watts: drums
Sonny Rollins: saxophone

A relaxed product of protracted sessions in the West Indies late in 1972 was the second *Tattoo You* 45, penetrating the US Top 20 while beginning a downward spiral after but one week at No. 50 in Britain. Only Jagger and Richards were seen in the correlated video, thus confirming the long-established power structure whereby every other Stone was to be subordinate to them for as long as the group stayed together.

STILL LIFE (AMERICAN CONCERT)

UK Release: 1 June 1982
US Release: 1 June 1982
Intl CD No: CBS CDCBS450204 2
Running Time: 40:15

Rolling Stones Records CUN 39115
Rolling Stones Records CUN 39113
Producers: The Glimmer Twins

SIDE ONE: Under My Thumb; Let's Spend the Night Together; Shattered; Twenty Flight Rock; Going To A Go-Go.

SIDE TWO: Let Me Go; Time Is On My Side; Just My Imagination (Running Away With Me); Start Me Up; (I Can't Get No) Satisfaction.

Exhuming old songs was becoming a common practice during the 80s. All it took was a swarthy youth removing his jeans to the accompaniment of Ben E. King's 'Stand By Me' in a TV advertisement and suddenly the whole of Britain was awash with nostalgia for the 60s. Time almost stopped when one week's Top Ten contained only one entry that wasn't either a reissue or a revival. In the latter half of 1982, The Rolling Stones' retread of The Miracles' 'Going To A Go-Go' was at No. 26, with another go at trusty old 'Time Is On My Side' bubbling under the Top 50.

Both A sides were taken from in-concert *Still Life*, which was topped and tailed by Duke Ellington's 'Take The A Train' signature tune and Jimi Hendrix's Woodstock Festival mauling of 'The Star-Spangled Banner'. Certain numbers came and went but the set was the same in essence throughout an international money-spinner that, in the wake of *Tattoo You*, focused on the USA and Europe.

Dead on time, the main event piled on a stage framed by sky-clawing scaffolding, giant video screens and lighting gantries like oil derricks. Beyond the three chief show-offs – Jagger, Richards and Wood – there was Charlie, his grins less bashful and rare than of yore whenever his eyes were teased from the drums; Ian Stewart, the one who hadn't looked enough like a 60s pop star, finally allowed out from the wings, and Bill Wyman, basking in the afterglow of '(Si Si) Je Suis Un Rock Star', a solid solo single in Britain's Top Ten only the previous summer.

ROLLING STONES
"STILL LIFE"
(AMERICAN CONCERT 1981)

Wyman had probably been the brains behind the delving into the past of two rock'n'rollers older than themselves – The Big Bopper (for 'Chantilly Lace') and Eddie Cochran ('Twenty Flight Rock') – which were slipped in to balance 'Start Me Up' and older smashes, spanning 20 years. The dark clouds and thickening twilight were suggestive of the witching hour and the Stones' approach to their shows had become lighter and friendlier since occurrences like Altamont had taken them out of their depth, obliging them to concentrate on the possible.

The crowds had seen it all before, but so what? The girls gasped rather than screamed when Mick took his shirt off and the music was still only one step from chaos, but the sound was crystal-clear and the Stones still rode 'em on down to howling approval, foot-stomping and girls removing their bras.

This was to be reflected in *Still Life*'s placing in the Top Fives of not only the territories covered by the tour, but those whose turn wasn't to come until much nearer the end of the century. Of the selected tracks, perhaps the aim of incorporating an equal balance of recent and time-honoured Jagger-Richards items was to show that songs from *Some Girls*, *Emotional Rescue* and *Tattoo You* were as durable as those that allowed the mums and dads in the audience to pretend they were swinging sixties teenagers again, lovestruck and irresponsible.

Apart from 'Let Me Go' with Keith Richards as lead singer, the line-up throughout was as follows:

Mick Jagger: guitar, lead vocals, harmonica
Keith Richards and Ronnie Wood: guitars and backing vocals
Ernie Watts: saxophone
Bill Wyman: bass guitar
Charlie Watts: drums
Ian Stewart and Ian McLagan: keyboards

Studio adjustments of errors and oversights were made by Wyman and Jagger on keyboards, among others.

As on all Rolling Stones in-concert albums, timing includes continuity and audience response.

Under My Thumb (Jagger-Richards) 4.18
The marimba was missing but the Aftermath arrangement was otherwise present and correct when this was recorded at the Brendan Byrne Area in New Jersey's Meadowlands.

Let's Spend The Night Together (Jagger-Richards) 3.51
At least as much cursory heed had been paid by Jagger to David Bowie's remake of this mid-60s hit on 1973's *Aladdin Sane* as Bob Dylan had to Bryan Ferry's rendition of his 'A Hard Rain's Gonna Fall' that same year.

Shattered (Jagger-Richards) 4.11
Apart from the energy of the performance at Hampton Roads Coliseum in Hampton, Virginia, this isn't much different from the 'Shattered' on Some Girls.

Twenty Flight Rock (Cochran-Fairchild) 1.48
A multi-talented Elvis-type from Oklahoma who was more adored in Europe than in his native land, Eddie Cochran died in a car accident near Chippenham, England in 1960. The Who paid respects on 1970's *Live At Leeds* that featured his 'Summertime Blues'. There was also an unreleased 1978 studio revival of the same by the Stones who also reworked this other audio snap-shot by Cochran of the trials of adolescence.

Going To A Go-Go (Robinson-Tarplin-Moore-Rogers) 3.21
The Miracles had been among the first Tamla-Motown acts to make the US Hot 100. Smokey Robinson, their high-pitched lead singer, had been the subsequent subject of 'Pure Smokey', a tribute song by George Harrison by the time the Stones gave this 1966 hit what it deserved on 5 November 1981. Six years later, ABC were to salute Robinson with their 'When Smokey Sings' hit.

Let Me Go (Jagger-Richards) 3.37
Though also taped at Tempe, Arizona's Sun Devil Stadium, this version of an *Emotional Rescue* item comes from the show at the Capitol Center in Largo, Madison on 7 December 1981.

Time Is On My Side (Meade) 3.39
Slightly slower than on *Got Live If You Want It*, the first Stones concert LP, this also has a more theatrical lead vocal underlined by organ and legato saxophone from Ernie Watts who'd been among central figures on the soundtrack to *Saturday Night Fever*.

Just My Imagination (Running Away With Me) (Whitfield-Strong) 5.23
From the same source as 'Shattered', the second Motown cover on the set-list was, if anything, more powerful than that heard on *Some Girls*.

Start Me Up (Jagger-Richards) 4.21
This latest smash was still in the US Hot 100 when it was heard at the New Jersey stop on 6 November 1981.

(I Can't Get No) Satisfaction (Jagger-Richards) 4.24
The fixed encore throughout the jaunt. What would have become of it had the main set in New Jersey ended with just a politely brief spattering of applause?

UNDERCOVER

UK Release: 7 November 1983
US Release: 8 November 1983
Intl CD No: CBS CDCBS450200 2
Producers: Chris Kimsey and The Glimmer Twins

Rolling Stones Records CUN 1654361
Rolling Stones Records 90120
Running Time: 45:02

SIDE ONE: Undercover Of The Night; She Was Hot; Tie You Up (The Pain Of Love); Wanna Hold You; Feel On Baby.

SIDE TWO: Too Much Blood; Pretty Beat Up; Too Tough; All The Way Down; It Must Be Hell.

Settling down and domestic upheavals can push both friendships and vocational partnerships into the background, often creating a void as piquant as a bereavement. The seeds for that scenario that all but finished The Rolling Stones would be planted during the *Undercover* period.

As Ronnie Wood's wife announced her pregnancy and Keith Richards was making plans to tie the knot and start a family with the longtime girlfriend that had succeeded Anita Pallenberg, Bill Wyman and Mick Jagger were either becoming temporarily estranged or finishing altogether with their respective constant companions.

Changes were afoot professionally too. As the US expiry date of Atlantic's contract crept closer, hearsay became a certainty that the group would not re-sign with a company that couldn't come up with the tens of millions of pounds required to keep them and their post-Decca back catalogue. Therefore representatives from every major label that had the resources, put forward serious bids, and 'it amused Mick Jagger to see so many record executives chasing him around the world,' noted CBS's Walter Yetnikoff, 'He was a skilled negotiator who never lost sight of his advantage as a pop icon.'

Jagger appeared most enticed by CBS who dangled the carrot of solo albums before him as well as the biggest advance ever proffered for a pop group. Yet, battled-hardened by the industry, he did not show too much eagerness, spoke in riddles and, cried Yetnikoff, 'kept me running for a year. Meetings in Europe, New York, California – the challenge of Jagger's

UNDER COVER

swagger and sinewy ways took all I had. One of my first had been in a swanky Parisian restaurant, ordering wine that cost more than the GNP of certain countries. We were both bombed – or at least I was. You could never tell with Mick. He liked to give the impression of inebriation while retaining control. When it came to numbers, Mick was as sober as St. Augustine and his image as the prancing prince of pop belied the side of his character that had seriously studied economics.'

During one business lunch Jagger and Yetnikoff calculated on table napkins a specific territory's VAT for a given royalty rate and numbers of albums sold. 'Two minutes later, he had an accurate reading' goggled Yetnikoff, 'while I was still struggling.'

'The highly complex contract was drafted,' he continued, 'It required a dozen lawyers and involved a Dutch Antilles holding company. After months of haggling, all we needed were signatures. That's when Mick balked.'

With the approbation of Keith Richards, Jagger's irresolution was chiefly over a clause concerning whether the Stones or CBS should select each album's singles. It is said that Jagger caved in after a frightful table-banging quarrel with Yetnikoff that you could hear all over the same French diner where the drawn-out discussions had started.

More often than not an album's most trite cut, a single was a fiddly little thing anyway, more likely to be a loss-leader than an unmistakable world-wide smash nowadays. No matter how they were packaged – 12-inch club mix or polkadot vinyl – 45s were becoming no more than radio play-list inducements to shell out for LPs.

During discussions, the Stones had also been attending to *Undercover*, their final obligation to Atlantic, in various studios in Paris, New York and the Bahamas with Chris Kimsey, a London studio engineer-turned-producer on the crest of a wave thanks to recent success with musically unadventurous but stadium-filling Peter Frampton. Among the skills that brought Kimsey to the Stones' attention was the way he gave the bass guitar more of a defined sound than the mere presence that it still was, even on other hit records, 'and that inspires you,' smiled Bill Wyman, 'and turns everyone on to your playing.'

Like a vicar in a BBC situation comedy, the presence of the first official outside producer since Jimmy Miller almost a decade ago was supposed to induce the biting back on shirtiness, provocative indifference and any other of the nonsenses that occur when human beings gather in recording studios. From day one it was evident that Richards and Jagger weren't in complete agreement over artistic direction. Sometimes light banter would erode to such stand-up indignation and cross-purpose that, after their eyes flickered from Mick to Keith as if watching a tennis match, the other Stones present would slope off for an embarrassed coffee break while defiance, hesitation, defiance again and final agreement chased across the face of either protagonist. Put crudely, Mick wanted the group to listen and learn from the latest sounds in and out of the charts while Keith was against change for the sake of change.

However, the growing internal problems were not yet indicative of something rotten in the state of the Stones and may even have been contributory to creative action. Certainly, critiques of *Undercover* were heartening enough, and the group left Atlantic on a high with the album topping the British list while not quite managing the same in the States. This was mildly disappointing, but the interrelated singles at least covered costs, some more quickly than others.

Regardless of sales the Stones had bolstered their position among certain pockets of the record-buying public by endeavouring to ensure that credible names could be printed in sleeve notes. Recovery from a near-fatal stomach operation had caused a lengthy halt to olde-tyme rock'n'roller Jerry Lee Lewis's concert schedule as well as his declining the Stones' kind invitation for him to play on *Undercover*. But this was mitigated by the presence of luminaries from another genre altogether. In the late 80s, Richards had been rubbing shoulders with Black Uhuru, an ensemble that contained Sly Dunbar and Robbie Shakespeare, the Jamaican drums-and-bass rhythm section that were an automatic choice for non-Caribbean pop icons wanting to dabble in reggae, even if James Brown, a bandleader of some discernment, reckoned they had no idea. Among these were Bob Dylan, Serge Gainsbourg and, when he struck out on his own in the later 80s, Mick Jagger.

Sly and Robbie were delighted when Keith asked them to assist on *Undercover* as were Moustapha Cisse and Brahms Coundoul from Xalam, a fusion group from Senegal who specialised in what was categorized as Afro-jazz. While completing *Goree,* their second album, in Paris in 1983, they entered the orbit of an intrigued Rolling Stones.

Undercover Of The Night (Jagger-Richards) 4.32

Mick Jagger: guitar, lead vocals
Bill Wyman: bass guitar
Moustapha Cisse and Brahms Coundoul: percussion
Keith Richards and Ronnie Wood: guitars
Charlie Watts: drums
Chuck Leavall: keyboards

The essence of this piece is a Jagger libretto about *nacht und nebel* raids that began the process of the vapourising of political dissidents in repressive South America republics. A dramatic video with himself as the victim was screened during an interview on *The Tube*, a Channel Four pop showcase intended to be the *Ready Steady Go* of its day. The cameras panned away from a particularly blood-stained sequence to Mick, whose staged wincing turned a promotional tool that might have passed without comment into something of a controversy. 'Undercover Of The Night' as an edited 45, commenced a scramble to the brink of the UK Top Ten, repeating this feat in North America.

She Was Hot (Jagger-Richards) 4.41

Mick Jagger: guitar, lead vocals
Bill Wyman: bass guitar
Ian Stewart and Chuck Leavell: keyboards
Keith Richards and Ronnie Wood: guitars
Charlie Watts: drums

As the follow-up 45 to 'Undercover Of The Night', this was also considered worthy of a video, a comparatively new marketing tool that projected the Stones in a supposedly amusing dramatic scenario rather than adhering to a straightforward synchronization with a musical performance. It hovered just outside the Top 40 in both Britain and the States.

Tie You Up (The Pain Of Love) (Jagger-Richards) 4.16
Mick Jagger: guitar, all vocals
Keith Richards: guitar
Ronnie Wood: bass guitar
Bill Wyman, Ian Stewart and Martin Ditcham: percussion
Charlie Watts: drums
Chuck Leavell: organ

From the title you may be able to deduce what this song concerns. Florid sexual vocabulary is given its expected head over a backing that at one point consists of just drums and minor percussion.

Wanna Hold You (Jagger-Richards) 3.52
Keith Richards: guitar, lead vocals
Bill Wyman: bass guitar
Keith Richards and Ronnie Wood: guitars
Charlie Watts: drums
Mick Jagger and Keith Richards: backing vocals

The CD re-issue contained an additional half-minute to what was now a customary inclusion of at least one lead vocal by Richards per album. Patti Hansen, the soon-to-be-second Mrs. Richards, was the muse for what might have been described in swinging sixties reviewer's parlance as a blues chaser as Keith ponders a golden future with a girl at his side and a song in his heart.

Feel On Baby (Jagger-Richards) 5.07
Mick Jagger: guitar, lead vocals
Charlie Watts: drums
Chuck Leavell: keyboards
Moustapha Cisse and Brahms Coundoul: percussion
Keith Richards and Ronnie Wood: guitars
Robbie Shakespeare: bass guitar
Sly Dunbar: synthesiser drums

An attempt at Rude Boy music was the merging of the Stones with Sly and Robbie. Thankfully, Jagger neither breaks into patois nor puts on a West Indian accent as Ray Davies did on 1970's 'Apeman' by the Kinks.

Too Much Blood (Jagger-Richards) 6.14

Mick Jagger: guitar, all vocals
Keith Richards, Ronnie Wood and Jim Barber: guitars
Moustapha Cisse and Brahms Coundoul: percussion
Bill Wyman: bass guitar
Chuck Leavel: keyboards
Various: brass and woodwinds
Charlie Watts and Sly Dunbar: drums

I hope Mick's poor old mother never heard this journey into Alice Cooper terrain. As horns blasted up the central riff, a tune that dissolved into monotonal and savage rap, albeit with a tang of grace-saving humour, posed the tacit question: was Jagger projecting himself into a situation or did it really happen? Subsequent research has uncovered a news story about a murder followed by cannibalism in Paris that is to 'Too Much Blood' as the utterances of the Boston Strangler were to 'Midnight Rambler'. There are also references to 1974's gory *Texas Chainsaw Massacre* movie.

Pretty Beat Up (Jagger-Richards-Wood) 4.04

Mick Jagger: guitar, lead vocals
Keith Richards: bass guitar
Ronnie Wood: backing vocals
Various: brass and woodwinds
Chuck Leavell and Martin Ditcham: percussion
Keith Richards and Ronnie Wood: guitars
Charlie Watts: drums
Bill Wyman and Chuck Leavell: keyboards
David Sanbourn: saxophone solo

This began as a doubtful contender when a shortlist was being compiled from the 18 tracks taped during the *Undercover* sessions. There is nothing particularly special about this song apart from Wyman and Richards crossing the instrumental demarcation lines of Stones tradition once again.

Too Tough (Jagger-Richards) 3.52
Mick Jagger: guitar, lead vocals
Bill Wyman: bass guitar
Chuck Leavell: piano
Keith Richards and Ronnie Wood: guitars
Charlie Watts: drums

The album's final US single, this was a mere mopping-up operation with only a solo by Wood against a propelling riff raising it above the ordinary.

All The Way Down (Jagger-Richards) 3.14
Mick Jagger: guitar, lead vocals
Ronnie Wood: bass guitar
Chuck Leavell: keyboards
Keith Richards and Ronnie Wood: guitars
Charlie Watts: drums
Mick Jagger and Keith Richards: backing vocals

Typical Rolling Stones up-tempo fare, the decision to position it and 'Pretty Beat Up' and 'Too Tough' in the middle section of Side Two was an entirely correct one.

It Must Be Hell (Jagger-Richards) 5.04
Mick Jagger: guitar, lead vocals
Bill Wyman: bass guitar
Ian Stewart and Martin Ditcham: percussion
Keith Richards and Ronnie Wood: backing vocals
Keith Richards and Ronnie Wood: guitars
Charlie Watts: drums
Chuck Leavel: keyboards

The thoughtful lyrics of this companion piece to 'Undercover Of The Night' were not matched by music that regurgitated maddeningly familiar aspects of previous Stones tracks.

DIRTY WORK

UK Release: 24 March 1986
US Release: 24 March 1986
Intl CD No: CBS CDCBS465953 2
Producer: Steve Lillywhite and The Glimmer Twins
Running Time: 40:04

CBS 86321
Rolling Stones Records 40250

SIDE ONE: One Hit (To The Body); Fight; Harlem Shuffle; Hold Back; Too Rude.

SIDE TWO: Winning Ugly; Back To Zero; Dirty Work; Had It With You; Sleep Tonight.

Partly because increasingly longer periods between tours had loosened bonds, the Glimmer Twins were no longer as inseparable as they once were. Keith Richards' perspective was that 'up until the beginning of the 80s, you could have called me up at the North Pole and Mick at the South Pole, and we would have said the same thing. We were that close. I didn't change, but he did. He became obsessed with age – his own and others. I don't see the point of pretending that you are 25 when you're not'.

Mick Jagger didn't retaliate with matching venom, but his schism with Keith didn't help the atmosphere that informed the overall spirit of *Dirty Work*. Before sessions had been so much as booked, a mere attempt at pre-production work had driven Charlie Watts, who was then trying to cope with grave domestic and personal turmoils, over the brink. A tipsy Jagger's reference to Watts as 'my drummer' was the ignition point for an outburst of swearing and fisticuffs in a hotel's dining room and a shouted 'I am not your drummer! You're my singer!' prior to a petering out that left Charlie glowering at Mick and Mick not daring to credit the glint in the eye of the standard-bearer of group stability.

If it hadn't been Jagger, Watts might have focused his resentment at life in general at that time at Keith's incurable lateness, Keith and Mick's disintegrating concord or a tape operator who hummed all the bloody time. Furthermore, Bill had been talking with increasing frequency of his long-mooted plan to quit the group and was surrendering more and more of the bass playing chores to others. However it wouldn't be possible to work out precisely who did what from *Dirty Work*'s scrawly sleeve information, that included a lyric sheet for the first time that looked as if it had been written in crayon by a child.

The Glimmer Twins brought in Steve Lillywhite as a third producer, whose previous clients had included Ultravox, Steel Pulse whose biggest-selling single was a reggae revival of 'Prodigal Son', and U2. But the underlying tension couldn't be directed towards a healthy commercial end. 'One Hit (To The Body)' was the first Stones single to miss the domestic Top 50 completely and struggled in the US Top 40 as well. The way had been paved by a resurrection of 'Harlem Shuffle', a turntable hit on pirate radio in the mid-60s for soul duo Bob and Earl. This turned out to be the last unarguable smash on both sides of the ocean for a near future invested with a suspicion that the Stones were in a slow but sure decline. CBS derived what gain it could from the situation, but the group's previous handlers considered themselves lucky to have milked the Stones when they did.

The scum of internal disharmony that had risen to the surface of the seemingly unsolvable problem boiled down to Mick and Keith. Even on the most superficial level, the guitarist's constant retakes and overdubbing of minor fills were starting to pall, and the vocalist's fastidiousness in other creative areas was just as irritating. 'If we're doing a video, it's never right,' complained Charlie Watts, 'He can never just leave it alone. He has to go and spend another four thousand pounds.' Yet Watts had sympathized with Jagger when Richards chose to go on a holiday in Jamaica in the middle of mixing sessions for *Undercover*.

Fanning dull embers, Keith was to steer the Stones towards a relatively uncluttered follow-up album, but brisker finesse could not dispel what he perceived as Mick's malcontented shiftlessness and the general muttering about the sessions' similarity to those for *Exile On Main Street*. 'Mick was there so infrequently for *Dirty Work*,' he'd sigh in retrospect, 'It was just Charlie, Ronnie and me trying to make a Stones record. It was very unprofessional of Mick'.

Other than Charlie's outburst and the most subtle sleights of social judo, there had been no outright animosity or any sense that Wyman, Watts and Wood were waiting for either Jagger or Richards to call time on the Stones. 'It's a very English relationship,' Jagger would discern with the candour of greater age, 'where not a lot is said'. Nevertheless, the wheels of the Stones' universe were no longer as interlocking as they had been during the

ROLLING
STONES
DIRTY WORK

intimacies of their life-defining adolescent friendship into adult life.

The outfit's junior partners didn't feel qualified to unravel the tangled web of a middle-aged Jagger and Richards' liaison. Watts attributed 'a combination of Keith's spirit and Mick's drive' as the key to the Stones' longevity: 'You could say Keith brings emotion and Mick brings direction. Mick on his own would have lost the way years ago if he hadn't had Keith to bounce off and vice-versa, because without Mick pushing, there's no way we would have been able to do it for this long'.

Jagger was coming to understand why Wyman didn't want to be a Rolling Stone unto the grave. He and the bass player seemed to be drifting apart too. 'Seven or eight years ago, I could talk with Mick about books, films and intelligent things,' agreed Bill, 'but now I just talk to him in asides'.

The mist of closure shrouding the Stones thickened as, between *Undercover* and *Dirty Work*, Jagger had been allocated several weeks at pricey Compass Point Studios for his first solo LP, *She's The Boss*. It was an undertaking guaranteed to generate more media interest than 1976's *Stone Alone*, Wyman's second in his own right, *Gimme Some Neck*, Ronnie's third, or Keith's pot-shot at the singles chart with Chuck Berry's 'Run Rudolph Run' in 1979. Even Charlie's extra-mural jazz combos had released records.

It wasn't possible to pour oil over the present troubled waters by insisting that Mick's maiden offering would enrich the group as a whole any more than another cliché defined as musical differences, would ring true if the sundering of the Stones had been announced formally. The split wasn't decisive enough for that although Keith apparently had opened a 'what if?' dialogue with Roger Daltrey.

Had it come to it, Daltrey might have jumped at the chance as the Who weren't much of a group anymore either. This had been painfully obvious to Jagger when he walked in on a backstage tongue-lashing that seemed bereft of any underlying affection: 'I learned a lesson from The Who being on the road when they were not getting on. It embarrassed me, and made me feel sad and I don't want to see The Rolling Stones like that. When you're not getting on, don't push it in public. I don't want to stand still and wait for the problems to go away, for everyone to come around and be in the right mood. I love the Stones, but it cannot be at my age the only thing in my life.'

An obvious indication of this was a resuscitation on 45 of Martha and the Vandellas'

'Dancing In The Street' by Jagger and David Bowie as a fund-raiser for the globally transmitted Live Aid. Created in eight hours, a video of Mick and David doing their bit was screened prior to the former's appearance in person at Philadelphia's JFK Stadium on 13 July 1985. It was 20 years to the day after the Stones were at No. 1 in the US with 'Satisfaction'. At the same outside broadcast from the same location, Richards and Wood had provided guitar accompaniment to three numbers by Bob Dylan that had preceded Live Aid's big finish.

Thus the century's final decade loomed with The Rolling Stones about to scatter like rats distrubed in a granary, and Jagger foreseen as the most engaging and commercially operative member, apparently under no economic or artistic pressure to ever tread the boards with the group again. He gave an outward impression too of a person completely in command of his faculties, an affluent family man in perfect health with only the most transient worries. However, Keith Richards perceived that his old pal was 'not living a happy life. Ninety-nine per cent of the male population of the Western World – and beyond – would give a limb to be him, but he's not happy being Mick Jagger'.

Still, he'd breezed into sessions in April 1985 at the new Pathe-Marconi complex in Paris with the self-possession to offer little in the the first instance beyond some notions computed in his brain, having expended – so Richards speculated – less nebulous ones on *She's The Boss*. Fortunately for Keith, Ronnie was only too pleased to help with the composition of no less than four *Dirty Work* tracks that emerged both before and after a two-month break.

When work resumed in New York's RPM Studios and at Right Track in another part of the same city, it was becoming clear that the album was to be commensurate with Keith's unwavering agenda that 'every number could be played live, simply, easy'. He'd been metaphorically rubbing his hands with the contemplation of recording it. 'Then we finished the record,' he grimaced, 'and Mick suddenly said, "I ain't going on no road" so that was the plug pulled from under me [sic].'

Though 'Lonely At The Top', co-written with Richards in 1979, had opened *She's The Boss*, Keith's discontent about this enterprise and Mick's open preparations for solo dates in Japan and Australasia taking precedent over the new Stones album and a possible tour impacted on a couple of *Dirty Work* pieces sung by Richards himself, 'Treat Me Like A Fool' and 'Knock

Your Teeth Out One By One'. They were, perhaps an extrapolation of a naked threat: 'If Mick tours without the band, I'll slit his throat.'

Jagger countered with 'Occasionally, you want to strangle even the closest of friends', and the two staged a fight for the benefit of hovering media during the shoot of the 'One Hit' video. This was passed off as a bit of a lark, but storm clouds were gathering. 'I couldn't deal with it any more,' shrugged Keith, 'It's like a marriage. Friction builds up over the years.'

Sibling rivalry intensified into railing at each other in the press, sometimes with almost audible sniggers. Over the next two years, there were periods when only the rare postcard filtered between Jagger and Richards. Other than these, they knew each other only by what was in the newspapers, the same as everyone else.

As 1987 got underway, Jagger made a second album without the other Stones and Richards recorded his first, *Talk Is Cheap*. Like *Dirty Work*, it was uninflated with gratuitous frills and had been designed to be performed on the boards without much difficulty because two could play at Jagger's game. In the same month as the final date of Mick's jaunt down under in November 1988, Keith embarked on a fortnight of engagements across the States with The X-Pensive Winos, an amalgam of the less illustrious *Talk Is Cheap* assistants.

Meanwhile, the unloved *Dirty Work* earned another platimum disc for The Rolling Stones, albeit a Rolling Stones who couldn't care less anymore.

One Hit (To The Body) (Jagger-Richards-Wood) 4.44
Mick Jagger: lead vocals
Keith Richards, Ronnie Wood and Jimmy Page: guitars
Beverly D'Angelo, Don Covay, Jimmy Cliff, Kirsty MacColl, Patti Scialfa and Bobby Womack: backing vocals
Bill Wyman: bass guitar
Charlie Watts: drums
Anton Fig: percussion
Chuck Leavell and Ivan Neville: keyboards

On this statement of intent, a diverse cast of big-name contributors included Covay – still much admired by Jagger – and MacColl, who happened to be Lillywhite's wife. She had just entered the UK Top Ten for the second time, but was quite willing to provide backing vocals. Ivan Neville is the son of New Orleans soul man Aaron. Jimmy Page had been involved with Bill Wyman in Willie and the Poor Boys, a supergroup formed in the mid-80s for events in aid of ARMS (Action For Muscular Sclerosis).

Fight (Jagger-Richards-Wood) 3.09
Mick Jagger: lead vocals
Keith Richards and Ronnie Wood: guitars
Ronnie Wood: bass guitar and pedal steel guitar
Keith Richards, Ronnie Wood, Kirtsy MacColl, Janis Pendarvis and Dolette MacDonald: backing vocals
Charlie Watts: drums
Chuck Leavell: organ

Symptomatic of Bill Wyman's waning interest, Wood throbs bass on this assault-in-song, having first switched to the instrument in 1968 when he joined The Jeff Beck Group, straight from playing lead guitar with The Creation.

Harlem Shuffle (Relf-Nelson) 3.24
Mick Jagger: lead vocals
Bill Wyman: bass guitar
Anton Fig: percussion
Keith Richards, Bobby Womack,
Ivan Neville, and Don Covay: backing vocals
Keith Richards and Ronnie Wood: guitars
Charlie Watts: drums
Chuck Leavell and Ivan Neville: keyboards

A fixture on Keith's car cassette player, Bob and Earl's floor-filler was, he said, 'probably the first disco record. The sound and beat were very connectable to that early disco stuff.' He'd first heard it pulsating in the Scotch Of St. James, the Bag O' Nails and similar London in-clubs in the dear, dead swinging sixties. Since then it had found its way time and time again onto the turntable at Up The Junction in Crewe, Stoke-on-Trent's Golden Torch and other early storm centres of what was to coalesce as Northern Soul when Wigan's celebrated Casino Soul Club opened in 1973. However, the Northern Soul scene and disco fever in general had become sufficiently passé for the Stones' revival of 'Harlem Shuffle' with guitars and keyboards replacing the original horns to bring much of the aura of a fresh sensation to the charts. Climbing to No. 13 in Britain and No. 5 in the US, it was the first non-original Stones A side single since 'Little Red Rooster' in 1964 apart from the live *Still Life* singles.

Hold Back (Jagger-Richards) 3.53
Mick Jagger: lead vocals
Ivan Neville: bass guitar
Charlie Watts: drums
Keith Richards and Ronnie Wood: guitars
Chuck Leavell: organ

If reduced to the acid-test of just voice and piano or guitar, this isn't much of a song. Indeed, it was saved from the cutting-room floor only by the forceful gusto of the drums and Neville's second attempt at a bass line.

Too Rude (Roberts) 3.11
Mick Jagger: lead vocals
Keith Richards and Ronnie Wood: guitars
Chuck Leavell: piano
Keith Richards, Ronnie Wood and Jimmy Cliff: backing vocals
Bill Wyman: bass guitar
Charlie Watts: drums
Phillippe Saisse: percussion

Montego Bay ska exponent Cliff's 'The Harder They Come' had been the B side of Keith's 'Run Rudolph Run' and much the same chopping reggae backbeat carries this item from the canon of Sly and Robbie.

Winning Ugly (Jagger-Richards) 4.32
Mick Jagger: lead vocals
Keith Richards and Ronnie Wood: guitars
Mick Jagger, Kirsty MacColl, Patti Schialfa, Janis Pendarvis and Dolette MacDonald: backing vocals
Bill Wyman: bass guitar
Charlie Watts: drums
Chuck Leavell: keyboards

Multiple guitar overdubs support a riff that in turn supports a song that wouldn't have been out of place on *She's The Boss*.

Back To Zero (Jagger-Richards-Leavell) 4.00
Mick Jagger: all vocals
Keith Richards, Ronnie Wood and Jimmy Page: guitars
Bill Wyman and Chuck Leavell: keyboards
Charlie Watts: drums
Ronnie Wood: bass guitar
Steve Jordan and Anton Fig: percussion
Dan Collette: trumpet

A drummer on albums by Joan Armatrading and a rejuvenated Link Wray in the late 70s, Fig and this song's co-writer Leavell figured on Jagger's first solo album also. An educated guess is that the libretto about impending nuclear holocaust was all Mick's own work.

Dirty Work (Jagger-Richards-Wood) 3.53
Mick Jagger: lead vocals
Charlie Watts: drums
Keith Richards, Ronnie Wood and Mick Jagger: guitars
Bill Wyman: bass guitar
Chuck Leavell: organ
Keith Richards and Tom Waits: backing vocals

Fans searching for autobiographical profundities in Stones lyrics would find much food for thought in this ditty. With a sub-flavour of animosity and severe irritation, it's about someone not pulling his or her weight in a relationship that could be personal, professional or both. It was getting beyond a joke.

Had It With You (Jagger-Richards-Wood) 3.19
Mick Jagger: all vocals, harmonica
Charlie Watts: drums
Keith Richards and Ronnie Wood: guitars
Ronnie Wood: saxophone

The f-word lacerates the very first line of an item that Stones-ologists might conclude was a Richards-Wood effort with 11th-hour adjustments by Jagger. A hard fact was that Ronnie honking a subtle sax undercurrent justified the decision to erase the bass guitar track.

Sleep Tonight (Jagger-Richards) 5.11
Keith Richards: lead vocals, piano
Ronnie Wood: drums
Chuck Leavell: synthesiser
Ronnie Wood, Kirsty MacColl, Patti Scialfa, Don Covay, Janis Pendarvis, Tom Waits and Dolette MacDonald: backing vocals
Bill Wyman: bass guitar
Keith Richards and Ronnie Wood: guitars
Tom Waits: piano

Richards had just guested on 1985's *Rain Dogs* by Waits, an artist whose public image of a booze-addled bohemian was akin to that of Richards who makes a fair fist of a countrified chastisement of a lover who's had too much fun. The talented Wood deputised for Watts who had broken his leg after a fall in the cellar of his Devon manor house.

Boogie-Woogie Dream (Ammons) 0.33
Ian Stewart: piano
The inclusion of an unlisted *Dirty Work* postscript, paid respects to Ian Stewart, the only true sixth Rolling Stone, who died suddenly on 12 December 1985 in London. This is him pounding out a solo instrumental by Albert Ammons, one of the most boisterous and compelling barrelhouse pianists of the 40s.

STEEL WHEELS

US Release: 28 August 1989
UK Release: 29 August 1989
Intl CD No: CBS CDCBS465752 2
Producers: Chris Kimsey and
The Glimmer Twins

Rolling Stones Records/CBS 4657521
Rolling Stones Records 45333
Running Time: 53:05

SIDE ONE: Sad Sad Sad; Mixed Emotions; Terrifying; Hold On To Your Hat; Hearts For Sale; Blinded By Love.

SIDE TWO: Rock And A Hard Place; Can't Be Seen; Almost Hear You Sigh; Continental Drift; Break The Spell; Slipping Away.

Mick Jagger's non-Stones ventures since *Dirty Work* had predictably been the most marketable though figures for Keith Richards' *Talk Is Cheap* had been healthy enough for moderate placings in Top 40s around the world. Nevertheless, after their longest period apart artistically, the estranged boyhood friends had experienced different revelations and arrived at the same conclusion: that there was to be no more circling round the issue with solo albums. They anchored themselves to the notion that they were going to be Rolling Stones once more and would have to put up with constantly being told that their best work was behind them. They may have been aware, for example, of *The Counterfeit Stones*, a tribute band then undertaking its first bookings with a repertoire containing nothing beyond the mid-70s.

It would be easier, so Mick and Keith had each thought independently, for the genuine articles to let go, stop trying to prove themselves, get out of step with the strident march of computer-proficient hip-hop, techno, acid house et al, and go back to making music that felt like it was hanging on a thread.

In part, time had healed, and there lingered memories of the struggle back in 1962 and its fantastic outcome when, on 18 May 1988, at the Savoy in London, Messrs. Richards, Wyman, Watts and Jagger with Ronnie Wood were in the same room for the first time in two years. There were moments when the meeting was more like corporation presidents discussing a merger than five old pals seeing how feasible it was to play together again. After loosening up with

ROLLING STONES STEEL WHEELS

selective reminiscences, it was agreed that the only barriers to picking up where they'd left off in 1986 were outstanding extra-curricular commitments and what Keith referred to as the 'family squabble. If I shout and scream at Mick, it's because no-one else has the guts to do it'.

Richards and Jagger each kept civil tongues in their heads over a drink in New York three months later when they decided to rent a house near Eddy Grant's studio in Barbados – neutral territory between respective spreads in Jamaica (Keith) and Mustique (Mick) – to see how full the Jagger-Richards songwriting well was and whether they could bear to be on the same lump of plastic as each other again. As his wife waved him off, Keith told her to expect him back in either two days or two months 'because I'll know within 48 hours whether this thing is going to work or if we are just going to be catting and dogging'.

The outcome was the two finding themselves working out chord changes and words for several new songs that were more Stones than *Primitive Cool* or *Talk Is Cheap* had been. Many of them were composed on a synthesiser that Jagger was to donate afterwards to Instruments International, a chidren's music charity.

These creations in Barbados and others that came later were to fill *Steel Wheels*, the recording of which was notable for accomplishing more in one evening than in the weeks of retakes and scrapped tracks that had had to be endured for *Dirty Work* and certain of its predecessors. 'In the past, we've spent too long looking at the ceiling,' explained Mick, 'getting really frustrated, waiting for the great inspiration. It makes for very long drawn-out sessions with not particularly good results. This inevitably leads to friction'.

The unadorned production criteria and sparser ensemble work coincided with a worldwide resurgence of garage bands. While the Stones weren't to tread the backwards path as much as British outfits of the genre like Thee (sic) Headcoats and The Inmates, the exhilaration of spontaneity was prized more than technical accuracy during the three months between the early spring and midsummer of 1989 that were needed to record *Steel Wheels*: 'the meanest rock'n'roll machine to hit the streets this summer', glowed the *New Musical Express*. Indeed, it could have been Keith talking about what he perceived as the rough-and-readiness of *Talk Is Cheap*, when, at the press conference at Grand Central Station, Mick concurred, 'Yes, a lot of it sounds really garagey. We didn't want it to sound too tidy, so we just followed our instincts'.

However, form didn't overrule content and the aim wasn't to make every track grippingly slipshod. As well as booking time at London's Olympic Sound and George Martin's Air Studios in

Monserrat where co-producer Chris Kimsey had been engaged on an album by the reconstituted Yes, the Stones also managed a side trip to Morocco in May to add icing to the backing track of the outstanding 'Continental Drift'. They dipped into this geographical casket of non-western culture as freely as Malcolm McLaren, Adam and the Ants and Peter Gabriel had over the previous ten years.

At Palais Ben Abbou in the Casbah just beyond Tangier, the Stones and their sound crew superimposed onto the *Steel Wheels* musical grid, the hand-drums and high-pitched rhaita pan-pipes played by The Master Musicians Of Joujouka, the tribal ensemble discovered by Brian Jones in 1966 and taped for the posthumously released *Brian Jones Presents The Pipes Of Pan At Joujouka*.

The Stones were also augmented by musicians who would remain with them for much longer. These were a variegated bunch. The two keyboard players had come from the most markedly different backgrounds. Matt Clifford, a former Gloucester cathedral chorister, had been working on the Yes project with Chris Kimsey while, from North America's deep south, Chuck Leavell had passed through the ranks of the laid-back Allman Brothers Band, who had been to New York what Delaney and Bonnie and Friends had been to Los Angeles.

Of the backing vocalists, Lisa Fischer had sung with Philly Soul lurve man Luther Vandross, and was destined for a modicom of solo stardom in the early 90s. She had also been part of the troupe on Jagger's solo tours, as had Bernard Fowler, a dreadlocked New Yorker. He wasn't old enough to be steeped in post-war jazz traditions, but was to become the singer with The Charlie Watts Quintet, having picked up the basic principles quickly enough to deliver the goods on *From One Charlie To Another*, an album genuflection by Watts to legendary bebop saxophonist Charlie Parker that was released in 1993.

While Leavell had been a Stones associate on and off since 1981, the injection of new blood may have had a subliminal effect on the critical weighing of *Steel Wheels*'s faults and merits. As it span its little vinyl life away, the rhetorical question on most lips was along the lines of 'Who'd have thought that the old boys still had it in them?' This was reflected in the album coming within an ace of topping the charts on both sides of the Atlantic and boded well for the world tour that tied-in with its release.

Sad Sad Sad (Jagger-Richards) 3.35

Mick Jagger: guitar, lead vocals
Keith Richards: guitar
Ronnie Wood: bass guitar
Charlie Watts: drums
Chuck Leavell: piano, organ
Bernard Fowler: backing vocals
The Kick Horns: brass and woodwinds

Nothing very constructive can be said about the musical content of this up-tempo rocker. Like railway lines or donkey's false teeth, it's just there. The lyrics, however, seem to involve Jagger projecting himself into the Chas character's situation in the opening scenes of *Performance* when a casual bedmate overstays her welcome.

Mixed Emotions (Jagger-Richards) 4.39

Mick Jagger: guitar, lead vocals, maraccas
Keith Richards and Ronnie Wood: guitars
Bill Wyman: bass guitar
Charlie Watts: drums
Chuck Leavell: piano, organ
Luis Jardim: percussion
Keith Richards, Bernard Fowler, Sarah Dash and Lisa Fischer: backing vocals
The Kick Horns: brass and woodwinds

Buoyed by a horn section assembled initially for a solo tour by Pink Floyd's Dave Gilmour, this was, reputedly, Jagger's response to 'You Don't Move Me', Richards's spelt-out swipe at him on *Talk Is Cheap*. More and more in those days, Mick was playing rhythm guitar in the studio, and it is particularly distinctive in this medium-tempo setting – as is Leavell's Hammond organ that is like a Saxon church in Manhattan when heard among the new-fangled synthesisers that crop up elsewhere.

Terrifying (Jagger-Richards) 4.53

Mick Jagger: lead vocals, maraccas
Keith Richards and Ronnie Wood: guitars
Bill Wyman: bass guitar
Charlie Watts: drums
Chuck Leavell: organ
Matt Clifford: keyboards
Keith Richards and Lisa Fischer: backing vocals
Roddy Corimer: trumpet

Initially this appears to open a Pandora's box of bestial predelictions, but was probably nothing more than a 'shopping list' lyric of similitudes to carry a slightly jazz-tinged tune strong enough to warrant the track's edit for release as an afterthought single in Britain.

Hold On To Your Hat (Jagger-Richards) 3.32
Mick Jagger: guitar, lead vocals
Keith Richards: guitar
Charlie Watts: drums
Ronnie Wood: bass guitar
Though uncredited, Watts had a hand in the creative development of a song in which drums are of finely-honed clarity.

Hearts For Sale (Jagger-Richards) 4.40
Mick Jagger: guitar, lead vocals, harmonica
Keith Richards and Ronnie Wood: guitars
Bill Wyman; bass guitar
Charlie Watts: drums
Matt Clifford: keyboards
Bernard Fowler: backing vocals
Jagger quotes a line from The Supremes' 'You Keep Me Hangin' On' out of context in a number with a more shadowy link to the Peggy Lee cabaret standard, 'When The World Was Young', concerning the strange depression of a cynical hedonist given to routine unfaithfulness.

Blinded By Love (Jagger-Richards) 4.37
Mick Jagger: guitar, lead vocals
Keith Richards and Ronnie Wood: guitars
Bill Wyman: bass guitar
Charlie Watts: drums
Chuck Leavell: organ
Matt Clifford: piano, harmonium
Luis Jardim: percussion
Phil Beer: violin, mandolin
Keith Richards and Bernard Fowler: backing vocals
Possibly with the aid of a word-processor, Jagger was now crafting his lyrics extremely carefully. On this occasion he picked the brains of younger brother Chris. This is *Steel Wheels* at its most folky, as instanced by the hiring of Beer, later half of Show Of Hands, a duo described in a press release as 'Britain's foremost acoustic group'.

Rock And A Hard Place (Jagger-Richards) 5.25

Mick Jagger: guitar, lead vocals
Keith Richards and Ronnie Wood: guitars
Bill Wyman: bass guitar
Charlie Watts: drums
Chuck Leavell and Matt Clifford: keyboards
The Kick Horns: brass and woodwinds
Bernard Fowler, Sarah Dash and Lisa Fischer: backing vocals

This concert favourite attempted to address in broad terms such recent issues as east mingling freely with west after the Berlin Wall came down in 1989. As the album's second single, it should have bucked the law of diminishing returns by climbing at least as high as the first, 'Mixed Emotions' (No. 36 in Britain and No. 5 in the US). But in the teeth of much radio play, it seized up at No. 23 in the States and a lowly No. 63 at home.

Can't Be Seen (Jagger-Richards) 4.10

Keith Richards: guitar, lead vocals
Bill Wyman: bass guitar
Charlie Watts: drums
Ronnie Wood: guitar
Bernard Fowler: backing vocals
Chuck Leavell: keyboards
Matt Clifford: clavinet

In a voice that was a Kentish cross between Bobs Dylan and Marley, Richards sings of the dangers of his fornication and his woman's greater sin of adultery becoming public knowledge on an item that could have been seated more comfortably around the middle of side two on *Talk Is Cheap*.

Almost Hear You Sigh (Jagger-Richards-Jordan) 4.37

Mick Jagger: lead vocals
Bill Wyman: bass guitar
Keith Richards and Ronnie Wood: guitars
Charlie Watts: drums
Chuck Leavell and Matt Clifford: keyboards
Luis Jardim: percussion
Keith Richards, Ronnie Wood, Bernard Fowler, Sarah Dash and Lisa Fischer: backing vocals

While Jagger received a mandatory composing credit, this ballad was almost entirely the work of Richards and Steve Jordan, a power behind the scenes on *Talk Is Cheap*. The sharp-eyed had spotted him beating drums in the 1980s Blues Brothers movie starring Keith's friend, John Belushi. As a single, it struggled wretchedly to No. 50 in the States, but crept to the edge of the Top 30 in Britain.

Continental Drift (Jagger-Richards) 5.14
Mick Jagger: guitar, lead vocals, keyboards
Keith Richards: guitar, percussion
Charlie Watts: drums
Ronnie Wood: double bass
Matt Clifford: synthesiser, orchestration
Bill Wyman: bass guitar
Sinia Morgan, Tessa Niles, Bernard Fowler, Sarah Dash and Lisa Fischer: backing vocals
Chuck Leavell and Matt Clifford: keyboards
The Master Musicians Of Jajouka: African instruments
That the album's most startling track was not one of its A sides may have been because of the difficulties inherent in reproducing it on stage. It had necessitated a twinning of the Stones and The Master Musicians of Jajouka to infuse it with an essential ingredient of North African mysticism. 'Brian Jones turned us onto it years ago,' admitted Mick Jagger, 'and I wanted to try something in the same vein myself. To be honest, I thought it would end up on one of my solo records. I never thought the Stones would buy it, but Keith was well into it. We worked something out on a keyboard first and then went to Morocco to record the real thing. In a way, it's a continuation of the 'Paint It Black' *Satanic Majesties* thing, but heading off a bit more into Brian's territory. It's the same group Brian recorded more than 20 years ago.'

'It is as though the spirit of Brian Jones has entered into the music,' agreed an *NME* appraisal, 'It is both a moving and an honest tribute to yet another master musician.' Nonetheless, handbills distributed outside London's Royal Festival Hall in May 1999 claimed that The Master Musicians Of Jajouka appearing there that month and, by implication, on 'Continental Drift' were not the genuine article.

Break The Spell (Jagger-Richards) 3.07

Mick Jagger: guitar, lead vocals, harmonica
Keith Richards: guitars
Ronnie Wood: dobro guitar
Charlie Watts: drums
Matt Clifford: keyboards

'Make me break this spell' had been the opening line of 'Shapes In My Mind', a 1966 solo 45 by Keith Relf of The Yardbirds. Perhaps a mental flash of this may have been the first shovel of coal in the furnace that inched Jagger and Richards' corporate train of thought forward. The result was a lyric freighted with seasonal metaphors for a broken love affair against a backing track that, compared to 'Continental Drift', was business as usual.

Slipping Away (Jagger-Richards) 4.30

Keith Richards: lead vocals
Keith Richards and Ronnie Wood: guitars
Chuck Leavell: piano, organ
Mick Jagger, Keith Richards, Bernard Fowler, Sara Dash and Lisa Fischer: backing vocals
Bill Wyman: bass guitar
Charlie Watts: drums
Matt Clifford: piano and synthesised strings
The Kick Horns: brass and woodwinds

Keith's relatively smooth singing suits a sombre, appositely titled and pretty-but-nothing opus about inevitable loss. It was probably remaindered from *Talk Is Cheap*.

FLASHPOINT

US Release: 2 April 1991

UK Release: 8 April 1991
Producer: The Glimmer Twins

Rolling Stones Records/Columbia RS 47456
Sony 468135.2
Running Time: 76.12

SIDE ONE: Continental Drift; Start Me Up; Sad Sad Sad; Miss You; Rock And A Hard Place; Ruby Tuesday; You Can't Always Get What You Want; Factory Girl; Can't Be Seen; Little Red Rooster.

SIDE TWO: Paint It Black; Sympathy For The Devil; Brown Sugar; Jumpin' Jack Flash; (I Can't Get No) Satisfaction; Highwire; Sex Drive.

The first in-concert album in a decade, this souvenir of the *Steel Wheels* tour was taken from stops in North America, Japan and Europe and supplemented by two studio tracks and a 12-page booklet. Mostly it was reprises of many old favourites, although the group explored a few remote pathways too on an offering that was well-received both critically and commercially. It reached No. 17 in the States and No. 6 in Britain, where it was also deemed to be worthwhile issuing it in a vinyl format (Sony 468135 1).

At times it had been just Watts, Wyman, Richards, Jagger and Wood pleasing themselves rather than their audience, seizing songs by the scruff of the neck and wringing the life out of them. But now they were showbiz enough to back-project and even line up to take a bow at the end. However, the starkly functional guitars-bass-drums-vocals core and the thrilling margin of error remained as potent as they had been in 1963. And on *Flashpoint* more than on any other of the outfit's live releases, it was almost the sound at any given moment that counted more than individual numbers.

Augmented by the now-customary horns, backing singers and keyboard players, the Stones had warmed up for the trek in front of a lucky few hundred in New Haven's Toad's Night Club. However, 55 minutes on its small stage, was roughly like a Channel swimmer crossing Dover harbour a few times. On the road, Mick Jagger especially would have to pace himself over three hours before a vast, self-instigated backdrop, 'quite industrial, quite moody', making the most of when his movements were restricted by stints on rhythm guitar and, to a greater degree, during Keith Richards' solitary lead vocal outing.

The customers still expected him to sweat away pounds as he goaded himself, the group and his onlookers to near-collapse. Never sacrificing impassioned content for technical virtuosity, he drew from an arsenal of facial expressions, flickering hand-ballets and more exertive antics, plus enhancements such as the inflatable Rottweiler that swallowed him during 'Street Fighting Man' as he bombarded the audience with the characters and scenarios of songs. 'Off stage, the problem is keeping your feet on the ground,' he mused, 'It's very, very difficult. You do get very prima-donna-ish and very wrapped up in your own inflated ego.'

No opera diva was more pampered. Daily voice-coaching sessions were yet to come, but his body was massaged by Dorothy 'Dr. Dot' Stein, as illustrious in her field as he was in his, and his make-up was applied by the similarly highly waged Pierre Laroche who also serviced David Bowie, Sophia Loren, Joan Collins, Charlotte Rampling and Anjelica Houston. 'If someone has droopy eyes,' explained Laroche,'I will work at making them even droopier. If someone has a big nose, I will emphasize that nose.' It is possible to guess which of Jagger's features received such attention.

US comedienne Joan Rivers delivered a televised monologue centred on Mick and his 'child-bearing lips' in the midst of the jaunt that touched its home base in summer 1990. One of three Wembley Stadium concerts coincided with a World Cup soccer match involving England, splitting the concentration of both those with transistor radios glued to their ears and those onstage, especially when a sudden burst of cheering when England scored a goal punctuated a hush between numbers.

The local-boys-made-good's time on the boards flew by as quickly as the reading of a page-turning thriller, and they pulled a far bigger audience than Frank Sinatra who was crooning to seven thousand on plastic seats at the London Arena that same night. Moreover, the Stones were to finish the year voted the Greatest Rockers of All Time in a poll by US periodical *Entertainment Weekly*. Bob Dylan was in second place and The Beatles were third.

RollingStones**Flashpoint**

Greatest Hits Live

Includes the single
Highwire

468135-1

THIS
ALBUM
CONTAINS
A 12 PAGE
BOOKLET

Except where otherwise stated, the line up throughout was as follows:

Mick Jagger: guitar, lead vocals, harmonica
Keith Richards and Ronnie Wood: guitars and backing vocals
Bobby Keyes and The Uptown Horns: brass and woodwinds
Bill Wyman: bass guitar
Charlie Watts: drums
Matt Clifford and Chuck Leavell: keyboards
Lisa Fischer, Bernard Fowler and Cindy Mizelle: backing vocals

As on all Rolling Stones in-concert albums, timing includes continuity and audience response.

Continental Drift (Jagger-Richards) 0.29
A pre-recorded clip from *Steel Wheels* ushers the principals onto the boards to the anticipated roar of the crowd.

Start Me Up (Jagger-Richards) 3.54
From Death Valley Stadium, Clemson, South Carolina, this was reportedly to be more remarkable for its pyrotechnical visual effects than its performance as vibrations in the air, but it still makes for a respectable start.

Sad Sad Sad (Jagger-Richards) 3.33
Jagger holds down guitar chords during the instrumental breaks on a work-out of a *Steel Wheels* item at Atlantic City Convention Centre.

Miss You (Jagger-Richards) 5.55
This was taken at a faster pace than usual but was extended not so much by soloing as repeated vocal lines.

Rock And A Hard Place (Jagger-Richards) 4.51
Caught in a coastline stadium in Florida, this neither adds nor subtracts from the *Steel Wheels* version. Once again, Jagger straps on an electric guitar.

Ruby Tuesday (Jagger-Richards) 3.34
This is a too premeditated modern reconstruction. The intrusion of technology, epitomised by a synthesised recorder/flute sound, leaves a peculiar afterglow, especially if the dusty old 1966 single holds emotional significance.

You Can't Always Get What You Want (Jagger-Richards) 7.26
The mob can't help but sing along with Mick during a painstakingly organic arrangement, even including a real as opposed to an electronically generated French horn, courtesy of the versatile Matt Clifford.

Factory Girl (Jagger-Richards) 2.48
Taped at Wembley Stadium, a resurrection of fourth track, side two of *Beggars Banquet* was a surprising, but an absorbing selection, judging by the relative hush from the ticket-holders.

Can't Be Seen (Jagger-Richards) 4.17
This rather routine Keith Richards lead-vocal outing and 'Rock And A Hard Place' were omitted from the vinyl pressing.

Little Red Rooster (Dixon) 5.15
A special treat at the Atlantic City stop on 19 December 1989 was the presence of Eric Clapton on the 1965 UK chart-topper.

Paint It Black (Jagger-Richards) 4.02
At Barcelona's Olympic Stadium, acoustic guitar rather than sitar opens another trip back to the swinging 60s.

Sympathy For The Devil (Jagger-Richards) 5.35
Beginning with what seems like an explosion, this excerpt from the show in Tokyo may have had Bill Wyman on backing vocals, because another recording in the States of the same opus the previous December certainly did.

Brown Sugar (Jagger-Richards) 4.10
The show at Stadio Delle Alpi in Turin, Italy was taped in its entirety, but only this fiery revisit to 1969 made it onto the album.

Jumpin' Jack Flash (Jagger-Richards) 5.00
Everyone within earshot of this finale during ten days at the same venue in Japan seems to be hostage to the beat, although Jagger deports himself as if he had all the time in the world.

(I Can't Get No) Satisfaction (Jagger-Richards) 6.08
We're back in the US for the encore, about which all I can say constructively is that it sounds like The Rolling Stones doing 'Satisfaction' and there will never be another like them.

Highwire (Jagger-Richards) 4.46
Mick Jagger: lead vocals and guitar
Keith Richards, Ronnie Wood, Mick Jagger and Bernard Fowler: backing vocals
Bill Wyman: bass guitar
Charlie Watts: drums
The first of the studio items was issued as a CD single and sneaked into the Top 30 in Britain and the US Top 20, despite unease among various media factions about the political opinions it expressed, which were as inflammable in their way as those in 'Street Fighting Man'. Plain but intense accompaniment.

Sex Drive (Jagger-Richards) 4.28
Mick Jagger: lead vocals
Keith Richards, Ronnie Wood and Mick Jagger: guitars
Mick Jagger, Katie Kissoon and Tessa Niles: backing vocals
Bill Wyman: bass guitar
Charlie Watts: drums
Various: brass and woodwinds
Love makes the world go round. Well, it often does when you're nearing 50 as Jagger was when, propelled by a hammered riff, he appears to allude to the sex therapy that was the crux of the jokey scenario in the associated video. Tessa Niles was a sometime member of Tina Turner's troupe while Trinidad's Katie Kissoon had, with her brother Mac, revived 'It's All Over Now' in 1971 as a flop prelude to five UK chart entries.

VOODOO LOUNGE

UK Release: 12 July 1994
US Release: 12 July 1994
Producers: Don Was and The Glimmer Twins

Virgin CDV2750
Virgin 39782
Running Time: 62:08

SIDE ONE: Love Is Strong; You Got Me Rocking; Sparks Will Fly;
SIDE TWO: The Worst; New Faces; Moon Is Up; Out Of Tears.

SIDE THREE: I Go Wild; Brand New Car; Sweethearts Together; Suck On The Jugular.
SIDE FOUR: Blinded By Rainbows; Baby Break It Down; Thru' And Thru'; Mean Disposition.

A general reawakening of enthusiasm for recording could be attributed to both a new recording partnership with Virgin Records and the long promised and amicable departure of 57-year-old Bill Wyman in spring 1993 after three decades as a Rolling Stone. This was regrettable rather than disastrous. The consequent change of personnel presented an opportunity to both refine known material and change stylistic habits.

After a moment's pause over the keys of their word-processors, some hacks reckoned that the most obvious candidates to replace Bill were John Entwistle and, once one-third of Cream, Jack Bruce, both at a loose end vocationally. The Who weren't much of a group any more, having not played together for three years. Since then, Entwistle had gone to ground on his Gloucestershire estate with slight deafness, a legacy of too many years of too many decibels. Putting his more avant-garde leanings on hold, Bruce was planning to take to the road in 1994 with a power trio completed by drummer Ginger Baker and guitarist Gary Moore. Focusing principally on the US, they'd break the ice each evening with an hour's worth of Cream favourites.

A list of other possibilities was pruned down and the final choice was left to Charlie Watts because, explained Keith Richards, 'what counts is what the drummer thinks. I said to Charlie, "You decide" – and he said, "You bastard, you put me in the hot seat!" and I said, "Yes, for once, Charlie, once in 30 years, you're going to be the supreme judge on this".'

Watts may have thought twice about Doug Wimbish from New York's Living Colour for

ROLLING STONES
VOODOO LOUNGE
WARNING!
THIS ALBUM
CONTAINS
LANGUAGE SOME
MAY FIND
OFFENSIVE
7243 8 39782 1 2
V 2750

whom an impressed Jagger had helped procure a recording contract and whose imput had left a mark on *Primitive Cool*, the solo album hot on the heels of *She's The Boss*. Indeed, Wimbish was to play on a couple of later Stones tracks after Watts' finger had pointed conclusively to Darryl Jones, another black North American who, if still in the cradle in his native Chicago when the Stones had first crept into the Top 30, wasn't exactly the pop equivalent of the chorus girl thrust into a sudden starring role. The main point in his favour for Charlie was that he'd played with Miles Davis, after attempting to audition over the telephone, and Gil Evans, not to mention Herbie Hancock and B.B. King. Indeed, there was nothing at all to suggest that Jones wasn't ideal. 'He's very comfortable to play with,' affirmed Watts, 'He's very quick to pick things up, very much a rhythm section within a rhythm section. He's underneath it – which is what we need really: foundation. He's a nice man as well'.

Another key long-term addition to the team was co-producer Don Was from Detroit who'd had a walk-on part in *Steel Wheels*. He was appointed mainly because, like the late Jimmy Miller, he combined supervisory skills with a background as a professional musician. Beginning as a multi-instrumental jazzer, the man born Donald Fagenson became richer after going pop in 1981 with the formation of Was (Not Was) and the assumption of his familiar alias. Was soon began making a name for himself as one of modern pop's most fashionable producers following his hand in 1989's flashy *Cosmic Thing* and 'Love Shack', its million-selling spin-off, by The B52s. Another feather in his cap for the Stones was a commission for *Under The Red Sky*, a Bob Dylan album with an all-star supporting cast.

Theoretically, Was was just what the Stones needed to steer them back into the brightest glare of the limelight, principally in his advocation of a leaner, more abandoned approach than on *Steel Wheels*. This, they agreed, would be commensurate with that of the leading executants of Britpop – a movement that borrowed heavily from a more optimistic age of British beat and was about to reach full bloom in the mid-90s before being reduced to mere chart ballast when absorbed into the main sequence of generalised pop.

Was recognised that the raw material he'd heard thus far was solid, even if the latest compositions were more 'Jagger and Richards' than 'Jagger-Richards'. On the run around the world, Keith and Mick couldn't have helped but get together in hotel rooms, tour buses and long-haul flight to tease songs from only a title or a melodic phrase but, dwelling on different land-masses, as they had been since *Steel Wheels*, they tended to present each other with numbers in more advanced states of completion. Nevertheless, they and Charlie Watts had spent a month in late spring of 1993 at Eddie Grant's complex in Barbados hammering out some workable ideas.

Throughout the summer, *Voodoo Lounge* shuddered into being at Ronnie Wood's home in St. Kildare, Ireland. From November to well into the New Year, further work was done in Dublin's Windmill Studios and then over in Los Angeles, commuting between Don Was's private Aladdin's cave of linked-up digital equipment and the A&M Recording Studios.

However, the sojourn in California could not wash away the effect of a creative environment. As Jagger affirmed, 'It's a good time-and-place album of what the Stones were about during that time in Ireland that year.' This was evidenced most blatantly in the hiring of indigenous violinist Frankie Galvin and the lyrical content of 'Blinded By Rainbows', referential to the Troubles in Ulster. When in the Emerald Isle too, the Stones were to guest on *Long Black Veil*, an album in preparation by The Chieftains, perhaps the most renowned virtuoso ambassadors of Irish traditional music.

That the momentum hadn't slackened despite the lay-off after *Steel Wheels* could be revealed in basic statistics. The group topped the British list for the first time since *Emotional Rescue* in 1980 and, in the States, *Voodoo Lounge* sold over five million within months and was on course to win a Grammy forthe year's Best Rock Album.

Love Is Strong (Jagger-Richards) 3.49
Mick Jagger: harmonica, lead vocals, maraccas
Charlie Watts: drums
Keith Richards, Bernard Fowler and Ivan Neville: backing vocals
Keith Richards and Ronnie Wood: guitars
Darryl Jones: bass guitar
Chuck Leavell: piano

This track derived from 'Wicked As It Seems', a track on *Main Offender*, Richards' second solo collection. Jagger's harmonica and unusually low-pitched vocal were strong selling points when this was picked as the first of no less than four *Voodoo Lounge* A sides, going straight in at No. 14 in Britain, but slipping from the Top 40 within a fortnight.

You Got Me Rocking (Jagger-Richards) 3.26
Mick Jagger: lead vocals, maraccas
Charlie Watts: drums
Keith Richards, Bernard Fowler and Ivan Neville: backing vocals
Keith Richards and Ronnie Wood: guitars
Darryl Jones: bass guitar
Chuck Leavell: piano

Of all the *Voodoo Lounge* items, this appeared to lend itself most readily to stage performance. It was largely Keith's baby and it was he who dominated a take in which the song was tried as a vocal duet. Moreover, now that the group was getting into its state-of-the-art stride with regard to re-mixes, this track would receive several such treatments when issued as a CD single. A percussion section by Steve Sidelnyk, an associate of The Soup Dragons, was layered onto all of them.

Sparks Will Fly (Jagger-Richards) 3.15
Mick Jagger: lead vocals
Charlie Watts: drums
Keith Richards and Bernard Fowler: backing vocals
Keith Richards and Ronnie Wood: guitars
Darryl Jones: bass guitar

A melody and dummy lyric were written virtually on the spot by Richards as a bonfire in Ronnie Wood's backyard subsided to glowing embers. Jagger penned new words that were too racy for much radio airplay until the mailing-out of an edited pressing.

The Worst (Jagger-Richards) 2.24
Keith Richards: guitar, lead vocals
Charlie Watts: drums
Darryl Jones: bass guitar
Frankie Gavin: violin
Ronnie Wood: pedal steel guitar
Chuck Leavell: piano
Mick Jagger: harmony vocal

Richards wrote this during the Barbados preliminaries. Lead guitar prevailed as the song developed, but this deferred to violin and a dose of quasi-country and western when the operation crossed the Atlantic.

New Faces (Jagger-Richards) 2.51
Mick Jagger: guitar, lead vocals
Charlie Watts: tambourine
Chuck Leavell: harpsichord
Luis Jardim: percussion
Keith Richards: guitar, harmony vocal
Darryl Jones: bass guitar
Frankie Gavin: penny-whistle

The quietest track on the album, this bears the most distinctive stamp of the Auld Sod, principally in the squeal of the penny-whistle, an instrument that surfaces as regularly as rocks in the stream in the output of Irish folk outfits as different in style as The Clancy Brothers and Celtic-speaking Na Fili.

Moon Is Up (Jagger-Richards) 3.40
Mick Jagger: harmonica, lead vocals, percussion
Darryl Jones: bass guitar
Benmont Tench: accordion
Keith Richards: guitars, tambourine
Ronnie Wood: pedal steel guitar
Chuck Leavell: harmonium
Bernard Fowler and Bobby Womack: backing vocals

Ronnie Wood applies wah-wah to his pedal steel on the opening bars that, though ear-catching, do not disguise the raw fact that this is one of *Voodoo Lounge*'s weaker tracks. Neither does one of Charlie's experiments with a metal litter bin, an instrument not generally thought of as musical.

Out Of Tears (Jagger-Richards) 5.27

Mick Jagger: guitar, lead vocals
Charlie Watts: drums
Chuck Leavell: piano
Lenny Castro: percussion
Keith Richards and Ronnie Wood: guitars
Darryl Jones: bass guitar
Benmont Tench: organ
David Campbell: string arrangement

Castro and Tench had been among Jagger's helpmates for *Wandering Spirit*, his most recent solo offering, and made insidious impact on this piquant *lied*, one of the most gripping vocal performances from the autumn of his career. Virgin issued it as a tear-shaped single.

I Go Wild (Jagger-Richards) 4.24

Mick Jagger: guitar, lead vocals
Charlie Watts: drums
Chuck Leavell: organ
Keith Richards, Bernard Fowler and Ivan Neville: backing vocals
Keith Richards and Ronnie Wood: guitars
Darryl Jones: bass guitar
Phil Jones: percussion

Penned almost entirely by Jagger, this nod in the direction of classic 50s rock sniped at hard-faced females with ruthless attitudes. As *USA Today* noted in a review on 2 August 1994, Jagger's voice was 'deeper and throatier now, but still a yowling menace, unmellowed by age.' Phil Jones was the former drummer with Crabby Appleton, a group that were signed to Elektra in 1970 before vanishing from the pages of history.

Brand New Car (Jagger-Richards) 4.14

Mick Jagger: guitar, lead vocals
Charlie Watts: drums
David McMurray: saxophone
Lenny Castro and Luis Jardim: percussion
Keith Richards: guitar and bass guitar
Chuck Leavell: piano
Mark Isham: trumpet
Keith Richards and Ivan Neville: backing vocals

In a variant on the ingenious libretto of 'Too Many Drivers', a mid-50s R&B single by Smiley Lewis, Jagger praises a woman's erotic performance during a discussion about a car. Personnel from Was (Not Was) were engaged to blow horns on this track and South American percussionist Jardim was a member of The Charlie Watts Tentet, a jazz combo in which he also sang.

Sweethearts Together (Jagger-Richards) 4.45

Mick Jagger: guitar, lead vocals
Keith Richards: guitars
Ronnie Wood: pedal steel guitar
Charlie Watts: drums
Chuck Leavell: organ
Max Baca: bajo sexto
Keith Richards, Bernard Fowler and Ivan Neville: backing vocals
Flaco Jiminez: accordion

Several attempts were made to record this number prior to an acceptable result that spotlighted Flaco Jiminez, the *enfant terrible* of a dynasty that dominated Tex-Mex conjunto music. Jiminez had also worked with Ry Cooder, Emmylou Harris and Los Lobos. Max Baca played a 12-string acoustic instrument resembling a lower-register guitar.

Suck On The Jugular (Jagger-Richards) 4.26

Mick Jagger: guitar, lead vocals, harmonica
Keith Richards and Ronnie Wood: guitars
Charlie Watts: drums
Ivan Neville: organ
David McMurray: saxophone
Mark Isham: trumpet
Lenny Castro and Luis Jardim: percussion
Keith Richards and Darryl Jones: bass guitars
Keith Richards, Ronnie Wood, Bernard Fowler and Ivan Neville: backing vocals

Laced with wah-wah guitar and relentless beat, call-and-response vocals enhance a lyric that had originally been called 'Holetown Prison' after a coastal location near the Barbados studio.

Blinded By Rainbows (Jagger-Richards) 4.33

Mick Jagger: guitar, lead vocals
Keith Richards and Ronnie Wood: guitars
Charlie Watts: drums
Darryl Jones: bass guitar
Benmont Tench: piano, organ
Lenny Castro: percussion
Keith Richards: harmony vocal

Because it exposes a point of view, the original lovey-dovey words of this item can be construed as political, but the attack on terrorism that drove the released version of 'Blinded By Rainbows' were far more so.

Baby Break It Down (Jagger-Richards) 4.07

Mick Jagger: lead vocals
Keith Richards: guitar, piano
Darryl Jones: bass guitar
Keith Richards, Bernard Fowler and Ivan Neville: backing vocals
Charlie Watts: drums
Ronnie Wood: pedal steel guitar
Ivan Neville: organ

While it was dismissed as a throwaway item by many critics that even bothered to mention it in the context of the album, this soothing ditty at fractionally less than mid-tempo, is my favourite post-Wyman Stones opus. If you stick with 'Baby Break It Down', you'll find yourself crooning it when engaged in some tedious task.

Thru' And Thru' (Jagger-Richards) 6.00

Keith Richards: guitar, lead vocals, piano
Darryl Jones: bass guitar
Mick Jagger, Bernard Fowler and Ivan Neville: backing vocals
Charlie Watts: drums
Pierre de Beauport: guitar
Mick Jagger: backing vocals

When investigating the sonic and spatial promise of places other than an isolation chamber, Charlie Watts captured an apt sepulchral echo for this track by miking up the drums in the well of a studio's four-flight staircase. One of the more interesting Stones items with Richards as lead singer, this featured in *The Sopranos,* the Channel Four gangster drama for which Watts refused a cameo role.

Mean Disposition (Jagger-Richards) 4.07

Mick Jagger: lead vocals
Darryl Jones: bass guitar
Keith Richards and Ronnie Wood: guitars
Chuck Leavell: organ

Sometimes, a new composition can be inspired by the mere title of another. An educated guess is that this song might be traceable to 'Cool Disposition' by Rice Miller, the second Sonny Boy Williamson, even if there is little further similarity in this fast, riff-driven play-out with a long instrumental coda dragging the listener deeper into the darkness.

STRIPPED

UK Release: 13 November 1995 **Virgin CDV 2801/V2801**
US Release: 13 November 1995 **Virgin 7243.8.41040-2-3**
Producers: Don Was and The Glimmer Twins **Running Time:** 59:34

Street Fighting Man; Like A Rolling Stone; Not Fade Away; Shine A Light; The Spider And The Fly; I'm Free; Wild Horses; Let It Bleed; Dead Flowers; Slipping Away; Angie; Love In Vain; Sweet Virginia; Little Baby.

These 14 mostly invigorating re-investigations utilized time intriguingly on the quaint audio postscript of a Stones round-the-world jaunt in 1995. Thus the Stones went as far as they ever would in boarding the unplugged bandwagon. Relaxed and primarily acoustic ambles down Memory Lane were what everyone, including Eric Clapton, Paul McCartney and Rod Stewart, were doing at the time. Moreover, from the now-defunct Led Zeppelin, Jimmy Page and Robert Plant had got together for *Unledded*, that was about to culminate in a best-selling album, *No Quarter*. It was comprised principally of Zeppelin favourites scored for exotic instrumentation that evoked visions of both Arabia and the ancient Celts.

Jagger, Richards et al hadn't the inclination to be as adventurous. Nevertheless, during rehearsals in the assembly hall of a Toronto school, empty of pupils during the 1994 summer recess, some try-outs were taped as an audible gauge of progress. So it was that an idea blossomed for recording items for what would become *Stripped* en route as the fancy took them. It did in various locations in England, Portugal, France, Holland and Japan, both in convenient studios and on the boards, particularly in the smaller venues that punctuated the itinerary.

'We're as accustomed to playing acoustic as we are electric,' Keith was to inform the *St. Louis Post-Despatch*, 'It's not just learning the songs or deciding which ones to play. It's the process of welding together. There's no pressure on you. It's all, "Play this. Try this. Try that" – like brainstorming sessions. That's the kind of feeling I wanted.'

While it was by no means completely acoustic, there was an almost downhome feel

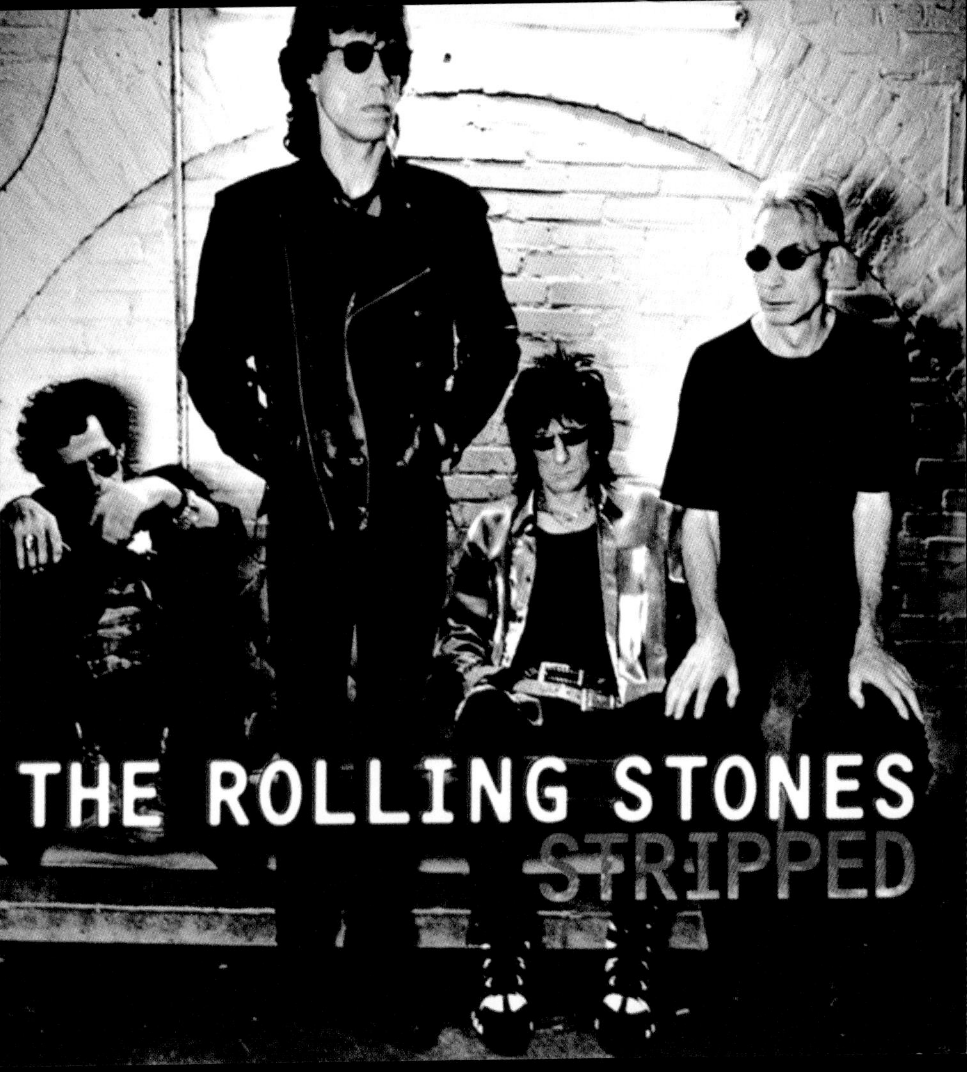
THE ROLLING STONES
STRIPPED

about the overhauls of blues throwbacks from the Crawdaddy, near-forgotten B sides and fourth-track-side-one of vinyl LPs, not to mention those of 'Street Fighting Man', 'Angie' and others that could not be dated past the early 70s, apart from a minor *Steel Wheels* item. Who could not derive pleasure from the Stones piling into Bob Dylan's 'Like A Rolling Stone' when the entourage hit England?

Whether looking to the past is healthy for any artist is open to conjecture, but the record-buying public were as delighted as the group with the results as exemplfied by *Stripped* reaching No. 9 in the States.

Except where otherwise stated, the line-up throughout was as follows:

Mick Jagger: guitar, lead vocals, harmonica
Charlie Watts: drums
Keith Richards, Bernard Fowler and Lisa Fischer: backing vocals
Keith Richards and Ronnie Wood: guitars
Darryl Jones: bass guitar
Chuck Leavell: keyboards
Various: brass and woodwinds

Street Fighting Man (Jagger-Richards) 3.41
With a capacity of only 700, Amsterdam's Paradiso was once as famous a European underground venue as Middle Earth in London. When the Stones appeared there decades later in mid-May 1995, they were seen via satellite on a giant video screen set up outside for the benefit of tens of thousands of fans. This excerpt was unrevised in essence and featured Bernard Fowler on percussion.

Like A Rolling Stone (Dylan) 5.39
According to Jagger's announcement, Bob Dylan had the Stones in mind when he composed this 1965 opus that brought him closest to topping the charts. The group finally got round to recording it at London's Brixton Academy on 19 July 1995. As the first of *Stripped*'s two singles, it almost penetrated the British Top 10.

Not Fade Away (Petty-Hardin) 3.06
Each show started with a newly concocted and percussion-heavy arrangement of the group's third UK chart entry. However, the driving acoustic rhythm guitar, the shave-and-a-haircut-six-pence beat and the ghost of Brian Jones on harmonica remained when Mick Jagger spent his 52nd birthday working with his colleagues in Lisbon's Estudios Valentim De Carvalho. The most striking difference was made by Charlie's tricky rim-shots and the incorporation of the bop-bop backing vocals that The Crickets sang on the 1957 original.

Shine A Light (Jagger-Richards) 4.38
On 3 July 1995, Don Was pumped the organ, Ronnie Wood took a solo, and Keith Richards strummed chords on this return to *Exile On Main Street* at the Paris Olympia, where the Stones first appeared in 1964. It was the City of Light's premier music hall, but was tiny in comparison to the stadiums the group played elsewhere in Europe that summer. Certainly they didn't need what was now their usual three million watts of power and eight miles of cable.

The Spider And The Fly (Jagger-Richards) 3.29
While psyching themselves up for seven nights at the Tokyo Dome in March 1995, the Stones spent two days in the local Toshiba-EMI studios. Among the consequences of this was a remake of the British B side of 'Satisfaction'. It was necessary for Jagger in his 50s to reconsider lyrics concerning a tryst with an older woman who, in the 1965 version, 'looked about 30'.

I'm Free (Jagger-Richards) 3.13
The Stones belatedly took another look at this 1965 B side in the light of it being the highest UK chart entry of several by The Soup Dragons in 1990.

Wild Horses (Jagger-Richards) 5.09
The album's second single was born of the Tokyo sessions. Looser than on *Sticky Fingers*, it also added vocal harmonies from Keith Richards and Chuck Leavell.

Let It Bleed (Jagger-Richards) 4.15
Although this was the title track of the transitional 1969 album, it couldn't hold a candle to most of its companion numbers. The Stones seemed to disagree, having included a performance of it on a video commemorating a 1981 tour, taking another crack at it during the Toshiba-EMI sojourn and selecting this rendition from the Olympia bash for *Stripped.*

Dead Flowers (Jagger-Richards) 4.13
This came from Brixton Academy. Bestowing the foreheads of both the group and the three thousand ticket-holders with pinpricks of sweat, the humidity was what The Lovin' Spoonful had sung about in 'Summer In The City'. Yet the mood was one of gaiety and this came across on all the items taped that evening.

Slipping Away (Jagger-Richards) 4.55
Darryl Jones and Chuck Leavell joined the backing chorale in Tokyo behind Keith Richards and Lisa Fischer's duet of this *Steel Wheels* song.

Angie (Jagger-Richards) 3.29
This was the 1972 ballad's first exposure as an in-concert recording and Jagger puts on the agony most effectively at the Paris Olympia in July 1995.

Love In Vain (traditional) 5.31
While needing little in the way of prior instruction, the group permitted mistakes that only old pros can make to go unretracted to the pressing plant on this Tokyo remake of Robert Johnson's gutbucket blues. This time round harmonica, keyboards and dobro guitar, courtesy of Ronnie Wood, enter after an introductory verse by just Mick and Keith.

Sweet Virginia (Jagger-Richards) 4.16
As an attempt at this *Exile On Main Street* track proved unsatisfactory at Brixton, the lads tried again a week later in the Lisbon studio. If anything, it was more of a stylized country-and-western send-up than in 1972. The only trick they missed were some blue yodels a la Jimmie Rodgers.

Little Baby (Dixon) 4.00
The only piece that the Stones had never recorded before had been recalled by Mick and Keith as the first Howlin' Wolf A side ever issued in Britain by Pye International in 1961. Keeping it appealingly ragged in places, the ensemble nailed 'Little Baby' in one take.

A version of 'Black Limousine' from *Tattoo You* made at Brixton Academy was included on the 'Like A Rolling Stone' single and as a bonus album track in Japan. It clocked in at 3.34. Reworkings of 'Tumbling Dice', 'Shattered' and a second 'Like A Rolling Stone' plus interviews with the four principals were listenable and viewable with the aid of a personal computer.

ROCK & ROLL CIRCUS

UK Release: 15 October 1996 **ABKCO 1268.2**
US Release: 18 October 1996 **ABKCO 1268.2**
Producers: The Rolling Stones **Running Time:** 59:05

Jumping Jack Flash; Parachute Woman; No Expectations; You Can't Always Get What You Want; Sympathy For The Devil; Salt Of The Earth plus spoken links by members of The Rolling Stones, and tracks by Jethro Tull, The Who, Taj Mahal, Marianne Faithfull and a group fronted by John Lennon and Yoko Ono.

This cancelled television spectacular was intended as a Christmas special on BBC television, as The Beatles' interesting-but-boring Magical Mystery Tour had been the previous winter. It was shot between the afternoon of 10 December 1968 and the following morning in the same Wembley Studios used for editions of *Ready Steady Go*, ITV's epoch-making pop series. The accumulated footage contained a sequential assortment of clowns, gymnasts, fire-eaters and a tiger. Most importantly, there was re-take after re-take of music that mashed up blues, rock, rock opera, ballads and a spin-off from an ad hoc quintet containing John Lennon, Yoko Ono, Eric Clapton, classical violinist Ivry Gitlis, Keith Richards on bass guitar and Jimi Hendrix's drummer, Mitch Mitchell. It was a piece that beggared precise categorization.

The show closed with a performance by the Stones that commenced an hour after midnight before a crowd that, if starstruck, had exercised patience above and beyond the call of duty. The musicians too were wilting slightly, especially Brian Jones, who'd found the entire proceedings as onerous as he had when the making of 'Sympathy For The Devil' was documented by Jean-Luc Godard a few months earlier.

With specific reference to Brian, the group's wearied musicianship on the graveyard shift was slammed by Ian Anderson, singing flautist in Jethro Tull, one of the support acts. The Stones weren't pleased with it either and the *Rock '&' Roll Circus* thus gathered dust for decades until it acquired sufficient historical interest to sneak into the lower reaches of the US Hot 100.

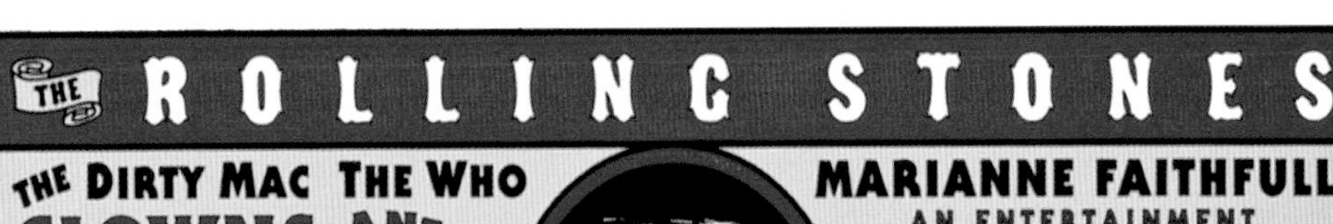

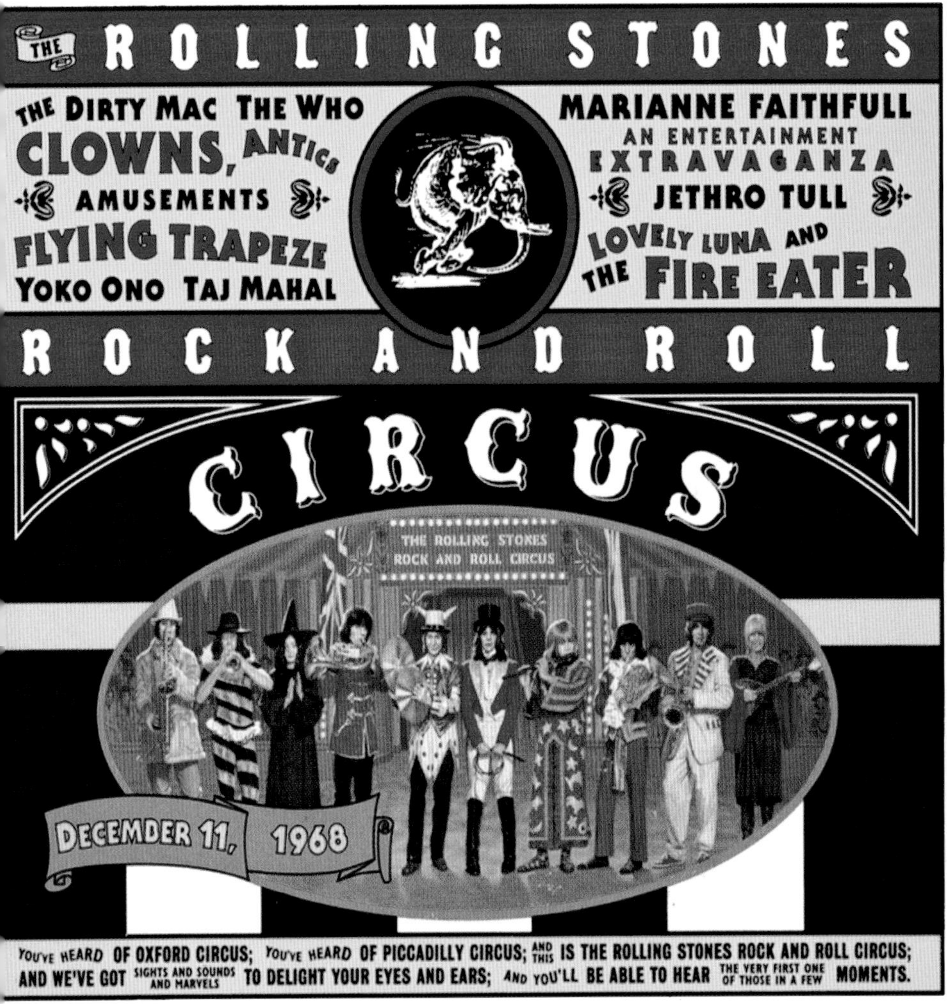
THE ROLLING STONES
THE DIRTY MAC THE WHO
CLOWNS, ANTICS
AMUSEMENTS
FLYING TRAPEZE
YOKO ONO TAJ MAHAL
MARIANNE FAITHFULL
AN ENTERTAINMENT EXTRAVAGANZA
JETHRO TULL
LOVELY LUNA AND THE FIRE EATER
ROCK AND ROLL
CIRCUS
THE ROLLING STONES ROCK AND ROLL CIRCUS
DECEMBER 11, 1968
YOU'VE HEARD OF OXFORD CIRCUS; YOU'VE HEARD OF PICCADILLY CIRCUS; AND THIS IS THE ROLLING STONES ROCK AND ROLL CIRCUS;
AND WE'VE GOT SIGHTS AND SOUNDS AND MARVELS TO DELIGHT YOUR EYES AND EARS; AND YOU'LL BE ABLE TO HEAR THE VERY FIRST ONE OF THOSE IN A FEW MOMENTS.

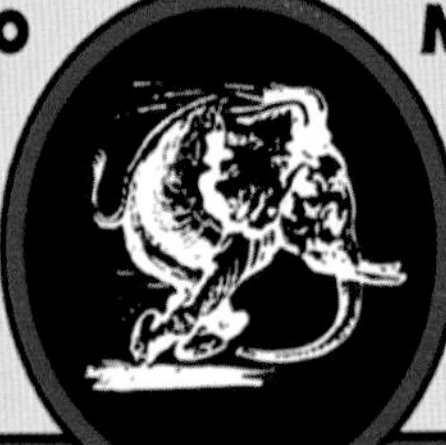

Mick Jagger: lead vocals, harmonica
Keith Richards: guitar, vocal
Brian Jones: guitar, percussion
Bill Wyman: bass guitar
Charlie Watts: drums
Nicky Hopkins: piano
Rocky Dijon: congas

As on all Rolling Stones in-concert albums, timing includes continuity and audience response.

Jumping Jack Flash (Jagger-Richards) 3.35
Following an introduction by John Lennon, the group attempted their most recent A side twice before achieving this passable result.

Parachute Woman (Jagger-Richards) 2.59
Richards solos while Jagger blows harmonica on the coda.

No Expectations (Jagger-Richards) 4.13
Keith strums an acoustic six-string, and Brian endeavours to emulate the adroit slide guitar he careened on the *Beggars Banquet* original.

You Can't Always Get What You Want (Jagger-Richards) 4.24
This first public unveiling took place at 4am and if not brilliant in absolute terms, this was probably the best they could have managed at the time, even if Brian appeared to struggle with the chords.

Sympathy For The Devil (Jagger-Richards) 8.49
As milk floats braved an icy dawn, Jones was reduced to shaking maraccas while Keith combined lead and rhythm guitar on this penultimate number for tired onlookers.

Salt Of The Earth (Jagger-Richards) 4.57
As Middlesex awoke, the audience were waved out of the premises to the sound of the backing track of the *Beggars Banquet* studio version with live vocals.

BRIDGES TO BABYLON

UK Release: 29 September 1997 **Virgin 2840/CDV 2840**
US Release: 29 September 1997 **Virgin 7243.8.44712.2.4**
Producers: Don Was, The Glimmer Twins and others
Running Time: 62:27

Flip The Switch; Anybody Seen My Baby; Low Down; Already Over Me; Gunface; You Don't Have To Mean It; Out Of Control; Saint Of Me; Might As Well Get Juiced; Always Suffering; Too Tight; Thief In The Night; How Can I Stop.

The final Stones studio album of the 20th century was the product of men who could afford to lark about. And that is what they did when they hired all three studios in Hollywood's Ocean Way complex from March to July in 1997. A consequent workshop ambience permitted Charlie Watts and Jim Keltner, a drummer with first refusal on virtually all Los Angeles record dates, to commandeer one of these studios to create idiosyncratic patterns of percussion while Mick and Keith were head-to-head on a multi-track desk elsewhere, mulling over degrees of reverberation on a keyboard part.

It wasn't all smiles between Jagger and Richards over an amorphous production criteria founded on a truce between the latest technology and their customary rough-and-readiness. Predictably, Keith was all for making a given song's point without any of the new-fangled trimmings, while Mick had got further into the swing of what made his children and their friends groove nowadays, especially the growing bond between the dance floor and electronica. He'd become sharp enough to spot the differences between the sub-divisions of what out-of-touch media critics lumped together as Modern Dance: jungle, ragga, ambient-techno, hardcore and all the rest of them.

He was therefore, keen on wheeling in some younger minds to apply the new methodology to what was to be *Bridges To Babylon*. Chief among these were Black Grape, leading lights of England's trendy Madchester party central and more so, The Dust Brothers, alias John King and Mike Simpson, esteemed within the industry for their skills as console

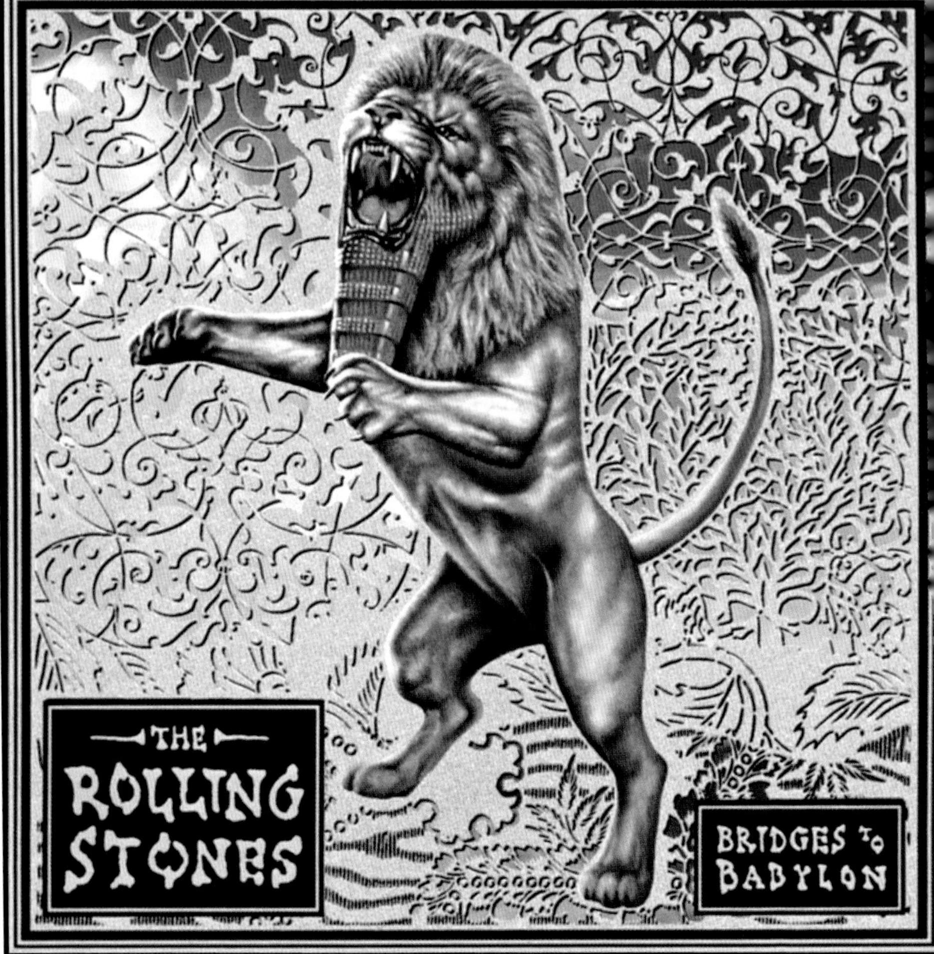
THE
ROLLING
STONES
BRIDGES TO
BABYLON

boffins with a flair for remixing. The Dust Brothers were on a roll after they had produced *Odelay*, released in 1996 by Beck. This was not Jeff Beck the British guitarist but an entertainer from Kansas and as the *Bridges To Babylon* sessions got underway, the brothers had an international chart-buster in Hanson's 'Mmm...Bop'.

Don Was and Richards were far from entirely convinced by Jagger's ideas. Nevertheless his enthusiasm was sufficient for The Dust Brothers, Black Grape's Danny Saber and John X. Voliatis plus other victims of the same passion were hired to attend to much of the technological donkey-work on some numbers. A spirit of give-and-take also accommodated an unprecedented three forays into lead vocals by Richards, and others present also found themselves occasionally with headphones on playing an unfamiliar instrument. For example, Pierre de Beauport, Keith's guitar technician, was flattered when asked to finger both electric and acoustic pianos on 'Thief In The Night', while Charlie Watts was persuaded to sing on 'Always Suffering'.

It provoked no friction either when Waddy Wachel, guitarist from The X-Pensive Winos, who were taken on the road by Richards to promote his *Talk Is Cheap* solo album, was present in some capacity on all but three tracks. It was OK too for Jim Keltner to add his touch to just about everything after the beat had been invested by Watts. As well as his long friendship with Charlie, another point in his favour in Jagger's eyes was Keltner's use of sampling and the programming of drum machines like those heard on Black Grape and Dust Brothers' records.

When ensconced away from the main creative events, Jim and Charlie were 'just mucking about,' explained Watts. 'Jim brought in some sequences he made from sampled sounds and asked me to play over them. He's been sampling stuff for years, household items, metal objects, pipes, all sorts of organic things, and we started to jam over them together. The thing with drums and percussion is that the overtones, after a while, become little melodies in themselves'.

After a while the two were using every minute, when not required elsewhere, to concentrate on what was turning into a project more intriguing than just sounding out Keith, Mick, Don and anyone else within earshot about whether their tiers of grooves and rhythms could be incorporated somewhere on *Bridges To Babylon*. On the day of the closing session Charlie flew back to Europe with 20 spools of tapes and floppy discs for moulding into

The Charlie Watts-Jim Keltner Project, a turn-of-the-millenium album that would prove to be too clever for the average Stones consumer who had assisted the clamber of *Bridges To Babylon* into the British and US Top Tens.

Flip The Switch (Jagger-Richards) 3.28
Mick Jagger: Lead vocals
Keith Richards, Ronnie Wood and Waddy Wachel: guitars
Blondie Chaplin and Bernard Fowler: backing vocals
Charlie Watts: drums
Jeff Sarli: double-bass
Jim Keltner: percussion
Joe Sublett: saxophone
To perhaps the fastest tempo since 'She Said Yeah' in 1965, Jagger's lyrics apparently were motivated by his educated guess that members of a North-American religious cult in the news would commit mass suicide. At one point, *Flip The Switch* was put forward as the album's title. Another possibility was *Blessed Poison*.

Anybody Seen My Baby (Jagger-Richards-Lang-Mink) 4.31
Mick Jagger: guitar, lead vocals
Don Was: keyboards
Keith Richards, Ronnie Wood and Waddy Wachel: guitars
Charlie Watts: drums
James Muhoberac: bass guitar, keyboards
Keith Richards, Blondie Chaplin and Bernard Fowler: backing vocals
As it had been with 'Satisfaction', Richards was worried about this song's stomach-knotting similarity to something else, namely 'Constant Craving' by guitarist Ben Mink and his long-time collaborator k.d. lang, a Canadian performer and country-and-western New Traditionalist. In 1992 she reached a global audience with *Ingenue*, that contained 'Constant Craving'. After groping for reasons why a suit for plagiarism would or would not be pursued, Richards and Jagger settled the matter out of court by persuading a flattered Mink and lang to permit their names to be included in the composing credits. An off-cut single, 'Anybody Seen My Baby' was a turntable hit in North America and made the Top 20 in Britain.

Low Down (Jagger-Richards) 4.26
Mick Jagger: lead vocals
Keith Richards and Waddy Wachel: guitars
Jim Keltner: percussion
Bernard Fowler and Blondie Chaplin: backing vocals
Charlie Watts: drums
Ronnie Wood: slide guitar
Blondie Chaplin: bass guitar, percussion
Joe Sublett: saxophone
Darrell Leonard: trumpet

The guitar ostinato played by Richards that kicks off this moderato shuffle does not re-surface. The results might have been more interesting if it had.

Already Over Me (Jagger-Richards) 5.24
Mick Jagger: guitar, lead vocals
Charlie Watts: drums
Don Was: bass guitar
Blondie Chaplin: piano
Keith Richards, Bernard Fowler and Blondie Chaplin: backing vocals
Keith Richards: guitar
Ronnie Wood: dobro guitar
Benmont Tench: keyboards
Jim Keltner and Kenny Aronoff: percussion

An initial attempt to record this item was too much like what Richards would dismiss as one of 'Mick's high-tech solo records'. The version selected for the album was more recognisable as traditional Rolling Stones fare but it did include Aronoff's thwacking of a bucket for one desired percussive effect.

Gunface (Jagger-Richards) 5.02
Mick Jagger: guitar, lead vocals
Ronnie Wood: slide guitar
Danny Saber: keyboards, guitar, bass guitar
Keith Richards: guitars
Jim Keltner: percussion

The subject wants to shoot both a false-hearted lover and the man who has cuckolded him. A feasible source of lyrical inspiration might have been an amused memory of the arrival of a burly West Indian at a residential studio complex in Oxfordshire where the Stones were working in 1978. He was waving a pistol and demanding an audience with Richards – who, he shouted, was fucking his wife. That this accusation was founded in fact became manifest when from rumpled bedclothes Keith and the lady concerned, both quite naked, bolted out of a sidedoor and across a lawn towards concealing undergrowth.

You Don't Have To Mean It (Jagger-Richards) 3.43

Keith Richards: lead vocals, guitar
Darryl Jones: bass guitar
Jim Keltner: percussion
Blondie Chaplin and Bernard Fowler: backing vocals
Ronnie Wood: guitar
Clinton Clifford: keyboards
Joe Sublett: saxophone
Darrell Leonard: trumpet

For the basic beat, Jagger favoured a pounding tom-tom rataplan as in 'Peggy Sue' by Buddy Holly, but this mutated into a chopping Caribbean feel with Jones's lithely contrapuntal bass as much a conduit of melody as rhythm.

Out Of Control (Jagger-Richards) 4.43

Mick Jagger: harmonica, lead vocals, guitar
Keith Richards, Ronnie Wood, Waddy Wachel: guitars
Blondie Chaplin: piano
Keith Richards, Bernard Fowler and Blondie Chaplin: backing vocals
Charlie Watts: drums
Jim Keltner: percussion
Danny Saber: bass guitar, clavinet
Don Was and James Muhoberac: keyboards

If searching for something that could be described as worth the whole price of the album, most reviewers homed in on what was mostly the brain child of Jagger, who was also responsible for its wah-wahed fretboard section. Other notable features include a bass line that nods towards the bass that propelled The Temptations' 'Papa Was A Rolling Stone', and an arrangement in which each subdued verse breaks into an explosive chorus.

Saint Of Me (Jagger-Richards) 5.15

Mick Jagger: guitar, lead vocals, keyboards
Billy Preston: organ
Pierre de Beauport and Me'Shell Mdegeocello: bass guitars
Charlie Watts: drums
Ronnie Wood and Waddy Wachel: guitars
James Muhoberac: keyboards
Bernard Fowler: Backing vocals

Richards was conspicuously absent on this attractive opus. Unleashed as a single, it entered the British charts so fleetingly that the attendant video was seen but once on BBC 1's *Top Of The Pops*. Routined by Jagger at The Dust Brothers' studio in a Los Angeles suburb, it was riddled with Biblical references stressed by Preston's holy organ, concerning betrayal and persecution.

Might As Well Get Juiced (Jagger-Richards) 5.23

Mick Jagger: harmonica, lead vocals, keyboards
Ronnie Wood: slide guitar
Keith Richards and Waddy Wachel: guitars
Charlie Watts: drums
Doug Wimbish: bass guitar

The first completed track to emerge from the sessions, this begins with synthesiser and drums establishing a rhythmic support structure for an account of someone seeking refuge in alcohol from the emotional ravages of middle age.

Always Suffering (Jagger-Richards) 4.44

Mick Jagger: guitar, lead vocals
Charlie Watts: drums
Ronnie Wood: guitar, pedal steel guitar
Benmont Tench: keyboards
Bernard Fowler, Blondie Chaplin, Doug Wimbish, Jim Keltner, Keith Richards, Charlie Watts and Doug Wimbish: backing vocals
Keith Richards and Waddy Wachel: guitars
Jim Keltner: percussion
Darryl Jones: bass guitar

With an acoustic emphasis, this is *Bridges To Babylon*'s most downbeat effort and does not reconcile easily with the overall climate of most of the other tracks.

Too Tight (Jagger-Richards) 3.33

Mick Jagger: lead vocals
Keith Richards, Ronnie Wood and Waddy Wachel: guitars
Blondie Chaplin: piano
Bernard Fowler and Blondie Chaplin: backing vocals
Charlie Watts: drums
Ronnie Wood: pedal steel guitar
Jeff Sarli: double bass
Jim Keltner: percussion

After a deceptively soft introduction on two guitars, this piles into a so-so crack at recreating olde-tyme rock'n'roll, complete with vamping piano and slapped double-bass.

Thief In The Night (Jagger-Richards-de Beauport) 5.16

Keith Richards: guitar, lead vocals, piano
Pierre de Beauport: keyboards
Darryl Jones: bass guitar
Bernard Fowler and Blondie Chaplin: backing vocals
Charlie Watts: drums
Ronnie Wood and Waddy Wachel: guitars
Jim Keltner: percussion
Darrell Leonard: trumpet
Joe Sublett: saxophone

On this slowish melancholia about lost love, de Beauport earned a composing credit for the riff in which it lives.

How Can I Stop (Jagger-Richards) 6.54

Keith Richards: guitar, lead vocals
Charlie Watts: drums
Don Was and Blondie Chaplin: pianos
Bernard Fowler and Blondie Chaplin: backing vocals
Ronnie Wood and Waddy Wachel: guitars
Jeff Sarli: double bass
Jim Keltner: percussion
Wayne Shorter: saxophone

Peep-parping his trademark soprano sax on this relaxed finale, Shorter who was brought in at the suggestion of Watts is the album's most illustrious guest musician, being a mainstay of Weather Report, behemoths of the jazz-rock that scored in university hostel rooms in the mid-70s.

NO SECURITY

UK Release: 9 November 1998
US Release: 16 November 1998
Producers: The Glimmer Twins

Virgin V-2880/CDV-2880
Virgin 7242.8.46740-21
Running Time: 67:50

You Got Me Rocking; Gimmie Shelter; Flip The Switch; Memory Motel; Corrina; Saint Of Me; Waiting On A Friend; Sister Morphine; Live With Me; Respectable; Thief In The Night; The Last Time; Out Of Control.

The sixth Rolling Stones in-concert album was drawn from shows at Amsterdam's Arena, the TWA Dome in St. Louis, the River Plate Stadium in Buenos Aires, Nuremburg's Zeppelinfield and the Capitol Theater in Chester, New York during a world tour that lasted from October 1997 to July 1998. It was reckoned to be the biggest-grossing enterprise of its kind ever undertaken, as exemplified by a web-cast audience of millions via a deal with a pay-to-view cable TV company for the TWA Dome show.

After rejecting a mooted title of *Bridges To Babylon Live At The Stadium*, the Stones assembled a representative mixture of plenty of hits, a couple of dredged-up obscurities and a handful of tracks from the latest studio effort. It wasn't a remarkable money-spinner, it struggled in the lower reaches of the charts in Britain and in the States, despite the group plunging into another tour for the very purpose of promoting it. Neither did *No Security* garner many commendations from reviewers. Perhaps agreeing with them, Jagger was to maintain that following a cursory spin, he never listened to it again. In retrospect, while it isn't vintage Stones, it's quite enjoyable and maybe that's the problem.

Excet where otherwise stated, the line up throughout was follows:

Mick Jagger: guitar, lead vocals, harmonica
Keith Richards: guitar, vocals
Charlie Watts: drums
Ronnie Wood: guitar
Darryl Wood: bass guitar
Chuck Leavell: keyboards
Bernard Fowler, Lisa Fischer and Blondie Chaplin: backing vocals
Various: brass and woodwinds

As on all Rolling Stones in-concert albums, timing includes continuity and audience response.

You Got Me Rocking (Jagger-Richards) 3.26
The group hit the ground running via a fiery romp through one of *Voodoo Lounge's* more up-tempo selections.

Gimmie Shelter (Jagger-Richards) 6.12
Taped at the New York stop on 25 October 1997 this is, more or less, a duet by Fischer and Jagger and was the sole content of the album's promotional CD mailed to relevant media the following November.

Flip The Switch (Jagger-Richards) 4.12
Fresh from *Bridges To Babylon*, this high-velocity raver was from a show on 12 December 1997 in St. Louis.

Memory Motel (Jagger-Richards) 5.52
Though the location was Amsterdam, Jagger shared lead vocals with Dave Matthews, a nominal leader of one of those heads-down-no-nonsense combos with a prosaic name that seem to thrive in North America.

CURITY

Corrina (Mahal-Davis) 3.56
The Stones and Massachusetts blues singer and dobro guitarist Taj Mahal went back a long way. Indeed, Mahal was on the bill of the Rock '&' Roll Circus in 1968. At St. Louis, he accepted an open invitation to join the group on the boards for a crack at one of his own songs that he had penned with Jesse Ed Davis, sometime guitarist in his Rising Sons backing outfit.

Saint Of Me (Jagger-Richards) 5.18
A second attempt to capture the essence of the most successful *Bridges To Babylon* single, with Jagger building it up into a rowdy singalong.

Waiting On A Friend (Jagger-Richards) 4.52
Beginning public life as a spin-off single from *Tattoo You*, this retains much the same arrangement but is played with more guts and embraces a deft saxophone obligato.

Sister Morphine (Jagger-Richards-Faithfull) 6.05
A daring choice but this is not up to the fighting weight of either the *Sticky Fingers* version or Marianne Faithfull's 1969 B side.

Live With Me (Jagger-Richards) 3.55
For reasons that have yet to become clear, the Stones liked this item from *Let It Bleed* enough to have re-made it for *Get Yer Ya-Yas Out* and, in 1995, for a Netherlands-only live four-track CD single. This third in-concert crack doesn't make 'Live With Me' any less nondescript in essence. Perhaps you had to be there.

Respectable (Jagger-Richards) 3.20
The Stones neither add nor subtract much from a *Some Girls* number that had previously popped up in live form on a 1978 bootleg.

Thief In The Night (Jagger-Richards-de Beauport) 5.37
From the first night of the tour's European leg in summer 1998, this is prefaced by an apology from Keith Richards, whose broken ribs following a domestic accident had caused the original date for the show to be rescheduled.

The Last Time (Jagger-Richards) 4.19
The first self-composed British No.1 is seized by the scruff of the neck in St. Louis, the extravaganza from which most of *No Security* is lifted.

Out Of Control (Jagger-Richards) 7.59
Chief road manager, Johnny Starbuck wields maraccas during this excerpt from one of five uproarious evenings in Buenos Aires. On the bill was Bob Dylan who joined in the fun when the Stones pitched into 'Like A Rolling Stone'.

LIVE LICKS

UK Release: 2 November 2004
US Release: 2 November 2004
Producers: Don Was and The Glimmer Twins

Virgin/EMI CDVDX3000
Virgin/EMI CDV2880
Running Time: 109:19

DISC ONE: Brown Sugar; Street Fighting Man; Paint It Black; You Can't Always Get What You Want; Start Me Up; Angie; It's Only Rock 'N' Roll (But I Like It); Honky Tonk Women; Happy; Gimmie Shelter; (I Can't Get No) Satisfaction.
DISC TWO: Neighbours; Monkey Man; Rocks Off; Can't You Hear Me Knocking; That's How Strong My Love Is; The Nearness Of You; Beast Of Burden; When The Whip Comes Down; Rock Me Baby; You Don't Have To Mean It; Everybody Needs Somebody To Love.

Another audio memento of a record-breaking world tour, this double-CD divides precisely into a cache of well-known crowd-pleasers and a host of items for which applause was more considered. Its release turned out to be a wiser merchandising strategy than *No Security*, eventually selling a million, entering the US Top 50, and climbing to No. 38 in Britain.

Charlie Watts in particular was much more pleased with this 'repetition of what I've been doing for 40 years', having been 'dragged into the excitement. I don't actually get excited myself. There's a minor flow of adrenaline seeping through my veins, but that's about it. I always get very nervous when they're filming because you can play a song 200 times, which we usually do and the night they choose to film the bloody thing, you muck it up.'

While no tangible errors protrude from *Live Licks*, it might not have altered an opinion expressed by Charlie with lugubrious affection years before: 'We're a terrible band really, but we are the oldest. That's some sort of distinction, isn't it? That's our claim to fame, you know. Carry on, lads, regardless!'

ROLLING STONES
LIVE LICKS

Except where otherwise stated, the line-up throughout is as follows:

Mick Jagger: guitar, lead vocals, harmonica
Charlie Watts: drums
Darryl Wood: bass guitar
Bernard Fowler, Lisa Fischer and Blondie Chaplin: backing vocals
Keith Richards: guitar, vocals
Ronnie Wood: guitar
Chuck Leavell: keyboards
Various: brass, woodwinds and additional keyboards

As on all Rolling Stones in-concert albums, timing includes continuity and audience response.

Brown Sugar (Jagger-Richard) 3.50
Once more with feeling for a number that was also selected for *Flashpoint*, the previous in-concert bash in 1991.

Street Fighting Man (Jagger-Richard) 3.43
This plants feet in both the version on *Beggar's Banquet* and that on the more recent *Stripped*.

Paint It Black (Jagger-Richard) 3.45
Electric guitar rather than sitar gnaws at this rendition of the 1966 chart-topper.

You Can't Always Get What You Want (Jagger-Richard) 6.46
Though minus the chorale introit of the 1969 original, this is stretched out like toffee, building from an almost conversational opening verse to boiling point.

Start Me Up (Jagger-Richard) 4.02
The lads wring the blood out of the last truly big hit single.

Angie (Jagger-Richard) 3.29
The *Stripped* arrangement is fitted out with a few garments.

It's Only Rock 'N Roll (But I Like It) (Jagger-Richard) 4.54
Thus far, this is the only appearance on a live album, although a 1997 version was seen on video and DVD.

Honky Tonk Women (Jagger-Richard) 3.24
Once a backing vocalist for the disparate likes of Michael Jackson and Sinead O' Connor, University of Missouri graduate Sheryl Crow's career had left the runway in 1993 with laid back *Tuesday Night Music Club*. Twelve years later, her hip status was such that she was invited onto the boards to duet with Jagger. You could understand the commercial motivation for including her on *Live Licks*, but Stones purists might have preferred a more typical honky tonk woman. Crow's slot certainly wasn't as appealing as that of Leah Wood, Ronnie's daughter, during the *Bridges To Babylon* jaunt.

Happy (Jagger-Richard) 3.38
Buoyed by goodwill, dear old Keith, drunk before breakfast, stoned before lunch time, according to the old image, gives 'em the only US Top 30 entry by the Stones with himself on lead vocal.

Gimmie Shelter (Jagger-Richard) 6.50
Compared to the guitars-bass-drums arrangement on 1969's celebrated *Live R Than You'll Ever Be* bootleg, this is as dairy butter to low-fat margarine.

(I Can't Get No) Satisfaction (Jagger-Richard) 4.55
Once they might have got away with it, but nowadays the Stones daren't leave the stage without at least encoring with this flash of past glory.

Neighbours (Jagger-Richard) 3.41
From *Tattoo You*, this had already been reprised on the 1983 video, *Let's Spend The Night Together.*

Monkey Man (Jagger-Richard) 3.41
This lesser *Let It Bleed* track had re-entered the stage repertoire ten years earlier.

Rocks Off (Jagger-Richard) 3.42
If not considered worthy of release as the A side of a single, this *Exile On Main Street* raver has been in and out of the set since the early 70s.

Can't You Hear Me Knocking (Jagger-Richard) 10.02
The long instrumental coda ventures beyond the Santana-esque blueprint on *Sticky Fingers,* mainly via interplay between harmonica and saxophone.

That's How Strong My Love Is (Roosevelt-Jamieson) 4.45
From an age almost as bygone as that bracketed by Hitler's suicide and 'Rock Around The Clock', this power ballad makes a return that, judging from the audience response, was triumphant.

The Nearness Of You (Hoagy Carmichael-Ned Washington) 4.34
Like a Viking longship docking in a hovercraft terminal, this cabaret standard from the 40s reared up mid-set. Yet the Stones slipping into Hoagy Carmichael mode might not have been as iconoclastic as first imagined. Since a version of 'My Resistance Is Low' by Robin Sarstedt had soared into the British Top Ten in 1976, George Harrison had included two Carmichael items on his *Somewhere In England* album, and Georgie Fame had recorded an entire 1983 tribute album to the fellow in collaboration with jazz-singing daredevil Annie Ross. And in the 90s, Eric Clapton would croon a customised verse of 'Gone Fishin'.

Beast Of Burden (Jagger-Richard) 4.09
Since its first appearance on *Some Girls* in 1978, the Stones' faith in the durability of this ditty has never wavered. This is its third rehashing on an official live release including video/DVD.

When The Whip Comes Down (Jagger-Richard) 4.28
Another *Some Girls* opus of which the group was excessively fond, makes a second appearance on an in-concert album.

Rock Me Baby (B.B. King-Joe Bihari) 4.35
Incomplete studio recordings of what amounts to bluesman B.B. King's signature tune were made during London sessions for *Beggar's Banquet* in March 1968. Very much in the air then, the number was in the stage set of many other outfits, notably The Jeff Beck Group. Here the Stones give it a workmanlike resurrection.

You Don't Have To Mean It (Jagger-Richard) 6.01
The most recent of all the *Live Licks* exhumations, this version is less reggaefied than that sung by Keith Richards on *Bridges To Babylon* in 1997.

Everybody Needs Somebody To Love (Burke-Russell-Wexler) 6.35
Of similar mid-60s vintage as 'That's How Strong My Love Is', this features none other than its co-writer, 78-year-old Solomon Burke – now reduced to performing seated – sharing vocals with Jagger in the expected testifying style during one of the more agreeable guest spots in the Stones' canon.

A BIGGER BANG

UK Release: 6 September 2005 **Virgin/EMI CDVX 3012**
US Release: 6 September 2005 **Virgin/EMI TOCP-66441**
Producers: Don Was and The Glimmer Twins **Running Time:** 64:23

Rough Justice; Let Me Down Slow; It Won't Take Long; Rain Fall Down; Streets Of Love; Back Of My Hand; She Saw Me Coming; Biggest Mistake; This Place Is Empty; Oh No Not You Again; Dangerous Beauty; Laugh I Nearly Died; Sweet Neo Con; Look What The Cat Dragged In; Driving Too Fast; Infamy.

The title referred to the primal cosmic explosion that most accept as the origin of the universe, but did *A Bigger Bang* constitute a rebirth or was it a glorious sunset mistaken for a dawn? A similar question had already been applied to every studio album since *Steel Wheels* and there had been no succinct answer in each of those cases either.

Preparation for this latest offering began when Jagger and Richards convened in the former's home in the Loire valley a few months after Mick, soberly attired, had been driven to Buckingham Palace on 12 December 2003 to be knighted by Prince Charles. Facing the press in the courtyard afterwards, cameras caught the flash of a diamond-studded front molar as he smiled while opining 'I don't think the establishment we knew exists any more.'

Neither does the generation gap on the strength of turn-out for the staggered back-to-back international tours, the second of which was the highest-grossing of all time by any act, pop or otherwise. It also coincided with the issue of *A Bigger Bang*. Inevitably, the Stones' advancing age had taken its toll. No longer able to rely on youthful metabolism, it was necessary for Jagger, prior to each show, to submit to two hours of vocal exercises, karaoke and the physical jerks that had been his habit from earliest youth. More seriously, even before rehearsals had been scheduled, 63-year-old Charlie Watts had been diagnosed with throat cancer, but still 'the greatest rock'n'roll band in the world' hit the road again, entertaining an audience drawn from a spectrum ranging from incorrigible old mods, rockers and hippies to those for whom *Steel Wheels* antedated consciousness.

'I can't see us stopping,' pontificated Jagger, 'Maybe we won't tour as we did – 16 months non-stop – but more regularly. I don't like to stay away from the stage too long, but I don't see us as just a live act. I think we have to do a record soon. Being a live act gives you instant gratification. Records don't.'

For Jagger, Richards and Watts it was elating when *A Bigger Bang*, recorded in France, the West Indies and California, swept to the top of the British chart – a triumph that was duplicated in other territories. Thus it was demonstrated that Charlie, Keith, Sir Mick and the others remained on a contemporary footing.

Nevertheless, as was becoming customary, there were rotten reviews, 'predictable, pedestrian and pointless,' reckoned *Record Collector* and nothing on the new album screamed out as an unmistakable smash-hit single, even by the fallen standards prevalent since the 80s. No 'Start Me Up' or so much as a 'Saint Of Me', though 'Streets Of Love' shot into the UK charts at No. 15 before an almost immediate departure.

Mick was in fine voice, the playing was solid with Jagger plucking bass on disc for the first time and the production polished, but endearingly muddied now and then with some musical dirt – something a bit crude to capsize the clever twiddling at the control room desk. Too many arrangements, however, hinged on a similar medium-to-fast tempo, and tended to make for much of a muchness when listening to 16 all-original tracks for the first and second and third times. This was the probable cause of the more vitriolic of what was, on balance, a mixed critical reaction.

Those dismissive of *A Bigger Bang* might have been so under the editorial lash to meet a deadline that they hadn't had time to get used to the overall drift. Repeated spins put individual items in sharper focus but because greater effort is needed to appreciate them it doesn't mean that they are somehow deeper than anything more instant from the old days. However, if not top-rate, *A Bigger Bang* is at least entertaining most of the time, and a promise of better things to come is as substantiated as it always has been since the first major disappointments of the post-Mick Taylor era – when fans began listening to each album before purchase and the concept of collecting every record the Stones ever made became economically unsound.

Gaps between releases might lengthen, but there's no reason why the group shouldn't still be making records for as long as Jagger, Richards and Watts remain alive, maybe placing some of them as high in the charts as they did in the swinging 60s. That's if we are to believe Keith Richards' prediction of a second golden age for a band that had once bared far sharper teeth to the world.

Rough Justice (Jagger-Richards) 3.11
Mick Jagger: guitar, lead vocals
Keith Richards: guitar
Charlie Watts: drums
Ronnie Wood: slide guitar
Darryl Jones: bass guitar
Chuck Leavell: piano
On this half of a double-A-side spin-off, Jagger spits out every word on a driving lecture in lust, establishing a vocal style that prevails on many other *Bigger Bang* items. During the associated tour, 'Rough Justice' proved the most popular of the new numbers that filled gaps between the ancient hits.

Let Me Down Slow (Jagger-Richards) 4.16
Mick Jagger: guitar, lead vocals
Keith Richards: guitar, vocals
Charlie Watts: drums
Ronnie Wood: slide guitar
Darryl Jones: bass guitar
If not particularly interesting musically, adroit lyrics hint at a lover's deceit prefacing her decision to dump him.

It Won't Take Long (Jagger-Richards) 3.54
Mick Jagger: guitar, lead vocals
Keith Richards: guitar, vocals
Charlie Watts: drums
Ronnie Wood: guitar
Darryl Jones: bass guitar
Chuck Leavell: organ
Rhythmically reminiscent of 'Honky Tonk Women', this anticipates the end of a fleeting affair and the other party becoming little more than a shadowy memory.

Rain Fall Down (Jagger-Richards) 4.53
Keith Richards: guitar, vocals
Mick Jagger: guitar, keyboards, vibraphone, lead vocals
Matt Clifford: keyboards, vibraphone, programming
Charlie Watts: drums
Ronnie Wood: guitar
Darryl Jones: bass guitar
A portrayal of a couple attempting to purchase respite from a frustrated, seedy flash life in a block of flats built by the book for those who had no choice.

Streets Of Love (Jagger-Richards) 5.10
Mick Jagger: guitar, lead vocals
Charlie Watts: drums
Darryl Jones: bass guitar
Keith Richards: guitar
Ronnie Wood: guitar
Chuck Leavell: piano, organ
Matt Clifford: piano, organ, strings, programming
This downbeat choice for a spin-off A side centres on a broken-hearted paramour stumbling along brightly lit streets at odds with his tearful mood.

Back Of My Hand (Jagger-Richards) 3.33
Mick Jagger: slide and bass guitars, lead vocals, harmonica, percussion
Keith Richards: guitar
Jagger is no slouch on bottleneck guitar on a blues track that evokes 'Hide Your Love' from *Goat's Head Soup* and wouldn't have been out of place on any other Stones album apart from *Satanic Majesties* or perhaps *Between The Buttons*.

She Saw Me Coming (Jagger-Richards) 3.32
Mick Jagger: bass guitar, lead vocals, percussion
Ronnie Wood: guitar
Keith Richards: guitar, vocals, piano
Charlie Watts: drums
Blondie Chaplin: vocals
Sometimes experience is recognising mistakes when they occur again, as they do when a calculating gold-digger's raw beauty rides roughshod over caution.

Biggest Mistake (Jagger-Richards) 3.12
Mick Jagger: guitar, lead vocals
Keith Richards: guitar, vocals
Charlie Watts: drums
Ronnie Wood: guitar
Darryl Jones: bass guitar
Chuck Leavell: organ

Echo-laden drumming high in the mix dominates *A Bigger Bang*, as exemplified most conspicuously on this account of true love arriving late only to be thrown away.

This Place Is Empty (Jagger-Richards) 4.06
Mick Jagger: slide guitar, vocals
Charlie Watts: drums
Keith Richards: guitar, lead vocals, piano, bass guitar
Don Was: piano

Richards is to the fore here, singing as if he's been gargling with iron filings on what is in part a laid-back lyrical update of 1963's 'Walk Right In', a million-selling revival by The Rooftop Singers of a jug band blues from the 30s.

Oh No Not You Again (Jagger-Richards) 3.16
Mick Jagger: guitar, lead vocals
Keith Richards: guitar, bass guitar
Charlie Watts: drums
Ronnie Wood: guitar
Darryl Jones: bass guitar

Replete with unremarkable lyrics and in-one-ear-and-out-the-other melody, this is a self-pastiche that Keith and Mick may have written on a muggy afternoon.

Dangerous Beauty (Jagger-Richards) 3.46
Mick Jagger: guitar, lead vocals, bass guitar
Keith Richards: guitar
Charlie Watts: drums

As uninspired as the preceding track, this seems too much like sham-tough-but-nothing syllables strung together to carry the tune.

Laugh I Nearly Died (Jagger-Richards) 4.54
Mick Jagger: guitar, lead vocals, bass guitar
Keith Richards: guitar
Charlie Watts: drums
Darryl Jones: bass guitar
The tempo drops on this impassioned cry of one whose global wanderings have brought ennui rather than wisdom in the context of a lost love.

Sweet Neo Con (Jagger-Richards) 4.33
Mick Jagger: guitar, lead vocals, bass guitar, harmonica, keyboards
Keith Richards: guitar
Charlie Watts: drums
Underscored by harmonica, this political number was advisedly not included in the stage set, swiping as it does at a certain world statesman and his foolish friendships.

Look What The Cat Dragged In (Jagger-Richards) 3.57
Mick Jagger: guitar, lead vocals, bass guitar
Keith Richards: guitar
Charlie Watts: drums
Ronnie Wood: guitar
Darryl Jones: bass guitar
Lenny Castro: percussion
The principal riff was a doctoring of INXS's 'Need You Tonight'; the influenced influencing the influencer. It serves as a support structure for verses in which a girlfriend, or possibly a child, is censured for staying out too late and indulging in pleasures that the singer knew only too well during an unquiet youth.

Driving Too Fast (Jagger-Richards) 3.56
Mick Jagger: guitar, lead vocals, percussion
Keith Richards: guitar
Charlie Watts: drums
Ronnie Wood: guitar
Darryl Jones: bass guitar
Chuck Leavell: piano
Somehow the most typical of the 21st century Stones' output, a basic rough-and-ready performance is processed at the console so that lead vocals and rhythmic pulse dominate layers of treated sound.

Infamy (Jagger-Richards) 3.47

Mick Jagger: guitar, vocals, harmonica, keyboards, percussion
Keith Richards: guitar, lead vocals, keyboards, bass guitar, percussion
Charlie Watts: drums
Blondie Chaplin: vocals

While Keith unveils a persecution complex, Sir Mick is in more insidious evidence as a multi-instrumentalist. Taped during the same block-booked sessions as 'She Saw Me Coming', Blondie Chaplin, a former Beach Boy, contributes a backing harmony.

RARITIES 1971-2003

UK Release: 22 November 2005 **Virgin/EMI CDV3015**
US Release: 22 November 2005 **Virgin/EMI CDV3015**
Producers: The Glimmer Twins, Chris Kimsey, Don Was, Steve Lillywhite
Running Time: 79:32

Fancy Man Blues; Tumbling Dice; Wild Horses; Beast Of Burden; Anyway You Look At It; If I Was A Dancer (Dance Part Two); Miss You; Wish I'd Never Met You; I Just Want To Make Love To You; Mixed Emotions; Through The Lonely Nights; Live With Me; Let It Rock; Harlem Shuffle; Mannish Boy; Thru' And Thru'.

Pop stars are two-a-penny. Jagger, Richards, Wyman, Watts – there are plenty more where they came from. Much rarer is the diehard fan who can tell you at a moment's notice the catalogue number of the Indonesian pressing of 'Love Is Strong'. He may have three cats called 'Angie', 'Downtown Suzie' and 'Lady Jane'; plan his life and bank balance around every Rolling Stones tour of Britain; and holiday in a different overseas country every year just to seek out and buy Stones recordings issued on an alien label.

The sounds in the grooves are the same, but there are visual differences. When 'Honky Tonk Women' was issued in the Netherlands, Dutch Decca was in the final weeks of using the old logo that had the firm's name in large capital letters across the top of the label. The second pressing stuck to the same fundamental design except that it was printed using a more compact typeface. This is most noticeable on the song title. Another intriguing feature is that it was still (Jagger-Richard) rather than (Jagger-Richards) in the composing credits. Also, the Dutch 'Honky Tonk Women' has a push-out rather than a solid centre.

Wanting to know everything about the Stones, no piece of information is too insignificant to be less than totally fascinating to a true fanatic. He can dwell very eloquently and with great authority on his interest but can't grasp why everyone else isn't as captivated. The floor of his converted attic groans beneath the weight of memorabilia and piles of records with label variations, foreign picture sleeves and the canons of associated artistes.

ROLLING STONES RARITIES 1971–2003

In the queue outside Seattle's Kingdome on the 1981 tour, a deranged woman attracted the attention of patrolling police by brandishing a revolver and spluttering about how she was going to worm her way to within point-blank range of Jagger. However, most of those for whom a hobby has turned into an obsession, even almost a religion, accept that their function is to remain uninvolved directly and just to absorb the signals as they come. For hundreds, thousands of hours, they file, catalogue and gloat over their acquisitions, finding much to study, notice and compare.

It was to such a person, rather than more marginal Stones devotees, that *Rarities* was targeted. That the fan is inclined to be North American is illustrated by the hoisting of this retrospective to No. 76 in the US Hot 100 while it hardly made a ripple at home.

Even so, it spread itself thinly enough to shift over half a million copies to date, a statistic all the more surprising because this curate's egg of an album is filled with nothing from the group's period of maximum artistic impact. The earliest track is from 1971; the majority have been exhumed from the past 20 years of the Stones answering often perfunctory questions about whatever current record a journalist would or wouldn't ever hear. They would, on these occasions be prompted, sometimes in vain, to retell the old, old story of a more ground-breaking past for the trillionth time.

Fancy Man Blues (Jagger-Richards) 4.48

Mick Jagger: harmonica and lead vocals
Charlie Watts: drums
Bill Wyman: bass guitar
Keith Richards: guitar
Ronnie Wood: guitar
Chuck Leavell: piano

The B side of 1989's 'Mixed Emotions', this boiled down to a standard 12-bar blues chord sequence, a walking bass line and a lyric about a two-timing girlfriend.

Tumbling Dice (Jagger-Richards) 4.02
Mick Jagger: lead vocals
Keith Richards: guitar
Charlie Watts: drums
Darryl Jones: bass guitar
Ronnie Wood: guitar
Chuck Leavell: piano
Bernard Fowler, Lisa Fischer and others: backing vocals
Bobby Keyes: saxophone

Remaindered from *Stripped*, this was taped during rehearsals for the *Voodoo Lounge* expedition in July 1995. Fractionally slower than the *Exile On Main Street* template, it was regarded by Keith Richards as the definitive arrangement.

Wild Horses (Jagger-Richards) 5.10
Mick Jagger: harmonica and lead vocals
Keith Richards: guitar
Charlie Watts: drums
Ronnie Wood: guitar
Darryl Jones: bass guitar
Chuck Leavell: keyboards

Incorporated into the set during the *Voodoo Lounge* tour, this version of the *Sticky Fingers* ballad was recorded before an invited audience in the EMI studio in Tokyo on 3 March 1995. It was issued as a single in the Netherlands the following spring.

Beast Of Burden (Jagger-Richards) 5.04
Mick Jagger: lead vocals
Keith Richards: guitar
Charlie Watts: drums
Bill Wyman: bass guitar
Ronnie Wood: guitar
Ian McLagan: keyboards
Ernie Watts: saxophone

Apparently this arrangement dates from a 1981 extravaganza in Los Angeles. Functioning mainly in Jagger's extrapolated verses and the duelling guitars of Richards and Wood, it was buried on the B side of another in-concert item, 'Goin' To A Go-Go', and also turned up on the *Sucking In The Seventies* compilation.

Anyway You Look At It (Jagger-Richards) 4.20

Mick Jagger: lead vocals
Keith Richards: guitar
Charlie Watts: drums
Ronnie Wood: guitar
Darryl Jones: bass guitar
Unknown: synthesised violin

On a rather ponderous *lied* that was the B side of 'Saint Of Me' in 1998, Jagger sounds not unlike a lower register Marianne Faithfull after her soprano had been shorn of its former purity by years of chain-smoking.

If I Was A Dancer (Dance Part Two) (Jagger-Richards-Wood) 5.50

Mick Jagger: lead vocals
Keith Richards: guitar
Charlie Watts: drums
Bill Wyman: bass guitar
Ronnie Wood: guitar
Bobby Keyes: saxophone
Max Romeo: backing vocals
Michael Shrieve: percussion

Freighted with a pot-pourri of polyrhythms – courtesy mostly of Shrieve – this version of *Emotional Rescue*'s opening 'Dance', the first song credited to Wood as an official Rolling Stone, was heard hitherto only on *Sucking In The Seventies*.

Miss You (Jagger-Richards) 7.32

Mick Jagger: lead vocals
Keith Richards: guitar
Charlie Watts: drums
Bill Wyman: bass guitar
Ronnie Wood: guitar
Ian McLagan: keyboards
Sugar Blue: harmonica
Mel Collins: saxophone

With assistance from US engineer Bob Clearmountain, Jagger made his debut as a remixer on a 'Miss You' that saw the light of day as the Stones' first 12-inch single, just as disco fever was sashaying to its John Travolta zenith.

Wish I'd Never Met You (Jagger-Richards) 4.39

Mick Jagger: lead vocals
Charlie Watts: drums
Ronnie Wood: guitar
Keith Richards: guitar
Bill Wyman: bass guitar
Chuck Leavell: keyboards

As a composition, this slow blues was in existence during sessions for *Dirty Work*. Finished at Monserrat's Air Studios in June 1989, it formed the UK B side of 'Almost Hear You Sigh' and in 1990, 'Terrifying'.

I Just Want To Make Love To You (Willie Dixon) 3.55

Mick Jagger: lead vocals
Charlie Watts: drums
Ronnie Wood: guitar
Lisa Fischer, Blondie Chaplin and Bernard Fowler: backing vocals
Keith Richards: guitar
Darryl Jones: bass guitar
Chuck Leavell: keyboards

Akin to the funereal-paced rendition by The Sensational Alex Harvey Band on 1972's *Framed* LP, this was a highlight of a show in Amsterdam on 1 July 1998.

Mixed Emotions (Jagger-Richards) 6.12

Mick Jagger: lead vocals
Keith Richards and Ronnie Wood: guitars
Chuck Leavell: keyboards
Bernard Fowler, Lisa Fischer, Sarah Dash and others: backing vocals
Bill Wyman: bass guitar
Charlie Watts: drums
The Kick Horns: brass and woodwinds

Having got the measure of this remix business, this overhaul of an A side from *Undercover* placed greater emphasis on keyboards. Sarah Dash from Labelle was prominent on *Talk Is Cheap,* Keith Richards' maiden solo album of 1988.

Through The Lonely Nights (Jagger-Richards) 4.12
Mick Jagger: lead vocals
Keith Richards, Mick Taylor and Jimmy Page: guitars
Bill Wyman: bass guitar
Charlie Watts: drums
Nicky Hopkins: keyboards

The B side of both British and US pressings of 'It's Only Rock 'N Roll', this has an acoustic emphasis. It was recorded during the London sessions for *Goat's Head Soup* in 1974. The purported presence of Jimmy Page may have been at the instigation of engineer Keith Harwood who worked principally with Led Zeppelin.

Live With Me (Jagger-Richards) 3.47
Mick Jagger: lead vocals
Charlie Watts: drums
Darryl Jones: bass guitar
Lisa Fischer, Bernard Fowler and Blondie Chaplin: backing vocals
Keith Richards: guitar
Ronnie Wood: guitar
Chuck Leavell: keyboards
Bobby Keyes: saxophone

This reworking of an over-valued track from *Let It Bleed* was immortalised at Amsterdam's Arena stadium on 1 July 1998 for possible inclusion on *No Security*.

Let It Rock (Chuck Berry) 3.47
Mick Jagger: lead vocals
Charlie Watts: drums
Mick Taylor: guitar
Bobby Keyes: saxophone
Keith Richards: guitar
Bill Wyman: bass guitar
Nicky Hopkins: keyboards
Jim Price: trumpet

Starting as the UK-only B side of the 'Brown Sugar'/'Bitch' maxi-single in 1971, it was a 1972 A side in its own right in Germany, having been captured on tape at the University of Leeds during the round-Britain trek in 1971 that prefaced the Stones' evacuation to France. The rest of the concert was also recorded but remains in the vaults.

Harlem Shuffle (Bob Relf-Ernest Nelson) 5.48

Mick Jagger: lead vocals
Keith Richards: guitar
Charlie Watts: drums
Bill Wyman: bass guitar
Ronnie Wood: guitar
Chuck Leavell: keyboards
Patti Scialfa, Bobby Womack, Don Covay, Tom Waits and others: backing vocals

This is the New York mix of the 1985 revival of Bob and Earl's 1969 sleeper hit. Among distinguished additional personnel are Womack, co-composer of 'It's All Over Now', chart-busting soul singer Covay and post-beatnik singing songwriter Waits.

Mannish Boy (McKinley Morganfield-Elias McDaniel-Mel London) 4.28

Mick Jagger: lead vocals
Keith Richards: guitar
Charlie Watts: drums
Bill Wyman: bass guitar
Ronnie Wood: guitar
Billy Preston: keyboards
Ollie Brown: congas

A set-work from the Crawdaddy days, this was taped at Toronto's El Mocambo club and short-listed for *Love You Live*. As it also surfaced on *Sucking In The Seventies*, it may be described as only a borderline rarity like companion tracks 'Beast Of Burden', 'Wild Horses' and 'Live With Me'.

Thru' And Thru' (Jagger-Richards) 6.39

Keith Richards: guitar, lead vocals
Charlie Watts: drums
Ronnie Wood: guitar
Darryl Wood: bass guitar
Mick Jagger, Bernard Fowler and others: backing vocals
Chuck Leavell: keyboards

One of Keith's stints at the central microphone, giving 'em a *Voodoo Lounge* opus, this was recorded at Madison Square Garden in January 2003.

THE US ALBUMS

ENGLAND'S NEWEST HITMAKERS

London LL 3373/PS 375
Release Date: 3 May 1964
Running Time: 31:21

Producer: Andrew Loog Oldham
Intl CD No: ABKCO 093752

SIDE ONE: Not Fade Away; Route 66; I Just Wanna Make Love To You; Honest I Do; Now I've Got A Witness; Little By Little.

SIDE TWO: I'm A King Bee; Carol; Tell Me (You're Coming Back); Can I Get A Witness; You Can Make It If You Try; Walking The Dog.

The day after 'Not Fade Away' entered the US Hot 100 at No. 98, it became a selling point of *England's Newest Hitmakers*, that began its own pedantic climb to No. 11 in the Billboard list.

Not Fade Away (Petty-Holly) 1.48

Mick Jagger: lead vocals
Keith Richards: guitar
Charlie Watts: drums
Brian Jones: harmonica
Bill Wyman: bass guitar
Mick Jagger and Phil Spector: percussion

As a schoolboy, Jagger had lent an intrigued ear to Buddy Holly and with Dick Taylor had seen the bespectacled Texan in concert with his accompanying Crickets in 1958. 'We both thought "Not Fade Away" was the best thing Buddy ever did,' enthused Dick, 'Although it was only a B side.' Six years later, the Rolling Stones version harried the British Top 10 and irritated the US Top 50. 'The way they arranged "Not Fade Away" was the beginning of Keith and Mick as songwriters,' remarked Andrew Oldham after the song had been reworked by Keith Richards on acoustic guitar to sound more like the previous summer's posthumous Buddy Holly solo hit, a vibrant revival of 'Bo Diddley' that retained the self-dedicating Bo's trademark shave-and-a-haircut-six-pence rhythm.

Route 66 2.20
See British *The Rolling Stones* album LK 4605.

I Just Wanna Make Love To You 2.17
See British *The Rolling Stones* album LK 4605.

Honest I Do 2.09
See British *The Rolling Stones* album LK 4605.

Now I've Got A Witness 2.29
See British *The Rolling Stones* album LK 4605.

Little By Little 2.39
See British *The Rolling Stones* album LK 4605.

I'm A King Bee 2.35
See British *The Rolling Stones* album LK 4605.

ENGLAND'S NEWEST HIT MAKERS

THE ROLLING STONES

Carol 2.33
See British *The Rolling Stones* album LK 4605.

Tell Me (You're Coming Back) 3.48
See British *The Rolling Stones* album LK 4605.

Can I Get A Witness 2.55
See British *The Rolling Stones* album LK 4605.

You Can Make It If You Try 2.01
See British *The Rolling Stones* album LK 4605.

Walking The Dog 3.10
See British *The Rolling Stones* album LK 4605.

12 X 5

London LL 3402/PS 402
Release Date: 23 October 1964
Running Time: 32:26

Producer: Andrew Loog Oldham
Intl CD No: ABKCO 94022

SIDE ONE: Around And Around; Confessin' The Blues; Empty Heart; Time Is On My Side; Good Times Bad Times; It's All Over Now.

SIDE TWO: 2120 South Michigan Avenue; Under The Boardwalk; Congratulations; Grown Up Wrong; If You Need Me; Suzie Q.

The Rolling Stones proved able to sustain and build upon their initial impact on North America when *12 X 5* – a mixture mostly of the contents of the British EP *Five By Five* and tracks from the second UK album – rose to No. 3 in the weekly chart published in *Billboard*, the Bible and Yellow Pages of the US music business.

Around And Around (Berry) 3.03
Mick Jagger: lead vocals
Brian Jones and Keith Richards: guitars
Ian Stewart: piano
Bill Wyman: bass guitar
Charlie Watts: drums

One of the first numbers to enter the Stones' repertoire, this 1958 Chuck Berry B side was sung by Mick Jagger, backed by Dick Taylor, Keith Richards and members of Blues Incorporated. Motionless except for trembling knees, Jagger found the nerve to mount a public stage for the first time. This took place in April 1962 at a newly opened blues club in Ealing and began the flight of Jagger and Richards to the very pinnacle of pop.

LONDON
THE ROLLING STONES
12 X 5
LL 3402 MONO

Confessin' The Blues (McShann-Brown) 2.47

Mick Jagger: lead vocals, harmonica
Bill Wyman: bass guitar
Ian Stewart: piano
Brian Jones and Keith Richards: guitars
Charlie Watts: drums

Such a confession was also an admission of the influence, however indirect, of lyricist Walter Brown who belted out the blues with Jay McShann's Kansas City Orchestra in the 40s. A point in this song's favour was that it was covered by Chuck Berry.

Empty Heart (Nanker-Phelge) 2.37

Mick Jagger: lead vocals, tambourine
Bill Wyman: bass guitar
Charlie Watts: drums
Brian Jones: harmonica
Keith Richards: guitar, backing vocals
Ian Stewart: organ

Nanker-Phelge efforts weren't just throwaway instrumentals as demonstrated by this solidly bona fide song that was to be the subject of a remarkable revival by an ageing ? and the Mysterions in the late 90s.

Time Is On My Side (Meade) 2.53

Mick Jagger: lead vocals, tambourine
Bill Wyman: bass guitar
Brian Jones, Bill Wyman and Keith Richards: backing vocals
Brian Jones and Keith Richards: guitars
Charlie Watts: drums
Ian Stewart: piano

With less emphasis on organ and more on Richards' lead guitar, this is noticably different from the version of the same number on *The Rolling Stones No. 2* that was recorded in Chicago rather than London.

Good Times Bad Times (Jagger-Richards) 2.30

Mick Jagger: lead vocals
Keith Richards: 12-string guitar
Charlie Watts: drums
Brian Jones: harmonica
Bill Wyman: bass guitar

A straightforward blues structure frames crackerbarrel philosophy in the context of a broken romance. It was also the B side of 'It's All Over Now' in almost all territories.

It's All Over Now (Womack-Womack) 3.26

Mick Jagger: lead vocals, tambourine
Brian Jones and Keith Richards: guitars
Bill Wyman: bass guitar
Charlie Watts: drums
Ian Stewart: piano
Keith Richards: backing vocals

Brian Jones was 'not that keen on the record. It's all right, but, I don't know...it's just something.' Yet this stirring improvement on a minor US hit by soul combo The Valentinos that was so minor that it didn't warrant a release in Europe, was the first of five consecutive UK No. 1s for the Stones. For weeks throughout 1964's high summer, 'It's All Over Now' and The Beatles' 'A Hard Day's Night' monopolised the first two positions in Britain's hit parade, necessitating the avoidance of such revenue-draining clashes in future.

2120 South Michigan Avenue (Nanker-Phelge) 3.38

Mick Jagger: tambourine
Brian Jones: harmonica
Keith Richards: guitar
Bill Wyman: bass guitar
Charlie Watts: drums
Ian Stewart: organ

Named after the postal address of the studio where it was taped, a streamlining of ideas that surfaced during a jam session resulted in an instrumental of similar persuasion to 'Now I've Got A Witness' on the first British LP. Because of the EP format's more restricted needle-time, the version on *Five By Five* suffered severe editing.

Under The Boardwalk

See British *The Rolling Stones* No. 2 LK 4661

Congratulations (Jagger-Richards) 2.29

Mick Jagger: lead vocals
Bill Wyman: bass guitar
Brian Jones and Keith Richards: guitars
Charlie Watts: drums
Ian Stewart: piano
Keith Richards: backing vocals

This had nothing to do with Cliff Richard's celebrated Eurovision Song Contest entry and was far from the greatest song that ever dripped from the Jagger-Richards pen. However, it was considered worthy of issue as a catchpenny A side in Germany.

Grown Up Wrong
See British *The Rolling Stones* No. 2 LK 4661.

If You Need Me (Bateman-Pickett-Sanders) 2.04
Mick Jagger: lead vocals
Keith Richards: guitar, backing vocals
Charlie Watts: drums
Brian Jones: tambourine
Bill Wyman: bass guitar
Ian Stewart: piano, organ
Legato organ chords intrude upon a soul ballad not dissimilar to 'Time Is On My Side'. On UK pirate radio, it competed with 'Around And Around' as the most played *Five By Five* track. It had been a small US chart strike for co-writer Wilson Pickett in 1961.

Susie Q
See British *The Rolling Stones No. 2* LK 4661.

THE ROLLING STONES NOW!

London LL 3420/PS 420
Release Date: 12 February 1965
Running Time: 36:00

Producer: Andrew Loog Oldham
Intl CD No: ABKCO 94202

SIDE ONE: Everybody Needs Somebody To Love; Down Home Girl; You Can't Catch Me; Heart Of Stone; What A Shame; Mona (I Need You Baby).

SIDE TWO: Down The Road Apiece; Off The Hook; Pain In My Heart; Oh Baby (We Got A Good Thing Goin'); Little Red Rooster; Surprise Surprise.

This reached No. 5 in the Billboard chart.

Everybody Needs Somebody To Love (Burke-Berns-Wexler) 2.58
Mick Jagger: lead vocals
Brian Jones and Keith Richards: guitars
Mick Jagger and Keith Richards: backing vocals
Bill Wyman: bass guitar
Charlie Watts: drums
Supposedly, the insertion of this shorter, and inferior, version of the track on the second British LP was the result of incompetence at the pressing plant.

Down Home Girl 4.12
See British *The Rolling Stones* No. 2 LK 4661.

You Can't Catch Me 3.39
See British *The Rolling Stones* No. 2 LK 4661.

Heart Of Stone 2.49
See British *Out Of Our Heads* LK/SKL 4733.

THE ROLLING STONES, NOW

What A Shame 3.05
See British *The Rolling Stones* No. 2 LK 4661.

Mona 3.35
See British *The Rolling Stones* LK 4605.

Down The Road Apiece 2.55
See British *The Rolling Stones* No. 2 LK 4661.

Off The Hook 2.34
See British *The Rolling Stones* No. 2 LK 4661.

Pain In My Heart 2.12
See British *The Rolling Stones* No. 2 LK 4661.

Oh Baby (We Got A Good Thing Goin') 2.08
See British *Out Of Our Heads* LK/SKL 4733.

Little Red Rooster (Dixon) 3.05
Mick Jagger: lead vocals, harmonica
Brian Jones: slide guitar
Keith Richards: guitars
Bill Wyman: bass guitar
Charlie Watts: drums

In November 1964, Willie Dixon topped the British charts by proxy as composer of the group's unrevised 'Little Red Rooster. The blues pedigree could be traced back through a rendition by Sam Cooke in 1963 to The Griffin Brothers' US sepia smash in 1951 to the first recording by Howlin' Wolf. The risk the Stones took in putting out a slow blues as an A side was confirmed when it caused of one of the biggest discrepancies between the two principal national music journal charts, entering at No. 15 in *Melody Maker* and going straight in at No.1 in the *New Musical Express*.

Surprise Surprise (Jagger-Richards) 2.31

Mick Jagger: lead vocals
Keith Richards: guitar
Charlie Watts: drums
Brian Jones: tambourine
Bill Wyman: bass guitar

Underproduced and tinged with the fading Merseybeat sound, this was not to be issued in Britain until buried as the third track on a 1971 maxi-single. Nevertheless, Sweden's Ola and the Janglers, re-invented as an ersatz British beat group, took a crack at it as did Scotland's Lulu and the Luvvers.

OUT OF OUR HEADS

London LL 3429/PS 429
Release Date: 30 July 1965
Running Time: 33:40

Producer: Andrew Loog Oldham
Intl CD No: ABKCO 94292

SIDE ONE: Mercy Mercy; Hitch Hike; The Last Time; That's How Strong My Love Is; Good Times; I'm Alright.

SIDE TWO: (I Can't Get No) Satisfaction; Cry To Me; The Under Assistant West Coast Promotion Man; Play With Fire; The Spider And The Fly; One More Try.

This was the first Rolling Stones LP to top the US chart. Its content was markedly different from the British album of the same title.

Mercy Mercy 2.45
See British *Out Of Our Heads* LK/SKL 4733.

Hitch Hike 2.25
See British *Out Of Our Heads* LK/SKL 4733.

The Last Time (Jagger-Richards) 3.41
Mick Jagger: lead vocals
Keith Richards and Brian Jones: guitars
Ian Stewart: piano
Jack Nitzsche: tambourine
Bill Wyman: bass guitar
Charlie Watts: drums
Keith Richards: backing vocals

The first Jagger-Richards A side for the group, this topped the British chart and entered the US Top 10. But, for all its rivetting guitar riff and Mick's bawling 'no-no-no' coda, it was a modest affair with basic boy-girl rhyming couplets and a chorus borrowed from 'This May Be The Last Time', a traditional song popularised in 1955 by The Five Blind Boys Of Mississippi, a gospel ensemble whose works could be bought in London record shops that specialised in imported merchandise from black America. Royalties from The Who's revival of 'The Last Time' as a single were donated to Mick and Keith's legal costs for their appeal against their respective gaol sentences in 1967.

That's How Strong My Love Is 2.25
See British *Out Of Our Heads* LK/SKL 4733.

Good Times 1.58
See British *Out Of Our Heads* LK/SKL 4733.

I'm Alright (Nanker-Phelge) 2.23
Mick Jagger: lead vocals
Keith Richards and Brian Jones: guitars
Bill Wyman: bass guitar
Charlie Watts: drums
A live track from the inaugural night at the Regal, Edmonton, part of a spring tour of Britain in 1965, this was a rethink of a Bo Diddley opus. It was also included on *Got Live If You Want It,* a UK-only EP that penetrated the singles Top 20. A US album of the same title was to embrace an 'I'm Alright' taped at another location.

(I Can't Get No) Satisfaction (Jagger-Richards) 3.43
Mick Jagger: lead vocals
Keith Richards and Brian Jones: guitars
Ian Stewart: piano
Bill Wyman: bass guitar
Charlie Watts: drums
Jack Nitzsche: tambourine
Mick Jagger and Keith Richards: backing vocals
Was this Beethoven's 5th of 60s pop a dissection of the Warhol-esque aesthetics of consumer culture or just Jagger moaning about the vicissitudes of his travelling life? He'd never offer a clue, 'because it's much more pleasurable for people to have their own interpretation of a song, novel, film and so on'. Thinking the worst, US TV's Ed Sullivan Show decreed the bleeping out of 'make' in the phrase 'trying to make some girl'. Similarly, radio and TV stations around the world were unhappy about other lines, and English teachers were trying to repair the damage caused by the double negative in the number's title.

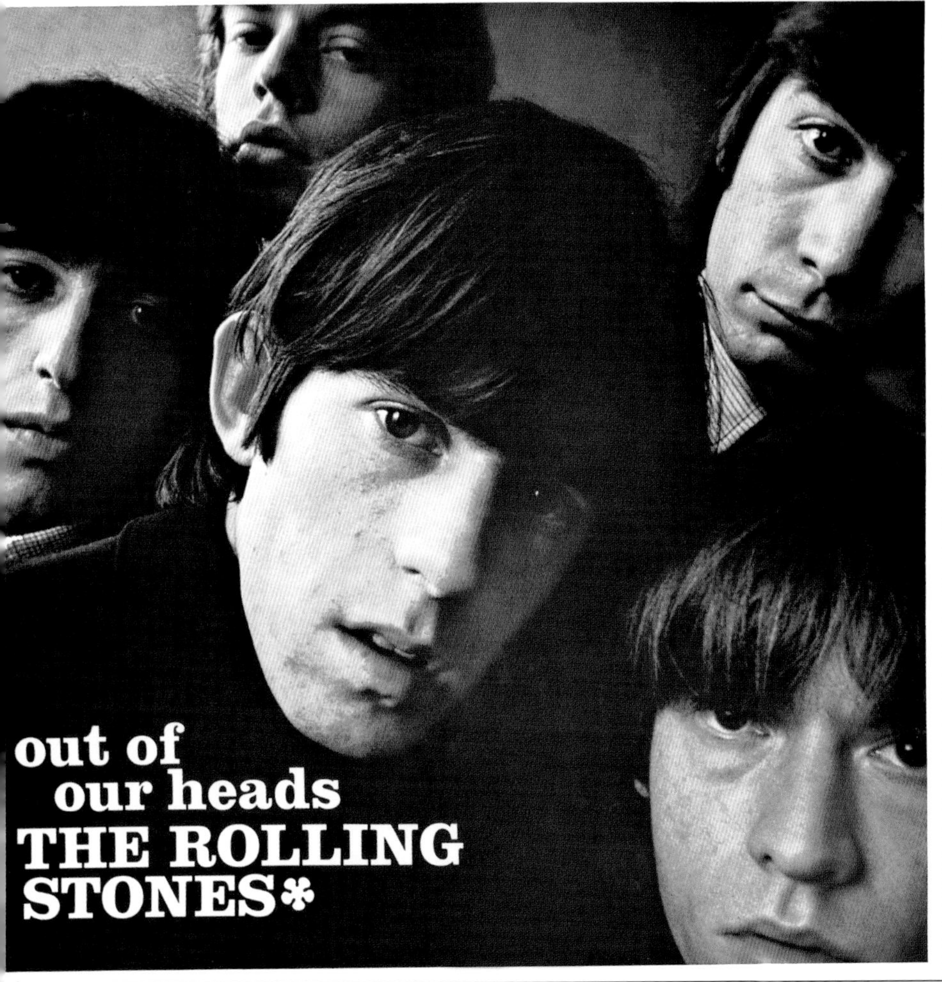
out of
our heads
THE ROLLING
STONES*

'Satisfaction' would be the Stones' first US No.1 and would be voted 1965's Best Single Of The Year in *New Musical Express*'s readers poll. It was little liked by Richards, to whom its defining ostinato occurred when he was jerked from sleep, bedevilled by an impulse to note it on the transistorised tape-recorder that had become as essential as a toilet-bag in his luggage. After the song had been launched into more tangible form, he fretted about what appeared to be its stomach-knotting similarity to 'Dancing In The Street' by Martha and the Vandellas. Another concern was that 'I can't get no satisfaction from the judge' had started a verse of the litigious Chuck Berry's 'Thirty Days' from 1955.

Cry To Me 3.09
See British *Out Of Our Heads* LK/SKL 4733.

The Under Assistant West Coast Promotion Man 3.07
See British *Out Of Our Heads* LK/SKL 4733.

Play With Fire (Nanker-Phelge) 2.14
Mick Jagger: lead vocals, tambourine
Keith Richards: guitar
Phil Spector: bass guitar
Jack Nitzsche: harpsichord, percussion
The B side of 'The Last Time', this song issued the same warning in so many words as 'Heart of Stone' to a sophisticate from a well-to-do but dysfunctional London family. It was recorded with whoever happened to be available and with whatever instruments were to hand, such as a tambourine apparently beaten with one of a dozing Bill Wyman's shoes.

The Spider And The Fly (Jagger-Richards) 3.38
Mick Jagger: lead vocals, harmonica
Keith Richards and Brian Jones: guitars
Bill Wyman: bass guitar
Charlie Watts: drums
Ian Stewart: piano
A walking-paced blues in structure, this concerned a roving minstrel's unchallenging procurement of illicit sexual gratification. Fame is a powerful aphrodisiac and, while admirable in many ways, The Rolling Stones had their share of young men's vices.

One More Try (Jagger-Richards) 1.58

Mick Jagger: lead vocals
Keith Richards and Brian Jones: guitars
Charlie Watts: drums
Brian Jones: harmonica
Bill Wyman: bass guitar
Ian Stewart: piano

This may have oozed more substance than its limited rhymes and chords suggest on paper had not the studio clock and overall fatigue dictated finishing it, and the album, in a hurry.

DECEMBER'S CHILDREN (AND EVERYBODY'S)

London LL 3431/PS 451
Release Date: 4 December 1965
Running Time: 29:06
Producer: Andrew Loog Oldham
Intl CD No: ABKCO 94512

SIDE ONE: She Said Yeah; Talkin' 'Bout You; You Better Move On; Look What You've Done; The Singer Not The Song; Route 66.

SIDE TWO: Get Off Of My Cloud; I'm Free; As Tears Go By; Gotta Get Away; Blue Turns To Grey; I'm Moving On.

Geared for the singles market as most pop stars were until the close of the decade, LPs containing a best-selling 45, in this case, 'Get Off Of My Cloud', could still do well in the States, even if programmed haphazardly and with as little as six weeks between each by a given artist. Image could render fans uncritical enough to digest sub-standard produce that testified to commercial expedience rather than quality. *December's Children* got to No. 4 and qualified for a gold disc.

She Said Yeah 1.34
See British *Out Of Our Heads* LK/SKL 4733.

Talkin' 'Bout You 2.31
See British *Out Of Our Heads* LK/SKL 4733.

PS 451
STEREO ELECTRONICALLY RE-PROCESSED
LONDON
december's
children
(and everybody's)
THE
ROLLING
STONES*

You Better Move On (Alexander) 2.39

Mick Jagger: lead vocals
Keith Richards and Brian Jones: guitars
Bill Wyman and Brian Jones; backing vocals
Bill Wyman: bass guitar
Charlie Watts: drums

This was dredged up from a session in November 1963, and had already been heard in Britain as the chief selling point of an eponymous debut EP that infiltrated the singles Top Ten. The group's first released attempt at a slow ballad, it was a belated cover of the first and biggest US hit by Arthur Alexander, a black vocalist from Alabama whose songs, if not his records, were brought to a European audience via the attentions of, among others, bands such as the Stones and Johnny Kidd and the Pirates and The Beatles, who'd already recorded 'A Shot Of Rhythm And Blues' and 'Anna' respectively.

Look What You've Done (Morganfield) 2.16

Mick Jagger: lead vocals
Keith Richards and Brian Jones: guitars
Charlie Watts: drums
Brian Jones: harmonica
Bill Wyman: bass guitar
Ian Stewart: piano

From the catalogue of Muddy Waters, who was present at the session in Chess, this is a slow and rambling blues with Stewart and Jones alternating solos.

The Singer Not The Song (Jagger-Richards) 2.22

Mick Jagger: lead vocals
Keith Richards and Brian Jones: guitars
Jack Nitzsche: organ
Bill Wyman: bass guitar
Charlie Watts: drums
Keith Richards: backing vocals

The group's corporate heart wasn't in this run-through of a twee jingle-jangle that should have been foisted on the type of also-ran acts who'd been interested in 'You Must Be The One', 'Shang-A-Doo-Lang', 'Will You Be My Lover Tonight' and other examples of Mick and Keith's early struggles as composers.

Route 66 (Troup) 2.39

Mick Jagger: lead vocals
Keith Richards and Brian Jones: guitars
Bill Wyman: bass guitar
Charlie Watts: drums

Like 'I'm Alright' from the US *Out Of Our Heads*, this whipped up a screeching rabble at the Edmonton Regal on 5 March 1965, and was selected for the *Got Live If You Want It* EP.

Get Off Of My Cloud (Jagger-Richards) 2.55

Mick Jagger: lead vocals
Keith Richards and Brian Jones: guitars
Jack Nitzsche: piano
Bill Wyman: bass guitar
Charlie Watts: drums
Mick Jagger and Keith Richards: backing vocals

In the mid-60s, the ordained strategy for keeping up a pop group's momentum was to rush-release as many 45s as possible, usually four per fiscal year. Under pressure to capitalise on 'Satisfaction', Keith and Mick came up with a similar-sounding ditty with Charlie's recurring rataplan a prominent feature that tramped a well-trodden path to the top at home and lasted a fortnight against the month its predecessor spent at No. 1 in the States. It was, opined Keith Richards, 'one of Andrew's worst productions. Actually, what I wanted to do was slow it down, but we rocked it up.' On many pressings, the title is rendered as 'Get Off My Cloud'.

I'm Free 2.23

See British *Out Of Our Heads* LK/SKL 4733.

As Tears Go By (Jagger-Richards) 2.45

Mick Jagger: lead vocals
Various: string quartet
Keith Richards: guitar

Penned to order, this roamed 1964's domestic Top 20 when sung by Marianne Faithfull, then a 17-year-old from Berkshire in whom Andrew Oldham had seen pop star potential and for whom Jagger entertained romantic designs. Though it resurfaced here as a sort of Stones 'Yesterday', Richards considered it 'the sort of song we'd never play. We were trying to write "Hoochie Coochie Man", and came out with a song that's almost like "Greensleeves"'. While relegated to a B side in Britain, it was a Top 10 entry in the US.

Gotta Get Away (Jagger-Richards) 2.07
Mick Jagger: all vocals
Keith Richards and Brian Jones: guitars
Ian Stewart: piano
Bill Wyman: bass guitar
Charlie Watts: drums
Woody Alexander: tambourine
Very much a filler, this is built round Charlie's pounding hi-hat, snare and bass drum in the same four-in-a-bar rhythm throughout, an in-one-ear-and-out-the-other effort.

Blue Turns To Grey (Jagger-Richards) 2.29
Mick Jagger: lead vocals
Keith Richards and Brian Jones: guitars
Jack Nitzsche: piano
Bill Wyman: bass guitar
Charlie Watts: drums
Mick Jagger and Keith Richards: backing vocals
Although this flopped in the hands of The Mighty Avengers, The Epics and, from California, Dick and Dee Dee, Cliff Richard took it to No. 15 in Britain. The Stones' version served as both a useful demo for the bachelor Boy and as a German flip-side not thought worthy of release at home.

I'm Moving On (Snow) 2.14
Mick Jagger: lead vocals
Keith Richards and Brian Jones: guitars
Bill Wyman: bass guitar
Charlie Watts: drums
Although speeded-up and thrust into a live context, this represented the Stones' first unquestionable venture into C&W on disc, being one of the best-known songs by Canada's Hank Snow who was to score over 60 entries in Billboard's country chart between 1950 and 1970.

AFTERMATH

London LL 3476/PS 476
Release Date: 2 July 1966
Running Time: 42:59

Producer: Andrew Loog Oldham
Intl CD No: ABKCO 94762

SIDE ONE: Paint It Black; Stupid Girl; Lady Jane; Under My Thumb; Dontcha Bother Me; Think.

SIDE TWO: Flight 505; High And Dry; It's Not Easy; I Am Waiting; Goin' Home.

Fourteen tracks was considered too long for the US pressing although it was thought prudent to kick off with a recent smash. This judgment proved correct as *Aftermath* stopped just one position short of No. 1.

Paint It Black (Jagger-Richards) 3.45
Mick Jagger: lead vocals
Brian Jones and Keith Richards: guitars
Brian Jones: sitar
Mick Jagger and Keith Richards: backing vocals
Charlie Watts: drums
Bill Wyman: bass guitar, organ
Jack Nitzsche: piano

To *Melody Maker* this follow-up to '19th Nervous Breakdown', also a chart-topper, was memorable for 'Charlie's driving tom-tom drumming, a sitar sound and Mick's special Indian lament voice. Charlie creates a galloping beat suggesting high-speed elephants, and Mick's accents get gradually more curried'. In an attempt to make the song exhale a further breath of the Orient, Watts confessed 'We ruined a marvellous pair of tablas trying to be Indians. You're not supposed to use sticks on them.' In the late 80s, 'Paint It Black' was back at No. 1 in Holland, having been employed as the theme to a TV series. On a 1967 A side by Chris Farlowe, produced by Jagger, Jones's masterful sitar obligato was traded for gypsy violins and a syncopated bolero passage.

Stupid Girl (Jagger-Richards) 2.55
See British *Aftermath* LK/SKL 4786.

Lady Jane (Jagger-Richards) 3.08
See British *Aftermath* LK/SKL 4786.

Under My Thumb (Jagger-Richards) 3.41
See British *Aftermath* LK/SKL 4786.

Dontcha Bother Me (Jagger-Richards) 2.41
See British *Aftermath* LK/SKL 4786.

Think (Jagger-Richards) 3.09
See British *Aftermath* LK/SKL 4786.

Flight 505 (Jagger-Richards) 3.27
See British *Aftermath* LK/SKL 4786.

High And Dry (Jagger-Richards) 3.08
See British *Aftermath* LK/SKL 4786.

It's Not Easy (Jagger-Richards) 2.56
See British *Aftermath* LK/SKL 4786.

I Am Waiting (Jagger-Richards) 3.11
See British *Aftermath* LK/SKL 4786.

Goin' Home (Jagger-Richards) 11.13
See British *Aftermath* LK/SKL 4786.

AFTERMATH

the rolling stones

INCLUDING PAINT IT, BLACK

GOT LIVE IF YOU WANT IT

London LL 3493/PS 493
Release Date: 9 December 1966
Running Time: 33:11

Producer: Andrew Loog Oldham
Intl CD No: ABKCO 94932

SIDE ONE: Under My Thumb; Get Off Of My Cloud; Lady Jane; Not Fade Away; I've Been Loving You Too Long; Fortune Teller.

SIDE TWO: The Last Time; 19th Nervous Breakdown; Time Is On My Side; I'm Alright; Have You Seen Your Mother Baby (Standing In The Shadow); (I Can't Get No) Satisfaction.

Pragmatism ruled on this first in-concert effort, reduced to a much higher-fidelity EP in Britain with two tracks unheard on the LP, whose title was a play on Slim Harpo's 'Got Love If You Want It'. This had just been released as a British single, but was known to British blues enthusiasts for years. Both The Yardbirds and The Kinks had released versions. Surprisingly The Rolling Stones didn't.

Neither did they record this LP at the London stop that was the Royal Albert Hall, contradicting what is printed on the sleeve. It wasn't completely live either. Cheap, tinny and fake though it was, *Got Live If You Want It* still earned a gold disc after falling from its zenith of No. 6. In mitigation it has to be said that conditions in the various auditoriums en route and their public-address systems, often involving equipment from the mediaeval period of sound technology, did not always allow engineer Glyn Johns to adjust recording levels. Moreover, as Keith Richards explained, 'Basically, we'd turn up, and all we'd think about is what's the exit strategy? Then we'd take bets on how many songs we'd get through before it all collapsed. Usually, it was ten minutes – three songs and it was all over. We'd walk into some of those places, and it was like they had the Battle of the Crimea [sic] going on. "Scream power" was the thing everybody was judged by. We couldn't hear each other for years.'

Keith had been one of 22 rendered unconscious after the first house at Manchester's ABC cinema on 3 October 1965, stunned by a flying lemonade bottle among votive offerings

got LIVE if you want it!
THE ROLLING STONES

that rained onto the stage. During the same expedition, some of those crammed nearest the front were able to wriggle though an inadequate barrier of stewards to almost kill Richards and Mick Jagger with kindness at the Albert Hall as Brian Jones and Bill Wyman fled into the wings, and Charlie Watts, pinioned behind his kit, had his new pink shirt so thoroughly ripped that he could never wear it again. On sodden carpeting afterwards, cleaners would come across soiled knickers among splintered rows of seating.

Except where otherwise stated, the line-up throughout is as follows:
Mick Jagger: guitar, lead vocals
Keith Richards and Brian Jones: guitars
Keith Richards: backing vocals
Bill Wyman: bass guitar
Charlie Watts: drums

As on all Rolling Stones in-concert albums, timing includes continuity and audience response.

Under My Thumb (Jagger-Richards) 2.54
After BBC Light Programme radio presenter Alan Freeman's introduction of 'the fantastic Rolling Stones' and Jagger's soulman utterances over what can be discerned of the opening instrumental bars, this sets the tone for the rest of the LP: prominent vocals over muffled accompaniment competing, often in vain, against pop hysteria at its most intense.

Get Off Of My Cloud (Jagger-Richards) 2.54
Like four other selections, this came from Newcastle's City Hall on 1 December 1966. Jagger's on-the-beat handclaps are louder than any other instrument.

Lady Jane (Jagger-Richards) 3.08
Charlie Watts emerged from behind the drums to announce a 'Lady Jane' in which Brian's dulcimer can just about be heard as Mick brazens out the ersatz-Elizabethan madrigal while perhaps suppressing an urge to laugh.

Not Fade Away (Petty-Holly) 2.04
The harmonica ostinatos are totally inaudible, prompting the question of whether one was actually being played. Tidal waves of screams – as if the girls had all sat on tin-tacks – well up to swamp the guitar break during Jagger's presumed cavortings away from the microphone.

I've Been Loving You Too Long (Redding-Butler) 2.55
Audience reaction was superimposed on this May 1965 studio recording of an Otis Redding US hit.

Fortune Teller (Neville) 1.57
Screams added after the event do not enhance the musical quality of a track dating from August 1963 and intended originally as a B side to 'Poison Ivy', a cancelled single. Hundreds of other British beat groups claimed rights over both these North American R&B hits. 'Fortune Teller', the discography of New Orleans-based singer Benny Spellman, for instance, was the B side of the 1963 debut 45 by The Merseybeats.

The Last Time (Jagger-Richards) 3.08
Jagger's 'no no no' coda is nowhere as frenzied as on the hit single and in common with other numbers previously heard only in studio form is taken at a faster pace.

19th Nervous Breakdown (Jagger-Richards) 3.31
Richards' vocal contributions are as loud as those of the mercurial Jagger, who causes the more detached onlookers to worry when he flags and glow when he rallies.

Time Is On My Side (Meade) 2.49
To the syllable, Mick proclaims his feelings in the talking bit just like he did on the two released studio versions.

I'm Alright (Jagger-Richards) 2.27
There have been allegations that this was a doctored studio recording but no concrete evidence exists. On other pressings, this song is attributed to either Nanker-Phelge or McDaniel (i.e. Bo Diddley).

Have You Seen Your Mother Baby (Standing In The Shadow) (Jagger-Richards) 2.19
It was almost decided to title the LP *Have You Seen Your Mother Live?* as this song was still in the British and US charts when the jaunt finished at the Gaumont in Southampton on 9 October 1966. It was to be another five years before the Stones toured Britain again.

(I Can't Get No) Satisfaction (Jagger-Richards) 3.05
Like the majority of *Got Live If You Want It* items, this was immortalised at Bristol's Colston Hall. However, rather than coming to a stop, it and the pandemonium fade into the run-out grooves.

BETWEEN THE BUTTONS

London LL 3499/PS 499
Release Date: 11 February 1967
Running Time: 38:51

Producer: Andrew Loog Oldham
Intl CD No: ABKCO 94992

SIDE ONE: Let's Spend The Night Together; Yesterday's Papers; Ruby Tuesday; Connection; She Smiled Sweetly; Cool Calm And Collected.

SIDE TWO: All Sold Out; My Obsession; Who's Been Sleeping Here; Complicated; Miss Amanda Jones; Something Happened To Me Yesterday.

This duplicated *Aftermath*'s chart feat of climbing to No. 2.

Let's Spend The Night Together (Jagger-Richards) 3.36
Mick Jagger: lead vocals
Keith Richards: guitar
Bill Wyman: bass guitar
Charlie Watts: drums
Brian Jones, Bill Wyman and Jack Nitzsche: keyboards
The host insisted that Mick Jagger change 'spend the night' to 'spend some time' when the Stones were booked to plug this number on The Ed Sullivan Show. That evening, Mick rolled his eyes in mock exasperation whenever he sang the doctored line. Composed largely by Keith Richards on the piano, the 45 reached No. 3 in Britain but partly because of the Ed Sullivan fuss, was demoted to the B side of 'Ruby Tuesday' in the States. David Bowie was to rehash 'Let's Spend The Night Together' on *Aladdin Sane* album of 1973.

Yesterday's Papers (Jagger-Richards) 2.04
See British *Between The Buttons* LK/SKL 4852.

Ruby Tuesday (Jagger-Richards) 3.17
Mick Jagger: lead vocals
Brian Jones: recorder, autoharp, piano
Charlie Watts: drums, tambourine
Keith Richards: guitar
Bill Wyman: bass guitar, 'cello
Mick Jagger and Keith Richards: backing vocals
According to Marianne Faithfull, while 'Jagger-Richards' was the composing credit for this US chart-topper, 'it was really Brian and Keith's song. It began, as I recall, from a bluesy Elizabethan fragment Brian was fiddling with in the studio. In his sheepish way, Brian very softly played a folkish, nursery rhyme melody on the recorder. It was nothing more than a wispy tune, but it caught Keith's attention. Brian said it was a hybrid of Thomas Dowland's "Air On The Late Lord Essex" [sic] and a Skip James blues'.

Connection (Jagger-Richards) 2.08 See British *Between The Buttons* LK/SKL 4852.

She Smiled Sweetly (Jagger-Richards) 2.44 See British *Between The Buttons* LK/SKL 4852.

Cool Calm And Collected (Jagger-Richards) 4.17 See British *Between The Buttons* LK/SKL 4852.

All Sold Out (Jagger-Richards) 2.17 See British *Between The Buttons* LK/SKL 4852.

My Obsession (Jagger-Richards) 3.17 See British *Between The Buttons* LK/SKL 4852.

Who's Been Sleeping Here (Jagger-Richards) 3.55 See British *Between The Buttons* LK/SKL 4852.

Complicated (Jagger-Richards) 3.15 See British *Between The Buttons* LK/SKL 4852.

Miss Amanda Jones (Jagger-Richards) 2.47 See British *Between The Buttons* LK/SKL 4852.

Something Happened To Me Yesterday (Jagger-Richards) 4.55
See British *Between The Buttons* LK/SKL 4852.

THE ROLLING STONES
BETWEEN THE BUTTONS

FLOWERS

London LL 3509/PS 509
Release Date: 15 July 1967
Running Time: 37:22

Producer: Andrew Loog Oldham
Intl CD No: ABKCO 95092

SIDE ONE: Ruby Tuesday; Have You Seen Your Mother Baby (Standing In The Shadow); Let's Spend The Night Together; Lady Jane; Out Of Time; My Girl.

SIDE TWO: Back Street Girl; Please Go Home; Mother's Little Helper; Take It Or Leave It; Ride On Baby; Sittin' On A Fence.

With a tacked-on title in keeping with the flower-power summer of love, this gave our colonial cousins the shortest measure of all, not in terms of actual needle-time, but in an audacious recycling of tracks from previous albums. It clambered high up the Top Ten as usual.

Ruby Tuesday (Jagger-Richards) 3.17
See US *Between The Buttons* LL 3499/PS 499.

Have You Seen Your Mother Baby (Standing In The Shadow) (Jagger-Richards) 2.34
Mick Jagger: lead vocals
Bill Wyman: bass guitar
Ian Stewart: piano
Mick Jagger, Keith Richards and Brian Jones: backing vocals
Keith Richards: guitar
Charlie Watts; drums
Jack Nitzsche: tambourine
Various: trumpets

Just as Decca's budget had stretched to the requisitioning of orchestral strings for 'As Tears Go By', it did likewise for the brass that blasted up the riff on this noisy 45, as Otis Redding-esque horns had on 'Got To Get You Into My Life' from *Revolver* The Beatles' new LP. Such an embellishment could not disguise the fact that 'Have You Seen Your Mother' wasn't much of a song. It stalled at No. 9 in the States and No. 5 at home.

DECCA

Let's Spend The Night Together (Jagger-Richards) 3.36
See US *Between The Buttons* LL 3499/PS 499.

Lady Jane (Jagger-Richards) 3.08
See British *Aftermath* LK/SKL 4786.

Out Of Time (Jagger-Richards) 3.41
See British *Aftermath* LK/SKL 4786.

My Girl (Robinson-White) 2.38
Mick Jagger: lead vocals
Brian Jones and Keith Richards: guitars
Jack Nitzsche: piano
Various: strings, woodwinds
Bill Wyman: bass guitar
Charlie Watts: drums
Mick Jagger and Keith Richards: backing vocals
A rather pointless copy of a soul item composed by Smokey Robinson of The Miracles and recorded to chart-busting effect by both The Temptations and Otis Redding. It was also covered as a US-only single by Birmingham's Carl Wayne and The Vikings who eventually became The Move.

Back Street Girl (Jagger-Richards) 3.26
See British *Between The Buttons* LK/SKL 4852.

Please Go Home (Jagger-Richards) 3.17
See British *Between The Buttons* LK/SKL 4852.

Mother's Little Helper (Jagger-Richards) 2.46
See British *Aftermath* LK/SKL 4786.

Take It Or Leave It (Jagger-Richards) 2.46
See British *Aftermath* LK/SKL 4786.

Ride On Baby (Jagger-Richards) 2.52

Mick Jagger: lead vocals
Brian Jones: marimba, dulcimer
Brian Jones, Ian Stewart and Jack Nitzsche: keyboards, congas and percussion
Mick Jagger and Keith Richards: backing vocals
Keith Richards: guitar
Bill Wyman: bass guitar
Charlie Watts: drums, timpani,

Of at least six more Jagger-Richards pieces Chris Farlowe recorded after his UK No. 1 with 'Out Of Time', only this one – much the same lyrical and musical vein – had so much as a glimpse at the Top 30. The Stones had tried it during the *Aftermath* sessions but the ragged result wasn't considered worthy of inclusion on that album.

Sittin' On A Fence (Jagger-Richards) 3.03

Mick Jagger: lead vocals
Brian Jones and Keith Richards: guitars
Brian Jones: harpsichord
Bill Wyman: bass guitar
Charlie Watts: drums, tambourine
Keith Richards: backing vocals

After a Top 10 strike with The McCoys' 'Hang On Sloopy' had fanfared the founding of *Immediate,* Richards and Jagger were employed as in-house composers and general factotums. Their clients ranged from hit-making Chris Farlowe to relative duds like Twice As Much, whose 'Sitting On A Fence' at No. 25 was the duo's highest and only chart performance. This mirrored the Stones' ersatz classical arrangement which was of the same vintage as 'Ride On Baby'.

THE BRITISH COMPILATION ALBUMS

BIG HITS (HIGH TIDE AND GREEN GRASS)

UK Release: 4 November 1966
Producer: Andrew Loog Oldham

Decca TXS 101
Running Time: 42.40

SIDE ONE: Have You Seen Your Mother Baby (Standing In The Shadow); Paint It Black; It's All Over Now; The Last Time; Heart Of Stone; (I Can't Get No) Satisfaction.

SIDE TWO: Get Off Of My Cloud; As Tears Go By; 19th Nervous Breakdown; Lady Jane; Time Is On My Side; Little Red Rooster.

All tracks previously released on albums except '19th Nervous Breakdown'.

19th Nervous Breakdown (Jagger-Richards) 3.57
Mick Jagger: lead vocals
Brian Jones and Keith Richards: guitars
Ian Stewart: piano
Bill Wyman: bass guitar
Charlie Watts: drums
Mick Jagger and Keith Richards: backing vocals

A floor-tom rumble brings in the vocal on the A side that followed its two predecessors almost to the top in Britain and in the States. Jim McCarty of The Yardbirds felt that it was symptomatic of 'a bit of a lull artistically then for the Stones, what with all those hits that were similar'. This latest smash did share the same heavy beat, mid-to fast tempo and rapid-fire verbosity as 'Satisfaction' and 'Get Off Of My Cloud'. There was also a gimmick in shuddering glissando descents on bass guitar towards the fade, and a compressed scream at the end of each bridge section. Manchester's Mike Sweeney and the Thunderbirds retrod '19th Nervous Breakdown' to agreeable effect on *Stoned Again*, a 1992 compilation album of chosen reworkings from The Rolling Stones' backlog.

big hits [high tide and green grass]

THE ROLLING STONES

DECCA

THROUGH THE PAST DARKLY (BIG HITS VOL. 2)

UK Release: 12 September 1969
Producers: Andrew Loog Oldham, The Rolling Stones, Jimmy Miller

Decca SKL 5019
Running Time: 42.30

SIDE ONE: Jumping Jack Flash; Mother's Little Helper; 2000 Light Years From Home; Let's Spend The Night Together; You Better Move On; We Love You.

SIDE TWO: Street Fighting Man; She's A Rainbow; Ruby Tuesday; Dandelion; Sittin' On A Fence; Honky Tonk Women.

All tracks previously released on albums except 'Jumping Jack Flash', 'We Love You', 'Dandelion' and 'Honky Tonk Women'.

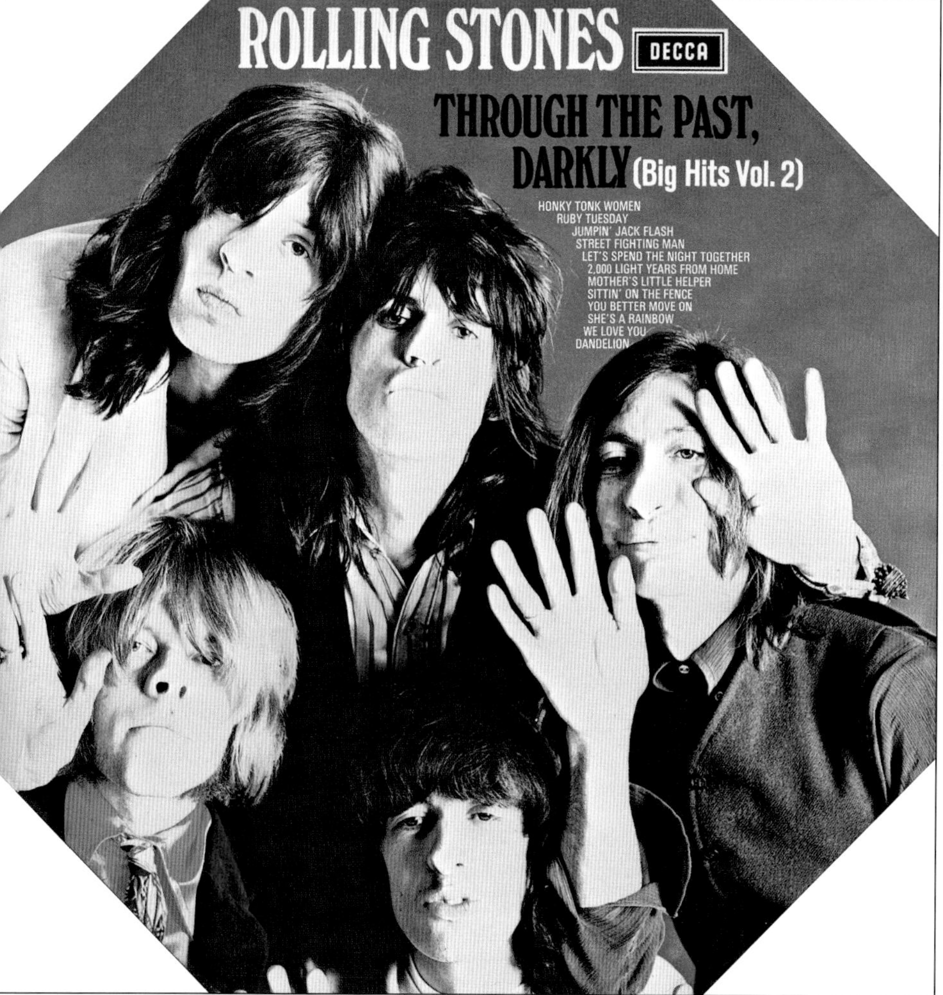
ROLLING STONES
DECCA
THROUGH THE PAST, DARKLY (Big Hits Vol. 2)
HONKY TONK WOMEN
RUBY TUESDAY
JUMPIN' JACK FLASH
STREET FIGHTING MAN
LET'S SPEND THE NIGHT TOGETHER
2,000 LIGHT YEARS FROM HOME
MOTHER'S LITTLE HELPER
SITTIN' ON THE FENCE
YOU BETTER MOVE ON
SHE'S A RAINBOW
WE LOVE YOU
DANDELION

Jumping Jack Flash (Jagger-Richards) 3.40
Mick Jagger: lead vocals
Keith Richards: bass guitar
Brian Jones and Keith Richards: guitars
Charlie Watts: drums
Bill Wyman and Ian Stewart: keyboards
Satanic Majesties was over-produced and too clever for most stones fans so The Rolling Stones turfed a raw three-chord bedrock with meaningful lyricism. This single was, therefore, as unvarnished and as natural as it was possible to be by marrying a return to the Crawdaddy primeval to advanced technology and post-psychedelic metaphysics. Into the bargain, rather than lose the drive inherent in the take used, a jarring couple of bars from the guitars in the middle instrumental passage were retained as an irritant factor. It was perhaps the group's most lasting and exciting artistic statement. It surfaces as frequently in 'Sounds Of The Sixties' nights as The Beatles' 'Yesterday' does in quality cabaret. Although it was the first domestic chart-topper since 1966, it couldn't duplicate this performance in other territories stopping, for instance, at No. 2 in Australia and 3 in the Irish republic and the USA. NB: On some pressings, it's spelt 'Jumpin' Jack Flash'.

We Love You (Jagger-Richards) 4.22
Mick Jagger: lead vocals
Brian Jones: mellotron
Keith Richards: guitar
Bill Wyman: bass guitar
Charlie Watts: drums
Nicky Hopkins: piano
Mick Jagger, Keith Richards, John Lennon and Paul McCartney: backing vocals
Rush-released as it was in the wake of all the unlooked-for publicity shrouding the dismissal of Jagger and Richards' jail sentences and the inter-related us-and-them divide between youth and the Establishment, this was one of the most plugged 45s on the playlist of pirate Radio London, then awaiting its final hour when the Marine Offences Act became law in August 1967. Laying it on with a trowel, the Stones' mock-conciliatory riposte to an ugly situation was bracketed by prison-door sound effects.

Dandelion (Jagger-Richards) 3.32

Mick Jagger: lead vocals
Brian Jones: saxophone, percussion
Brian Jones, Ian Stewart and Nicky Hopkins: keyboards
Mick Jagger, Keith Richards, John Lennon and Paul McCartney: backing vocals
Keith Richards: guitar
Bill Wyman: bass guitar
Charlie Watts: drums

This reflected a musical 'Honky Tonk Women' scenario pertinent to the commercialisation of flower power that pervaded the summer charts. The coupling of 'Dandelion' with 'We Love You' may be seen as a concept single, what with a segment of the former serving as a coda for the latter. Keith Richards was to name his eldest daughter Dandelion.

Honky Tonk Women (Jagger-Richards)

Mick Jagger: lead vocals
Keith Richards and Mick Taylor: guitars
Jimmy Miller: percussion
Keith Richards, Doris Troy and others: backing vocals
Bill Wyman: bass guitar
Charlie Watts: drums
Various: brass and woodwinds

Jimmy Miller tapped a cowbell in slightly awry counterpoint to a stomping and not-quite-medium tempo Watts introit. If technically wrong with a rhythm that had all but doubled in speed by the final chorus, this million-seller went unchanged to the pressing plant for much the same reasons as The Dave Clark Five's percussion-driven 'Bits And Pieces' did in 1964. 'Sometimes you make mistakes,' confessed Clark, 'and out of them, good things happen.' Indeed, they did, 'Honky Tonk Women' was to be another Rolling Stones 'Best Single Of The Year' in 1969's *New Musical Express* poll. It was also at an opportune No.1 in the States, and still in the Hot 100 when the Stones hit the road as a working band again. Furthermore, the hit song of 1970 was to be Free's 'All Right Now', that had appropriated the salient points of 'Honky Tonk Women'.

STONE AGE

UK Release: 6 March 1971
Producer: Andrew Loog Oldham

Decca SKL 5084

SIDE ONE: Look What You've Done; It's All Over Now; Confessin' The Blues; One More Try; As Tears Go By; The Spider And The Fly.

SIDE TWO: My Girl; Paint It Black; If You Need Me; The Last Time; Blue Turns To Grey; Around And Around.

All tracks previously released on an album.

After the loss of The Rolling Stones, Decca realigned its scruples about the rejected cover submitted originally for *Beggars Banquet*. This depicted a toilet wall festooned by Mick Jagger and Keith Richards in felt-tipped graffiti and it was decided to use something like it for *Stone Age*, one of many compilations the company chose to release. Despite the Stones' sour-faced endeavours at damage limitation that extended to posting music-journal adverts expressing their displeasure, *Stone Age* and further vinyl odds-and-ends proved worthwhile market exercises.

STEREO L20P1029

LONDON

Stone Age

The Rolling Stones

GIMME SHELTER

UK Release: 29 August 1971 **Decca SKL 5101**
Producers: Andrew Loog Oldham, Jimmy Miller

SIDE ONE: Jumpin' Jack Flash; Love In Vain; Honky Tonk Women; Street Fighting Man; Sympathy For The Devil; Gimme Shelter.

SIDE TWO: Under My Thumb; Time Is On My Side; I've Been Loving You Too Long; Fortune Teller; Lady Jane; (I Can't Get No) Satisfaction.

All tracks previously released on albums.

This almost resembled a mispressing with its cover shot from a London show in July 1972 and the mingling of the audio content of a handful of late 60s items with excerpts and their atrocious sound quality untreated from the US *Got Live If You Want It* LP from 1966.

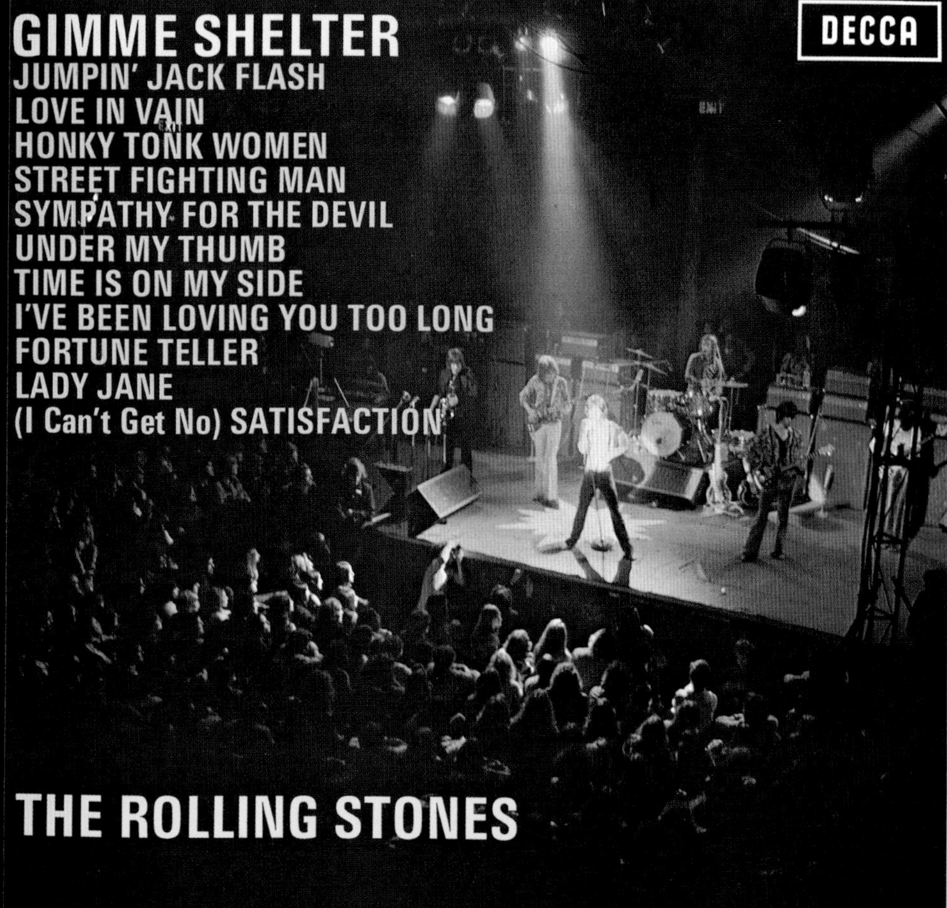
GIMME SHELTER
JUMPIN' JACK FLASH
LOVE IN VAIN
HONKY TONK WOMEN
STREET FIGHTING MAN
SYMPATHY FOR THE DEVIL
UNDER MY THUMB
TIME IS ON MY SIDE
I'VE BEEN LOVING YOU TOO LONG
FORTUNE TELLER
LADY JANE
(I Can't Get No) SATISFACTION
DECCA
THE ROLLING STONES
Including 6 LIVE tracks never before released in the U.K.

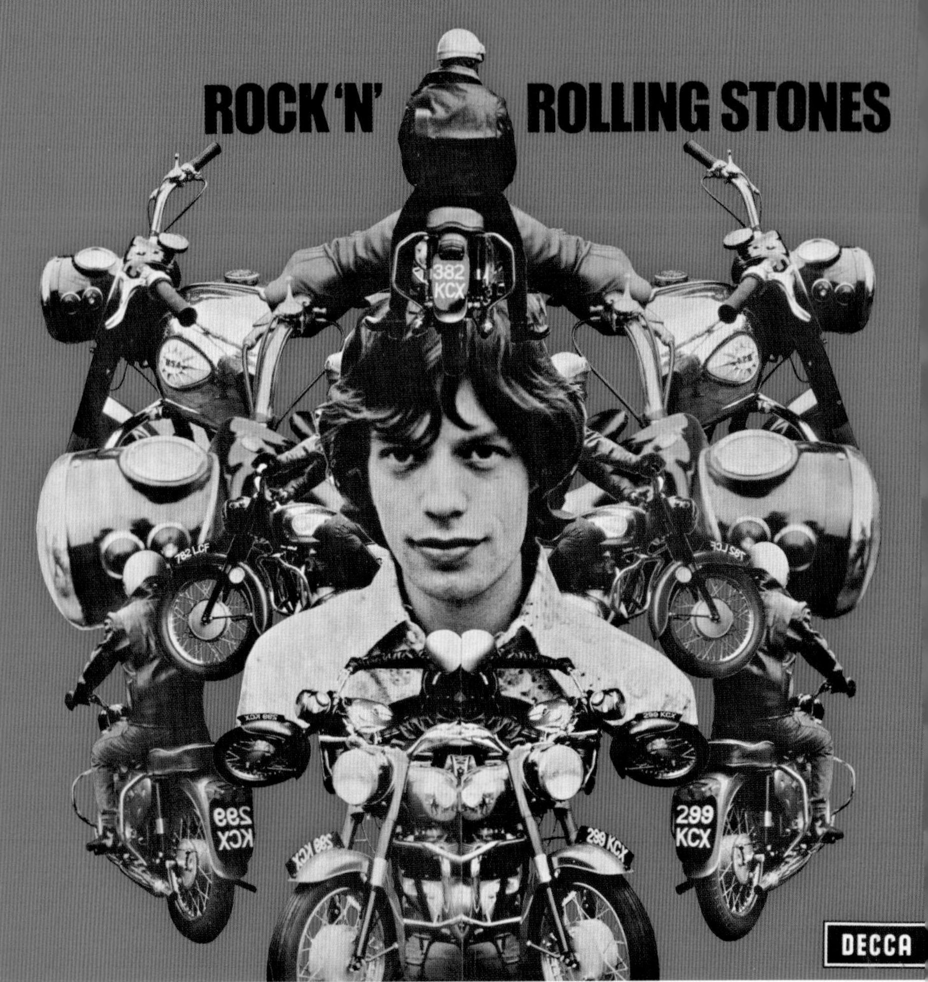
ROCK 'N' ROLLING STONES
382
KCX
782 LCF
299
KCX
299 KCX
DECCA

ROCK 'N' ROLLING STONES

UK Release: 13 October 1972
Producer: Andrew Loog Oldham

Decca SKL 5149

SIDE ONE: Route 66; The Under Assistant West Coast Promotion Man; Come On; Talkin' 'Bout You; Bye Bye Johnny; Down The Road Apiece.

SIDE TWO: I Just Wanna Make Love To You; Everybody Needs Somebody To Love; Oh Baby (We Got A Good Thing Goin'); 19th Nervous Breakdown; Little Queenie; Carol.

All tracks previously released on albums except 'Bye Bye Johnny'.

Bye Bye Johnny (Berry) 2.10
Mick Jagger: lead vocals
Brian Jones and Keith Richards: guitars
Brian Jones and Bill Wyman: backing vocals
Bill Wyman: bass guitar
Charlie Watts: drums

Emulation of heroes is a vital part of growing up and the essence of Keith Richards' fretboard style was formed with Chuck Berry lurking in the background. 'When I started,' Keith admitted, 'I pinched virtually all his riffs'. On this track from the Stones' eponymous debut EP, his dexterity matches that of his idol who released the song as a 1960 A side.

NO STONE UNTURNED

UK Release: 5 October 1973 **Decca SKL 5173**
Producer: Andrew Loog Oldham, Jimmy Miller

SIDE ONE: Poison Ivy; The Singer Not The Song; Surprise, Surprise, Child Of The Moon; Stoned; Sad Day; Money.

SIDE TWO: Congratulations; I'm Moving On; 2120 South Michigan Avenue; Long Long While; Who's Driving Your Plane.

All tracks previously released on albums except 'Poison Ivy', 'Child Of The Moon', 'Stoned', 'Sad Day', 'Money', 'Long Long While' and 'Who's Driving Your Plane'.

Poison Ivy (Leiber-Stoller) 2.34
Mick Jagger: lead vocals, guiro
Brian Jones and Keith Richards: guitars
Bill Wyman: bass guitar
Charlie Watts: drums
Brian Jones and Bill Wyman: backing vocals
This was the second released version of the number scheduled to be the Stones' second single in 1963 but was subsequently cancelled. A British Top 20 hit for The Coasters in 1959, it was going the rounds with many other beat groups including The Dave Clark Five with Rick Huxley, Mick Jagger's cousin by marriage, on bass guitar, and The Paramounts, a Southend combo from which would spring Procol Harum. A previous 'Poison Ivy' by the Stones was 28 seconds shorter. It was issued in January 1964 on a various artists LP named after *Saturday Club*, the BBC Light Programme's weekly pop magazine.

Child Of The Moon (Jagger-Richards) 3.12

Mick Jagger: lead vocals
Brian Jones and Keith Richards: guitars
Brian Jones: saxophone
Mick Jagger, Keith Richards and Jimmy Miller: backing vocals
Bill Wyman: bass guitar
Charlie Watts: drums
Nicky Hopkins: organ

Alhough attempts were made at recording this number during the *Satanic Majesties* period, it bridges a gap between psychedelia and the pastoral element embraced on *Beggars Banquet* with a hint that someone had skip-read Aleister Crowley's *Moonchild*. For a very short while, 'Child Of The Moon' shared A side status with its 'Jumping Jack Flash' coupling.

Stoned (Nanker-Phelge) 2.09

Mick Jagger: lead vocals
Brian Jones and Keith Richards: guitars
Charlie Watts: drums
Brian Jones: harmonica
Bill Wyman: bass guitar
Ian Stewart: piano

The B-side of 'I Wanna Be Your Man', this instrumental was in essence Brian blowing over a riff borrowed from the reptilian crawl of Booker T and the MGs' 'Green Onions'. It also adhered to the contemporary cliche of a spoken utterance breaking a silence at the end of each verse. The Dave Clark Five reworked the basic idea of 'Stoned' for 'Move On', flip-side of 1965's 'Catch Us If You Can'.

Sad Day (Jagger-Richards) 3.00

Mick Jagger: lead vocals
Brian Jones and Keith Richards: guitars
Charlie Watts: drums
Mick Jagger and Keith Richards: backing vocals
Keith Richards: guitar
Bill Wyman: bass guitar
Brian Jones and Jack Nitzsche: keyboards

This rockaballad started life as the US B side of '19th Nervous Breakdown' but was elevated belatedly to the A side of a 1973 single for British fans for whom it had previously been unavailable. As a pot-shot at the charts however, it missed completely.

Money (Gordy Jnr-Bradford) 2.32
Release date: 10 January 1964
Mick Jagger: lead vocals, harmonica, tambourine
Brian Jones and Keith Richards: guitars
Bill Wyman: bass guitar
Charlie Watts: drums

From The Beatles downwards, it seemed that every beat group that had ever been formed tried this Merseybeat standard, historically, the first Tamla-Motown disc ever released. However, the general intention was to make it sound different from any other outfit's version. In this, the Stones succeeded chiefly by substituting harmonica for the usual guitar or piano lead instrument. It was included on the same EP as 'Bye Bye Johnny'.
See British Rock 'N' Rolling Stones SKL 5149.

Long Long While (Jagger-Richards) 2.32
Mick Jagger: lead vocals
Bill Wyman: bass guitar
Brian Jones and Keith Richards: guitars
Charlie Watts: drums
Ian Stewart: organ
Jack Nitzsche: piano, tambourine

If too strong to be buried on the UK B side of 'Paint It Black', this likeable blues-boogie hardly extended the limits of the avant-garde, being almost a throwback in spirit to the sulky balladeering in which 50s rock'n'rollers indulged on occasions.

Who's Driving Your Plane (Jagger-Richards) 3.14
Mick Jagger: lead vocals, harmonica
Brian Jones and Keith Richards: guitars
Bill Wyman: bass guitar
Charlie Watts: drums
Ian Stewart and Jack Nitzsche: keyboards

Recorded in Hollywood, this is a complaint about a girlfriend's passiveness towards her parents' dictates – over a swirling backing track that nods towards the blues and, less precisely, at Bob Dylan's new electric approach. It was the B side of 'Have You Seen Your Mother' in all territories.

ROLLED GOLD

UK Release: 14 November 1975
Producer: Andrew Loog Oldham, The Rolling Stones, Jimmy Miller

Decca ROST 1/2

SIDE ONE: Come On; I Wanna Be Your Man; Not Fade Away; Carol; It's All Over Now; Little Red Rooster.

SIDE TWO: Time Is On My Side; The Last Time; (I Can't Get No) Satisfaction; Get Off Of My Cloud; 19th Nervous Breakdown; As Tears Go By.

SIDE THREE: Under My Thumb; Lady Jane; Out Of Time; Paint It Black; Have You Seen Your Mother Baby (Standing In The Shadow); Let's Spend The Night Together; Ruby Tuesday.

SIDE FOUR: Yesterday's Papers; We Love You; She's A Rainbow; Jumpin' Jack Flash; Honky Tonk Women; Sympathy For The Devil; Street Fighting Man; Midnight Rambler; Gimme Shelter.

All tracks previously released on albums except 'I Wanna Be Your Man'.

I Wanna Be Your Man (Lennon-McCartney) 1.43
Mick Jagger: lead vocals
Keith Richards: guitar
Brian Jones: slide guitar and backing vocals
Bill Wyman: bass guitar
Charlie Watts: drums

'We weren't going to give them anything great, were we?' was John Lennon's rhetorical confession in one of his last interviews. After The Beatles had impinged upon national consciousnes in 1963, the gift of a Lennon-McCartney composition became like a licence to print banknotes. Thus every original track on *With The Beatles* was covered by another artist including this one as the Stones' career-stabilising second single. While it was to be their first venture into the Top 20, implied association with the Fab Four was a double-edged sword. Described in one *New Musical Express* article as 'a London group with the Liverpool sound', the Stones were pigeon-holed for convenience as a southern wing of fast-fading Merseybeat.

Rolled Gold

the very best of the Rolling Stones

DECCA

GET STONED: 30 GREATEST HITS 30 ORIGINAL TRACKS

UK Release: 21 October 1977 **Arcade ADEP 32**
Producer: Andrew Loog Oldham, The Rolling Stones, Jimmy Miller

SIDE ONE: Not Fade Away; It's All Over Now; Tell Me (You're Coming Back); Good Times Bad Times; Time Is On My Side; Little Red Rooster; The Last Time; Play With Fire.

SIDE TWO: (I Can't Get No) Satisfaction; Get Off Of My Cloud; I Wanna Be Your Man; As Tears Go By; 19th Nervous Breakdown; Mother's Little Helper; Have You Seen Your Mother Baby (Standing In The Shadow).

SIDE THREE:
Paint It Black; Lady Jane; Let's Spend The Night Together; Ruby Tuesday; Dandelion; We Love You; She's A Rainbow; 2000 Light Years From Home.

SIDE FOUR:
Jumpin' Jack Flash; Gimme Shelter; Street Fighting Man; Honky Tonk Women; Sympathy For The Devil; Wild Horses; Brown Sugar.

All tracks previously released on albums.

This was released during the same month as *Brian Jones Presents The Pipes Of Pan At Joujouka* on Rolling Stones Records.

THE ROLLING STONES

GET STONED

30 greatest hits. 30 original tracks.

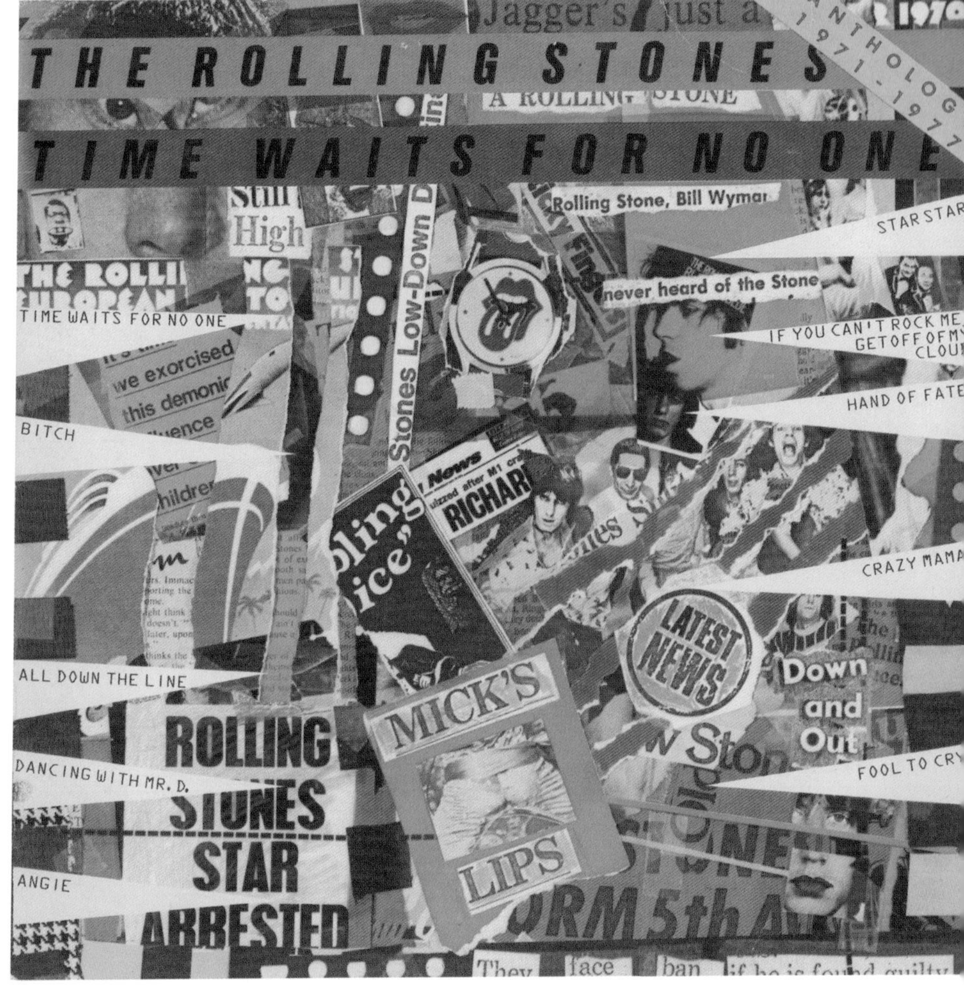
THE ROLLING STONES
ANTHOLOGY 1971-1977
TIME WAITS FOR NO ONE
TIME WAITS FOR NO ONE
BITCH
ALL DOWN THE LINE
DANCING WITH MR. D.
ANGIE
STAR STAR
IF YOU CAN'T ROCK ME, GET OFF OF MY CLOUD
HAND OF FATE
CRAZY MAMA
FOOL TO CRY
Jagger's just a
A ROLLING STONE
Rolling Stone, Bill Wyman
never heard of the Stone
Stones Low-Down
we exorcised
this demonic
LATEST NEWS
RICHARD
MICK'S LIPS
Down and Out
ROLLING STONES STAR ARRESTED
They face ban if he is found guilty

TIME WAITS FOR NO-ONE

UK Release: 1 June 1979
Producers: Jimmy Miller, The Glimmer Twins

Rolling Stones Records COC 59107

SIDE ONE: Time Waits For No-One; Bitch; All Down The Line; Dancing With Mr. D; Angie; Star Star.

SIDE TWO: If You Can't Rock Me; Get Off Of My Cloud; Hand Of Fate; Crazy Mama; Fool To Cry.

All tracks previously released on albums.

This was the last Rolling Stones release under a distribution contract with WEA.

REWIND 1971-1984 (THE BEST OF THE ROLLING STONES)

UK Release: 29 June 1984
Intl CD No: CBS CDCBS450199 2
Running Time: 55:55

Rolling Stones Records CUN 1
Producers: Jimmy Miller, The Glimmer Twins

SIDE ONE: Miss You; Brown Sugar; Undercover Of The Night; Start Me Up; Tumbling Dice; Hang Fire; Emotional Rescue.

SIDE TWO: Beast Of Burden; Fool To Cry; Waiting On A Friend; Angie; It's Only Rock 'N Roll; She's So Cold.

All tracks previously released on albums.

Bill Wyman and Mick Jagger collborated on the associated video for this compilation from the EMI years.

OLLING STONES
REWI

JUMP BACK: THE BEST OF THE ROLLING STONES '71-'93

UK Release: 22 November 1993 **Virgin CDV2726**
Producers: Jimmy Miller, The Glimmer Twins

Start Me Up; Brown Sugar; Harlem Shuffle; It's Only Rock 'N Roll; Mixed Emotions; Angie; Tumbling Dice; Fool To Cry; Rock And A Hard Place; Miss You; Hot Stuff; Emotional Rescue; Respectable; Beast Of Burden; Waiting On A Friend; Wild Horses; Bitch; Undercover Of The Night.

All tracks previously released on albums.

This reached No. 15, and remained in the album charts for nearly three months.

The best of the Rolling Stones

Jump Back

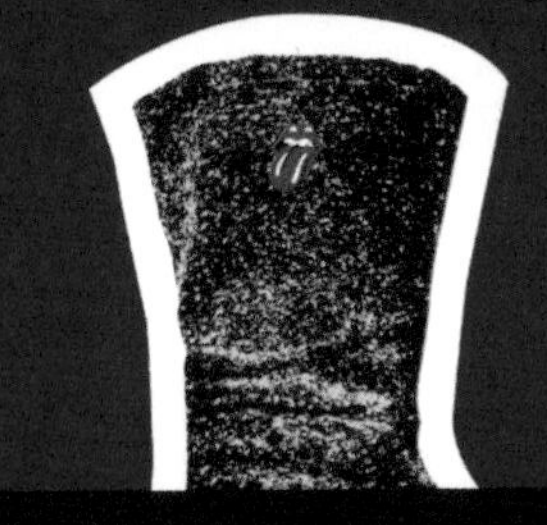

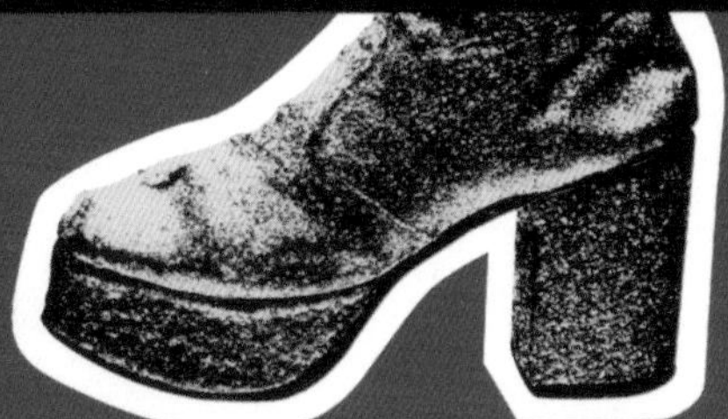

'71 '93

THE BRITISH AND US COMPILATION ALBUMS

MADE IN THE SHADE

UK Release: 6 June 1975
US Release: 6 June 1975
Intl CD No: CBS CDCBS 450201 2
Running Time: 39:56

Rolling Stones Records COC 59104
Rolling Stones Records COC 79101
Producers: Jimmy Miller, The Glimmer Twins

SIDE ONE: Brown Sugar; Tumbling Dice; Happy; Dance Little Sister; Wild Horses.

SIDE TWO: Angie; Bitch; It's Only Rock 'N Roll; Doo Doo Doo Doo (Heartbreaker); Rip This Joint.

All tracks previously released on albums.

This was issued in direct competition to *Metamorphosis*. It climbed to No. 6 in the States.

Rolling Stones
Made In The Shade

SUCKING IN THE 70s

UK Release: 12 March 1981
US Release: 13 April 1981
Intl CD No: CBS CDCBS450 205 2
Running Time: 42:39

Rolling Stones Records CUN 39112
Rolling Stones Records CUN 16028
Producers: The Glimmer Twins

SIDE ONE: Shattered; Everything Is Turning Into Gold; Hot Stuff; Time Waits For No-One; Fool To Cry.

SIDE TWO: Mannish Boy; When The Whip Comes Down; If I Was A Dancer (Dance Part Two): Crazy Mama; Beast Of Burden.

All tracks previously released on albums except 'If I Was A Dancer (Dance Part Two)'.

If I Was A Dancer (Dance Part Two) 5.50
See *British and US Rarities* CDV3015.

Many stockists in the USA would not take the album because of its suggestive title. Nevertheless, it entered the national Top 30, lingering there for six weeks.

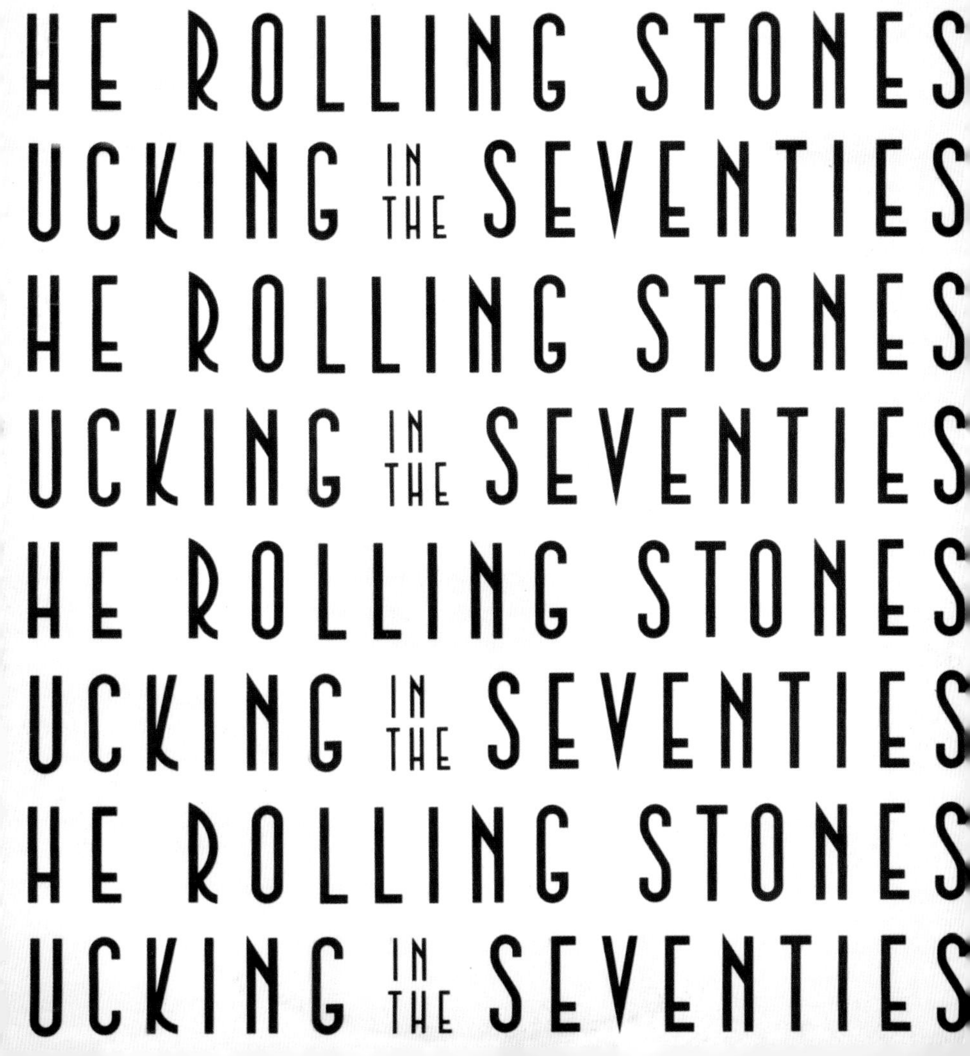
HE ROLLING STONES
UCKING IN THE SEVENTIES
HE ROLLING STONES
UCKING IN THE SEVENTIES
HE ROLLING STONES
UCKING IN THE SEVENTIES
HE ROLLING STONES
UCKING IN THE SEVENTIES

THE ROLLING STONES
Slow Rollers

SLOW ROLLERS

UK Release: 19 August 1981 **Decca TAB 30**
US Release: 21 August 1981 **London 820 455-1**
Producers: Andrew Loog Oldham, Jimmy Miller

SIDE ONE: You Can't Always Get What You Want; Take It Or Leave It; You Better Move On; Time Is On My Side; Pain In My Heart; Dear Doctor; Con Le Mie Lagrime Cosi (As Tears Go By).

SIDE TWO: Ruby Tuesday; Play With Fire; Lady Jane; Sittin' On A Fence; Back Street Girl; Under The Boardwalk; Heart Of Stone.

All tracks previously released on albums except 'Con Le Mie Lagrime Cosi (As Tears Go By)'.

Con Le Mie Lagrime Cosi (As Tears Go By) 2.42
Mick Jagger: lead vocals
Keith Richards: guitar
Mike Leander: harpsichord
Various: orchestral strings

The Searchers and The Beatles had each released German-language arrangements of certain of their hits by 1966 when The Rolling Stones got round to trying one of theirs in Italian. Mick Jagger tackles the job with confidence and without any of that clipped solemnity of someone singing in a tongue not his own. The orchestral scoring on this Italian A side was by Mike Leander, producer of Marianne Faithfull's 1964 version of the song.

THE ROLLING STONES SINGLES COLLECTION: THE LONDON YEARS

UK Release: 15 August 1989
US Release: 15 August 1989
Producers: Andrew Loog Oldham, The Rolling Stones, Jimmy Miller

ABKCO 92312
ABKCO 1218-1

SIDE ONE: Come On; I Want To Be Loved; I Wanna Be Your Man; Stoned; Not Fade Away; Little By Little.

SIDE TWO: It's All Over Now; Good Times Bad Times; Tell Me (You're Coming Back; I Just Want To Make Love To You; Time Is On My Side; Congratulations.

SIDE THREE: Little Red Rooster; Off The Hook; Heart Of Stone; What A Shame; The Last Time; Play With Fire.

SIDE FOUR: (I Can't Get No) Satisfaction; The Under Assistant West Coast Promotion Man; The Spider And The Fly; Get Off Of My Cloud; I'm Free; The Singer Not The Song; As Tears Go By; Gotta Get Away.

SIDE FIVE: 19th Nervous Breakdown; Sad Day; Paint It Black; Stupid Girl; Long Long While; Have You Seen Your Mother Baby (Standing In The Shadow; Who's Driving Your Plane.

SIDE SIX: Let's Spend The Night Together; Ruby Tuesday; We Love You; Dandelion; She's A Rainbow; 2000 Light Years From Home; In Another Land; The Lantern.

SIDE SEVEN: Jumpin' Jack Flash; Child Of The Moon; Street Fighting Man; No Expectations; Surprise Surprise; Honky Tonk Women; You Can't Always Get What You Want.

SIDE EIGHT: Memo From Turner; Brown Sugar; Wild Horses; I Don't Know Why; Try A Little Harder; Out Of Time; Jiving Sister Fanny; Sympathy For The Devil.

All tracks previously released on albums except 'Come On' and 'I Want To Be Loved'.

COME ON
THE ROLLING STONES
I wanna be your man
NOT FADE AWAY
THE ROLLING STONES
THE ROLLING STONES
IT'S ALL OVER NOW
TELL ME
ROLLING STONES
THE ROLLING STONES
THE LAST TIME
ANDREW LOOG OLDHAM
SATISFACTION
"get off of my cloud"
THE ROLLING STONES

THE ROLLING STONES
TIME IS ON MY SIDE
3 COMPACT DISC SET
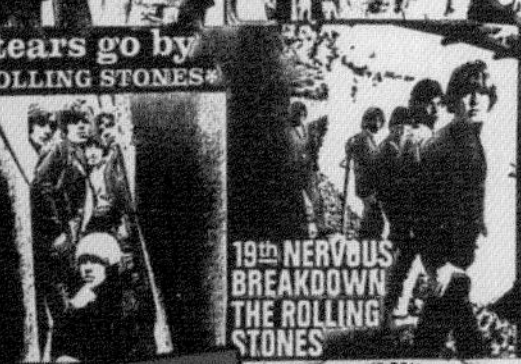
as tears go by
THE ROLLING STONES*
19th NERVOUS
BREAKDOWN
THE ROLLING
STONES

the rolling stones
singles collection*
the london years

ROLLING STONES
I DON'T KNOW WHY
TRY A LITTLE HARDER

NO EXPECTATIONS

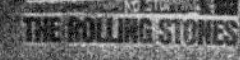
THE ROLLING STONES

as tears go by
THE ROLLING STONES*

LET'S SPEND
THE NIGHT TOGETHER
RUBY TUESDAY

Come On (Berry) 1.48

Mick Jagger: lead vocals
Keith Richards: guitar
Charlie Watts: drums
Brian Jones: harmonica
Bill Wyman: bass guitar
Brian Jones and Bill Wyman: backing vocals

An accelerated cover of a Chuck Berry B side, it was gingered up with Brian's wah-wah-wah harmonica and a corny key change for the last verse. To the Crawdaddy crowd, 'Come On' was hardly a show-stopper, and *Record Mirror* confirmed that 'it's not the fanatical R&B sound that audiences wait hours to hear.' However, scattered radio spins allied with the buzz from London began a progression to the edge of the Top 20, so fulfilling *Record Mirror*'s prophecy that 'it should make the charts in a small way'.

I Want To Be Loved (Dixon) 1.52

Mick Jagger: lead vocals
Keith Richards: guitar
Charlie Watts: drums
Brian Jones: harmonica
Bill Wyman: bass guitar

Jagger sounded a little like Elvis Presley of whom he wasn't particularly fond, on this Muddy Waters-via-Willie Dixon opus that was the B side of 'Come On' and bore a passing resemblance to Jimmy Reed's 'I Ain't Got You'. 'We do not use any original material,' Mick had told *Jazz News*, 'Can you imagine a British-composed R&B number? It just wouldn't make it.'

FORTY LICKS

UK Release: 30 September 2002
US Release: 1 October 2002
Producers: Andrew Loog Oldham, The Rolling Stones, Jimmy Miller, The Glimmer Twins

Virgin 13325.1.1/13378.2.0
Virgin 13325.1.1/13378.2.0
Running Times: 77:32 78:20

Street Fighting Man; Gimme Shelter; (I Can't Get No) Satisfaction; The Last Time; Jumping Jack Flash; You Can't Always Get What You Want; 19th Nervous Breakdown; Under My Thumb; Not Fade Away; Have You Seen Your Mother Baby (Standing In The Shadow); Sympathy For The Devil; Mother's Little Helper; She's A Rainbow; Get Off Of My Cloud; Wild Horses; Ruby Tuesday; Paint It Black; Honky Tonk Women; It's All Over Now; Let's Spend The Night Together; Start Me Up; Brown Sugar; Miss You; Beast Of Burden; Don't Stop; Happy; Angie; You Got Me Rocking; Fool To Cry; Shattered; Anybody Seen My Baby; Keys To Your Love; Stealing My Heart; Tumbling Dice; Undercover Of The Night; Emotional Rescue; It's Only Rock 'N Roll (But I Like It); Losing My Touch.

All tracks previously released on albums except 'Stealing My Heart', 'Losing My Touch' and 'Key To Your Love'.

Stealing My Heart (Jagger-Richards) 3.42
Mick Jagger: lead vocals
Keith Richards, Ronnie Wood and Mick Jagger: guitars
Chuck Leavell: keyboards
Charlie Watts: drums
Brian Jones and Keith Richards: guitars
Darryl Jones: bass guitar

Like the other two bonus items, this was recorded in the summer of 2002 at the Guillaume Tell Studios, Suresne, near Paris. Mainly the work of Jagger, it may have been a sound choice for a single had a little more work been done to bring out its inherent bombast.

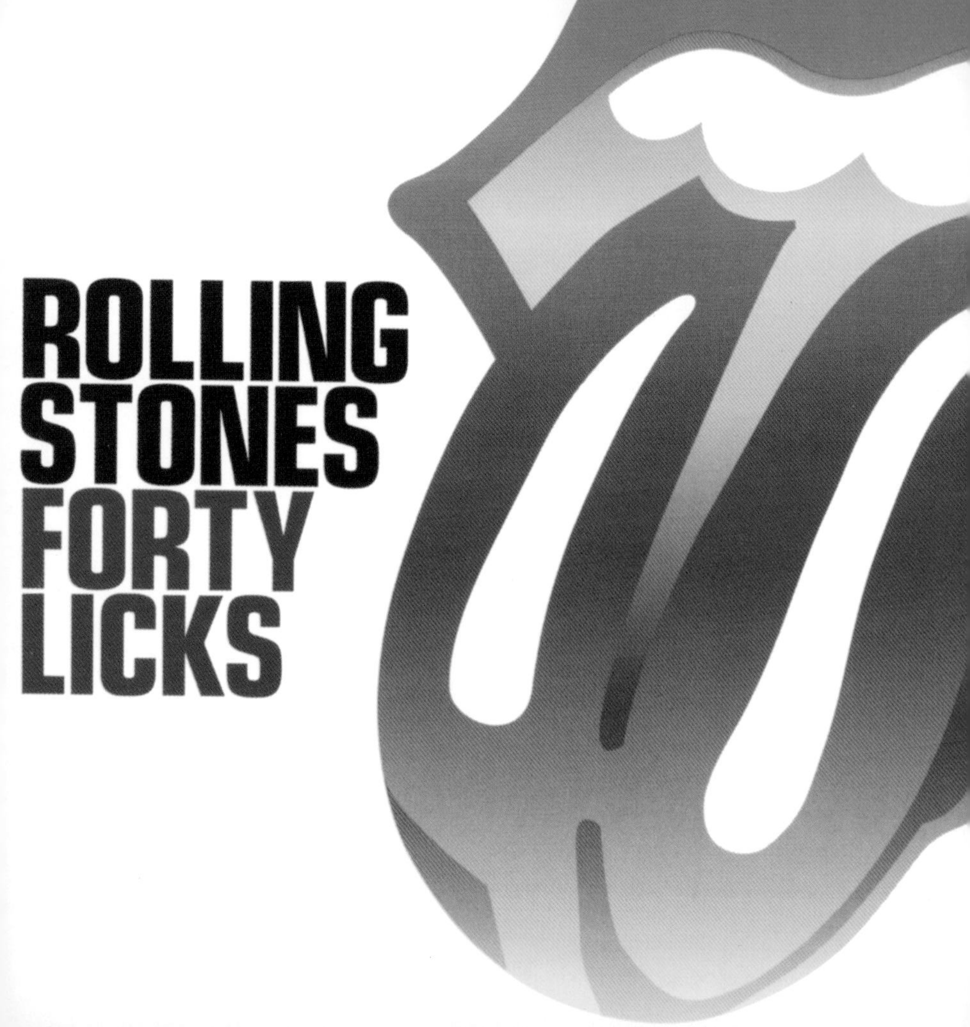
ROLLING
STONES
FORTY
LICKS

Losing My Touch (Jagger-Richards) 5.06
Keith Richards: lead vocals, guitar
Ronnie Wood: pedal steel guitar
Chuck Leavell: keyboards
Charlie Watts: drums
Darryl Jones: bass guitar
Richards overstays his welcome slightly on a slow melancholia composed in his Jamaican fortress after the *No Security* tour was over.

Keys To Your Love (Jagger-Richards) 4.11
Mick Jagger: lead vocals
Keith Richards, Ronnie Wood and Mick Jagger: guitars
Chuck Leavell: keyboards
Charlie Watts: drums
Brian Jones and Keith Richards: guitars
Darryl Jones: bass guitar
Veering into falsetto at times, Jagger comes close to relocating 60s soul balladry in the new century, albeit with a touch of late 70s vintage Stones.

US COMPILATION ALBUMS

BIG HITS (HIGH TIDE AND GREEN GRASS)

London NP/NPS 1
Release Date: 11 March 1966
Running Time: 36:55

Producer: Andrew Loog Oldham
Intl CD No: ABKCO 90012

SIDE ONE: (I Can't Get No) Satisfaction; The Last Time; As Tears Go By; Time Is On My Side; It's All Over Now; Tell Me (You're Coming Back).

SIDE TWO: 19th Nervous Breakdown; Heart Of Stone; Get Off Of My Cloud; Not Fade Away; Good Times Bad Times; Play With Fire.

All tracks previously released on albums.

BIG HITS
(HIGH TIDE AND GREEN GRASS)
THE ROLLING STONES
LONDON
MONO NP-1

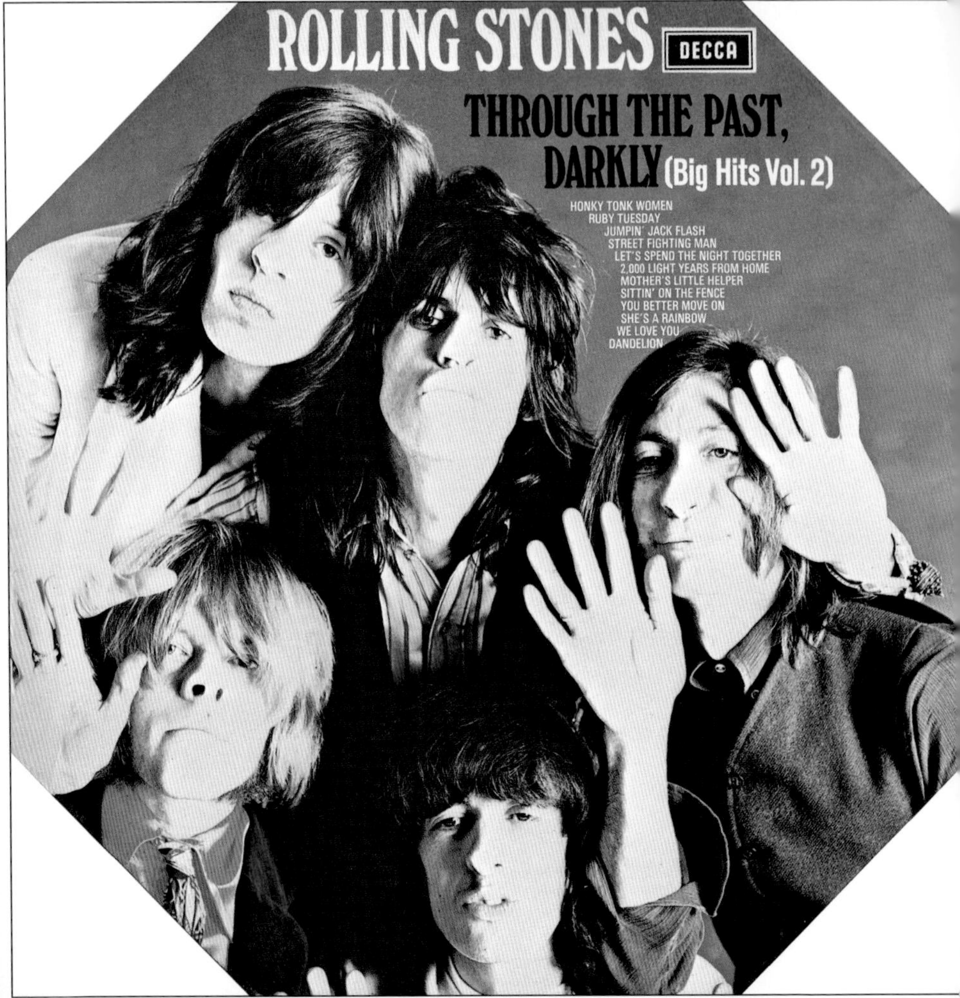
ROLLING STONES
DECCA
THROUGH THE PAST, DARKLY (Big Hits Vol. 2)
HONKY TONK WOMEN
RUBY TUESDAY
JUMPIN' JACK FLASH
STREET FIGHTING MAN
LET'S SPEND THE NIGHT TOGETHER
2,000 LIGHT YEARS FROM HOME
MOTHER'S LITTLE HELPER
SITTIN' ON THE FENCE
YOU BETTER MOVE ON
SHE'S A RAINBOW
WE LOVE YOU
DANDELION

THROUGH THE PAST DARKLY (BIG HITS VOL. 2)

US Release: 12 September 1969
Intl CD No: ABKCO 90032
Running Time: 38:17

London NPS-3
Producers: Andrew Loog Oldham, The Rolling Stones, Jimmy Miller

SIDE ONE: Paint It Black; Ruby Tuesday; She's A Rainbow; Jumpin' Jack Flash; Mother's Little Helper; Let's Spend The Night Together.

SIDE TWO: Honky Tonk Women; Dandelion; 2000 Light Years From Home; Have You Seen Your Mother Baby (Standing In The Shadow); Street Fighting Man.

All tracks previously released on albums.

HOT ROCKS 1964-1971

US Release: 11 January 1972
Intl CD No: ABKCO 96672
Running Time: 38:27 47:13

London 2PS 606/607
Producers: Andrew Loog Oldham, The Rolling Stones, Jimmy Miller

SIDE ONE: Time Is On My Side; Heart Of Stone; Play With Fire; (I Can't Get No) Satisfaction; As Tears Go By.

SIDE TWO: Get Off Of My Cloud; Mother's Little Helper; 19th Nervous Breakdown; Paint It Black; Under My Thumb.

SIDE THREE: Ruby Tuesday; Let's Spend The Night Together; Jumpin' Jack Flash; Street Fighting Man; Sympathy For The Devil.

SIDE FOUR: Honky Tonk Women; Gimme Shelter; Midnight Rambler; You Can't Always Get What You Want; Brown Sugar, Wild Horses.

All tracks previously released on albums.

MORE HOT ROCKS (BIG HITS AND FAZED COOKIES)

London 2PS 626/627
INTL CD No: ABKCO 96262
Running Times: 38:15 52:30

Release Date: 1 December 1972
Producer: Andrew Loog Oldham, The Rolling Stones; Jimmy Miller

SIDE ONE: Tell Me (You're Coming Back); Not Fade Away; The Last Time; It's All Over Now; Good Times Bad Times; I'm Free.
SIDE THREE: She's A Rainbow; 2000 Light Years From Home; Child Of The Moon; No Expectations; Let It Bleed; What To Do; Money.

SIDE TWO: Out Of Time; Lady Jane; Sittin' On A Fence; Have You Seen Your Mother Baby (Standing In The Shadow); Dandelion; We Love You.
SIDE FOUR: Come On; Fortune Teller; Poison Ivy; Bye Bye Johnny; I Can't Be Satisfied; Long Long While.

All tracks previously released on albums except 'Fortune Teller'.

Fortune Teller 2.18
Mick Jagger: lead vocals
Keith Richards: guitar
Mick Jagger, Brian Jones and Keith Richards: backing vocals

Brian Jones: tambourine
Bill Wyman: bass guitar
Charlie Watts: drums

With overdubbed audience reaction, this was crowbarred into the US-only *Got Live If You Want It* LP.
See US *Got Live If You Want It* (3493/PS 493).

ROLLING STONES

MORE HOT ROCKS

(big hits & fazed cookies)

JAMMING/SPOKEN WORD ALBUMS

There have been several spoken-word products that contain no Rolling Stones music. None of them was authorised by the group or any of its present or past record companies or managements.

Among the more notable are *Who Are The Stones?*, issued by Arabesque in 1994; *Loose Talk* (Laserlight, 1996) and *The Rolling Stones Interviews* (Delta, 1996). However, the most interesting is *As It Happened* (Chrome Dreams CIS 2002), a four-CD package released in 2002 and based on extant press conferences and one-to-one interviews, starting with Mick Jagger coming on like a workin' class 'ero when discussing his family background, and concluding with genuine article Bill Wyman speaking about why he left the group.

JAMMING WITH EDWARD

US Release: 12 December 1971 **Rolling Stones Records COC 39100**
UK Release: 12 December 1971 **Rolling Stones Records COC 39100**
Producer: Glyn Johns

Boudoir Stomp; It Hurts Me Too; Edward's Thrump Up; Blow With Ry; The Loveliest Night Of The Year; Highland Fling.

During one May 1969 session for the transitional *Let It Bleed* album, jamming consumed more time than usual as late arrivals set up their equipment and console technicians twiddled. Nothing was seen of Keith Richards for the entire time that Charlie Watts, Mick Jagger, Bill Wyman and two auxiliary players were there. Nevertheless, it was thought prudent to keep the tape rolling so that edited highlights could be cobbled together for release nearly three years later as *Jamming With Edward*. While Jagger managed a slightly muted revival of an Elmore James blues, the proceedings were dominated by the catalytic familiars, namely pianist Nicky Hopkins to the fore on 'Highland Fling', titled for its aptly Hibernian pentatonic overtones on piano and Ry Cooder on bottleneck guitar.

'Blow With Ry' was cast adrift on the vinyl oceans as a German single in 1972, but in common with 'Edward's Thrump Up', 'Boudoir Stomp' and the rest of *Jamming With Edward*, it revealed little more remarkable than any idle studio crew's wanderings after one of them kicks off an extemporization that lives principally in its riff. Nevertheless, it wasn't entirely an immortalisation of the participants' own arrogance as it made for cheaper and far less tedious listening than George Harrison's similarly motivated 'Apple Jam' third of 1970's *All Things Must Pass* triple-album.

SOLO ALBUMS

MICK JAGGER SOLO ALBUMS

SHE'S THE BOSS

US and UK Release: 4 March 1985 **CBS 86310**
Producers: Mick Jagger, Bill Laswell and Nile Rodgers

Lonely At The Top; Half A Loaf; Running Out Of Luck; Turn The Girl Loose; Hard Woman; Just Another Night; Lucky In Love; Secrets; She's The Boss.

The first overt indication that Mick Jagger was contemplating a recording career as a non-Stone was his acceptance of an invitation to duet with Michael Jackson on 'State Of Shock', the hit single from 1984's *Victory* by the former Tamla-Motown child star and his elder brothers as The Jacksons.

Teaming up with other artists often proved a viable strategy during the 80s. Alliances on 45 by Jackson and Paul McCartney; McCartney and Stevie Wonder; Queen and David Bowie; Bowie and Bing Crosby (!); gnarled Joe Cocker and fresh-faced Jennifer Warnes; Don Everly and Cliff Richard; Cliff Richard and Van Morrison and Gene Pitney and crypto-punk vocalist Marc Almond had all yielded chartbusting bonanzas.

Backed by local lads Hall and Oates and their band, Mick's first ever show without the Stones – his appearance on the US section of Live Aid – embraced 'Miss You' and a 'State Of Shock' that segued into 'It's Only Rock 'n' Roll'. This duet with Tina Turner reached boiling point with him ripping off her skirt just like the male members had those of the female half of Bucks Fizz during 1981's Eurovision Song Contest – which Mick knew none of the Americans would have seen.

He also inserted a couple of numbers from *She's The Boss*, the long-awaited solo album that, still in record shop windows months after it was 'shipped out' in March, had spawned 'Just Another Night'. This Top 30 entry in Britain achieved a high of Number ten in the States. Meanwhile a second *She's The Boss* single, 'Lucky In Love' was lingering still in the Hot 100.

We never see the man. We only see his art. I mean this most sincerely, friends. So how could we ever know if Jagger at Live Aid was motivated by a simple desire to help the starving – to which end he also recorded a spoken link on the associated video compilation – or if he was seizing an unforeseeable but welcome opportunity to trumpet *She's The Boss*?

Whatever his motivation, Mick had allowed the album the best possible chance by bolstering the credits with credible and negotiable names, among them Pete Townshend of The Who, jazz-rock behemoths Herbie Hancock and Jan Hammer. Trend-setting producer Nile Rodgers and, supplier of music for two Jagger lyrics, Carlos Alomar, had also been credited. Alomar, like Keith Richards, had became known principally as a rhythm guitarist. Alomar's apprenticeship in James Brown's Famous Flames and his tenure in the house band at the Sigma Sound complex – from which emanated Philadephia's feathery soul style in the 70s – had led an irregular Sigma client, David Bowie, to retain Alomar as a full-time accompanist and sometime bandleader on tour and on disc.

While Carlos wasn't heard on *She's The Boss*, the influence of his urgent fretboard precision and his terse ostinati picking pervaded the tracks 'Lucky In Love', 'Turn The Girl Loose' and accompanied instances of Mick slipping into a James Brown-esque groove. Overall, however, it was what you might have imagined the Stones sounding like if Jeff Beck had filled the post left vacant by Mick Taylor in 1974. Loud and clear on 'Lonely At The Top' (once earmarked for *Tattoo You*), 'Running Out Of Luck' – where he played finger-style acoustic six-string – 'Lucky In Love' and three more of the LP's nine tracks, Beck's solos and passagework were as indelible a signature as Jagger's baritone.

Dubbed 'the Paganini of the guitar' by no less than Malcolm McLaren, Beck kept his devotees guessing what he'd be up to next while at the same time sweating over something new. At the same time, more famous contemporaries – like his Yardbirds predecessor Eric Clapton – were turning out increasingly more ordinary albums. 'I just like to condition my audience to be ready for anything,' averred Jeff, 'rather than turn their noses up because I've done a weird album.'

A pot calling a kettle black, Beck found Jagger a very moody guy: 'He would strum chords for about three hours to get into the mood. By that time, I was tired – and he wouldn't show any signs of appreciation or pleasure at what you were doing. "Oh yeah, that was all right. Let's call it a day". You go home and you feel dejected. It was difficult.'

Both in between sessions and prior to flying to the Bahamas, Mick crafted his lyrics as carefully as a cementer would a mosaic, sometimes picking the brain of brother Chris. These covered a broad waterfront from the Hollywood hopeful rapidly saddened by brush-offs and unreturned calls in 'Lonely At The Top' to the frustrated smoke-screening of an affair in 'Half A Loaf', to the pleading despair and submissiveness of 'Hard Woman' and the title song. Self-regret about a cash-haemorrhaging addiction to gambling is mitigated by success with the ladies in harmonica-tinged 'Lucky In Love', while 'Running Out Of Luck' seems to be riven with intimations about division of property with a former lover.

The words were printed on the inner sleeve of a package that garnered mixed reviews. Headlined HE'S THE BOSS!, the most favourable was from *Melody Maker*, but the bulk of its two million sales were overseas. Every silver lining has a cloud, however, and a multi-million dollar suit for plagiarism – because reggae executant Patrick Alley detected too great a similarity between 'Just Another Night' and his own 1982 opus of the same title – was to haunt Jagger until May 1988 when it was thrown out of a New York court – though not before he delighted the public gallery by singing a few bars to demonstrate his counsel's argument.

Most of the *She's The Boss* dust had, however, settled when Jagger – with Hall and Oates – was prominent on the soundtrack to the 1986 film comedy *Ruthless People*. Nevertheless, that Mick's extra-mural activities seemed to be taking precedence over his Rolling Stones duties was the source of increasing disenchantment within the group.

There were more subjective worries too. Keith Richards, referring to him privately as 'Brenda' – after Brenda Jagger's English bookshop in Paris – surmised: 'he doesn't have many close male friends apart from me, and he keeps me at a distance. There is something of a siege mentality, so that whenever anyone comes up to Mick, he's thinking, "What do they want out of me?"'. Self-protecting psychological tactics were, if you like, in keeping with a characteristic of Aries, his astrological sign. Thus few could ever gauge if he'd be hail-fellow-well-met or stonewalling towards them. 'I'd be with him from ten in the morning until ten at night,' affirmed David Sanderson, a latter-day Stones employee, 'but the next day, he'd behave almost as if we'd never met before – like, "Who are you, and who are you calling 'Mick'?"'

It wasn't advisable to put on such airs with Jeff Beck, who Mick transparently hoped would join him on the road as well as on disc. A Jagger tour of Japan was on the cards for the beginning of 1988, with Australasia and a side-trip to Indonesia for the autumn, prior, presumably, to cracking the harder nut of North America. Jeff's participation seemed likely as he'd been game enough to let himself be seen in the video for 'Throwaway', the second single from *Primitive Cool*, the album that came hot on the heels of *She's The Boss*.

PRIMITIVE COOL

US and UK Release: 14 September 1987 **CBS 4601232**
Producers: Mick Jagger, Keith Diamond and Dave Stewart

Throwaway; Let's Work; Radio Control; Say You Will; Primitive Cool; Kow Tow; Shoot Off Your Mouth; Peace For The Wicked; Party Doll; War Baby.

This album smouldered into form under the aegis of the co-writer of three of the ten tracks, Dave Stewart of The Eurythmics, a post-punk combo whose musical policy and subsequent chart entries had been founded on a truce between synthesiser trickery and minor-key human emotion. New advances in studio technology informed *Primitive Cool* too. So did the input of even younger minds than Stewart's; among them personnel from Living Colour, a black New York ensemble. Impressed by their stint in a city club, Jagger had overseen the tape that had procured Living Colour a recording deal. Paying close heed to what made his now teenage daughters, Karis and Jade, groove too, he had also assisted Strange Things From Tackhead, a local 'collective' of hip-hop persuasion. His recreational listening lay in the same direction as he reiterated his falling-out-of-love with 'traditional rock music. 'I've done it to death'.

He was as scornful of aspects of a new development in country and western, marketed as New Tradition, even though it was finding favour with young consumers by rescuing C&W from its rhinestoned tackiness. Mick, while confessing that he didn't mind Dwight Yoakam and Ofra Haza, found Randy Travis 'deadly dull, this year's Jim Reeves, but all the girls like Randy'.

As well as a demonstrative awareness of modern pop, there was some lyrical soul-baring – for example that he'd found true love after a lifelong search in 'Throwaway'. There was also a dig at Keith in 'Shoot Off Your Mouth' and he fielded questions from his children about his past in the title song. These were all major ingredients in the *Primitive Cool* cauldron. It invited fair-to-middling critiques, typified by *Q*'s 'an improvement...respectable but not earthed'. For once, these were reflected in chart positions – because fair-to-middling was also the performance of the inaugural single, the bolt-upright 'Let's Work'. Its entry at No. 35 in Britain was also its watermark, despite Mick taking the trouble to plug it with a *Top Of The Pops* slot that was more like a keep-fit class.

A recent hit, however modest, still kept him in the public eye, and two shows at Tokyo's 55,000-capacity Kerakuen Dome – the biggest venue on the Japanese itinerary – sold out on the day they were announced. For the second of these, Tina Turner was an unexpected pleasure for the fans, jogging on to join in 'Brown Sugar' and 'It's Only Rock 'n' Roll'.

For some, this made up for the non-appearance of Jeff Beck, then recovering from a domestic accident that had almost cost him the thumb on his left hand. This mishap, nevertheless, wasn't why he'd cried off. The warning signs had been the inventive but petulant Jeff's disgruntlement at the *Primitive Cool* selections being presented to him and the other musicians as more of a fait accompli than had been the case on *She's The Boss*. 'I wanted to be in an experimental Rolling Stones with Jagger singing,' he gloomed, 'and I was sure that was what he wanted, but as time time drifted by, I realised he was determined to put the songs on tape the way he wanted them. He wanted a very stylized album. I was just slotted in as a guest, a studio-type guy'.

Beck was bemused too by the large amount of old material in the proposed set list for the tour: 'It turned out there were fifteen Rolling Stones songs, and I didn't want to go to Australia and Japan to play a load of Keith Richards licks'. Neither did the ace guitarist wish to skulk beyond the main spotlight as one of a backing band in which 'we were all planetary kinds of people' . Though named The Brothers Of Sodom, the band included 'two chicks prancing around doing "Tumbling Dice",' raged Keith Richards, 'It was very sad that a high percentage of his show was Stones songs. If you're going to do stuff on your own, do stuff off the two albums you did.' Perhaps it was erring on the side of caution by a Jagger who, moments before his Japanese concert debut, had come nearly as close to vomiting with nerves as he had before that hesitant 'Around And Around' with Blues Incorporated back in nineteen-sixty-forget-about-it.

Of the same vintage was 'the four-headed monster' (as Mick had dubbed the representatives of The Beatles: George Harrison and Ringo Starr plus John Lennon's widow and elder son), who he coaxed to say a few words at 1988's annual Rock 'n' Roll Hall Of Fame gala in the banqueting room of New York's Waldorf-Astoria Hotel. Afterwards he made his way back onto the stage for the 'surprise' all-star blow at the end, bunching round a single microphone with Harrison and Bob Dylan for a raucous 'I Saw Her Standing There'. The strains of a 'Like A Rolling Stone' led by Dylan and Jagger and 'Satisfaction' with Jagger and Jeff Beck to the fore also dominated the joyous proceedings.

Eighteen months earlier, Mick had been on camera too at a Prince's Trust Concert at Wembley Pool, delivering 'Dancing In The Street' with David Bowie. Despite this, he never quite became one of the usual shower – Eric Clapton, Elton John, Annie Lennox, Phil Collins et al – expected to show their faces on such occasions as a contrast to the processed frenzy of Curiosity Killed The Cat, Bros, Wet Wet Wet and other Me-Generation chart-riders of the 80s.

Nevertheless, he laid out a dry-cleaned suit, shampooed his hair and polished his shoes on 18 January 1989 when it was The Rolling Stones' turn to be inducted into Rock 'n' Roll Hall Of Fame. With him on the podium stood Keith, Ron Wood and Mick Taylor, and on their behalf he made the acceptance speech, cracking, 'It's slightly ironic that tonight you see us on our best behaviour, but we've been awarded for twenty-five years of bad behaviour'. He also paid tribute to Brian Jones and the more recently deceased Ian Stewart.

Back home, as well as the R&B oldies on the juke-box, disco turntable and bar band repertoire, some of their original perpetrators would still be labouring to set up equipment at opening time, as was fifty-something John Mayall at London's Town-and-Country where, though his name had been mis-spelt on the ticket, he was as ecstatic as his cramped devotees that he was so rabidly remembered.

This gave Jagger pause for thought. In Japan and Australasia, all the majority of customers had wanted to hear were the sounds of yesteryear, as the poorer sales for *Primitive Cool* against the *Rewind* compilation and its by-products testified. If the next Mick Jagger album – if there was to be one – gave the profit graph another downward turn, what then?

How could Mick have possibly visualised too the loneliness and disappointment that his breaking free had brought him? As for Keith, he had channelled some of his disenchantment with the Stones' disintegration into reactivating the waning careers of certain of his boyhood idols, realising his wildest dream via his organisation of an all-star backing group for a televised concert starring Chuck Berry – who, Keith had to admit grudgingly 'gave me more headaches than Mick Jagger'.

It was pointless, continued Keith, for Mick to 'keep looking back over his shoulder at

Michael Jackson, Prince and George Michael. I've told him it's ludicrous to try to pretend you're twenty when you're forty-five'. Like a cat that has tried in vain to catch a mouse before walking away as if he'd never had any such idea, Jagger seemed to be refuting his forays into the latest sounds: 'It's not that I don't like that music. I just don't think it has any relevance within the Stones. Maybe I'm old-fashioned, but I don't think the writing, certainly the lyric writing, is particularly interesting.' He had a point. Some exponents were given to either repeating one line ad nauseum or just 'emoting' wordlessly whenever rhymes and scansion seemed too much like hard work.

WANDERING SPIRIT

US and UK Release: 8 February 1993 **Atlantic 7567824362**
Producers: Mick Jagger and Rick Rubin

Wired All Night; Sweet Thing; Out Of Focus; Don't Tear Me Up; Put Me In The Trash; Use Me; Evening Gown; Mother Of A Man; Think; Wandering Spirit; Hang On To Me Tonight; I've Been Lonely For So Long; Angel In My Heart; Handsome Molly.

Mick was also soft-pedalling his measureless celebrity nowadays – even if England's cricket XI were delighted to have their picture taken with him, and national broadsheets to publish it. The Stones were judged by Richard Branson to be 'Mick Jagger plus three others' when, after periodic attempts since 1975, he signed them to his Virgin label in November 1991. It would be Atlantic, however, that would press Jagger's *Wandering Spirit*, a solo album of more downbeat kidney than its predecessors. While it included a revival of James Brown's 'Think', a traditional ditty, 'Handsome Molly', was its finale, symptomatic perhaps of an abiding, if covert, interest in folk music.

Wandering Spirit's self-penned singles – 'Sweet Thing', 'Don't Tear Me Up' and 'Out Of Focus' – spread themselves thinly enough to be worthwhile marketing exercises without actually troubling the charts, and it was to make the most commercial headway of all Jagger's solo ventures – in Europe anyway, where it gained a gold disc in Germany – the world's third most vital sales territory and sliced to No. 5 in Britain.

GODDESS IN THE DOORWAY

US and UK Release: 19 November 2001 **Virgin 8112882**
Producers: Mick Jagger, Matt Clifford, Marti Frederiksen and others

Visions Of Paradise; Joy; Dancing In The Starlight; God Gave Me Everything; Hide Away; Don't Call Me Up; Goddess In The Doorway; Lucky Day; Everybody Getting High; Gun.

When the millenium turned, though, Mick's 30-minute performance in Los Angeles' El Rey Theatre to launch a fourth solo album was an industry event. *Goddess In The Doorway* sold in thousands rather than tens of thousands until the broadcast of a television documentary entitled *Being Mick*, an interlacing of mostly studio and domestic scenes.

Eventually, it teetered on the edge of Britain's Top 40 and the US Top 30, though the principal single, 'God Gave Me Everything', was a flop. Nonetheless, most reviewers agreed that the album was an entertaining mixture of styles that, while not always reconciling easily, indicated a still-lively imagination at work. This was particularly evident in lyrics that, as well as domestic issues, reflected a deeper concern with spiritual matters. It's a preoccupation that may become more pronounced on future solo offerings as eternity beckons for one who, whatever else he does in the years left to him, will be forever visualised by Joe Public in some fixed attitude, doing what he did during some optimum moment as lead singer of The Rolling Stones.

KEITH RICHARDS SOLO PROJECTS

TALK IS CHEAP

US and UK Release: 4 October 1988 **Virgin CDV 2554**
Producers: Keith Richards and Steve Jordan

Big Enough; Take It So Hard; Struggle; I Could Have Stood You Up; Make No Mistake; You Don't Move Me; How I Wish; Rockawhile; Whip It Up; Locked Away; It Means A Lot.

A footloose period of excursions back and forth across the Atlantic during the late 70s was notable for sightings of Keith Richards, perhaps at the Bottom Line in Greenwich Village, sharing a backstage joke with McGuinn-Clark-Hillman, a reconstitution of three-fifths of the original Byrds. There he was again with Ronnie Wood, ambling across the boards at the Elysee Matignon in Paris to shake hands with Leonard Bernstein during an extravaganza in honour of the composer of *West Side Story*, who'd planted successful feet in both the classical and pop camps.

Richards was also assisting on albums by such respected names as Steve Cropper – Booker T's guitarist – and Peter Tosh, by then an artiste in his own right too. Keith had already dabbled in a solo project himself – a single that coupled self-produced tracks taped whenever studio time had gone begging over the past two years.

With Ian Stewart and Mick Taylor's drummer, Mike Driscoll, the A-side was a fiery revival of a 1960 Chuck Berry flip-side, 'Run Rudolph Run'. Since Bing Crosby's 'White Christmas' had sold by the ton in 1942, the Christmas single has been, with the 'death disc', one of pop's hardiest forms. Gene Autry, The Goons, Dickie Valentine, Elvis Presley, The Beverley

Sisters, Freddie and the Dreamers, Max Bygraves, Slade, John Lennon, Wizzard, Jethro Tull and Showaddywaddy had been among multitudinous entertainers trying their luck with seasonal platters aimed directly at a time of year when the usual chart rules don't apply. How else had Valentine's 'Christmas Alphabet' knocked 'Rock Around The Clock' from No. 1 in Britain in December 1955? Why did repromotions of Slade's 'Merry Christmas Everybody' keep registering in the list years after the disc's optimum moment in 1973?

'Run Rudolph Run' had all the credentials of a Yuletide smash, but none that actually grabbed the public, mainly because it missed the December sell-in altogether, issued as it was in February 1979. Though it tumbled into the bargain bin, Keith seemed to have enjoyed committing this old favourite to vinyl. Others better known for their own compositions too were releasing non-originals in the mid- to late-70s, either to display their skills as 'interpreters' or simply because they were running out of ideas. Bryan Ferry, Jonathan King, John Lennon and The Hollies had all issued entire LPs of oldies after David Bowie had set the ball rolling with 1973's *Pin-Ups*, an affectionate trawl through British beat group classics. Renewed interest in 60s instrumentals had put elderly guitarist Bert Weedon abruptly at the top of the British album list in 1976 with *22 Golden Guitar Greats*. There were also singles of old chestnuts by the likes of Zoot Money, Traffic's Jim Capaldi, The Troggs (an incredible 'Good Vibrations') and Colin Blunstone of The Zombies.

Keith compounded his own retrospection with a workmanlike cover of Jimmy Cliff's 'The Harder They Come', demonstrating an adept absorption of that chopping reggae afterbeat, on the flip-side of 'Run Rudolph Run'. It had been realised during sessions for *Emotional Rescue*, and a general period when Keith was lending his celebrity to further the causes of various boyhood heroes, both alive and dead. He was, for example, a laconic 'talking head' on *The Real Buddy Holly Story*, a documentary screened on BBC 2 in 1985, but this was a mere bagatelle compared to what should have been his finest hour in this respect: *Hail! Hail! Rock 'n' Roll*, the sanctification of Chuck Berry's 60th birthday on celluloid and in the back-slapping attendance by himself and other famous musicians who'd grown up to the Brown-Eyed if now less Handsome Man's music.

The idea of *Hail! Hail! Rock 'n' Roll* had come to Keith on 23 January the previous year when he inducted Berry at the first ever Rock'n'Roll Hall Of Fame ceremony. Mounting the podium at New York's deluxe Wardorf-Astoria Hotel, Keith, with several stiff drinks on board, delivered a heart-felt citation ('I lifted every lick he ever played') and presented the statuette. Later, the stage heaved with stars and starlets for an 'impromptu' valedictory jam. Amid the musical clutter that characterized such affairs, Keith caught several bars of unadulterated magic when Chuck was able to take over at the central microphone. Eyes met and telepathic communication seemed to read, 'I know you and you know me. We understand each other in a secret way'. The idol and his worshipper had become as one.

Somehow, Keith wanted to recapture and protract the sensation of those few moments at the big finish because 'I felt I owed him so much'. Contacting an unexpectedly genial Chuck before the week was out, he enthused about the feasibility of either a bio-pic or a project along the lines of *The Real Buddy Holly Story*.

Consequent brain-storming boiled down to the pencilling in of a Berry concert in his home-town of St. Louis to tie in with the publication of his autobiography. The results were to be immortalized on film – with Keith overseeing a thoroughly drilled and illustrious backing combo rather than trusting his hero's usual policy of employing a pick-up group that had little or no time to rehearse or even sound-check with their paymaster.

Keith was determined to summon whatever willingness and energy was needed to give the best of everything to his first authorised stint on the boards with Berry. More than a week of rehearsals at the fellow's house in Wentzville on the outskirts of St. Louis were, however, freighted with Richards' ruthlessness at sticking to the task in hand and Berry's alternate grouchiness and bored indolence as if he couldn't wait to knock off for the day from some run-of-the-mill job he'd done for decades – which it was. Keith was affronted by the criticisms and reprimands that preceded his withdrawals into abstracted indifference. His hackles rose time and time again, but he was determined not to stride out, insulted, but poured himself a whiskey and dissected the host's character and ability with bitter intensity.

On the night, only naked pleas would cajole Chuck to test vocal balance for Johnnie Johnson, Bobby Keyes and the rest of the hand-picked instrumentalists from every trackway of his career. The special guests, among them Eric Clapton, Julian Lennon and Etta James all agreed to appear at the Fox, the theatre where Berry's teenage self had been refused admission. This was an age when any admixture of negro blood was deemed sufficient to restrict its owner to 'colored' public conveniences, and launderettes displayed the sign 'Whites Only Or Maids In Uniform'.

This time, Chuck Berry stepped beneath its very proscenium, and an almost palpable wave of goodwill washed over him as it always did, regardless of who shared the same stage. With a dotage rich in material comforts earned from a golden past, Berry had nothing to lose by serving his present accompanists as he had the pick-up outfits, launching impetuously into songs not in the ordered modus operandi, changing key mid-song if he felt like it, and ripping prescribed arrangements to shreds, leaving a panicking Keith and the others to busk behind him. Like, what key's this one in, man? Like Z minus, man.

Yet, from theoretical disaster came forth a hysterical gaiety, with cavorting onlookers assuming the role of rhythm section during the up-tempo rockers, and Chuck tumbling about, skylarking and pulling out every ham trick in the book.

All's well that ended well, Keith supposed, and before the fond gaze of those in the green room, he and Chuck had bear-hugged each other, but 'I couldn't warm to him if I was cremated next to him – a big chip on his shoulder and, now and again, it's knocked off, and he's a fascinating, sweet guy, but suddenly he checks himself like he's given away too much, having too much fun, and the armour goes back on.'

The experience faded, and Richards was so able to disassociate music from the individual personal weaknesses of its practitioners that he remained as well-meaning when trying to throw down a line to other olde-tyme rock 'n' rollers.

He was, of course, turning into one himself – and so, much more unwillingly, was Mick Jagger, who was thinking aloud about a professional life beyond The Rolling Stones. The possibility that Jagger might slip his cable permanently may have been as real as it was for all four Beatles, who had been well into solo careers long before their partnership had been dissolved in the High Court.

While it was unlikely that customers would be obliged to pay their money and take a choice between The Rolling Stones and Mick Jagger's Rolling Stones – with maybe Mick Taylor leading an ensemble earning ovations with versions of Stones classics on which he may or may not have been heard – Keith was long-faced about Mick's now open preparations for solo dates in Japan and Australasia: 'I couldn't deal with it any more. It's like a marriage. Friction builds up over the years.'

Keith was driven beyond desultory sabre-rattling. With drummer Paul Shaffer – one of NBC's satirical *Saturday Night Live*'s resident musicians – and session bass player Marcus Miller, he registered a protest of sorts by delivering old Stones numbers with rueful affection on the same television channel's *Friday Night Videos*. He also appeared sniping at Jagger in the media, sometimes with almost audible sniggers.

To what extent it was sincerely bitter, grist to the publicity mill or just half-serious mind games is unfathomable. In any case, the enigma of the sunshine and showers of Mick and Keith's friendship couldn't be formulated in plain terms any more than any long and intimate relationship, coalesced by common ordeal and jubilation, that has endured from childhood to middle age. 'Mick's and my battles are not exactly as perceived through the press or other people,' elucidated Keith, 'They're far more convoluted – because we've known each other for most of our lives. So they involve more subtleties and ins and outs than could possibly be explained.'

Those within or on the periphery of the Stones' inner circle came to realize that, as it was with the messiest of divorces, you had to side with one or the other – though David Bowie was able to hedge his bets by duetting with Mick on the 'Dancing In The Street' charity single for the Live Aid relief fund, and seizing the opportunity to be photographed with Keith at some apres-concert gathering for publication in the New Musical Express. The feeling was that, though Jagger was the most engaging and commercially operable of the two, Richards could pull some unexpected stroke that would bring about his ascendancy. Soon, there came reports of both a fire that necessitated total evacuation on the final day of sessions and, less specifically, intriguing sounds emitting from New York's then unfashionable Studio 900. It was one of the locations where Keith was recording *Talk Is Cheap*, his first bona fide solo album, in accordance with a deal covering only him which he was about to wrap up with Virgin Records. Personnel was drawn mainly from The New Barbarians, the Hail! Hail! Rock 'n' Roll stage fixtures and Dirty Work auxiliaries, but more notable bit-part players were Mick Taylor, The Memphis Horns (derived from The Markeys, who'd preceded Booker T and the MGs as Stax's house band) and Bootsy Collins, former James Brown bass guitarist-turned-solo attraction. Johnny Marr, guitarist with The Smiths, was alleged to have played on a Richards session around this time too.

As it had been with Dirty Work, *Talk Is Cheap*'s 11 selections – co-written with Steve Jordan – were designed to be reproduced on the boards without much difficulty. The most contrived studio artifice was some backwards-running instrument fading in and out of the opening 'Big Enough', otherwise perhaps the most typical track with its murky deliberation and a snare drum almost as prominent as a lead vocal. It was like a Kentish cross between Bobs Dylan and Marley with a hint of post-war bluesman Slim Harpo.

On 'Rockawhile' and 'Make No Mistake', Sarah Dash (from Labelle) was as loud as Keith in what amounted to virtual duets. Yet, if she outclassed him technically, his inability to stray far beyond his central two octaves reinforced an idiosyncratic allure peculiar to certain singers who warp an intrinsically limited range and eccentric delivery to their own devices. In this oligarchy are David Bowie, Bob Dylan – and, of course, Mick Jagger. A Caruso-loving fly on the Studio 900 wall may well have blocked his ears, but, rather than try and fail to hit notes, Richards had discovered the knack of extemporizing huskily like a soul man, as though a random couplet's sentiment couldn't be expressed through orthodox articulation.

Keith's controlled guitar solos and obligatos were less of a revelation. Constructed to integrate with each piece's melodic and lyrical intent, these were refreshingly unfussed when compared to other players' de rigeur reaction with face-pulling flash to underlying chord patterns rather than the more obvious aesthetics of a song. That puts Keith Richards in a different rather than lower league to Eric Clapton and his sort with blisteringly high-velocity string-bending.

As a production – with Steve Jordan, who the sharp-eyed had spotted beating drums in The *Blues Brothers* movie – *Talk Is Cheap* was characterized by not so much gratuitous soloing as 'laying down a groove' via repeated choruses and extended fades which put some in a mantric (or stoned) trance, while others wondered, 'How much longer?' However, constant replay was necessary for details – such as the understated violin in downbeat 'Locked Away' and *sotto voce* muttering in 'Struggle' – to assume sharper focus.

Comprising only in riffs and perfunctory syllables strung together, to carry a tune, some of the compositions worked less as separate entities than the summoning of atmospheres in which it was the rough-and-ready sound at any given moment that counted. 'I have more exact, more perfect or skilful takes of each of the songs,' said Richards, before reiterating the old mantra, 'The more you try to literally perfect them, the more you lose the instinctive thing. Instinct is what I want.'

Much of *Talk Is Cheap* was maddeningly – and probably unavoidably – familiar – a 'Street Fighting Man'-ish ostinato here, a Bo Diddley inflection there, vamping Chuck Berry-like piano triplets (courtesy of Johnnie Johnson) elsewhere. There are ample helpings of dub-reggae, Cajun-Zydeco and Buddy Holly and the Crickets-like backing chorale (in 'I Could Have Stood You Up'), Missa Luba jungle mass and James Brown anguish were served up too. 'Big Enough' wouldn't have been out of place on a Police album and, by Keith's own admission,

The Beatles surfaced obliquely in 'Whip It Up'.

Yet an inbred originality rode roughshod over all the stylistic borrowing – and, while Frank Sinatra, jackpot of all songwriters, was unlikely to cover them, certain compositions *per se* could be reduced most servicably to the acid test of just voice and piano, overtly the 'Take It So Hard' and 'Make No Mistake' singles and, catchier still, 'You Don't Move Me', a supposed dig at Jagger, spelt out in its diminuendo coda.

LIVE AT THE HOLLYWOOD PALLADIUM DECEMBER 15 1988

US Release: 10 December 1991 **Virgin CDVU545**
UK Release: 8 February 1992 **Virgin CDVU545**
Producers: Keith Richards, Steve Jordan and Don Smith

Take It So Hard; How I Wish, I Could Have Stood You Up; Too Rude; Make No Mistake; Time Is On My Side; Big Enough; Whip It Up; Struggle; Happy.

[

Two could play at Jagger's game, and in the same month as the final date of Mick's jaunt Down Under in November 1988, Keith embarked on a fortnight of engagements across the States with The X-Pensive Winos, an amalgam of the less illustrious *Talk Is Cheap* assistants. As well as the album *in toto*, they gave 'em 'Happy', 'Time Is On My Side' – featuring Sarah Dash – and, most bygone of all, 'Connection' from the Stones canon plus 'Run Rudolph Run' – which became more and more fitting as the tour crept nearer to its climax. This was a week before Christmas Day in New Jersey in front of a crowd of over 20, 000. This took place two days after the show at Los Angeles' Hollywood Palladium, containing more or less the same set, taped for an in-concert album.

This was heralded by a publicity blitz conspicuous for a spot on Smile Jamaica, a concert in London for victims of an unforeseen hurricane that had damaged properties – including Keith's – throughout the island. Patiently puffing a perpetual cigarette, Richards also gave unblinking off-stage copy, frequently tormenting questioners with hints of a Stones comeback.

This wasn't as mischievous as it seemed – because the parts hadn't equalled the whole. Of all the non-Stones ventures, Mick's had, as predicted, been the most saleable, albeit on a law of diminishing returns – though figures for *Talk Is Cheap* had been healthy enough for moderate placings in Top 40 charts across the globe.

When the Stones became a functional entity again, Keith was recast by certain key pundits as an unlikely Judy Garland of pop. He was no longer a human rag being blown pedantically across a terrible desert with an empty canteen, buoyed by a drug-begotten and surreal mirage of a rescue ship surging through the scorching rocks and flash-lacerating cacti. Awaiting him on the other side of the desert in the first instance was morbid inquisitiveness from those who looked and wondered. Onstage was not a common-or-garden pop star, but a man who'd been to hell and back. Others cognisant with Richards' personal vulnerability and turbulent life worried when he seemed to flag, cheered when he recovered and glowed when his lead vocal spot went down especially well. Rather than 'Happy', this tended to be 'Before They Make Me Run', 'Little T & A' from *Tattoo You* – also quasi-autobiographical (as exemplified by its observation that pushers were disgruntled because he was no longer interested in hard drugs) – or, later, 'The Worst' from 1994's *Voodoo Lounge*.

Every day he still lived was a bonus. Whatever had been wrong was righting itself now that most of the mainly self-invoked devils had been sweated from him, even if he continued to play up to an old image. At some awards ceremony or other of the many he attended nowadays as both presenter and nominee, Richards was sober and coherent at his table, but, like the late Oliver Reed, his opposite number in the world of drama, he pretended to be real, real gone when called to the podium – cosmetic fish-hooks and amulets dangling from his hair: dear, old Keith, drunk before breakfast, stoned before lunch time...

MAIN OFFENDER

UK and US Release: 20 October 1992 **Virgin CDVUS59**
Producers: Keith Richards, Steve Jordan and Waddy Wachtel

999; Wicked As It Seems; Eileen; Words Of Wonder; Yap Yap; Bodytalks; Hate It When You Leave; Runnin' Too Deep; Will But You Won't; Demon.

It had been noted that Keith was imbibing mineral water in preference to his hitherto-customary off-duty vodka-with-orange soda when back at Studio 900 in August 1992 recording a second solo album, *Main Offender*. Its making was symptomatic not of internal dissent in the Stones any more, but a more mature attitude within not so much a group, as perhaps an artistic kolkhoz in which members could plough this or that extra-mural furrow with the blessing of the rest – unless, of course, they considered that it threatened direct rivalry to the integral unit. This was to extend as far as Keith headlining a concert on behalf of the Rain Forest Alliance at New York's Beacon Theatre – where he was lauded by compere Jackson Browne as 'one of the finest singer-songwriters of our time' – though there had been little evidence of this on *Main Offender*.

Completed with, more or less, the *Talk Is Cheap* personnel in attendance, *Main Offender* was hailed by younger critics for whom it was given that Keith was The Rolling Stones, but was otherwise deemed unexciting – certainly not as ear-catching as *Talk Is Cheap*. Repeated spins put individual tracks – notably '999', 'Eileen' and soulful 'Demon' – in sharper focus, but nothing screamed out as a blatant single that might or might not irritate the Top 50, let alone be an unmistakable 'Happy'-like smash. The most fundamental flaws were the dragging out of songs – with 'Words Of Wonder' almost touching the seven-minute mark – to a greater degree than *Talk Is Cheap*, and certain lyrics that may have contained opaque gems of worldly wisdom, but were more likely just words to sing.

To be brutal, *Main Offender* was a much of a muchness, though the playing and production was proficient, and Keith, within his limits, in fine voice. Yet who the hell am I to criticise an album that spread itself thinly enough over a long period to sell moderately well whilst dithering on the edge of the charts in both Britain and the States?

No-one could moan either that Keith had let the album fend for itself. Its promotion included X-Pensive Winos shows in Argentina, a short European tour – that took in an engagement at the Marquee – and some US showcases, notably two numbers at the first International Rock Awards televised from New York's Armory. Here, Eric Clapton handed Richards an award – a twelve-inch statuette of Elvis Presley – for being a 'Living Legend'.

Keith also submitted to a signing session at Tower Records in New York – which sucked in a crowd of over 3, 000, as well as making himself pleasant at *Rolling Stone* magazine's 25th anniversary party in one of the city's restaurants, and speaking to *Kerrang*, a chief mouthpiece of heavy metal – in which he dismissed fame as 'a mind-rotting thing'.

CHARLIE WATTS' SOLO PROJECTS

His membership of The Rolling Stones will always remain central to any consideration of Charlie Watts as a figure in time's fabric. Yet, under less extraordinary circumstances, he might have won a place in British cultural history as a truly great jazz drummer.

THE PEOPLE BAND (1970)

UK and US Release: 6 February 1970 **Transatlantic TRA 214**
Producer: Charlie Watts

Part 1; Part2; Part 3; Part 4; Part 5; Part 6; untitled track.

His first venture into the form of jazz on disc was in 1970 as producer of an eponymous album by The People Band, who roamed Britain's furthest reaches of jazz-rock – or jazz-something. This entity was connected to both The Battered Ornaments – unfortunates who'd been booed venomously during a spot just before the Stones at Hyde Park – and North London's avant-garde theatre group, The People Show, who were resident in one of the Arts Laboratories that had come into being circa 1967.

Whenever The People Band ventured beyond this underground security, a minority absorbed their free-form recitals in a knowing, nodding sort of way, whilst blocking out the impure thought in the tacit question, 'How could anyone like this stuff?'. They clapped politely this 'spontaneous music', that others enjoyed for 'the wrong reasons' rather than comprehending that the more effort needed to appreciate it, the more 'artistic' it must be.

Though often cynosures of an unnerving stare from what looked like a gigantic photograph of silent and undemonstrative onlookers, The People Band's core personnel was distinguished after a retrospective fashion, containing as it did drummer Rob Tait and keyboard player Charlie Hart, who was to work with Ronnie Lane of the Small Faces, The Who's Pete Townshend and, via art school pal Ian Dury, Wreckless Eric – while Roger Potter and George Kahn, respectively on bass and woodwinds, were ever-present session players in London. Guest musicians on the Band's long-player included saxophonist Lyn Dobson, once of Manfred Mann and, more recently, Soft Machine, and Mike Figgis, who cut his teeth as trumpeter in Newcastle soul band, The Gas Board with whom Bryan Ferry had been awaiting his destiny with Roxy Music.

Finally, there was Charlie Watts, who not only oversaw the album, but drummed on it. Yet, regardless of big name approbation – and intrinsic content – for it was the sound at any given moment that counted more than the six individual excerpts from a continuous performance – The People Band's LP had breadth of sonic expression that, if confident and clean, didn't detract from the forceful gusto. Neither was it pat, dovetailed and American with neatly-executed solos floating effortlessly over layers of treated sound.

As the decade progressed, Charlie Watts added further to credits on album covers, being heard on Ronnie Wood's *Gimme Some Neck*, and *Rough Mix* by Pete Townshend and Ronnie Lane and, for old time's sake – *A Dark Horse* by Brian Knight, one of the Ealing club crowd when the world was young. Another assistant on the Townshend-Lane and Knight offerings was Ian Stewart, a chief catalyst in Rocket 88, a project in which he and Charlie Watts remained mainstays for as long as it didn't interfere too much with Stones matters. Essentially, however, it was the brainchild of Bob 'Big Sunflower' Hall, a boogie-woogie pianist who was of sufficient eminence to call upon such luminaries as Fleetwood Mac's Peter Green and leading British blues chanteuse Jo Ann Kelly for assistance when recording three albums in the late 1960s for, admittedly, labels of no great merit.

Swindon's cosy Wyvern Theatre was the venue of the first manifestation of what became Rocket 88 on 12 June 1977. 'It was originally The Bob Hall Band,' outlined the artist formerly known as Big Sunflower, 'and was formed to play a farewell concert for me when I was living and working in Swindon, and planning to move back to London. I suggested to Ian Stewart we might do a charity concert. He said, "I might know a drummer who's quite good" - and that was Charlie Watts. We got a local bass player and a brass section. We never practiced at all, just went on stage and did this show.'

ROCKET 88 (1981)

UK Release: 8 January 1981 **Atlantic KS0776**
US Release: 11 March 1981 **Atlantic CD 19293**
Producer: Ian Stewart

Rocket 88; Waiting For The Call; St. Louis Blues; Roll 'Em Pete; Swindon Swings; Roadhouse Boogie; Talking About Louise.

It was an intense discussion that took place as old friendships and rivalries were renewed at Alexis Korner's 50th birthday party on 19 April 1978. Guests at this affair included Paul Jones – and Ian Stewart who, recalled Jones, 'wanted to get together an R&B outfit like the Ellington or Basie "small group", and he didn't want any guitarists unless they could play like Freddie Green – which meant that the only guitarist who could be in it was Alexis.'

Putting deeds over debate, Stewart was behind the organisation of a show just before Christmas in the image of those at the Wyvern but relocated to Dingwall's Dance Hall in London to celebrate what he'd calculated to be half a century of boogie-woogie. The major change to the personnel was that Jack Bruce was now plucking upright bass.

Bruce's presence as much as that of Charlie Watts and Alexis Korner – who'd become a pop star at last when singer on early 70s hits with CCS – added to the turn-out at Dingwall's. Indeed, hundreds were turned away at the tail-end of a queue that stretched round the block. Many were genuine boogie-woogie enthusiasts, but quite a few had only the vaguest notion about what they were paying to hear, convincing themselves perhaps that some of that Stones, Cream and, if you like, CCS magic was going to radiate from the stage. Instead of magic, however, there was mere music played for the benefit of the musicians almost as much as the audience.

Enough people, however, lapped it up to make reconvenings viable. Billed as Rocket 88 – this was a genuflection to a 1951 Chess single by Ike Turner's Kings of Rhythm, cited by some cultural historians as a specific harbinger of rock'n'roll. Dates in Holland, Germany and back in Britain followed, largely on the strength of the famous names promised, particularly

that of a delighted Watts. 'I can't keep up being a Rolling Stone all the time,' he grinned at a scribbling scribe from the *Daily Mail*, 'I like the people involved, but not the whole showbiz thing.'

'If Charlie said he could do it,' agreed Bob Hall, 'We'd get major shows.' They also gained an Atlantic recording contract for an in-concert album.

If nothing else, Charlie, Jack and most of the other participants seemed to have fun to the degree that Watts and Stewart hurtled from a Stones studio session in Paris for Rocket 88's spot at the North Sea Jazz Festival in the Netherlands. The next afternoon, they were back in the studio, Ian's eyes bloodshot after nigh on two days at the wheel. Fine if unambitious music – 12-bar chord changes and a four-four backbeat that a half-wit couldn't lose – it was played for sheer enjoyment by the ablest practitioners of the form.

Though Rocket 88 vanished in a haze of one-nighters sur le continent, its impact would continue to ripple for as long as Charlie Watts remained an entertainer. The most immediate evidence of this was the use of bouncy 'Take The "A" Train', Duke Ellington's signature tune, as the introit to Rolling Stones stage appearances in the early 80s.

LIVE AT FULHAM TOWN HALL (1986)

UK Release: 1 December 1986 **CBS 450243**
US Release: 22 November 1986 **Columbia 40570**
Producers: Charlie Watts and John Stevens

Stomping At The Savoy; Moonglow; Robbin's Nest; Lester Leaps In; Scrabble From The Apple; Flying Home.

'Take the 'A'-Train' would rear up too in the repertoire of The Charlie Watts Jazz Orchestra, whose multi-millionaire instigator had the wherewithal to fulfil a pragmatic dream. He and a hand-picked ensemble kicked off a 1985 week – rented by Charlie – at no less than London's Ronnie Scott's club.

What struck the crowd first was the sheer size of the band – 'all my favourite players, people I've admired for years'. There were nigh on thirty players which, without a synthesizer in sight, included two vibraphonists, a flautist doubling on clarinet, a brass section (including four trombonists), two singers, and a pianist – who was none other than sixty-year-old Stan Tracey, resident at the place for most of the 60s, during which time he worked with Sonny Rollins, Roland Kirk and every other visiting jazz giant. Finally, Charlie had hired a sensational array of a dozen saxophonists chosen from both veterans and up-and-coming talent.

Charlie beamed at the salvos of clapping whenever one or other of them wrapped up a particularly bravura solo, but, as expected, he preferred not to indulge himself, choosing instead to keep smooth pace with the blowing of others. Indeed, he was flanked by two other drummers who, like everyone else in The Charlie Watts Jazz Orchestra, were committed, even delighted, participants. While no-one could pretend that they'd been lifted by time-machine from the Cotton Club, it was great fun to make music to which you could lindy-hop and jitterbug rather than break-dance, music in a zoot-suit that was nowhere to be found on the map of present-day pop, coinciding as it did with the golden age of swing as the spirits of Ellington, Krupa, Goodman, Hampton, Herman, Lester Young and Artie Shaw effused from the bandstand.

Though one of those 'Greatest Nights Anyone Could Ever Remember', in fact the momentum was sustained for the rest of the week and next, a rebooking was arranged for the following April, and wheels set in motion for a reprise at Fulham Town Hall on 23 March 1986 as well as a short US tour. Before the dramatis personnae dispersed to individual activities, it was thought prudent to immortalise the show with a CD (and associated video) release, Live At Fulham Town Hall, remarkable for a front cover depicting just the founder of the feast's face, an old-young countenance beautified by the skill of the photographer.

Of course, Charlie's Jazz Orchestra was too expensive and cumbersome to last. Nevertheless, a twenty-two piece version honoured the negotiated dates in the USA. At one of these, Andrew Loog Oldham seemed quite buoyant with rose-tinted sentiment for the old days as well as genuine pleasure at Charlie 'being exactly where he wanted to be'.

FROM ONE CHARLIE... (1991)

UK Release: 5 April 1991
US Release: 6 June 1991
Producer: Roger Wake

UFO UF0002
Continuum 10104

Practicing Practicing; Black Bird White Chicks; Bluebird; Terra De Pajaro; Bad Seeds Rye Drinks; Relaxing At Camarillo; Going Going Going Gone.

In summer 1992, Watts resumed his moonlighting as a jazzer with a less ambitious labour of love when he and Keith Richards were heard on *Weird Nightmare*, an uneven tribute album to Charlie Mingus. However, of more import – if as tangential to contemporary pop as the Orchestra – was the following year's *From One Charlie To Another*, a genuflection by the newly-formed Charlie Watts Quintet to Charlie 'Yardbird' Parker and, less directly, the bebop combos that put so many of the big bands out of business.

This time, Watts presided over Peter King and David Green from the earliest Orchestra and three new – or not so new – faces. The most venerable was that of pianist Brian Lemon, a Midlander who'd rated as a rising jazz star in a *Melody Maker* poll in 1959. Largely on his recommendation, Watts had taken on trumpeter Gerard Presencer, an 18-year-old prodigy from London who, with the candour of his fourth decade, was to cite Charlie as 'the best bandleader I've ever worked with. He's almost quite angelic, despite going through all the stuff with The Rolling Stones'.

One who went through a little of that stuff was the Quintet's chanteur, Bernard Fowler, who'd been among the backing singers with the Stones both in the studio and on stage since the late 80s. While he wasn't old enough to be steeped in post-war jazz traditions, he picked up the basic principles quickly and, to Charlie's satisfaction, delivered what vocals were necessary when the outfit repaired in February 1991 to West London's Lansdowne Studio – as Olympic wasn't available – to tape 'Lover Man', 'Dancing In The Dark', 'Bound For New York', 'Just Friends' and further selections from Parker's catalogue. It was released several weeks later in a CD package that also embraced a reproduction of Charlie's long out-of-print book about Parker, *Ode To A High-Flying Bird*.

Bereft of commercial pressure, Watt's motives for *From One Charlie...* were rooted in a commitment to keeping Parker's work before the public, and to touch base somehow with the emotions that fuelled him when his adolescent self used to spin the vinyl of 'Bird At St. Nick's', 'April In Paris' et al to dust. Yet the overall intention of The Charlie Watts Quintet, nevertheless, was not to sound just like the Parker blueprint when they gave 'em 'Perdido', 'Bluebird', 1954's 'Cool Blues'. The gigs were at such disparate venues as Tokyo's Spiral Hall, both the Birmingham and London branches of Ronnie Scott's and, poignantly, two electrifying engagements in June 1991 at the Blue Note in New York. There, they dared to open with a slow Ellington ballad, 'Sunset And The Mockingbird', and include a Presencer original, 'Changing Reality'. If not expected to be astounding, these shows were very well-received both pleased and confused Charlie: 'So many English players are world class. Yet they're not that known elsewhere. In New York, people loved them, but they never offered these guys other gigs. I don't know why.'

A TRIBUTE TO CHARLIE PARKER (1992)

UK and US Release: 18 May 1991 **Continuum 19201**
Producer: Roger Wake

Practicing Practicing Just Great; Black Bird Whire Chicks; Bluebird; Bound For New York; Terra De Pajaro; Bad Seeds Rye Drinks; Relaxing At Camarillo; Going Going Going Gone; Just Friends; Cool Blues; Dancing In The Dark; Dewey's Square; Rocker; Lover Man; Perdido.

As it had been with the Orchestra, there were frequent long gaps between bookings, but ten dates in Brazil the following May and a short coast-to-coast trek across the States hot on its heels, turned the Quintet into a polished and thoroughly road-drilled unit on the crest of glowing critiques of *From One Charlie...* ('Light years better than anything Watts's day job has produced in fifteen years... a fabulous jazz recording,' reckoned *Option* magazine). A 'live' album that belied its prosaic title, *A Tribute To Charlie Parker*, it testified to more intrinsic virtues in an industry where sales figures are arbiters of success.

It was a truism that the drummer's status as a *Rolling Stone* guaranteed the ensemble more attention than would have been warranted in the normal course of events. Certainly, cash returns for the two oblations to Charlie Parker were healthy enough for two further Quintet albums – and even a 1993 single, 'You Go To My Head' – to be considered worthwhile marketing exercises.

WARM AND TENDER (1993)

UK and US Release: 26 October 1993 **Continuum 19310**
Producer: Roger Wake

My Ship; Bewitched Bothered And Bewildered; My Foolish Heart; Someone To Watch Over Me; I'll Be Around; Love Walked In; It Never Entered My Mind; My One And Only Love; I'm Glad There Is You; If I Should Lose You; Ill Wind; Time After Time; Where Are You; For All We Know; They Didn't Believe Me; You Go To My Head.

They had progressed from Parker to more generalised post-swing 'modern' jazz, and hinged on a tasteful, if stubbornly North American, choice of standards, principally from the annals of the type of Hollywood movies that crop up on midweek TV during the lonely hours between the lunchtime news and the children's programmes. Songs covered included Gershwin's 'Someone To Watch Over Me' (from *Young At Heart*), Sammy Cahn's 'I Should Care' (from *Thrill Of A Romance*) – as well as numbers from Broadway musicals ('Bewitched' from *Pal Joey*), some of which predated the first Billboard chart in 1940. Any one of them might be crucified by publand's answer to Tony Bennett on a beer-sodden evening in your local Red Lion.

Patiently puffing a cigarette, Charlie overcame his known aversion to the dazzle of flash bulbs and the scratch of biros on notebooks by showing willing at *Warm And Tender's* press launch on 11 October 1993 at New York's Algonquin Hotel. There he deadpanned the foreseeably stupid and damned impertinent questions – many of the same ones he'd listened to in the mid-60s – and, mouth moving mechanically, retelling the old, old story of him and the Stones for the trillionth time whilst trying to steer the wry shallowness round to the Quintet.

LONG AGO AND FAR AWAY (1996)

UK and UK Release: 11 June 1993 **Cema/Virgin 41695**
Producer: Roger Wake

I've Got A Crush On You; Long Ago And Far Away; More Than You Know; I Should Care; Good Morning Heartache; Someday; I Get Along Without You Very Well; What's New; Stairway To The Stars; In The Still Of The NIght; All Or Nothing At All; I'm In The Mood For Love; In A Sentimental Mood; Never Let Me Go.

There were three years between *Warm And Tender* and 1996's *Long Ago And Far Away*, on which the five were augmented by The London Metropolitan Orchestra, provoking comparisons with jazzer-turned-easy listening maestro Henry Mancini.

Just as they had expected Charlie Watts to play down his own part in *Warm And Tender*, in this respect, he wasn't to play the iconoclast with the few words he'd be persuaded to utter on behalf of Long Ago And Far Away. Lauding the contributions of the others, especially Bernard who, he said, 'sings beautifully'. He added, 'Of its type, it's a great album.'

Fundamentally, however, that *Warm And Tender* and its belated follow-up were critical triumphs was neither here nor there to Charlie. It wasn't anything to do with arrogance or over-confidence about his own or his colleagues' abilities, far from it. No matter how much the pundits on broadsheet arts pages smirked at each other's cleverness, it was the bane of their existence that, thanks to the financial safety net provided by his membership of an internationally-renowned pop group, someone like Charlie Watts could afford to do something that they couldn't do – and that he couldn't have cared less about their tin-pot reviews.

THE CHARLIE WATTS-JIM KELTNER PROJECT (2000)

UK and US Release: 23 May 2000 **Virgin VHOCD69**
Producers: Charlie Watts and Jim Keltner

Shelly Manne; Art Blakey; Kenny Clarke; Tony Williams; Roy Haynes; Max Roach; Airto; Billy Higgins; Elvin Suite.

Charlie Watts continued in the same vein with this project with Jim Keltner, wheeled in ostensibly to add idiosyncratic patterns of percussion onto *Bridges To Babylon* tracks after the beat had been invested by Charlie in Hollywood's Ocean Studios. He had taught himself the button-pushing new idioms of electronic drum devices and sampling, but had remained open-minded enough for organic experimentation such as whacking a refrigerator's wire grille with brushes on *Volume One* by The Traveling Wilburys, a 'supergroup' that included George Harrison, Bob Dylan and Roy Orbison.

Keltner brought a far greater abundance of such ideas to *The Charlie Watts-Jim Keltner Project*, an album of two years gestation that began during the recording of *Bridges To Babylon*. After a while, the two were using every minute that they were not required by the Stones to work on something that, if not potentially remunerative, was too intriguing to just amuse Keith, Mick and anyone else within earshot of the grooves and rhythms that effused from their tiers of processed sound. 'The percussion and the various electronic things make the music here,' Charlie would tell them, 'and that was kind of the interest because I'm not normally into that. I'm not playing any differently from anything I've ever done. Jim's parts are very techno sequences. It was very exciting, very interesting. I don't know if I'd ever choose to do it again either.'

Flesh was layered onto the Hollywood skeleton when Watts flew 20 boxes of tapes and floppy discs over to Twin Studios in Paris for moulding into items of sharper definition for release on a nine-track CD. As he wasn't as sufficiently schooled in the aural possibilities of state-of-the-art equipment, Watts received practical instruction *in situ* from Philippe Chauveau, a French drummer, who earned a credit with Charlie as the album's co-producer.

Much depended too on the proficiency of the other instrumentalists needed. Given this brief, Chauveau had picked and chosen violinist Marek Czerwiaski, bass guitarist Remy Vignolo, pianist Emmanuel Sourdeix and others whose names are as obscure now as they were then in English-speaking territories. But they were the finest Paris could offer, and Charlie did not presume to dictate notes and nuances to them or the players of a pot-pourri of melodic exotica including a berimbau, a cuica and a Moroccan souk.

He delegated much of the technological donkey-work, furthermore, to Chauveau because 'Jim told me I needed a computer editing system called Pro Tools. It's another world to me. I thought, "What are they talking about?", but I found Phillipe and we used some great Parisian jazz and world music musicians he knew. Then we started chopping and editing the tracks, and I sent them back across the Atlantic for Jim to hear.'

There would be parts of the Project that he'd have changed had he not been busy with the Stones and other matters, but some sections had been assembled literally second by second, and, belying any private anxieties about his console skills during the repeated re-running of each taped mile, the engineers – if showing neither enthusiasm nor distaste – were impressed by the visitor's learned suggestions about amplitude, stereo placement, degeneration et al, though correct terminology might have deferred sometimes to wordless vocal expressions like snatches of a Dada poem.

On one track, Mick Jagger's cinematic string synthesizer dominates the framing of Keltner reading – through a megaphone – quotes from Tony Williams, with something about the ride cymbal being the centre of the universe among one of the few discernable lines. Keltner's text wasn't self-created, but from a drumming magazine's eulogy for Williams, who'd just died at the age of 52. 'It was meant as a sort of requiem,' shrugged Charlie.

Actually titled 'Tony Williams', it had precipitated the naming of each of nearly all the other items after a North American jazz drummer admired by both – 'Max Roach', 'Shelly Mann', 'Art Blakey', 'Kenny Clarke' and so forth. 'If this project had come about in London,' reckoned Watts, 'I'm sure it would have been "Phil Seaman", "Tony Oxley", "John Stevens" and the others.' Nevertheless, like abstract impressionism in modern art, the purpose was for every piece not to illustrate the sound and style of its subject – records took care of that – but to convey an essence of him in some non-specific way, perhaps for reasons you couldn't articulate – or, in Charlie's words, 'It's not anything to do with them as players. It's more the feeling I get from just watching them play or hearing their records. It's in honour of them.'

'If the demand came,' Watts continued, 'I might get it together and do it like a Philip Glass concert I once saw in New York. I'd have Phillipe programming on one side, and Jim and I in the middle, mucking about with some guests – but the only thing I wouldn't want to happen is for people to think that because these tracks are named after these great drummers, I'm going to play like them.'

WATTS AT SCOTTS (2004)

UK Release: 14 June 2004 **Sanctuary BBJ3000**
US Release: 24 August 2004 **Sanctuary BBJ3000**
Producer: Charlie Watts

Main Stem; Bemsha SWing; Anthony's Dice; Roll 'Em Charlie; What's New; Body And Soul; Here's That Rainy Day; Tin Tin Deo; Sunset And The Mockingbird; Little Willie Leaps; Airto II; Chasing Reality; Faction (Satisfaction); Elvin's Song; Take The A Train.

Arrangements of two items from the Keltner collaboration were to be integrated into the set after Watts formed a new jazz outfit, The Charlie Watts Tentet, who commenced a fortnight at London's Ronnie Scott's in June 2001. Striking a balance between the unwieldy Orchestra and the limitations of the Quintet, Watts had selected personnel from both plus newcomers like South American percussionist Luis Jardim and, on vibraphone, Anthony Kerr. The line-up varied only slightly as most were happy to let other ventures take care of themselves in order to play with Charlie at home – and abroad in autumn with a one-nighter in Barcelona and residencies at the respective Blue Note clubs in Tokyo and New York where the bandleader proved a proficient if laconic interlocutor, developing quite a polished patter. In New York, he gave a particularly good account of himself when responding to backchat from Keith Richards, seated with his retinue near the front on the first evening.

As the tension had built on the opening night at Ronnie Scott's, Watts might not have minded swapping the unsettling hush for the uproar on the 60s 'scream circuit' with just Keith, Brian, Bill and Mick. 'I hate that silence,' he shuddered, 'When they come to listen. I hope people talk. It's got good acoustics. You can hear everything – so it's more exposed for me than being on one of those bloody great big stages in front of 90, 000. I don't play that loud, even with the Stones, so they mike you pretty closely.'

He was, therefore, glad of Richards's phoney insults at the Blue Note, and this with Charlie's own disarming wit made for a hugely entertaining evening that included the expected Parker, Ellington and Miles Davis preferences and a solitary vocal performance, courtesy of Luis Joachim, of Dizzy Gillespie's 'Tin Tin Deo'. The set concluded with an encore of 'Take The A Train', a number that, while he didn't risk being lynched if he omitted it, had become to Charlie and his jazz groups as 'Jumpin' Jack Flash' to the Stones.

DISCOGRAPHY

SINGLES, 12-inch SINGLES, CD SINGLES AND EPs

BRITISH RELEASES – SINGLES

Decca *

Rolling Stones Records §

London #

F 11675*	**Come On/I Want To Be Loved** (7 June 1963)
F 11764*	**I Wanna Be Your Man/Stoned** (1 November 1963)
F 11845*	**Not Fade Away/Little By Little** (21 February 1964)
F 11934*	**It's All Over Now/Good Times Bad Times** (26 June 1964)
F 12014*	**Little Red Rooster/Off The Hook** (13 November 1964)
F 12104*	**The Last Time/Play With Fire** (26 February 1965)

F 12220*	**(I Can't Get No) Satisfaction/The Spider And The Fly** (20 August 1965)
F 12263*	**Get Off Of My Cloud/The Singer Not The Song** (22 October 1965)
F 12331*	**19th Nervous Breakdown/As Tears Go By** (4 February 1966)
F 12395*	**Paint It Black/Long Long While** (13 May 1966)
F 12497*	**Have You Seen Your Mother Baby (Standing In The Shadow)/ Who's Driving Your Plane** (23 September 1966)
F 12546*	**Ruby Tuesday/Let's Spend The Night Together** (13 January 1967)
F 12654*	**We Love You/Dandelion** (18 August 1967)
F 12782*	**Jumping Jack Flash/Child Of THe Moon** (23 May 1968)
F 12952*	**Honky Tonk Women/You Can't Always Get What You Want** (11 July 1969)
RS 19100§	**Brown Sugar/Bitch/Let It Rock** (16 April 1971)

F 13195* **Everybody Needs Somebody To Love/Street Fighting Man/ Surprise Surprise** (30 June 1971)

F 13203* **Street Fighting Man/Surprise Surprise** (20 July 1971)

RS 19103§ **Tumbling Dice/Sweet Black Angel** (14 April 1972)

F 13404* **Sad Day/You Can't Always Get What You Want** (29 April 1973)

RS 19105§ **Angie/Silver Train** (20 August 1973)

RS 19114§ **It's Only Rock 'N Roll (But I Like It)/Through The Lonely Nights** (26 July 1974)

F 13584* **I Don't Know Why/Try A Little Harder** (23 May 1975)

F 13597* **Out Of Time/Jiving Sister Fanny** (5 September 1975)

RS 19121§ **Fool To Cry/Crazy Mama** (20 April 1976)

RSR EMI 2802/ RSR 12 EMI 2802§	**Miss You/Far Away Eyes** (19 May 1978)
RSR EMI 2861§	**Respectable/When The Whip Comes Down** (15 September 1978)
RSR 105§	**Emotional Rescue/Down In The Hole** (20 June 1980)
RSR 106§	**She's So Cold/Send It To Me** (19 September 1980)
RSR 108§	**Start Me Up/No Use In Crying** (17 August 1981)
RSR 109§	**Waiting On A Friend/Little T & A** (30 November 1981)
RSR 110§	**Going To A Go-Go/Beast Of Burden** (1 June 1982)
RSR 111§	**Time Is On My Side/Twenty Flight Rock** (14 September 1982)
RSR 113§	**Undercover Of The Night/All The Way Down** (1 November 1983)
RSR 113§	**Undercover Of The Night (version)/Feel On Baby** (instrumental version) (1 November 1983)

RSR 114§	**She Was Hot/I Think I'm Going Mad** (24 January 1984)
RSR SUGAR 1§	**Brown Sugar/Bitch** (29 June 1984)
RSR CBS A 6864§	**Harlem Shuffle/Had It With You** (10 March 1986)
CBS A 7160§	**One Hit To The Body/Fight** (19 May 1986)
FX 102*	**Jumping Jack Flash/Child Of The Moon** (25 May 1987)
FX 102*	**Jumping Jack Flash/Child Of The Moon/Sympathy For The Devil** (25 May 1987)
CBS 655193§	**Mixed Emotions/Fancyman Blues** (21 August 1989)
CBS 655422§	**Rock And A Hard Place/Cook Cook Blues** (13 November 1989)
LONX# 264	**Paint It Black/Honky Tonk Women** (11 June 1990)
CBS RSR 656065-7§	**Almost Hear You Sigh/Beast Of Burden/Angie** (18 June 1990)

Sony 656892.2	**Ruby Tuesday/Play With Fire** (24 May 1991)
Virgin VS 1503	**Love Is Strong/The Storm** (5 July 1994)
Virgin VS 1518	**You Got Me Rocking/Jump On Top Of Me** (26 September 1994)
Virgin VS 1524	**Out Of Tears** (edit)/**I'm Gonna Drive** (28 November 1994)
Virgin VS 1653	**Anybody Seen My Baby** (edit)/**Anybody Seen My Baby** (version) 22 September 1997
Virgin VSY 1667	**Saint Of Me** (edit)/**Anyway You Look At It** (26 January 1998)
Virgin VS 1838	**Don't Stop** (edit)/**Don't Stop** (version) (red vinyl, 16 December 2002)
Virgin VS 1905	**Streets Of Love/Rough Justice** (22 August 2005)

12-INCH SINGLES

RSR 12 RSR 111§	**Time Is On My Side/Twenty Flight Rock/Under My Thumb** (14 September 1982)
CBS QTA 6864§	**Harlem Shuffle** ('New York' version)/**Harlem Shuffle** ('London' version) (10 March 1986)
CBS 655193 8§	**Mixed Emotions** (version)/**Mixed Emotions** (21 August 1989)
CBS RSR 655422.2§	**Rock And A Hard Place** (edit)/ **Rock And A Hard Place** (version)/**Cook Cook Blues** (13 November 1989)
CBS RSR 655422.2§	**Rock And A Hard Place** (version 2)/ **Rock And A Hard Place** (version 3)/**Cook Cook Blues** (13 November 1989)
CBS RSR 655422.2§	**Rock And A Hard Place** (version 3)/ **Rock And A Hard Place** (version 4)/**Rock And A Hard Place** (edit) (13 November 1989)
CBS RSR 656122.6§	**Rock And A Hard Place** (version 5)/**Rock And A Hard Place** (version 1)/**Harlem Shuffle** ('London' version) (30 July 1990)

Sony RSR 656756.6§	**Highwire/2000 Light Years From Home/ Sympathy For The Devil/I Just Want To Make Love To You** (21 March 1991)
Sony 656892.6	**Ruby Tuesday/Play With Fire/You Can't Always Get What You Want/Rock And A Hard Place** (24 May 1991)
Virgin VSCDG-1518	**You Got Me Rocking/You Got Me Rocking** (version)**/You Got Me Rocking** (version 2)**/You Got Me Rocking** (version 3) (26 September 1994)

CD SINGLES

CBS RSR 656065-7§	**Almost Hear You Sigh/Beast Of Burden/Angie/Fool To Cry** (18 June 1990)
CBS RSR 6561122.2§	**Terrifying/Rock And A Hard Place** (version 1)/**Harlem Shuffle** ('London' version) (30 July 1990)
CBS RSR 656122.2§	**Terrifying** (version 1)/**Terrifying** (version 2)/ **Rock And A Hard Place/Harlem Shuffle** (30 July 1990)
CBS RSR 656756.2§	**Highwire/2000 Light Years From Home/ Sympathy For The Devil/I Just Want To Make Love To You** (21 March 1991)
CBS RSR 656756.5§	**Highwire/2000 Light Years From Home/ Play With Fire/Factory Girl** (21 March 1991)
Sony 656892.5	**Ruby Tuesday/Play With Fire/Harlem Shuffle/ Winning Ugly** (version) (24 May 1991)

Sony 656892.2	**Ruby Tuesday/Play With Fire/You Can't Always Get What You Want/Undercover Of The Night** (24 May 1991)
Sony 656892.6	**Ruby Tuesday/Play With Fire/You Can't Always Get What You Want/Rock And A Hard Place** (24 May 1991)
Virgin VSCDT-1503	**Love Is Strong/The Storm/So Young/Love Is Strong** (version) (5 July 1994)
Virgin VSCDT-1503	**Love Is Strong** (version 2)/**Love Is Strong** (version 3)/**Love Is Strong** (version 4)/**Love Is Strong** (version 5)/**Love Is Strong** (version 6) (5 July 1994)
Virgin VSCDG-1518	**You Got Me Rocking/You Got Me Rocking** (version)/**You Got Me Rocking** (version 2)/**Jump On Top Of Me** (26 September 1994)
Virgin VS 1524	**Out Of Tears** (edit)/**I'm Gonna Drive/Out Of Tears** (edit 2)/**Out Of Tears** (version) (28 November 1994)

Virgin V25H-38478	**I Go Wild/I Go Wild** (version)/**I Go Wild** (version 2)/**I Go Wild** (version 3)/**I Go Wild** (version 4) (15 May 1995)
Virgin VSCDT-1562	**Like A Rolling Stone/All Down The Line/Black Limousine/ Like A Rolling Stone** (edit) (30 October 1995)
Virgin VSCDT 1653	**Anybody Seen My Baby** (edit)/**Anybody Seen My Baby** (version 2)/**Anybody Seen My Baby** (version 3)/**Anybody Seen My Baby** (version 4) 22 September 1997
Virgin VSCDT 1667	**Saint Of Me** (edit)/**Gimmie Shelter/Anybody Seen My Baby** (version 5)/**Saint Of Me** (version) (26 January 1998)
Virgin VSCDX 1667	**Saint Of Me** (edit)/**Anyway You Look At It/Saint Of Me** (version) (26 January 1998)
Virgin VSCDX 1700	**Out Of Control** (version)/**Out Of Control** (version 2)/**Out Of Control** (version 3) (17 August 1998)

Virgin VUSCDJ-145	**Memory Motel** (edit)/Memory Motel (3 May 1999)
Virgin VSCDX 1838	**Don't Stop** (edit)/**Don't Stop** (version) (16 December 2002)
Virgin VSCDT 1905	**Streets Of Love/Rough Justice** (22 August 2005)
Virgin VSCDT 1907	**Rain Fall Down** (version)/**Rain Fall Down** (edit)/**Rain Fall Down** (version 2) (22 November 2005)

EXTENDED PLAY

DFE 8560* **The Rolling Stones**
Bye Bye Johnny; Money; You Better Move On; Poison Ivy. (10 January 1964)

DFE 8590* **Five By Five**
If You Need Me; Empty Heart; 2120 South Michigan Avenue; Confessin' The Blues; Around And Around. (15 August 1964)

DFE 8620* **Got Live If You Want It**
We Want The Stones: Everybody Needs Somebody To Love; Pain In My Heart; Route 66; I'm Moving On; I'm Alright. (11 June 1965)

LONG PLAY

(including various artists albums) August 1963 – March 1967

LK 4554* **Thank Your Lucky Stars**
Come On; tracks by other artists. (27 September 1963)

LK 4583* **Saturday Club**
Poison Ivy; Fortune Teller; tracks by other artists. (24 January 1964)

LK 4577* **Ready Steady Go**
Come On; I Wanna Be Your Man; tracks by other artists. (24 January 1964)

LK 4605* **The Rolling Stones**
Side One: Route 66; I Just Wanna Make Love To You; Honest I Do; Mona; Now I've Got A Witness; Little By Little.
Side Two: I'm A King Bee; Carol; Tell Me (You're Coming Back); Can I Get A Witness; You Can Make It If You Try; Walking The Dog. (17 April 1964)

LK 4695* **Fourteen**
Surprise Surprise; tracks by other artists. (21 May 1965)

LK 4661* **The Rolling Stones No. 2**

Side One: Everybody Needs Somebody To Love; Down Home Girl; You Can't Catch Me; Time Is On My Side; What A Shame; Grown Up Wrong.
Side Two: Down The Road Apiece; Under The Boardwalk; I Can't Be Satisfied; Pain In My Heart; Off The Hook; Susie Q. (30 January 1965).

LK 4733* **Out Of Our Heads**

Side One: She Said Yeah; Mercy Mercy; Hitch Hike; That's How Strong My Love Is; Good Times; Gotta Get Away; Talkin' 'Bout You.
Side Two: Cry To Me; Oh Baby (We Got A Good Thing Goin'); Heart Of Stone; The Under Assistant West Coast Promotion Man; I'm Free. (24 September 1965)

SKL 4786* **Aftermath**

Side One: Mother's Little Helper; Stupid Girl; Lady Jane; Under My Thumb; Dontcha Bother Me; Goin' Home.
Side Two: Flight 505; High And Dry; Out Of Time; It's Not Easy; I Am Waiting; Take It Or Leave It; Think; What To Do. (15 April 1966)

LK 4852* **Between The Buttons**

Side One: Yesterday's Papers; My Obsession; Back Street Girl; Connection; She Smiled Sweetly; Cool Calm And Collected.
Side Two: All Sold Out; Please Go Home; Who's Been Sleeping Here; Complicated; Miss Amanda Jones; Something Happened To Me Yesterday. (20 January 1967)

US RELEASES – SINGLES

9657# **Not Fade Away/I Wanna Be Your Man** (6 March 1964)

9682# **Tell Me (You're Coming Back)/I Just Want To Make Love To You** (19 June 1964)

9687# **It's All Over Now/Good Times Bad Times** (2 July 1964)

9708# **Time Is On My Side/Congratulations** (25 September 1964)

9725# **Heart Of Stone/What A Shame** (19 December 1964)

9741# **The Last Time/Play With Fire** (13 March 1965)

9766# **(I Can't Get No) Satisfaction/The Under Assistant West Coast Promotion Man** (5 June 1965)

9792# **Get Off Of My Cloud/I'm Free** (24 September 1965)

9808#	**As Tears Go By/Gotta Get Away** (18 December 1965)
901#	**Paint It Black/Stupid Girl** (7 May 1966)
902#	**Mother's Little Helper/Lady Jane** (2 July 1966)
904#	**Let's Spend The Night Together/Ruby Tuesday** (13 January 1967)
905#	**Dandelion/We Love You** (18 August 1967)
906#	**In Another Land/The Lantern** (4 December 1967)
907#	**2000 Light Years From Home/She's A Rainbow** (23 December 1967)
908#	**Jumping Jack Flash/Child Of The Moon** (24 May 1968)
910#	**Honky Tonk Women/You Can't Always Get What You Want** (11 July 1969)
RLS§ 19100	**Brown Sugar/Bitch** (7 May 1971)

RLS§ 101 **Wild Horses/Sway** (12 June 1971)

RLS 19103§ **Tumbling Dice/Sweet Black Angel** (14 April 1972)

RLS 19104§ **Happy/All Down The Line** (14 July 1972)

RLS 19105§ **Angie/Silver Train** (20 August 1973)

RS 19109§ **Doo Doo Doo Doo (Heartbreaker)/Dancing With Mr. D** (14 December 1973)

RS 19302§ **It's Only Rock 'N Roll (But I Like It)/Through The Lonely Nights** (26 July 1974)

RS 19302§ **Ain't Too Proud To Beg/Dance Little Sister** (25 October 1974)

ABKCO 4701 **I Don't Know Why/Try A Little Harder** (23 May 1975)

ABKCO 4702 **Out Of Time/Jiving Sister Fanny** (5 September 1975)

RS 19304§ **Fool To Cry/Hot Stuff** (20 April 1976)

RS 19306§ **Miss You/Far Away Eyes** (19 May 1978)

RS 19309§ **Beast Of Burden/When The Whip Comes Down** (27 August 1978)

RS 19310§ **Shattered/Everything Is Turning To Gold** (28 November 1978)

RS 20001§ **Emotional Rescue/Down In The Hole** (20 June 1980)

RS 21001§ **She's So Cold/Send It To Me** (19 September 1980)

RS 21003§ **Start Me Up/No Use In Crying** (19 August 1981)

RS 21004§ **Waiting On A Friend/Little T & A** (30 November 1981)

RS 21300§ **Hang Fire/Neighbours** (11 April 1982)

RS 21301§ **Going To A Go-Go/Beast Of Burden** (1 June 1982)

RSR RS 21302§ **Time Is On My Side/Twenty Flight Rock** (14 September 1982)

RSR 7-99813§	**Undercover Of The Night/Feel On Baby** (instrumental version) (1 November 1983)
RSR 7-99788§	**She Was Hot/I Think I'm Going Mad** (24 January 1984)
RSR 7-99724§	**Too Tough/Miss You** (3 July 1984)
RSR 38-05802§	**Harlem Shuffle/Had It With You** (11 March 1986)
RSR 38-05906§	**One Hit (To The Body)/Fight** (19 May 1986)
RSR 38-69008§	**Mixed Emotions/Fancyman Blues** (21 August 1989)
RSR 38-73057§	**Rock And A Hard Place/Cook Cook Blues** (13 November 1989)
Columbia RSR 38-73742§	**Highwire/2000 Light Years From Home** (21 March 1991)
Columbia RSR ZSS 73789§	**Sexdrive** (edit)/**Undercover Of The Night** (19 August 1991)
Virgin NR 38446§	**Love Is Strong/The Storm** (5 July 1994)

12-INCH SINGLES

RSR DK 4609 **Miss You/Far Away Eyes** (19 May 1978)

RSR 0-96902 **Too Much Blood** (version)/
Too Much Blood (version 2)/
Too Much Blood (version 3)
(11 December 1984)

RSR 44-05365§ **Harlem Shuffle** ('New York' version)/
Harlem Shuffle
('London' version) (10 March 1986)

RSR 44-05388 **One Hit (To The Body)** (version)/
One Hit (To The Body/**Fight** (19 May 1986)

Columbia CAS 1765§
Mixed Emotions (version)/
Mixed Emotions (21 August 1989)

RSR 44-73133§ **Rock And A Hard Place** (version)/
Rock And A Hard Place (version 2)/
Rock And A Hard Place (version 3)/
Rock And A Hard Place (version 4)
(13 November 1989)

LONX 264# **Paint It Black/Honky Tonk Women/Sympathy For The Devil**
(11 June 1990)

CD SINGLES

Virgin V25H-38459 **Out Of Tears** (edit)/
I'm Gonna Drive/Out Of Tears (edit 2)/
So Young
(28 November 1994)

Virgin V25H-38468 **You Got Me Rocking** (version)/
You Got Me Rocking (version 2)/
You Got Me Rocking (version 3)/
You Got Me Rocking (version 4)/
Jump On Top Of Me (3 January 1995)

Virgin VSCDX-1539 **I Go Wild/I Go Wild** (version)/
I Go Wild (version 2)/
I Go Wild version 3)/
I Go Wild (version 4)
(4 April 1995)

Virgin DPRO-12746 **Anybody Seen My Baby** (edit)/
Anybody Seen My Baby (version 2)/
Anybody Seen My Baby (version 3)
22 September 1997

Virgin V25H-38627 **Saint Of Me** (edit)/ **Anyway You Look At It/Gimmie Shelter/Saint Of Me** (version)/**Saint Of Me** (version 2) (26 January 1998)

Virgin V25D-38626 **Saint Of Me** (edit)/**Anyway You Look At It** (26 January 1998)

Virgin V25H-38625 **Don't Stop** (edit)/ **Don't Stop** (version) (16 December 2002)

Virgin V25H-38624 **Streets Of Love/Rough Justice** (22 August 2005)

LONG PLAY (April 1964 – August 1967)

PS 375# **England's Newest Hitmakers**
Side One: Not Fade Away; Route 66; I Just Wanna Make Love To You; Honest I Do; Mona; Now I've Got A Witness; Little By Little.
Side Two: I'm A King Bee; Carol; Tell Me (You're Coming Back); Can I Get A Witness; You Can Make It If You Try; Walking The Dog.
(3 May 1964)

PS 402# **12 x 5**
Side One: Around And Around; Confessin' The Blues; Empty Heart; Time Is On My Side; Good Times Bad Times; It's All Over Now.
Side Two: 2120 South Michigan Avenue; Under The Boardwalk; Congratulations; Grown Up Wrong; If You Need Me; Susie Q.
(23 October 1964)

PS 420# **The Rolling Stones Now!**
Side One: Everybody Needs Somebody To Love; Down Home Girl; You Can't Catch Me; Heart Of Stone; What A Shame; Mona (I Need You Baby).
Side Two: Down The Road Apiece; Off The Hook; Pain In My Heart; Oh Baby (We Got A Good Thing Goin'); Little Red Rooster; Surprise Surprise
(12 February 1965)

PS 429# **Out Of Our Heads**
Side One: Mercy Mercy; Hitch Hike; The Last Time; That's How Strong My Love Is; Good Times; I'm Alright.
Side Two: (I Can't Get No) Satisfaction; Cry To Me; The Under Assistant West Coast Promotion Man; Play With Fire; The Spider And The Fly; One More Try. **(30 July 1965)**

PS 451# **December's Children**
Side One: She Said Yeah; Talkin' 'Bout You; You Better Move On; Look What You've Done; The Singer Not The Song; Route 66.
Side Two: Get Off Of My Cloud; I'm Free; As Tears Go By; Gotta Get Away; Blue Turns To Grey; I'm Moving On. **(4 December 1965)**

PS 476# **Aftermath**
Side One: Paint It Black; Stupid Girl; Lady Jane; Under My Thumb; Dontcha Bother Me; Think.
Side Two: Flight 505; High And Dry; It's Not Easy; I Am Waiting; Goin' Home. **(2 July 1966)**

PS 493# **Got Live If You Want It**
Side One: Under My Thumb; Get Off Of My Cloud; Lady Jane; Not Fade Away; I've Been Loving You Too Long; Fortune Teller.
Side Two: The Last Time; 19th Nervous Breakdown; Time Is On My Side; I'm Alright; Have You Seen Your Mother Baby (Standing In The Shadow); (I Can't Get No) Satisfaction. **(9 December 1966)**

PS 499# **Between The Buttons**

Side One: Let's Spend The Night Together; Yesterday's Papers; Ruby Tuesday; Connection; She Smiled Sweetly; Cool Calm And Collected.
Side Two: All Sold Out; My Obsession; Who's Been Sleeping Here; Complicated; Miss Amanda Jones; Something Happened To Me Yesterday.
(11 February 1967)

PS 509# **Flowers**

Side One: Ruby Tuesday; Have You Seen Your Mother Baby (Standing In The Shadow); Let's Spend The Night Together; Lady Jane; Out Of Time; My Girl.
Side Two: Back Street Girl; Please Go Home; Mother's Little Helper; Take It Or Leave It; Ride On Baby; Sittin' On A Fence. **(15 July 1967)**

BRITISH (UK) AND US LONG PLAY

(non-compilations, August 1967 – April 1986)

UK: TXS 103*/US: NPS 2#

Their Satanic Majesties Request
Side One: Sing This All Together; Citadel; In Another Land; 2000 Man; Sing This All Together (See What Happens).
Side Two: She's A Rainbow; The Lantern; Gomper; 2000 Light Years From Home; On With The Show.
(UK: 8 December 1967/US: 9 December 1967)

UK: SKL 4955*/US: PS 539#

Beggars Banquet
Side One: Sympathy For The Devil; No Expectations; Dear Doctor; Parachute Woman; Jigsaw Puzzle.
Side Two: Street Fighting Man; Prodigal Son; Stray Cat Blues; Factory Girl; Salt Of The Earth.
(UK: 6 December 1968/7 December 1967)

UK: SKL 5025*/US: NPS 4#

Let It Bleed
Side One: Gimmie Shelter; Love In Vain; Country Honk; Live With Me; Let It Bleed.
Side Two: Midnight Rambler; You Got The Silver; Monkey Man; You Can't Always Get What You Want.
(UK: 5 December 1969/US: 28 November 1969)

UK: SKL 5065*/US: NPS 5#

Get Yer Ya-Yas Out
Side One: Jumpin' Jack Flash; Carol; Stray Cat Blues; Love In Vain; Midnight Rambler.
Side Two: Sympathy For The Devil; Live With Me; Little Queenie; Honky Tonk Women; Street Fighting Man.
(UK: 4 September 1970/US: 4 September 1970)

COC 59100§

Sticky Fingers
Side One: Brown Sugar; Sway; Wild Horses; Can't You Hear Me Knocking; You Gotta Move.
Side Two: Bitch; I Got The Blues; Sister Morphine; Dead Flowers; Moonlight Mile. **(23 April 1971)**

UK: COC 69100§/
US: COC 2-2900§

Exile On Main Street
Side One: Rocks Off; Rip This Joint; Hip Shake; Casino Boogie; Tumbling Dice.
Side Two: Sweet Virginia; Torn And Frayed; Black Angel; Loving Cup.
Side Three: Happy; Turd On The Run; Ventilator Blues; Just Wanna See His Face; Let It Loose.
Side Four: All Down The Line; Stop Breaking Down; Shine A Light; Soul Survivor.
(12 May 1972)

COC 59101§

Goat's Head Soup
Side One: Dancing With Mr. D; 100 Years Ago; Coming Down Again; Doo Doo Doo Doo (Heartbreaker); Angie.
Side Two: Silver Train; Hide Your Love; Winter; Can You Hear The Music; Star Star. **(31 August 1973)**

COC 59103§

It's Only Rock 'N Roll
Side One: If You Can't Rock Me; Ain't Too Proud To Beg; It's Only Rock 'N' Roll; Till The Next Goodbye; Time Waits For No-One.
Side Two: Luxury; Dance Little Sister; If You Really Want To Be My Friend; Short And Curlies; Fingerprint File. **(18 October 1974)**

UK: SKL 5212*/
US: ABKCO ANA 1

Metamorphosis
Side One: Out Of Time; Don't Lie To Me; Some Things Just Stick In Your Mind; Each And Every Day Of The Year; Heart Of Stone; I'd Much Rather Be With The Boys; (Walkin' Thru') The Sleepy City; We're Wastin' Time; Try A Little Harder.
Side Two: I Don't Know Why; If You Let Me; Jiving Sister Fanny; Downtown Suzie; Family; Memo From Turner; I'm Going Down.
(6 June 1975)

UK: COC 59106§/
US: COC 79104§

Black And Blue
Side One: Hot Stuff; Hand Of Fate; Cherry Oh Baby; Memory Motel.
Side Two: Hey Negrita; Melody; Fool To Cry; Crazy Mama.
(20 April 1976)

UK: COC 89101§/
US: COC 79104§

Love You Live
Side One: Honky Tonk Women; If You Can't Rock Me; Get Off Of My Cloud; Happy; Hot Stuff.
Side Two: Star Star; Tumbling Dice; Fingerprint File; You Gotta Move.
Side Three: You Can't Always Get What You Want; Mannish Boy; Crackin' Up; Little Red Rooster.
Side Four: Around And Around; It's Only Rock 'N Roll; Brown Sugar; Jumpin' Jack Flash; Sympathy For The Devil. **(23 September 1977)**

UK: CUN 39108§/
US: TP 39108§

Some Girls
Side One: Miss You; When The Whip Comes Down; Just My Imagination (Running Away With Me); Some Girls; Lies.
Side Two: Far Away Eyes; Respectable; Before They Make Me Run; Beast Of Burden; Shattered. **(19 May 1978)**

UK: CUN 39111§/
US: CUN 16015§

Emotional Rescue
Side One: Dance; Summer Romance; Send It To Me; Let Me Go; Indian Girl.
Side Two: Where The Boys Go; Down In The Hole; Emotional Rescue; She's So Cold; All About You. **(22 June 1980)**

UK: CUNS 39114§/
US: COC 16052§

Tattoo You
Side One: Start Me Up; Hang Fire; Slave; Little T & A; Black Limousine; Neighbours.
Side Two: Worried About You; Tops; Heaven; No Use In Crying; Waiting On A Friend. Neighbours. **(24 August 1981)**

UK: CUN 39115§/
US: CUN 39113§

Still Life (American Concert)
Side One: Under My Thumb; Let's Spend The Night Together; Shattered; Twenty Flight Rock; Going To A Go-Go.
Side Two: Let Me Go; Time Is On My Side; Just My Imagination (Running Away With Me); Start Me Up; (I Can't Get No) Satisfaction. **(1 June 1982)**

UK: CUN 1654361§/
UK: 90120§

Undercover
Side One: Undercover Of The Night; She Was Hot; Tie You Up (The Pain Of Love); Wanna Hold You; Feel On Baby.
Side Two: Too Much Blood; Pretty Beat Up; Too Tough; All The Way Down; It Must Be Hell. **(7 November 1983)**

UK: CBS 86321/
US: 40250§

Dirty Work
Side One: One Hit (To The Body); Fight; Harlem Shuffle; Hold Back; Too Rude.
Side Two: Winning Ugly; Back To Zero; Dirty Work; Had It With You. Sleep Tonight. **(24 March 1986)**

BRITISH (UK) AND US CD LONG PLAY

(non-compilation, April 1986 – April 2006)

UK: CBS 4657521§/US: 45333§ Steel Wheels
Sad Sad Sad; Mixed Emotions; Terrifying; Hold On To Your Hat; Hearts For Sale; Blinded By Love; Rock And A Hard Place; Can't Be Seen; Almost Hear You Sigh; Continental Drift; Break The Spell; Slipping Away. **(UK: 29 August 1989/US: 28 August 1989)**

UK: Virgin CDV2750/US: Virgin 39782 Voodoo Lounge
Love Is Strong; You Got Me Rocking; Sparks Will Fly; The Worst; New Faces; Moon Is Up; Out Of Tears; I Go Wild; Brand New Car; Sweethearts Together; Suck On The Jugular; Blinded By Rainbows; Baby Break It Down; Thru' And Thru'; Mean Disposition. **(12 July 1994)**

UK: Virgin CDV 2801/V2801/US: Virgin 7243.8.41040-2-3 Stripped
Street Fighting Man; Like A Rolling Stone; Not Fade Away; Shine A Light; The Spider And The Fly; I'm Free; Wild Horses; Let It Bleed; Dead Flowers; Slipping Away; Angie; Love In Vain; Sweet Virginia; Little Baby. **(13 November 1995)**

ABKCO 1268.2 Rock & Roll Circus
Jumping Jack Flash; Parachute Woman; No Expectations; You Can't Always Get What You Want; Sympathy For The Devil; Salt Of The Earth; tracks by other artists. **(15 October 1996)**

UK: Virgin 2840/CDV 2840/US: Virgin 7243.8.44712.2.4 Bridges To Babylon
Flip The Switch; Anybody Seen My Baby; Low Down; Already Over Me; Gunface; You Don't Have To Mean It; Out Of Control; Saint Of Me; Might As Well Get Juiced; Always Suffering; Too Tight; Thief In The Night; How Can I Stop. **(29 September 1997)**

UK: Virgin V-2880/CDV-2880/US: Virgin 7242.8.46740-21 No Security
You Got Me Rocking; Gimmie Shelter; Flip The Switch; Memory Motel; Corrina; Saint Of Me; Waiting On A Friend; Sister Morphine; Live With Me; Respectable; Thief In The Night; The Last Time; Out Of Control. **(UK: 9 November 1998/US: 16 November 1998)**

UK: Virgin/EMI CDVDX3000/US: Virgin/EMI CDV2880 Live Licks
Disc One: Brown Sugar; Street Fighting Man; Paint It Black; You Can't Always Get What You Want; Start Me Up; Angie; It's Only Rock 'N Roll (But I Like It); Honky Tonk Women; Happy; Gimmie Shelter; (I Can't Get No) Satisfaction.
Disc Two: Neighbours; Monkey Man; Rocks Off; Can't You Hear Me Knocking; That's How Strong My Love Is; The Nearness Of You; Beast Of Burden; When The Whip Comes Down; Rock Me Baby; You Don't Have To Mean It; Everybody Needs Somebody To Love.
(2 November 2004)

UK: Virgin/EMI CDVX 3012/US: Virgin/EMI TOCP-66441) A Bigger Bang
Rough Justice; Let Me Down Slow; It Won't Take Long; Rain Fall Down; Streets Of Love; Back Of My Hand; She Saw Me Coming; Biggest Mistake; This Place Is Empty; Oh No Not You Again; Dangerous Beauty; Laugh I Nearly Died; Sweet Neo Con; Look What The Cat Dragged In; Driving Too Fast; Infamy. **(6 September 2005)**

Virgin/EMI CDV3015 Rarities 1971-2003

Fancy Man Blues; Tumbling Dice; Wild Horses; Beast Of Burden; Anyway You Look At It; If I Was A Dancer (Dance Part Two); Miss You; Wish I'd Never Met You; I Just Want To Make Love To You; Mixed Emotions; Through The Lonely Nights; Live With Me; Let It Rock; Harlem Shuffle; Mannish Boy; Thru' And Thru'. **(22 November 2005)**

BRITISH COMPILATION LONG PLAY

TXS 101* **Big Hits (High Tide And Green Grass)**
Side One: Have You Seen Your Mother Baby (Standing In The Shadow); Paint It Black; It's All Over Now; The Last Time; Heart Of Stone; (I Can't Get No) Satisfaction.
Side Two: Get Off Of My Cloud; As Tears Go By; 19th Nervous Breakdown; Lady Jane; Time Is On My Side; Little Red Rooster. **(4 November 1966)**

SKL 5019* **Through The Past Darkly (Big Hits Vol. 2)**
Side One: Jumpin' Jack Flash; Mother's Little Helper; 2000 Light Years From Home; Let's Spend The Night Together; You Better Move On; We Love You.
Side Two: Street Fighting Man; She's A Rainbow; Ruby Tuesday; Dandelion; Sittin' On A Fence; Honky Tonk Women. **(12 September 1969)**

SKL 5084* **Stone Age**
Side One: Look What You've Done; It's All Over Now; Confessin' The Blues; One More Try; As Tears Go By; The Spider And The Fly.
Side Two: My Girl; Paint It Black; If You Need Me; The Last Time; Blue Turns To Grey; Around And Around. **(6 March 1971)**

SKL 5101* **Gimmie Shelter**
Side One: Jumpin' Jack Flash; Love In Vain; Honky Tonk Women; Street Fighting Man; Sympathy For The Devil; Gimmie Shelter.
Side Two: Under My Thumb; Time Is On My Side; I've Been Loving You Too Long; Fortune Teller; Lady Jane; (I Can't Get No) Satisfaction.
(29 August 1971)

SKL 5149*	**Rock 'n' Rolling Stones** **Side One:** Route 66; The Under Assistant West Coast Promotion Man; Come On; Talkin' 'Bout You; Bye Bye Johnny; Down The Road Apiece. **Side Two:** I Just Wanna Make Love To You; Everybody Needs Somebody To Love; Oh Baby (We Got A Good Thing Goin'); 19th Nervous Breakdown; Little Queenie; Carol. **(13 October 1972)**
SKL 5173*	**No Stone Unturned** **Side One:** Poison Ivy; The Singer Not The Song; Child Of The Moon; Stoned; Sad Day; Money. **Side Two:** Congratulations; I'm Moving On; 2120 South Michigan Avenue; Long Long While; Who's Driving Your Plane. **(5 October 1973)**
ROST 1/2*	**Rolled Gold** **Side One:** Come On; I Wanna Be Your Man;Not Fade Away; Carol; It's All Over Now; Little Red Rooster. **Side Two:** Time Is On My Side; The Last Time; (I Can't Get No) Satisfaction; Get Off Of My Cloud; 19th Nervous Breakdown; As Tears Go By **Side Three:** Under My Thumb; Lady Jane; Out Of Time; Paint It Black; Have You Seen Your Mother Baby (Standing In The Shadow); Let's Spend The Night Together; Ruby Tuesday. **Side Four:** Yesterday's Papers; We Love You; She's A Rainbow; Jumpin' Jack Flash; Honky Tonk Women; Sympathy For The Devil; Street Fighting Man; Midnight Rambler; Gimmie Shelter. **(14 November 1975)**

Arcade ADEP 32 — **Get Stoned: 30 Greatest Hits 30 Original Tracks**

Side One: Not Fade Away; It's All Over Now; Tell Me (You're Coming Back); Good Times Bad Times; Time Is On My Side; Little Red Rooster; The Last Time; Play With Fire.

Side Two: (I Can't Get No) Satisfaction; Get Off Of My Cloud; I Wanna Be Your Man; As Tears Go By; 19th Nervous Breakdown; Mother's Little Helper; Have You Seen Your Mother Baby (Standing In The Shadow).

Side Three: Paint It Black; Lady Jane; Let's Spend The Night Together; Ruby Tuesday; Dandelion; We Love You; She's A Rainbow; 2000 Light Years From Home.

Side Four: Jumpin' Jack Flash; Gimmie Shelter; Street Fighting Man; Honky Tonk Women; Sympathy For The Devil; Wild Horses; Brown Sugar. **(21 October 1977)**

COC 59107§ — **Time Waits For No-One**

Side One: Time Waits For No-One; Bitch; All Down The Line; Dancing With Mr. D; Angie; Star Star.

Side Two: If You Can't Rock Me; Get Off Of My Cloud; Hand Of Fate; Crazy Mama; Fool To Cry. **(1 June 1979)**

CUN 1§ — **Rewind 1971-1984 (The Best Of The Rolling Stones)**

Side One: Miss You; Brown Sugar; Undercover Of The Night; Start Me Up; Tumbling Dice; Hang Fire; Emotional Rescue.

Side Two: Beast Of Burden; Fool To Cry; Waiting On A Friend; Angie; It's Only Rock 'N Roll; She's So Cold. **(29 June 1984)**

BRITISH CD COMPILATION LONG PLAY

Virgin CDV2726 — **Jump Back: The Best Of The Rolling Stones '71-'93**
Start Me Up; Brown Sugar; Harlem Shuffle; It's Only Rock 'N Roll; Mixed Emotions; Angie; Tumbling Dice; Fool To Cry; Rock And A Hard Place; Miss You; Hot Stuff; Emotional Rescue; Respectable; Beast Of Burden; Waiting On A Friend; Wild Horses; Bitch; Undercover Of The Night. **(22 November 1993)**

US COMPILATION LONG PLAY

NPS 1# **Big Hits (High Tide And Green Grass)**
Side One: (I Can't Get No) Satisfaction; The Last Time; As Tears Go By; Time Is On My Side; It's All Over Now; Tell Me (You're Coming Back).
Side Two: 19th Nervous Breakdown; Heart Of Stone; Get Off Of My Cloud; Not Fade Away; Good Times Bad Times; Play With Fire. **(11 March 1966)**

NPS-3# **Through The Past Darkly (Big Hits Vol. 2)**
Side One: Paint It Black; Ruby Tuesday; She's A Rainbow; Jumpin' Jack Flash; Mother's Little Helper; Let's Spend The Night Together.
Side Two: Honky Tonk Women; Dandelion; 2000 Light Years From Home; Have You Seen Your Mother Baby (Standing In The Shadow); Street Fighting Man. **(12 September 1969)**

2PS 606/607# **Hot Rocks 1964-1971**
Side One: Time Is On My Side; Heart Of Stone; Play With Fire; (I Can't Get No) Satisfaction; As Tears Go By.
Side Two: Get Off Of My Cloud; Mother's Little Helper; 19th Nervous Breakdown; Paint It Black; Under My Thumb.
Side Three: Ruby Tuesday; Let's Spend The Night Together; Jumpin' Jack Flash; Street Fighting Man; Sympathy For The Devil.
Side Four: Honky Tonk Women; Gimmie Shelter; Midnight Rambler; You Can't Always Get What You Want; Brown Sugar, Wild Horses. **(11 January 1972)**

2PS 626/627# **More Hot Rocks (Big Hits And Fazed Cookies)**

Side One: Tell Me (You're Coming Back); Not Fade Away; The Last Time; It's All Over Now; Good Times Bad Times; I'm Free.
Side Two: Out Of Time; Lady Jane; Sittin' On A Fence; Have You Seen Your Mother Baby (Standing In The Shadow); Dandelion; We Love You.
Side Three: She's A Rainbow; 2000 Light Years From Home; Child Of The Moon; No Expectations; Let It Bleed; What To Do; Money.
Side Four: Come On; Fortune Teller; Poison Ivy; Bye Bye Johnny; I Can't Be Satisfied; Long Long While. **(1 December 1972)**

BRITISH (UK) AND US COMPILATION LONG PLAY

UK: COC 59104§/ US: COC 79101§	**Made In The Shade** **Side One:** Brown Sugar; Tumbling Dice; Happy; Dance Little Sister; Wild Horses. **Side Two:** Angie; Bitch; It's Only Rock 'N Roll; Doo Doo Doo Doo (Heartbreaker); Rip This Joint. **(6 June 1975)**
UK: CUN 39112#§/ US: CUN 16028§	**Sucking In The 70s** **Side One:** Shattered; Everything Is Turning Into Gold; Hot Stuff; Time Waits For No-One; Fool To Cry. **Side Two:** Mannish Boy; When The Whip Comes Down; If I Was A Dancer (Dance Part 2); Crazy Mama; Beast Of Burden. **(12 March 1981)**
UK: TAB 30*/ US: 820 455-1#	**Slow Rollers** **Side One:** You Can't Always Get What You Want; Take It Or Leave It; You Better Move On; Time Is On My Side; Pain In My Heart; Dear Doctor; Con Le Mie Lagrime Cosi (As Tears Go By). **Side Two:** Ruby Tuesday; Play With Fire; Lady Jane; Sittin' On A Fence; Back Street Girl; Under The Boardwalk; Heart Of Stone. **(UK: 19 August 1981/US: 21 August 1981)**

UK: ABKCO 92312/
US: ABKCO 1218-1

The Rolling Stones Singles Collection: The London Years
Side One: Come On; I Want To Be Loved; I Wanna Be Your Man; Stoned; Not Fade Away; Little By Little.
Side Two: It's All Over Now; Good Times Bad Times; Tell Me (You're Coming Back); I Just Want To Make Love To You; Time Is On My Side; Congratulations.
Side Three: Little Red Rooster; Off The Hook; Heart Of Stone; What A Shame; The Last Time, Play With Fire.
Side Four: (I Can't Get No) Satisfaction; The Under Assistant West Coast Promotion Man; The Spider And The Fly; Get Off Of My Cloud; I'm Free; The Singer Not The Song; As Tears Go By; Gotta Get Away.
Side Five: 19th Nervous Breakdown; Sad Day; Paint It Black; Stupid Girl; Long Long While; Have You Seen Your Mother Baby (Standing In The Shadow); Who's Driving Your Plane.
Side Six: Let's Spend The Night Together; Ruby Tuesday; We Love You; Dandelion; She's A Rainbow; 2000 Light Years From Home; In Another Land; The Lantern.
Side Seven: Jumpin' Jack Flash; Child Of The Moon; Street Fighting Man; No Expectations; Surprise Surprise; Honky Tonk Women; You Can't Always Get What You Want.
Side Eight: Memo From Turner; Brown Sugar; Wild Horses; I Don't Know Why; Try A LIttle Harder; Jiving Sister Fanny; Sympathy For The Devil. **(15 August 1989)**

BRITISH (UK) AND US CD LONG PLAY

UK: Columbia RS 47456§/ US: Sony 468135.2

Flashpoint
Continental Drift; Start Me Up; Sad Sad Sad; Miss You; Rock And A Hard Place: Ruby Tuesday; You Can't Always Get What You Want; Factory Girl; Can't Be Seen; Little Red Rooster; Paint It Black; Sympathy For The Devil; Brown Sugar; Jumpin' Jack Flash; (I Can't Get No) Satisfaction; Highwire; Sex Drive.
(UK: 2 April 1991/US: 8 April 1991)
This was also issued in vinyl format in the UK (Sony 468135.1) minus 'Rock And A Hard Place' and 'Can't Be Seen'.

Virgin 13325.1. 1/13378.2.0

Forty Licks
Disc One: Street Fighting Man; Gimmie Shelter; (I Can't Get No) Satisfaction; The Last Time; Jumping Jack Flash; You Can't Always Get What You Want; 19th Nervous Breakdown; Under My Thumb; Not Fade Away; Have You Seen Your Mother Baby (Standing In The Shadow); Sympathy For The Devil; Mother's Little Helper; She's A Rainbow; Get Off Of My Cloud; Wild Horses; Ruby Tuesday; Paint It Black; Honky Tonk Women.
Disc Two: It's All Over Now; Let's Spend The Night Together; Start Me Up; Brown Sugar; Miss You; Beast Of Burden; Don't Stop; Happy; Angie; You Got Me Rocking; Fool To Cry; Shattered; Anybody Seen My Baby; Stealing My Heart; Tumbling Dice; Undercover Of The Night; Emotional Rescue; It's Only Rock 'N Roll (But I Like It); Losing My Touch. **(UK: 30 September 2002/US: 1 October 2002)**

MISCELLANEOUS

ITALIAN SINGLE
F 22270* Con Le Mie Lacrime/Heart Of Stone (5 April 1966)

BRITISH FLEXI-DISC
New Musical Express
All Down The Line (edit)/
Tumbling Dice (edit)/
Shine A Light (edit)/
Happy (edit)/
tracks by other artists
(free with 29 April 1972 edition)

CANADIAN 12-INCH SINGLE
Columbia 12CXP-7191
Winning Ugly (version)/
Winning Ugly (version 2)
(5 November 1986)

JAPANESE CD SINGLE
Sony SRCS 5322
Sexdrive (version)/
Sexdrive (edit)/
Sexdrive (edit 2)/
Undercover Of The Night (18 July 1991)

NETHERLANDS SINGLE
Sony 657334
Sexdrive (edit)/
Sexdrive (version 2)
(19 August 1991)

NETHERLANDS 12-INCH SINGLE
Sony RSR 657334 7§
Sexdrive
(version)/**Sexdrive**
(version 2)/**Sexdrive** (edit) (19 August 1991)

BRITISH CASSETTE SINGLE
EMI TC ORDER 1
Gimmie Shelter
(live)/tracks by other artists

JAPANESE CD LONG PLAY
Virgin CJCP 25426
No Security
(includes 'I Just Want To Make Love To You', 21 November 1998)

GERMAN LONG PLAY
FOR COLLECTOR'S ONLY
820722-1
(includes the 1965 studio version of 'I've Been Loving You Too Long', 4 June 1980)

REST OF THE BEST (THE ROLLING STONES STORY PART 2)
Polygram 6.30125
(11 September 1983)
Side One: Stoned; Come On; I Want To Be Loved; Poison Ivy; Fortune Teller; Money; Surprise Surprise.
Side Two: Little Red Rooster; Tell Me Baby; Time Is On My Side; Congratulations; I've Been Loving You Too Long; 2 Andrew Oldham Orchestra tracks.
Side Three: We Want the Stones/ Everybody Needs Somebody To Love; Pain In My Heart; Route 66; I'm Moving On; I'm Alright; Everybody Needs Somebody To Love; One More Try.
Side Four: The Last Time; Play With Fire; (I Can't Get No) Satisfaction; The Spider And The Fly; Get Off Of My Cloud; The Singer Not The Song.
Side Five: 19th Nervous Breakdown; Look What You've Done; Blue Turns to Grey; Sad Day; Con Le Mie Lacrime (As Tears Go By).
Side Six: Paint it Black; Long Long While; Have Your Seen Your Mother Baby (Standing In the Shadow); Who's Driving Your Plane; Let's Spend the Night Together; Ruby Tuesday.
Side Seven: We Love You; Dandelion; Sittin' on a Fence; Ride On Baby; My Girl.
Side Eight: Jumping Jack Flash; Child Of The Moon; Honky Tonk Women; You Can't Always Get What You Want.

All tracks previously released on album except 'Tell Me Baby', 'I've Been Loving You Too Long' and 'We Want The Stones'/ 'Everybody Needs Somebody To Love'.

Tell Me Baby 1.54

Mick Jagger: lead Vocals
Brian Jones and Keith Richards: guitars
Brian Wyman: bass guitar
Charlie Watts: drums

A nondescript 1964 run-through of a Big Bill Bronzy blues.

I've Been Loving You Too Long 2.54

Mick Jagger: lead vocals
Brian Jones and Keith Richards: guitars
Ian Stewart: organ
Bill Wyman: bass guitar
Charlie Watts: drums

This is the US-only *Got Live if You Want It* album track minus the overdubbed screams and plus organ. See US *Got Live If You Want It* (3493/ PS 493).

We Want The Stones (Nanker-Phelge)/
Everybody Needs Somebody to Love (Russell-Burke-Wxler) 0.45

Various: vocals on 'We Want the Stones'
Brian Jones and Keith Richards: guitars
Mick Jagger: lead vocals
Bill Wyman: bass guitar
Charlie Watts: drums

The chanting of near hysterical girls that preceeds a fragment of the Stones opening number in concert during a two-week UK tour in March 1965, was credited as a group original. Both items were selected for the *Got Live if You Want It* Britain-only EP.

Some mispressings of *Rest Of The Best* are believed to contain 'Cocksucker Blues', a burst of obscene nonsense, spotlighting just Jagger and an acoustic guitarist, offered to an appalled Decca in 1969 when the delivery of one more single was the only barrier to The Rolling Stones' complete freedom from the company. Then unreleased, the master tape was not destroyed but locked in a safe, where it would lie as forgotten as Serge Gainsbourg and Brigitte Bardot's cancelled 'Je T'Aime…Moi No Plus' and, also from 1969, 'The Troggs Tape'an illicit recording of a cross-purpose studio discussion with a swear-word in nearly every sentence.

INDEX

For entries in bold read as italics (albums, larger works etc.)

ACKNOWLEDGEMENTS

As Horace reminds us, 'quandoque bonus domitat Homerus' - which, given a free translation, means even the wisest can make mistakes. Those who devote their recreational time to collating facts about The Rolling Stones may have pounced on errors and omissions while scrutinising this work. All I can say to them is that it's as accurate as it can be after the synthesis of primary research and conversations with some of the dramatis personnae – not to mention too many folders with labels like 'Decca', 'US compilations' and 'Jagger solo' on them, and exercise books full of doctor's prescription-like scribble drawn from press archives – some of them quite obscure.

Please put your hands together for Joanne Wilson, Iain MacGregor, Karen Dolan, the rest of the team at Cassell, Laura Brudenell and everyone who went far beyond the call of duty from this book's genesis to its final publication.

I am also very grateful to Pat Andrews, Alan Barwise, Dave Berry, Mike Cooper, Don Craine, Keith Grant-Evans, Richard Hattrell, Rick Huxley, the late Carlo Little, Phil May, Jim McCarty, Brian Poole, Dick Taylor and Art Wood for their pragmatism, candour, reminiscences, clear insight and intelligent argument.

Thanks are in order too for Mick Avory, Jonathan Meades and Trevor Hobley.

Whether they were aware of providing assistance or not, let's also have a round of applause for the following musicians: Frank Allen, Roger Barnes, Cliff Bennett, Arthur Brown, Clem Cattini, Pete Cox, Paul Critchfield, Tony Dangerfield, the late Lonnie Donegan, Chris Dreja, Alan Franks, 'Wreckless' Eric Goulden, Tom McGuiness, John Harries, Brian Hinton, Alan Holmes, Robb Johnson, Garry Jones, Barb Jungr, Graham Larkbey, Andy Lavery, Andy Pegg, the late Noel Redding, Twinkle Rogers, Paul Samwell-Smith, Jim Simpson, Mike and Anja Stax, John Steel, the late Lord David Sutch, Andy Taylor, John Townsend, Fran Wood, Paul Tucker, Patty Vetta and Ron Watts.

It may be obvious to the reader that I have received much information from sources that prefer not to be mentioned. Nevertheless, I wish to acknowledge their contribution – as well as those of Robert Cross of Bemish Business Machines, Stuart and Kathryn Booth, Ian Drummond, Tim Fagan, Katy Foster-Moore, Paul Hearne, Michael Heatley, the late Susan Hill, Dave and Graham Humphreys, Rob Johnstone, Allan Jones, Iris and Giselle Little, Elisabeth McCrae, Russell Newmark, Percy Perrett, Mike Robinson, the late David Sanderson, Anna Taylor, Warren Walters and Gina Way as well as Inese, Jack and Harry Clayson.

Finally, I would like to say a big 'hello' to Kevin Delaney.

The Publishers are grateful to Robin at Impactive for his help in tracking down albums. Thank you also to Brian Hinton for taking on another impossible challenge at short notice. Many thanks to Terence Kelsey and also to Mike Evans and John Bailey for tying up many loose ends.

Picture Credits

Abum artwork copyright Virgin/ ABKCO/ Decca/ London Records/ Rolling Stones Records/ Arcade

Every effort has been made to contact the copyright holders however please contact the publishers if any omissions have inadvertently been made.